WORDSWORTH CLASSICS
OF WORLD LITERATURE

General Editor: Tom Griffith MA, MPhil

FIVE GREAT TRAGEDIES

D0845505

William Shakespeare
Five Great Tragedies

Romeo and Juliet, Hamlet, Othello,
King Lear and Macbeth

❖

Introduction
by Emma Smith

WORDSWORTH CLASSICS
OF WORLD LITERATURE

This edition published 1998 by Wordsworth Editions Limited
Cumberland House, Crib Street, Ware, Hertfordshire SG12 9ET

ISBN I 85326 799 6

© Wordsworth Editions Limited 1998

Wordsworth® is a registered trade mark of
Wordsworth Editions Ltd

Typeset by Antony Gray
Printed and bound in Great Britain by
Mackays of Chatham, Chatham, Kent

CONTENTS

INTRODUCTION

When Shakespeare's works were gathered together for post-humous publication in the First Folio edition of 1623, the volume's title-page divided them into comedies, histories and tragedies. How John Heminges and Henry Condell, Shakespeare's fellow-actors who collected the plays, came at this tripartite division, we will never really know, but as an early attempt at categorisation it has been remarkably resilient. However, what was understood by the genres, especially by the label 'tragedy', can only be surmised. It is unlikely that Shakespeare wrote with any tragic blueprint in mind, still less that Aristotle's influential pronouncements on Greek tragedy's flawed hero, whose downfall arouses pity and fear among the spectators, were a consideration. Among the eleven plays which the First Folio calls tragedies there are as many differences as similarities, and by 1623 there has been some shifting so that a play such as *Richard II*, described as a tragedy when it was first published in 1597, is catalogued as a history, whereas the opposite has happened to *King Lear*, a history in 1608 but a tragedy by 1623. This fluidity may register the fluidity of generic boundaries in the period, and Polonius's ridiculous sub-division of drama – 'tragedy, comedy, history, pastoral, pastoral-comical, historical-pastoral, tragical-historical, tragical–comical-historical-pastoral' (*Hamlet* 2.2.388–91) is a cautionary reminder both that genres are frequently indistinct and that any attempt to list all their possible permutations is folly.

This is not to say that there is no such thing as tragedy, rather that its definition, both in the context of Renaissance England and more modern times, is itself open to debate. In fact, the heterogeneity of tragedy is probably the only firm conclusion to be drawn from the welter of differing, even contradictory, assertions about its particular qualities. The Elizabethan courtier-poet Sir Philip Sidney called 'the high and excellent tragedy' a form that 'showeth forth the ulcers that are covered with tissue', making 'kings fear to be tyrants' and showing 'upon how weak foundations gilden roofs are builded'. Some years later, Sidney's friend and biographer Fulke Greville described contemporary tragedy's demonstration of 'God's revenging aspect upon every particular sin, to the despair, or confusion, of mortality'. About the same date, the playwright Thomas Heywood put forward a definition based on formal, rather than thematic or moral, criteria, defining tragedy with reference to its apparent opposite, comedy. According to Heywood, the two forms 'differ thus: in comedies *turbulenta prima, tranquilla ultima*; in tragedies *tranquilla prima, turbulenta ultima*: comedies begin in trouble and end in peace; tragedies begin in calms and end in tempest'. Set against Shakespeare's tragedies, these contemporary definitions seem at best inadequate and at worst misleading. Greville's belief that tragedy displays God's omniscient vengeance on mortal sin sits uneasily with the conclusion of, say, *King Lear*; *Macbeth*'s supernatural opening or the brawl which begins *Romeo and Juliet* do not seem to fit Heywood's 'tragedies begin in calms' formula; and it seems unlikely that Shakespeare's nuanced and complex representations of internal and external conflict could ever be didactic in the uncomplicated way Sidney asserts.

If definitions are evasive, however, the plays themselves give some sense of a unified grouping. There is no doubt that we approach a tragedy with different expectations from those with which we approach a comedy, and that these expectations may include a fundamental seriousness, high tone, and corpse-strewn finale. The five plays in this volume, *Romeo and Juliet*, *Hamlet*, *Othello*, *King Lear* and *Macbeth*, encompass all these elements to differing degrees, but they also contain a surprising amount of black humour, and wordplay, as well as a taste for the sensational. The often-cited porter scene in *Macbeth* (2.3), Hamlet's wit, the shock of Gloucester's blinding in *King Lear*, all push at tragic expectations in different ways. Together the plays span about a dozen years of Shakespeare's writing career over the reigns of two monarchs, Elizabeth I and James I. Although the continuing popularity of the tragedies, and their exalted place in the literary canon, mean that those aspects which seem to transcend the historical moment of their composition tend to be the most valued, the plays are, in their different ways, indelibly marked with the concerns of their period. Such concerns are registered in many ways, from the specific topicality of *Macbeth*'s Scottishness to the more general resonances of the plays' concern with the operations of authority and governance. Specific details of language or plot may seem obscure, and the fact that, since the seventeenth century, the plays have been repeatedly rewritten for contemporary audiences is evidence that elements of their particular historical mindset do not always travel across time and cultures. A version of *King Lear*, for example, adapted in 1681 by Nahum Tate to spare Cordelia and end with her marriage to Edgar, held the stage for almost a century and a half, and more recently the play has been updated in Jane Smiley's novel *A Thousand Acres* (1992). On the other hand, the tragedies' capacity to speak to modern concerns ensures their lasting relevance, especially in performance. From a Soviet film of *Hamlet* by Grigori Kozintsev (1964), in which the tortured hero stood for a generation of dissident intellectuals oppressed by the Stalinist regime, to a production of *Othello* directed by Janet Suzman in Johannesburg under apartheid, a context in which the kiss of a white Desdemona and a black Othello was charged with social taboo and legal prohibition, Shakespeare's tragedies maintain the power to express and to challenge social, personal and political realities.

EMMA SMITH
New Hall
Cambridge

FURTHER READING

Dympna Callaghan, *Women and Gender in Renaissance Tragedy* (1989)

John Drakakis (ed.), *Shakespearean Tragedy* (1992)

Michael Mangan, *A Preface to Shakespeare's Tragedies* (1991)

Tom McAlindon, *Shakespeare's Tragic Cosmos* (1991)

Adrian Poole, *Tragedy: Shakespeare and the Greek Example* (1987)

NOTE ON THE TEXT

None of Shakespeare's plays exists in an original manuscript. Ever since the earliest sixteenth- and seventeenth-century editions, therefore, the plays have been shaped, in small but significant ways, by publication. There is no 'original' – except a printed one – to revert to. Different editors see their role in different ways, but most modern editions try to balance authenticity with accessibility. Thus, most modern editions, like this one, have modernised spelling and punctuation, *dramatis personae*, and additional stage directions. Where two early texts of a play exist, as, for example, in the cases of *King Lear* or *Hamlet*, the editor must adjudicate between their competing claims in order to draw up his or her own text.

This edition is derived from the New Shakespeare series produced under the general editorship of Sir Arthur Quiller-Couch and John Dover Wilson. In it the following typographical conventions have been adopted to indicate editorial intervention:

Original stage directions are indicated between two single quotation marks; all other stage directions are editorial.

Where two differing versions of the play exist, passages which are not found in both are enclosed in square brackets.

Readers who would like to find out more about the early texts of Shakespeare's plays and the issues involved in editing are referred to Stanley Wells and Gary Taylor, *William Shakespeare: A Textual Companion* (Oxford, 1987).

ROMEO AND JULIET

INTRODUCTION

The Most Excellent and Lamentable Tragedy of Romeo and Juliet was first printed in 1597, and probably written in 1594 or 1595. Shakespeare based his tale of 'star-cross'd lovers' on a well-known story. Arthur Brooke's long poem 'The Tragicall Historye of Romeus and Juliet' was translated from the Italian and first printed in 1562, although the tale of fated young love is archetypal and has numerous mythic analogues. Brooke's version of the tale has a definite didactic impulse, as is conveyed in its prefatory epistle 'To the Reader': 'this tragical matter [is] written to describe unto thee a couple of unfortunate lovers, thralling themselves to unhonest desire, neglecting the authority and advice of parents and friends, conferring their principal counsels with drunken gossips, and superstitious friars (the naturally fit instruments of unchastity) attempting all adventures of peril, for the attaining of their wished lust, using auricular confession (the key of whoredom, and treason) for furtherance of their purpose, abusing the honourable name of lawful marriage, to cloak the shame of stolen contracts, finally, by all means of unhonest life, hasting to most unhappy death.' Shakespeare takes the main narrative elements of Brooke's poem and develops them into a much warmer, more sympathetic play whose central couple are the victims, rather than the perpetrators, of wickedness.

The play tells the story of Romeo, a Montague, and Juliet, a Capulet. They meet, fall in love, and secretly marry despite the implacable feuding of their two families. In a fight with Tybalt, Juliet's cousin, Romeo kills him and is banished from Verona. To avoid marrying Paris, her father's choice of husband, Juliet takes a drug given her by a friar, and the sleep which results so resembles death that she is placed in her family tomb. The friar's plan to bring back Romeo, wake Juliet and reunite the pair misfires. Romeo finds Juliet and believes her dead; he kills himself with poison and she wakes to find him dead, only to kill herself on his dagger. The couple are buried together as the Montagues and Capulets vow to bury their enmity with them.

The choric sonnet which prefaces the play establishes what follows as a tragedy of fate. Two causes, one immediate and human (the warring families), the other distant and horoscopic (the 'star-crossed lovers'), are intertwined to form the governing dynamic of the story. The audience is given a superior knowledge of events at the outset, and thus the tragic effectiveness of the play rests on the inevitability of its conclusion rather than on suspense. We know what will happen in the end, but what is compulsive, in one of tragedy's most unpleasant truths, is watching its horror unfold. The familiarity of its story together with this statement of predetermination gives a double sense of unavoidable destiny, although many viewers and readers of the play have found it difficult to accept the role of coincidence in bringing about its catastrophe. As Michael Attenborough, who directed the play for the Royal Shakespeare Company in Stratford-on-Avon in 1997–8, put it: 'Most directors would try and persuade Shakespeare to find something more profound to cause everything to go so appallingly wrong. The erratic nature of the ecclesiastical postal service seems a bit limp as a dramatic device.' One of the play's characteristic features, and one of its great challenges in the theatre, is this audacious incorporation of banality and accident into its tragic mode.

In fact the play can claim a kind of hybrid generic status. Setting aside the Prologue (which was omitted from the play when it was printed in the First Folio of 1623), it begins more in a spirit of comedy than tragedy. The story of parental opposition to young love is a common theme of Shakespeare's comedies. *A Midsummer Night's Dream*, for example, written at about the same time as *Romeo and Juliet*, fulfils its comic promise as the lovers are united in the end. Even its inset tragedy, the play-within-a-play of Pyramus and Thisbe which probably also informed Shakespeare's conception of his own love tragedy *Romeo and Juliet*, is an opportunity for merriment. *Romeo and Juliet* ends, too, with the union of the lovers but subverts the comic finale by staging this as an entombed nuptial with death. Perhaps it is the death of Mercutio, Shakespeare's most brilliant addition to his source material, at almost exactly halfway through the play, which shifts its hitherto comic mood into irreversible tragedy. His dying curse 'A plague o' both your houses' (3.1.89) hangs in the air as the play lurches towards catastrophe through Romeo's revenge killing of Tybalt and his subsequent banishment. The play manages to combine inevitability – things are bound to go wrong – with the tantalising but never-allowed possibility that tragedy can be avoided. There is always the feeling that perhaps this time Juliet will wake up just a fraction sooner, and the awful spectacle of the double sacrifice to the 'ancient grudge' between the Montagues and the Capulets may thus be avoided. It is a hope which, of course, the play must always cruelly dash.

The events which lead to the final tragedy seem to gain momentum and become unstoppable as the play proceeds. Time is a crucial player in Shakespeare's play, where the dilatory narrative of Brooke's poem is tightened into a compact drama, which, while not quite the 'two hours' promised by the prologue, is characterised by a fierce energy. Time is inescapable, and seems to speed up as the play progresses. Juliet wills time onwards in the famous headlong cadences of her impatient 'Gallop apace, you fiery-footed steeds' (3.2.1), but then cannot put off the dawn and Romeo's flight after their wedding night together; Capulet tells Paris that Juliet will not be of marriageable age for 'two more summers' and then, a couple of acts later, brings their wedding forward to Thursday; Friar Lawrence's *sententiae* advise caution ('Wisely and slow. They stumble that run fast' 2.3.94; 'Too swift arrives as tardy as too slow' 2.6.15), but go unheeded in the helter-skelter pace towards the play's denouement.

This momentum contributes to the play's careful structure and symmetry. The dual focus suggested by its title is emphasised in the Prologue's 'Two households, both alike in dignity'. Brawls between the warring families punctuate the brief narrative of Romeo and Juliet's meeting, secret marriage, consummation, separation and reunion in the Capulet tomb. Within this structure, Shakespeare incorporates a diversity of language, from the regular rhyming of the Prologue, appropriately delivered in the anodyne cadences of a newscaster at the start of Baz Luhrmann's 1996 film *William Shakespeare's Romeo & Juliet*, to the weird inventiveness of

Mercutio's Queen Mab reverie, 'begot of nothing but vain fantasy' (1.4.98). The inspired bawdy of the Nurse's rambling prose contrasts with the formal sonnet the young lovers complete as their first exchange (1.5.90–103); the menacing prose exchanges of encounters between the two families are emphasised by their juxtaposition with the lyric intensity of love poetry; Tybalt's vaunting tragic idiom is matched by Mercutio's punning. Language is also a theme in a play concerned with the fatal consequences of names. Juliet's 'what's in a name' marks her naivety: names are all-important in a play which turns, fatally, on their inescapability. The language of *Romeo and Juliet* includes both formal verse and colloquial prose, and thus marks a development of the rhetorical artifice of Shakespeare's early plays and points towards the muscular lyricism and emotional immediacy of the mature playwright. Images of light and of fire suggest the 'violent passions' which, quite literally, burn themselves out. The symphonic quality of the play's variety and linguistic leitmotifs may explain the popularity of musical renditions of the story, from Berlioz, Prokofiev and Tchaikovsky to Dire Straits and Leonard Bernstein's *West Side Story*.

Romeo and Juliet's familiarity may be misleading. Like the play's original audiences, we almost all know the story before we read or see it. The two lovers have become cultural icons, embodiments of love in countless stories and songs. Every year from around the world thousands of letters, mostly asking for advice on matters of the heart or telling of other forbidden courtships, are sent to Verona for the attention of 'Juliet', and the town employs a team to answer them. A 1990s advertisement for a British dating agency offered to find lonely hearts their Romeo or Juliet, apparently unaware of the practical unsuitability, and fatal consequences, of the famous match. Romeo and Juliet represent a kind of perfect love immune to the rhythms of real life, fixed in the exquisite masochism of their double death in the tomb. Reading the play itself, however, we find that the characters do not quite stand up to their towering reputations. For one thing, they are very young. It is not accidental that both use comparisons drawn from childhood to articulate their new feelings, as their only experiences are those of children. For Romeo, parting from Juliet is like a boy's unwilling steps 'toward school with heavy looks' (2.2.157), and Juliet likens her frustration waiting for news of her lover 'As is the night before some festival To an impatient child that hath new robes And may not wear them' (3.2.29–31). The pace of their love may suggest an infatuation of which, were it allowed to run its natural course, they would soon tire. The illicit nature of their relationship gives it an added frisson; they are married within days – minutes, in performance – of meeting, egged on by the dubious encourage-ment of the Nurse, whose role retains some vestigial ambiguity from her culpability in Brooke's poem. Romeo is an incurable romantic, who is lovesick for the quickly-forgotten 'fair Rosaline' at the beginning of the play. He may seem to be in love less with Juliet as an individual than with love itself, a rather narcissistic young man whose earnest protestations satirise the hyperbolic rhetoric of Elizabethan sonnets and love conventions. Juliet is the younger of the pair, captivated by her ardent lover, rapt with the bittersweet emotions of first love. Neither seems fully to appreciate what they are doing, nor to know the other save as an idealised object of teenage desire. Characterisation, particularly of the cen-tral couple, is subservient to the relentless plot; Romeo and Juliet represent lovers rather than rounded personalities. Perhaps only the Nurse and Mercutio really take full flight as dramatic characters against a background of duller plot functionaries: lovers, parents, servants. *Romeo and Juliet* is a young person's play, a play about the integrity and intensity of immaturity in an irrational and powerful adult world, and perhaps its immediacy and energy can only be fully appreciated by young people. This is not to say that the play looks down on its heroes: they represent, more than any of Shakespeare's other tragic characters, the innocent victims of a malign machinery they did nothing to activate and can do nothing to avert.

The scene: Verona and Mantua

CHARACTERS IN THE PLAY

ESCALUS, *prince of Verona*

PARIS, *a young nobleman, kinsman to the prince*

MONTAGUE

CAPULET } *heads of two houses at enmity with each other*

An old man, kinsman to Capulet

ROMEO, *son to Montague*

MERCUTIO, *kinsman to the prince, and friend to Romeo*

BENVOLIO, *nephew to Montague, and friend to Romeo*

TYBALT, *nephew to Lady Capulet*

FRIAR LAWRENCE, *a Franciscan*

FRIAR JOHN, *of the same order*

BALTHASAR, *servant to Romeo*

SAMPSON

GREGORY } *servants to Capulet*

PETER, *servant to Juliet's Nurse*

ABRAHAM, *servant to Montague*

An Apothecary

Three Musicians

Page to Paris, another Page, an Officer

LADY MONTAGUE, *wife to Montague*

LADY CAPULET, *wife to Capulet*

JULIET, *daughter to Capulet*

Nurse to Juliet

*Citizens, Kinsfolk of both houses, Guards, Watchmen,
Servants and Attendants*

CHORUS

The Prologue

Enter Chorus

CHORUS   Two households, both alike in dignity,
In fair Verona, where we lay our scene,
From ancient grudge break to new mutiny,
Where civil blood makes civil hands unclean.
From forth the fatal loins of these two foes
A pair of star-crossed lovers take their life;
Whose misadventured piteous overthrows
Doth with their death bury their parents' strife.
The fearful passage of their death-marked love,
And the continuance of their parents' rage,   10
Which, but their children's end, nought could remove,
Is now the two hours' traffic of our stage;
The which if you with patient ears attend,
What here shall miss, our toil shall strive to mend.

                                                    [exit

ACT I SCENE I

Verona. A public place

'Enter SAMPSON and GREGORY *of the house of* CAPULET,
with swords and bucklers'

SAMPSON   Gregory, on my word we'll not carry coals.

GREGORY   No, for then we should be colliers.

SAMPSON   I mean, an we be in choler we'll draw.

GREGORY   Ay, while you live draw your neck out of collar.

SAMPSON   I strike quickly, being moved.

GREGORY   But thou art not quickly moved to strike.

SAMPSON   A dog of the house of Montague moves me.

GREGORY   To move is to stir, and to be valiant is to stand:
therefore if thou art moved thou runn'st away.

SAMPSON   A dog of that house shall move me to stand: I will take   10
the wall of any man or maid of Montague's.

GREGORY	That shows thee a weak slave, for the weakest goes to the wall.
SAMPSON	'Tis true, and therefore women, being the weaker vessels, are ever thrust to the wall: therefore I will push Montague's men from the wall, and thrust his maids to the wall.
GREGORY	The quarrel is between our masters, and us their men.
SAMPSON	'Tis all one; I will show myself a tyrant: when I have fought with the men, I will be cruel with the maids; I will cut off their heads.
GREGORY	The heads of the maids?
SAMPSON	Ay, the heads of the maids, or their maidenheads; take it in what sense thou wilt.
GREGORY	They must take it in sense that feel it.
SAMPSON	Me they shall feel while I am able to stand, and 'tis known I am a pretty piece of flesh.
GREGORY	'Tis well thou art not fish; if thou hadst, thou hadst been poor John. Draw thy tool; here comes two of the house of Montagues.

Enter ABRAHAM *and another serving man*

SAMPSON	My naked weapon is out: quarrel; I will back thee.
GREGORY	How? Turn thy back and run?
SAMPSON	Fear me not.
GREGORY	No, marry; I fear thee!
SAMPSON	Let us take the law of our sides; let them begin.
GREGORY	I will frown as I pass by, and let them take it as they list.
SAMPSON	Nay, as they dare. I will bite my thumb at them, which is disgrace to them if they bear it.
ABRAHAM	Do you bite your thumb at us, sir?
SAMPSON	I do bite my thumb, sir.
ABRAHAM	Do you bite your thumb at us, sir?
SAMPSON	Is the law of our side if I say ay?
GREGORY	No.
SAMPSON	No, sir, I do not bite my thumb at you, sir, but I bite my thumb, sir.
GREGORY	Do you quarrel, sir?
ABRAHAM	Quarrel, sir? No, sir.
SAMPSON	But if you do, sir, I am for you: I serve as good a man as you.

ABRAHAM No better.   50
SAMPSON Well, sir.

'Enter BENVOLIO*' on one side,* TYBALT *on the other*

GREGORY [*seeing Tybalt*] Say 'better': here comes one of my
         master's kinsmen.
SAMPSON Yes, better, sir.
ABRAHAM You lie.
SAMPSON Draw, if you be men. Gregory, remember thy washing
         blow.   ['*they fight*'
BENVOLIO: [*intervening from behind*] Part, fools!
         Put up your swords; you know not what you do.

                    TYBALT *comes up*

TYBALT: What, art thou drawn among these heartless hinds?   60
         Turn thee, Benvolio; look upon thy death.
BENVOLIO I do but keep the peace: put up thy sword,
         Or manage it to part these men with me.
TYBALT   What, drawn, and talk of peace? I hate the word,
         As I hate hell, all Montagues, and thee:
         Have at thee, coward.

         They fight. Enter several of both houses, joining in the
              fray. Then 'enter three or four Citizens with
                   clubs or partisans', and an Officer

OFFICER Clubs, bills, and partisans! Strike, beat them down.
         Down with the Capulets, down with the Montagues!

         'Enter old CAPULET *in his gown, and his wife'*

CAPULET What noise is this? Give me my long sword, ho!
LADY CAP. A crutch, a crutch! Why call you for a sword?   70
CAPULET My sword, I say! Old Montague is come,
         And flourishes his blade in spite of me.

              'Enter old MONTAGUE *and his wife'*

MONTAG. Thou villain Capulet! – Hold me not, let me go.
LADY MON. Thou shalt not stir one foot to seek a foe.

              'Enter PRINCE ESCALUS*, with his train'*

PRINCE   Rebellious subjects, enemies to peace,
         Profaners of this neighbour-stainéd steel, –
         Will they not hear? What ho! you men, you beasts,

That quench the fire of your pernicious rage
With purple fountains issuing from your veins,
On pain of torture, from those bloody hands   80
Throw your mistempered weapons to the ground,
And hear the sentence of your movéd prince.
Three civil brawls, bred of an airy word
By thee, old Capulet, and Montague,
Have thrice disturbed the quiet of our streets,
And made Verona's ancient citizens
Cast by their grave beseeming ornaments
To wield old partisans, in hands as old,
Cankered with peace, to part your cankered hate:
If ever you disturb our streets again,   90
Your lives shall pay the forfeit of the peace.
For this time, all the rest depart away:
You, Capulet, shall go along with me;
And, Montague, come you this afternoon,
To know our farther pleasure in this case,
To old Freetown, our common judgment-place.
Once more, on pain of death, all men depart.
            [all but Montague, Lady Montague, and Benvolio depart

MONTAG. Who set this ancient quarrel new abroach?
         Speak, nephew, were you by when it began?

BENVOLIO Here were the servants of your adversary   100
         And yours, close fighting ere I did approach:
         I drew to part them; in the instant came
         The fiery Tybalt, with his sword prepared,
         Which, as he breathed defiance to my ears,
         He swung about his head, and cut the winds,
         Who, nothing hurt withal, hissed him in scorn:
         While we were interchanging thrusts and blows,
         Came more and more, and fought on part and part,
         Till the prince came, who parted either part.

LADY MON.O where is Romeo? Saw you him today?   110
         Right glad I am he was not at this fray.

BENVOLIO Madam, an hour before the worshipped sun
         Peered forth the golden window of the east,
         A troubled mind drave me to walk abroad,
         Where, underneath the grove of sycamore

That westward rooteth from this city's side,
So early walking did I see your son:
Towards him I made, but he was ware of me,
And stole into the covert of the wood:
I, measuring his affections by my own,   120
Which then most sought where most might not be
                                                    found,
Being one too many by my weary self,
Pursued my humour, not pursuing his,
And gladly shunned who gladly fled from me.

MONTAG. Many a morning hath he there been seen,
With tears augmenting the fresh morning's dew,
Adding to clouds more clouds with his deep sighs;
But all so soon as the all-cheering sun
Should in the farthest east begin to draw
The shady curtains from Aurora's bed,   130
Away from light steals home my heavy son,
And private in his chamber pens himself,
Shuts up his windows, locks fair daylight out,
And makes himself an artificial night:
Black and portentous must this humour prove,
Unless good counsel may the cause remove.

BENVOLIO My noble uncle, do you know the cause?

MONTAG. I neither know it, nor can learn of him.

BENVOLIO Have you importuned him by any means?

MONTAG. Both by myself and many other friends: 140
But he, his own affections' counsellor,
Is to himself – I will not say how true –
But to himself so secret and so close,
So far from sounding and discovery,
As is the bud bit with an envious worm,
Ere he can spread his sweet leaves to the air,
Or dedicate his beauty to the sun.
Could we but learn from whence his sorrows grow,
We would as willingly give cure as know.

                    'Enter ROMEO'

BENVOLIO See where he comes: so please you, step aside;   150
I'll know his grievance or be much denied.

MONTAG. I would thou wert so happy by thy stay

To hear true shrift. Come, madam, let's away.

[*Montague and his wife depart*

BENVOLIO Good morrow, cousin.

ROMEO   Is the day so young?

BENVOLIO But new struck nine.

ROMEO   Ay me, sad hours seem long.
Was that my father that went hence so fast?

BENVOLIO It was. What sadness lengthens Romeo's hours?

ROMEO Not having that which, having, makes them short.

BENVOLIO In love?

ROMEO Out –   160

BENVOLIO Of love?

ROMEO Out of her favour where I am in love.

BENVOLIO Alas that Love, so gentle in his view,
Should be so tyrannous and rough in proof!

ROMEO Alas that Love, whose view is muffled still,
Should without eyes see pathways to his will!
Where shall we dine? – O me! What fray was here?
Yet tell me not, for I have heard it all:
Here's much to do with hate, but more with love:
Why, then, O brawling love, O loving hate,   170
O anything of nothing first create!
O heavy lightness, serious vanity,
Misshapen chaos of well-seeming forms,
Feather of lead, bright smoke, cold fire, sick health,
Still-waking sleep, that is not what it is!
This love feel I, that feel no love in this.
Dost thou not laugh?

BENVOLIO   No, coz, I rather weep.

ROMEO Good heart, at what?

BENVOLIO   At thy good heart's oppression.

ROMEO Why, such is love's transgression.
Griefs of mine own lie heavy in my breast,   180
Which thou wilt propagate, to have it pressed
With more of thine. This love that thou hast shown
Doth add more grief to too much of mine own.
Love is a smoke made with the fume of sighs:
Being purged, a fire sparkling in lovers' eyes;
Being vexed, a sea nourished with lovers' tears.

What is it else? A madness most discreet,
A choking gall and a preserving sweet.
Farewell, my coz.

BENVOLIO   Soft, I will go along:
And if you leave me so, you do me wrong.   190

ROMEO   Tut, I have lost myself, I am not here,
This is not Romeo, he's some other where.

BENVOLIO Tell me in sadness, who is that you love?

ROMEO   What, shall I groan and tell thee?

BENVOLIO   Groan? Why no:
But sadly tell me, who?

ROMEO   Bid a sick man in sadness make his will –
A word ill urged to one that is so ill.
In sadness, cousin, I do love a woman.

BENVOLIO I aimed so near when I supposed you loved.

ROMEO   A right good markman! And she's fair I love.   200

BENVOLIO A right fair mark, fair coz, is soonest hit.

ROMEO   Well, in that hit you miss. She'll not be hit
With Cupid's arrow: she hath Dian's wit,
And, in strong proof of chastity well armed,
From Love's weak childish bow she lives unharmed.
She will not stay the siege of loving terms,
Nor bide th' encounter of assailing eyes,
Nor ope her lap to saint-seducing gold.
O, she is rich in beauty, only poor
That, when she dies, with beauty dies her store.   210

BENVOLIO Then she hath sworn that she will still live chaste?

ROMEO   She hath, and in that sparing makes huge waste:
For beauty, starved with her severity,
Cuts beauty off from all posterity.
She is too fair, too wise, wisely too fair,
To merit bliss by making me despair:
She hath forsworn to love, and in that vow
Do I live dead, that live to tell it now.

BENVOLIO Be ruled by me; forget to think of her.

ROMEO   O, teach me how I should forget to think.   220

BENVOLIO By giving liberty unto thine eyes;
Examine other beauties.

ROMEO   'Tis the way

To call hers (exquisite) in question more.
These happy masks that kiss fair ladies' brows,
Being black, puts us in mind they hide the fair.
He that is strucken blind cannot forget
The precious treasure of his eyesight lost.
Show me a mistress that is passing fair:
What doth her beauty serve but as a note
Where I may read who passed that passing fair?   230
Farewell, thou canst not teach me to forget.

BENVOLIO I'll pay that doctrine, or else die in debt.   [*they go*

SCENE 2

The same; later in the day

'*Enter* CAPULET, *County* PARIS, *and the* CLOWN', *servant to Capulet*

CAPULET But Montague is bound as well as I,
In penalty alike; and 'tis not hard, I think,
For men so old as we to keep the peace.

PARIS Of honourable reckoning are you both,
And pity 'tis you lived at odds so long.
But now, my lord, what say you to my suit?

CAPULET But saying o'er what I have said before:
My child is yet a stranger in the world ;
She hath not seen the change of fourteen years:
Let two more summers wither in their pride   10
Ere we may think her ripe to be a bride.

PARIS Younger than she are happy mothers made.

CAPULET And too soon marred are those so early made.
Earth hath swallowed all my hopes but she;
She is the hopeful lady of my earth.
But woo her, gentle Paris, get her heart;
My will to her consent is but a part:
And, she agreed, within her scope of choice
Lies my consent and fair according voice.
This night I hold an old accustomed feast,   20
Whereto I have invited many a guest,
Such as I love; and you among the store,
One more most welcome, makes my number more.

At my poor house look to behold this night
Earth-treading stars that make dark heaven light.
Such comfort as do lusty young men feel
When well-apparelled April on the heel
Of limping winter treads, even such delight
Among fresh female buds shall you this night
Inherit at my house: hear all, all see,   30
And like her most whose merit most shall be:
Which on more view, of many mine being one
May stand in number, though in reckoning none.
Come, go with me. [*To the Clown*] Go, sirrah,
                                        trudge about
Through fair Verona; find those persons out
Whose names are written there, [*giving him a paper*]
                                        and to them say
My house and welcome on their pleasure stay.
                                [*Capulet and Paris go*

CLOWN   [*turns the paper about*] Find them out whose names are
          written here! It is written that the shoemaker should
          meddle with his yard and the tailor with his last, the   40
          fisher with his pencil and the painter with his nets. But
          I am sent to find those persons whose names are here
          writ, and can never find what names the writing person
          hath here writ. I must to the learned. In good time!

                    '*Enter* BENVOLIO AND ROMEO'

BENVOLIO Tut, man, one fire burns out another's burning,
          One pain is lessened by another's anguish;
          Turn giddy, and be holp by backward turning;
          One desperate grief cures with another's languish;
          Take thou some new infection to thy eye,
          And the rank poison of the old will die.   50
ROMEO   Your plantain leaf is excellent for that.
BENVOLIO For what, I pray thee?
ROMEO   For your broken shin.
BENVOLIO Why, Romeo, art thou mad?
ROMEO   Not mad, but bound more than a madman is:
          Shut up in prison, kept without my food,
          Whipped and tormented, and – God-den, good fellow.
CLOWN   God gi' god-den. I pray, sir, can you read?

ROMEO   Ay, mine own fortune in my misery.

CLOWN   Perhaps you have learned it without book: but, I pray,
         can you read anything you see?   60

ROMEO   Ay, if I know the letters and the language.

CLOWN   Ye say honestly: rest you merry.

                                              [*he turns to go*

ROMEO   Stay, fellow; I can read.   [*he reads the list*
         'Signior Martino and his wife and daughters,
         County Anselmo and his beauteous sisters,
         The lady widow of Vitruvio,
         Signior Placentio and his lovely nieces,
         Mercutio and his brother Valentine,
         Mine uncle Capulet, his wife and daughters,
         My fair niece Rosaline and Livia,   70
         Signior Valentio and his cousin Tybalt,
         Lucio and the lively Helena.'
         A fair assembly: whither should they come?

CLOWN   Up.

ROMEO   Whither?

CLOWN   To supper; to our house.

ROMEO   Whose house?

CLOWN   My master's.

ROMEO   Indeed I should have asked thee that before.

CLOWN   Now I'll tell you without asking. My master is the   80
         great rich Capulet; and, if you be not of the house of
         Montagues, I pray come and crush a cup of wine. Rest
         you merry.   [*goes*

BENVOLIO At this same ancient feast of Capulet's
         Sups the fair Rosaline whom thou so loves,
         With all the admiréd beauties of Verona:
         Go thither, and with unattainted eye
         Compare her face with some that I shall show,
         And I will make thee think thy swan a crow.

ROMEO   When the devout religion of mine eye   90
         Maintains such falsehood, then turn tears to fires:
         And these who, often drowned, could never die,
         Transparent heretics, be burnt for liars.
         One fairer than my love! The all-seeing sun
         Ne'er saw her match since first the world begun.

BENVOLIO Tut, you saw her fair, none else being by,
　　　　 Herself poised with herself in either eye:
　　　　 But in that crystal scales let there be weighed
　　　　 Your lady's love against some other maid
　　　　 That I will show you shining at this feast,   100
　　　　 And she shall scant show well that now seems best.
ROMEO　　I'll go along, no such sight to be shown,
　　　　 But to rejoice in splendour of mine own.   [*they go*

SCENE 3

Within Capulet's house

'Enter Capulet's Wife, and NURSE*'*

LADY CAP. Nurse, where's my daughter? Call her forth to me.
NURSE　　Now, by my maidenhead at twelve year old,
　　　　 I bade her come. What, lamb! What, lady-bird!
　　　　 God forbid! Where's this girl? What, Juliet!

'Enter JULIET*'*

JULIET　　How now, who calls?
NURSE　　Your mother.
JULIET　　Madam, I am here. What is your will?
LADY CAP. This is the matter. Nurse, give leave awhile:
　　　　 We must talk in secret. Nurse, come back again:
　　　　 I have remembered me; thou's hear our counsel.   10
　　　　 Thou knowest my daughter's of a pretty age.
NURSE　　Faith, I can tell her age unto an hour.
LADY CAP. She's not fourteen.
NURSE　　　　　　　　　　　　I'll lay fourteen of my teeth –
　　　　 And yet, to my teen be it spoken, I have but four –
　　　　 She's not fourteen. How long is it now
　　　　 To Lammas-tide?
LADY CAP.　　　　　　　　　A fortnight and odd days.
NURSE　　Even or odd, of all days in the year,
　　　　 Come Lammas-Eve at night shall she be fourteen.
　　　　 Susan and she – God rest all Christian souls –
　　　　 Were of an age. Well, Susan is with God;   20
　　　　 She was too good for me. But, as I said,

On Lammas-Eve at night shall she be fourteen:
That shall she, marry; I remember it well.
'Tis since the earthquake now eleven years,
And she was weaned – I never shall forget it –
Of all the days of the year, upon that day:
For I had then laid wormwood to my dug,
Sitting in the sun under the dove-house wall.
My lord and you were then at Mantua –
Nay, I do bear a brain! But, as I said, 30
When it did taste the wormwood on the nipple
Of my dug, and felt it bitter, pretty fool,
To see it tetchy and fall out with the dug!
'Shake,' quoth the dove-house: 'twas no need, I trow,
To bid me trudge.
And since that time it is eleven years:
For then she could stand high-lone; nay, by th' rood,
She could have run and waddled all about:
For even the day before, she broke her brow,
And then my husband – God be with his soul, 40
'A was a merry man – took up the child:
'Yea,' quoth he, 'dost thou fall upon thy face?
Thou wilt fall backward when thou hast more wit;
Wilt thou not, Jule?' And, by my holidame,
The pretty wretch left crying, and said 'Ay'.
To see now how a jest shall come about!
I warrant, an I should live a thousand years,
I never should forget it: 'Wilt thou not, Jule?' quoth he;
And, pretty fool, it stinted, and said 'Ay'.

LADY CAP. Enough of this; I pray thee hold thy peace. 50

NURSE   Yes, madam, yet I cannot choose but laugh,
To think it should leave crying, and say 'Ay':
And yet, I warrant, it had upon it brow
A bump as big as a young cockerel's stone,
A perilous knock: and it cried bitterly.
'Yea', quoth my husband, 'fallst upon thy face?
Thou wilt fall backward when thou comest to age:
Wilt thou not, Jule?' It stinted, and said 'Ay'.

JULIET   And stint thou too, I pray thee, Nurse, say I.

NURSE   Peace, I have done. God mark thee to his grace! 60

            Thou wast the prettiest babe that e'er I nursed:
            An I might live to see thee married once,
            I have my wish.

LADY CAP. Marry, that 'marry' is the very theme
            I came to talk of. Tell me, daughter Juliet,
            How stands your dispositions to be married?

JULIET   It is an honour that I dream not of.

NURSE   An honour! Were not I thine only nurse,
            I would say thou hadst sucked wisdom from thy teat.

LADY CAP. Well, think of marriage now; younger than you   70
            Here in Verona, ladies of esteem,
            Are made already mothers. By my count,
            I was your mother much upon these years
            That you are now a maid. Thus then in brief:
            The valiant Paris seeks you for his love.

NURSE   A man, young lady! Lady, such a man
            As all the world – Why, he's a man of wax.

LADY CAP. Verona's summer hath not such a flower.

NURSE   Nay, he's a flower; in faith, a very flower.

LADY CAP. What say you? Can you love the gentleman?   80
            This night you shall behold him at our feast:
            Read o'er the volume of young Paris' face,
            And find delight writ there with beauty's pen;
            Examine every married lineament,
            And see how one another lends content;
            And what obscured in this fair volume lies
            Find written in the margent of his eyes.
            This precious book of love, this unbound lover,
            To beautify him, only lacks a cover.
            The fish lives in the sea; and 'tis much pride   90
            For fair without the fair within to hide.
            That book in many's eyes doth share the glory,
            That in gold clasps locks in the golden story:
            So shall you share all that he doth possess,
            By having him making yourself no less.

NURSE   No less! Nay, bigger women grow by men!

LADY CAP. Speak briefly, can you like of Paris' love?

JULIET   I'll look to like, if looking liking move;
            But no more deep will I endart mine eye

Than your consent gives strength to make it fly.   100
'Enter Servingman'

SERV'MAN Madam, the guests are come, supper served up, you
called, my young lady asked for, the nurse cursed in
the pantry, and everything in extremity. I must hence
to wait; I beseech you follow straight.

LADY CAP. We follow thee. Juliet, the County stays.

NURSE   Go, girl, seek happy nights to happy days.   [*they go*

SCENE 4

Without Capulet's house

'Enter ROMEO, MERCUTIO, BENVOLIO, *with five or six
other masquers; torch-bearers'*

ROMEO   What, shall this speech be spoke for our excuse?
          Or shall we on without apology?

BENVOLIO The date is out of such prolixity:
          We'll have no Cupid hoodwinked with a scarf,
          Bearing a Tartar's painted bow of lath,
          Scaring the ladies like a crow-keeper:
          Nor no without-book prologue, faintly spoke
          After the prompter, for our entrance:
          But, let them measure us by what they will,
          We'll measure them a measure and be gone.   10

ROMEO   Give me a torch: I am not for this ambling;
          Being but heavy, I will bear the light.

MERCUTIO Nay, gentle Romeo, we must have you dance.

ROMEO   Not I, believe me: you have dancing shoes
          With nimble soles; I have a soul of lead
          So stakes me to the ground I cannot move.

MERCUTIO You are a lover: borrow Cupid's wings,
          And soar with them above a common bound.

ROMEO   I am too sore enpiercéd with his shaft
          To soar with his light feathers and so bound;   20
          I cannot bound a pitch above dull woe:
          Under love's heavy burden do I sink.

MERCUTIO And, to sink in it, should you burden love –

          Too great oppression for a tender thing.

ROMEO   Is love a tender thing? It is too rough,
          Too rude, too boisterous, and it pricks like thorn.

MERCUTIO   If love be rough with you, be rough with love;
          Prick love for pricking, and you beat love down.
          Give me a case to put my visage in:
          A visor for a visor! What care I   30
          What curious eye doth quote deformities?
          Here are the beetle-brows shall blush for me.
                                 [putting on a mask

BENVOLIO   Come, knock and enter, and no sooner in
          But every man betake him to his legs.

ROMEO   A torch for me; let wantons light of heart
          Tickle the senseless rushes with their heels.
          For I am proverbed with a grandsire phrase,
          I'll be a candle-holder, and look on.
          The game was ne'er so fair, and I am done.

MERCUTIO   Tut, dun's the mouse, the constable's own word   40
          If thou art Dun, we'll draw thee from the mire,
          Or save-your-reverence love, wherein thou stickest
          Up to the ears. Come, we burn daylight, ho.

ROMEO   Nay, that's not so.

MERCUTIO   I mean, sir, in delay
          We waste our lights in vain, like lights by day.
          Take our good meaning, for our judgment sits
          Five times in that ere once in our five wits.

ROMEO   And we mean well in going to this masque,
          But 'tis no wit to go.

MERCUTIO   Why, may one ask?

ROMEO   I dreamt a dream tonight.

MERCUTIO   And so did I.   50

ROMEO   Well, what was yours?

MERCUTIO   That dreamers often lie.

ROMEO   In bed asleep while they do dream things true.

MERCUTIO   O then I see Queen Mab hath been with you.
          She is the fairies' midwife, and she comes
          In shape no bigger than an agate-stone
          On the fore-finger of an alderman,
          Drawn with a team of little atomi

Over men's noses as they lie asleep.
Her chariot is an empty hazel-nut,
Made by the joiner squirrel or old grub   60
Time out o' mind the fairies' coachmakers:
Her waggon-spokes made of long spinners' legs,
The cover of the wings of grasshoppers,
Her traces of the smallest spider-web,
Her collars of the moonshine's watery beams,
Her whip of cricket's bone, the lash of film;
Her waggoner a small grey-coated gnat,
Not half so big as a round little worm
Pricked from the lazy finger of a maid.
And in this state she gallops night by night   70
Through lovers' brains, and then they dream of love;
O'er courtiers' knees, that dream on curtsies straight;
O er lawyers' fingers who straight dream on fees;
O'er ladies' lips, who straight on kisses dream,
Which oft the angry Mab with blisters plagues
Because their breaths with sweetmeats tainted are.
Sometime she gallops o'er a courtier's nose,
And then dreams he of smelling out a suit:
And sometime comes she with a tithe-pig's tail
Tickling a parson's nose as 'a lies asleep,   80
Then dreams he of another benefice.
Sometime she driveth o'er a soldier's neck,
And then dreams he of cutting foreign threats,
Of breaches, ambuscadoes, Spanish blades,
Of healths five fathom deep; and then anon
Drums in his ear, at which he starts and wakes,
And being thus frighted swears a prayer or two,
And sleeps again. This is that very Mab
That plats the manes of horses in the night,
And bakes the elf-locks in foul sluttish hairs,   90
Which once untangled much misfortune bodes:
This is the hag, when maids lie on their backs,
That presses them and learns them first to bear,
Making them women of good carriage:
This is she —

ROMEO   Peace, peace, Mercutio, peace!

Thou talkst of nothing.

MERCUTIO   True, I talk of dreams,
Which are the children of an idle brain,
Begot of nothing but vain fantasy,
Which is as thin of substance as the air,
And more inconstant than the wind, who woos   100
Even now the frozen bosom of the north,
And, being angered, puffs away from thence,
Turning his side to the dew-dropping south.

BENVOLIO This wind you talk of blows us from ourselves:
Supper is done, and we shall come too late.

ROMEO   I fear, too early: for my mind misgives
Some consequence, yet hanging in the stars,
Shall bitterly begin his fearful date
With this night's revels, and expire the term
Of a despiséd life closed in my breast,   110
By some vile forfeit of untimely death.
But He that hath the steerage of my course
Direct my sail! On, lusty gentlemen.

BENVOLIO Strike, drum.

> [*they march into the house*

SCENE 5

The hall in Capulet's house; musicians waiting.
Enter the masquers, march round the hall, and stand aside.
'Servingmen come forth with napkins'

1 SER'MAN Where's Potpan, that he helps not to take away? He
shift a trencher! He scrape a trencher!

2 SER'MAN When good manners shall lie all in one or two men's
hands, and they unwashed too, 'tis a foul thing.

1 SER'MAN Away with the joined-stools, remove the court-cup-
board, look to the plate – Good thou, save me a piece of
marchpane; and, as thou loves me, let the porter let in
Susan Grindstone and Nell – Antony and Potpan!

3 SER'MAN Ay, boy, ready.

1 SER'MAN You are looked for and called for, asked for and sought   10
for, in the great chamber.

4 SER'MAN We cannot be here and there too. Cheerly, boys; be
          brisk a while, and the longer liver take all.
                                    [*Servingmen withdraw*

      'Enter' CAPULET, *and* JULIET, *with 'all the guests and*
                    gentlewomen to the masquers'

CAPULET   Welcome, gentlemen! Ladies that have their toes
          Unplagued with corns will walk a bout with you.
          Ah, my mistresses, which of you all
          Will now deny to dance? She that makes dainty,
          She I'll swear hath corns: am I come near ye now?
          Welcome, gentlemen! I have seen the day
          That I have worn a visor and could tell   20
          A whispering tale in a fair lady's ear,
          Such as would please: 'tis gone, 'tis gone, 'tis gone.
          You are welcome, gentlemen! Come, musicians, play.
          A hall, a hall! Give room. And foot it, girls.
                              [*'music plays and they dance'*
          More light, you knaves, and turn the tables up,
          And quench the fire – the room is grown too hot.
          Ah, sirrah, this unlooked-for sport comes well. –
          Nay sit, nay sit, good cousin Capulet,
          For you and I are past our dancing days.
          How long is't now since last yourself and I   30
          Were in a masque?
2 CAPUL'T   By'r Lady, thirty years.
CAPULET   What, man! 'tis not so much, 'tis not so much:
          'Tis since the nuptial of Lucentio,
          Come Pentecost as quickly as it will,
          Some five and twenty years, and then we masqued.
2 CAPUL'T 'Tis more, 'tis more; his son is elder, sir:
          His son is thirty.
CAPULET   Will you tell me that?
          His son was but a ward two years ago.
ROMEO   [*to a servingman*]
          What lady's that which doth enrich the hand
          Of yonder knight?
SERV'MAN   I know not, sir.   40
ROMEO   O she doth teach the torches to burn bright!
          It seems she hangs upon the cheek of night

As a rich jewel in an Ethiop's ear –
Beauty too rich for use, for earth too dear!
So shows a snowy dove trooping with crows,
As yonder lady o'er her fellows shows.
The measure done, I'll watch her place of stand,
And, touching hers, make blesséd my rude hand.
Did my heart love till now? Forswear it, sight!
For I ne'er saw true beauty till this night.   50

TYBALT   This, by his voice, should be a Montague.
          Fetch me my rapier, boy. [*his page goes*]
                              What dares the slave
          Come hither, covered with an antic face,
          To fleer and scorn at our solemnity?
          Now, by the stock and honour of my kin,
          To strike him dead I hold it not a sin.

CAPULET   Why, how now, kinsman! wherefore storm you so?

TYBALT   Uncle, this is a Montague, our foe:
          A villain that is hither come in spite,
          To scorn at our solemnity this night.   60

CAPULET   Young Romeo is it?

TYBALT   'Tis he, that villain Romeo.

CAPULET   Content thee, gentle coz, let him alone,
          'A bears him like a portly gentleman:
          And, to say truth, Verona brags of him
          To be a virtuous and well-governed youth.
          I would not for the wealth of all this town
          Here in my house do him disparagement
          Therefore be patient, take no note of him.
          It is my will, the which if thou respect,
          Show a fair presence and put off these frowns,   70
          An ill-beseeming semblance for a feast.

TYBALT   It fits when such a villain is a guest:
          I'll not endure him.

CAPULET   He shall be endured.
          What, goodman boy? I say he shall. Go to,
          Am I the master here, or you? Go to,
          You'll not endure him? God shall mend my soul!
          You'll make a mutiny among my guests!
          You will set cock-a-hoop! You'll be the man!

TYBALT	Why, uncle, 'tis a shame.
CAPULET	Go to, go to,

TYBALT Why, uncle, 'tis a shame.

CAPULET   Go to, go to,
You are a saucy boy. Is't so indeed?   80
This trick may chance to scathe you, I know what.
You must contrary me! Marry, 'tis time –
Well said, my hearts! – You are a princox: go,
Be quiet, or – More light, more light, for shame! –
I'll make you quiet. What, cheerly, my hearts!

TYBALT Patience perforce with wilful choler meeting
Makes my flesh tremble in their different greeting.
I will withdraw, but this intrusion shall,
Now seeming sweet, convert to bitterest gall. [goes

ROMEO [takes Juliet's hand]
If I profane with my unworthiest hand   90
This holy shrine, the gentle pain is this:
My lips, two blushing pilgrims, ready stand
To smooth that rough touch with a tender kiss.

JULIET Good pilgrim, you do wrong your hand too much,
Which mannerly devotion shows in this:
For saints have hands that pilgrims' hands do touch,
And palm to palm is holy palmers' kiss.

ROMEO Have not saints lips, and holy palmers too?

JULIET Ay, pilgrim, lips that they must use in prayer.

ROMEO O then, dear saint, let lips do what hands do, 100
They pray: grant thou, lest faith turn to despair.

JULIET Saints do not move, though grant for prayers' sake.

ROMEO Then move not, while my prayer's effect I take.
Thus from my lips by thine my sin is purged.
                [kissing her

JULIET Then have my lips the sin that they have took.

ROMEO Sin from my lips? O trespass sweetly urged!
Give me my sin again.   [kissing her

JULIET   You kiss by th' book.

NURSE Madam, your mother craves a word with you.

ROMEO What is her mother?

NURSE   Marry, bachelor,
Her mother is the lady of the house,   110
And a good lady, and a wise and virtuous.
I nursed her daughter that you talked withal.

I tell you, he that can lay hold of her
Shall have the chinks.

ROMEO   Is she a Capulet?
O dear account! My life is my foe's debt.

BENVOLIO Away be gone; the sport is at the best.

ROMEO Ay, so I fear; the more is my unrest.

CAPULET Nay, gentlemen, prepare not to be gone;
We have a trifling foolish banquet towards.

The masquers excuse themselves, whispering in his ear

Is it e'en so? Why, then, I thank you all: 120
I thank you, honest gentlemen; good night.
More torches here; come on! then let's to bed.

Servants bring torches to escort the masquers out

Ah, sirrah, by my fay, it waxes late:
I'll to my rest.   [*all leave but Juliet and Nurse*

JULIET Come hither, nurse. What is yond gentleman?

NURSE The son and heir of old Tiberio.

JULIET What's he that now is going out of door?

NURSE Marry, that I think be young Petruchio.

JULIET What's he that follows there, that would not dance?

NURSE I know not.   130

JULIET Go ask his name. – If he be marriéd,
My grave is like to be my wedding bed.

NURSE His name is Romeo, and a Montague,
The only son of your great enemy.

JULIET My only love sprung from my only hate!
Too early seen unknown, and known too late!
Prodigious birth of love it is to me,
That I must love a loathéd enemy.

NURSE What's this, what's this?

JULIET   A rhyme I learned even now
Of one I danced withal.

'One calls within, "Juliet" '

NURSE   Anon, anon!   140
Come, let's away; the strangers all are gone.

[*they go*

ACT 2

Prologue

Enter Chorus

CHORUS   Now old desire doth in his deathbed lie,
       And young affection gapes to be his heir;
       That fair for which love groaned for and would die,
       With tender Juliet matched, is now not fair.
       Now Romeo is beloved and loves again,
       Alike bewitchéd by the charm of looks,
       But to his foe supposèd he must complain,
       And she steal love's sweet bait from fearful hooks:
       Being held a foe, he may not have access
       To breathe such vows as lovers use to swear;   10
       And she as much in love, her means much less
       To meet her new belovéd anywhere:
       But passion lends them power, time means, to meet,
       Tempering extremities with extreme sweet.   [*exit*

SCENE I

*Capulet's orchard; to the one side the outer wall with a lane beyond,
to the other Capulet's house showing an upper window*

'Enter ROMEO *alone' in the lane*

ROMEO   Can I go forward when my heart is here?
       Turn back, dull earth, and find thy centre out.
               [*he climbs the wall and leaps into the orchard*

'Enter BENVOLIO *with* MERCUTIO*' in the lane.
Romeo listens behind the wall*

BENVOLIO Romeo, my cousin Romeo!

MERCUTIO   He is wise,
       And on my life hath stolen him home to bed.

BENVOLIO He ran this way and leapt this orchard wall.
       Call, good Mercutio.

MERCUTIO: Nay, I'll conjure too.

Romeo, humours, madman, passion, lover!
Appear thou in the likeness of a sigh;
Speak but one rhyme and I am satisfied:
Cry but 'Ay me!', pronounce but 'love' and 'dove';   10
Speak to my gossip Venus one fair word,
One nickname for her purblind son and heir,
Young Abraham Cupid, he that shot so trim
When King Cophetua loved the beggar maid.
He heareth not, he stirreth not, he moveth not;
The ape is dead, and I must conjure him.
I conjure thee by Rosaline's bright eyes,
By her high forehead and her scarlet lip,
By her fine foot, straight leg, and quivering thigh,
And the demesnes that there adjacent lie,   20
That in thy likeness thou appear to us.

BENVOLIO An if he hear thee, thou wilt anger him.

MERCUTIO This cannot anger him. 'Twould anger him
To raise a spirit in his mistress' circle
Of some strange nature, letting it there stand
Till she had laid it and conjured it down;
That were some spite. My invocation
Is fair and honest; in his mistress' name
I conjure only but to raise up him.

BENVOLIO Come! He hath hid himself among these trees   30
To be consorted with the humorous night:
Blind is his love and best befits the dark.

MERCUTIO If love be blind, love cannot hit the mark.
Now will he sit under a medlar tree,
And wish his mistress were that kind of fruit
As maids call medlars when they laugh alone.
O Romeo, that she were, O that she were
An open-arse and thou a poperin pear!
Romeo, goodnight. I'll to my truckle-bed;
This field-bed is too cold for me to sleep.   40
Come, shall we go?

BENVOLIO   Go then, for 'tis in vain
To seek him here that means not to be found.

                                        [they go

SCENE 2

ROMEO   He jests at scars that never felt a wound.

            JULIET *appears aloft at the window*

But soft! What light through yonder window breaks?
It is the east, and Juliet is the sun.
Arise, fair sun, and kill the envious moon,
Who is already sick and pale with grief
That thou, her maid, art far more fair than she.
Be not her maid, since she is envious.
Her vestal livery is but sick and green,
And none but fools do wear it: cast it off.
It is my lady, O it is my love;   10
O that she knew she were.
She speaks, yet she says nothing. What of that?
Her eye discourses: I will answer it.
I am too bold: 'tis not to me she speaks.
Two of the fairest stars in all the heaven,
Having some business, do entreat her eyes
To twinkle in their spheres till they return.
What if her eyes were there, they in her head?
The brightness of her cheek would shame those stars
As daylight doth a lamp; her eyes in heaven   20
Would through the airy region stream so bright
That birds would sing and think it were not night.
See how she leans her cheek upon her hand!
O that I were a glove upon that hand,
That I might touch that cheek.

JULIET   Ay me!

ROMEO   She speaks.
O speak again, bright angel, for thou art
As glorious to this night, being o'er my head,
As is a wingéd messenger of heaven
Unto the white-upturnéd wondering eyes
Of mortals that fall back to gaze on him   30
When he bestrides the lazy-passing clouds

          And sails upon the bosom of the air.

JULIET   O Romeo, Romeo! Wherefore art thou Romeo?
          Deny thy father and refuse thy name:
          Or, if thou wilt not, be but sworn my love,
          And I'll no longer be a Capulet.

ROMEO   Shall I hear more, or shall I speak at this?

JULIET   'Tis but thy name that is my enemy.
          Thou art thy self, though not a Montague.
          O be some other name! What's Montague?   40
          It is nor hand, nor foot, nor arm, nor face,
          Nor any part belonging to a man.
          What's in a name? That which we call a rose
          By any other name would smell as sweet.
          So Romeo would, were he not Romeo called,
          Retain that dear perfection which he owes,
          Without that title. Romeo, doff thy name;
          And for thy name, which is no part of thee,
          Take all myself.

ROMEO   I take thee at thy word.
          Call me but love, and I'll be new baptized;   50
          Henceforth I never will be Romeo.

JULIET   What man art thou that, thus bescreened in night,
          So stumblest on my counsel?

ROMEO   By a name
          I know not how to tell thee who I am.
          My name, dear saint, is hateful to myself
          Because it is an enemy to thee.
          Had I it written, I would tear the word.

JULIET   My ears have yet not drunk a hundred words
          Of thy tongue's uttering, yet I know the sound.
          Art thou not Romeo, and a Montague?   60

ROMEO   Neither, fair maid, if either thee dislike.

JULIET   How camest thou hither, tell me, and wherefore?
          The orchard walls are high and hard to climb,
          And the place death, considering who thou art,
          If any of my kinsmen find thee here.

ROMEO   With love's light wings did I o'erperch these walls;
          For stony limits cannot hold love out,
          And what love can do, that dares love attempt:

	Therefore thy kinsmen are no stop to me.

JULIET If they do see thee, they will murther thee.   70
ROMEO   Alack, there lies more peril in thine eye
        Than twenty of their swords. Look thou but sweet,
        And I am proof against their enmity.
JULIET I would not for the world they saw thee here.
ROMEO   I have night's cloak to hide me from their eyes;
        And but thou love me, let them find me here:
        My life were better ended by their hate
        Than death proroguéd, wanting of thy love.
JULIET By whose direction foundst thou out this place?
ROMEO   By love, that first did prompt me to enquire.   80
        He lent me counsel, and I lent him eyes.
        I am no pilot; yet, wert thou as far
        As that vast shore washed with the farthest sea,
        I should adventure for such merchandise.
JULIET Thou knowest the mask of night is on my face;
        Else would a maiden blush bepaint my cheek,
        For that which thou hast heard me speak tonight.
        Fain would I dwell on form; fain, fain deny
        What I have spoke: but farewell compliment!
        Dost thou love me? I know thou wilt say 'Ay',   90
        And I will take thy word. Yet, if thou swearst,
        Thou mayst prove false. At lovers' perjuries
        They say Jove laughs. O gentle Romeo,
        If thou dost love, pronounce it faithfully.
        Or, if thou think'st I am too quickly won,
        I'll frown and be perverse and say thee nay,
        So thou wilt woo; but else, not for the world.
        In truth, fair Montague, I am too fond,
        And therefore thou mayst think my haviour light;
        But trust me, gentleman, I'll prove more true   100
        Than those that have more cunning to be strange.
        I should have been more strange, I must confess,
        But that thou overheardst, ere I was ware,
        My true-love passion. Therefore pardon me,
        And not impute this yielding to light love,
        Which the dark night hath so discoveréd.
ROMEO   Lady, by yonder blesséd moon I vow,

That tips with silver all these fruit tree tops –

JULIET   O swear not by the moon, th' inconstant moon,
That monthly changes in her circled orb,   110
Lest that thy love prove likewise variable.

ROMEO   What shall I swear by?

JULIET   Do not swear at all:
Or, if thou wilt, swear by thy gracious self,
Which is the god of my idolatry,
And I'll believe thee.

ROMEO   If my heart's dear love –

JULIET   Well, do not swear. Although I joy in thee,
I have no joy of this contract tonight:
It is too rash, too unadvised, too sudden,
Too like the lightning, which doth cease to be
Ere one can say 'It lightens'. Sweet, goodnight: 120
This bud of love, by summer's ripening breath,
May prove a beauteous flower when next we meet.
Goodnight, goodnight! As sweet repose and rest
Come to thy heart as that within my breast.

ROMEO   O wilt thou leave me so unsatisfied?

JULIET   What satisfaction canst thou have tonight?

ROMEO   Th'exchange of thy love's faithful vow for mine.

JULIET   I gave thee mine before thou didst request it:
And yet I would it were to give again.

ROMEO   Would'st thou withdraw it? For what purpose, love?   130

JULIET   But to be frank and give it thee again:
And yet I wish but for the thing I have.
My bounty is as boundless as the sea,
My love as deep: the more I give to thee,
The more I have: for both are infinite.
I hear some noise within. Dear love, adieu –

                           [*Nurse calls within*

Anon, good nurse! – sweet Montague, be true.
Stay but a little; I will come again.   [*Juliet goes in*

ROMEO   O blessed, blessed night! I am afeared,
Being in night, all this is but a dream,   140
Too flattering sweet to be substantial.

       JULIET *reappears at the window*

JULIET   Three words, dear Romeo, and good night indeed.

             If that thy bent of love be honourable,
             Thy purpose marriage, send me word tomorrow,
             By one that I'll procure to come to thee,
             Where and what time thou wilt perform the rite;
             And all my fortunes at thy foot I'll lay,
             And follow thee my lord throughout the world.

NURSE   [*within*] Madam!

JULIET   I come, anon. – But if thou meanest not well,   150
             I do beseech thee –

NURSE   [*within*]   Madam!

JULIET   By and by I come –
             To cease thy suit, and leave me to my grief.
             Tomorrow will I send.

ROMEO   So thrive my soul –

JULIET   A thousand times good night!
                                    [*she goes in*

ROMEO   A thousand times the worse, to want thy light!
             Love goes toward love as schoolboys from their books,
             But love from love, toward school with heavy looks.

                    JULIET *returns to the window*

JULIET   Hist, Romeo, hist! O for a falconer's voice
             To lure this tassel-gentle back again!
             Bondage is hoarse and may not speak aloud,   160
             Else would I tear the cave where Echo lies,
             And make her airy tongue more hoarse than mine
             With repetition of my "Romeo!"

ROMEO   It is my soul that calls upon my name.
             How silver-sweet sound lovers' tongues by night,
             Like softest music to attending ears!

JULIET   Romeo!

ROMEO   My niëss!

JULIET   What o'clock tomorrow
             Shall I send to thee?

ROMEO   By the hour of nine.

JULIET   I will not fail. 'Tis twenty year till then.
             I have forgot why I did call thee back.   170

ROMEO   Let me stand here till thou remember it.

JULIET   I shall forget, to have thee still stand there,

        Rememb'ring how I love thy company.

ROMEO   And I'll still stay, to have thee still forget,
        Forgetting any other home but this.

JULIET   'Tis almost morning. I would have thee gone,
        And yet no farther than a wanton's bird,
        That lets it hop a little from her hand,
        Like a poor prisoner in his twisted gyves,
        And with a silk thread plucks it back again,   180
        So loving-jealous of his liberty.

ROMEO   I would I were thy bird.

JULIET   Sweet, so would I;
        Yet I should kill thee with much cherishing.
        Goodnight, goodnight! Parting is such sweet sorrow,
        That I shall say goodnight till it be morrow.

ROMEO   Sleep dwell upon thine eyes, peace in thy breast!
        Would I were sleep and peace, so sweet to rest!

                                           [*she goes in*

        Hence will I to my ghostly sire's close cell,
        His help to crave, and my dear hap to tell.   [*he goes*

SCENE 3

Friar Lawrence's cell

'Enter FRIAR *alone with a basket*'

FRIAR   The grey-eyed morn smiles on the frowning night,
        Check'ring the eastern clouds with streaks of light:
        And darkness fleckéd like a drunkard reels
        From forth day's pathway, made by Titan's wheels:
        Now ere the sun advance his burning eye,
        The day to cheer and night's dank dew to dry,
        I must upfill this osier cage of ours,
        With baleful weeds and precious-juicéd flowers.
        The earth that's nature's mother is her tomb;
        What is her burying grave, that is her womb;   10
        And from her womb children of divers kind
        We sucking on her natural bosom find:
        Many for many virtues excellent,
        None but for some, and yet all different.

O mickle is the powerful grace that lies
In plants, herbs, stones, and their true qualities:
For nought so vile that on the earth doth live
But to the earth some special good doth give:
Nor aught so good but, strained from that fair use,
Revolts from true birth, stumbling on abuse.   20
Virtue itself turns vice, being misapplied,
And vice sometime by action dignified.

       ROMEO *approaches, unseen by the Friar*

Within the infant rind of this weak flower
Poison hath residence, and medicine power:
For this, being smelt, with that part cheers each part;
Being tasted, stays all senses with the heart.
Two such opposéd kings encamp them still
In man as well as herbs – grace and rude will:
And where the worser is predominant,
Full soon the canker death eats up that plant.   30

ROMEO	Good morrow, father.
FRIAR	Benedicite!

What early tongue so sweet saluteth me?
Young son, it argues a distempered head,
So soon to bid goodmorrow to thy bed.
Care keeps his watch in every old man's eye,
And where care lodges sleep will never lie:
But where unbruiséd youth with unstuffed brain
Doth couch his limbs, there golden sleep doth reign.
Therefore thy earliness doth me assure
Thou art uproused with some distemperature   40
Or if not so, then here I hit it right –
Our Romeo hath not been in bed tonight.

ROMEO	That last is true – the sweeter rest was mine.
FRIAR	God pardon sin! Wast thou with Rosaline?
ROMEO	With Rosaline? My ghostly father, no;
	I have forgot that name, and that name's woe.
FRIAR	That's my good son! But where hast thou been then?
ROMEO	I'll tell thee ere thou ask it me again.
	I have been feasting with mine enemy,
	Where on a sudden one hath wounded me 50
	That's by me wounded. Both our remedies

	Within thy help and holy physic lies.	
	I bear no hatred, blessed man, for lo,	
	My intercession likewise steads my foe.	
FRIAR	Be plain, good son, and homely in thy drift.	
	Riddling confession finds but riddling shrift.	
ROMEO	Then plainly know my heart's dear love is set	
	On the fair daughter of rich Capulet:	
	As mine on hers, so hers is set on mine,	
	And all combined save what thou must combine	60
	By holy marriage: when and where and how	
	We met, we wooed, and made exchange of vow	
	I'll tell thee as we pass; but this I pray,	
	That thou consent to marry us today.	
FRIAR	Holy Saint Francis, what a change is here!	
	Is Rosaline, that thou didst love so dear,	
	So soon forsaken? Young men's love then lies	
	Not truly in their hearts but in their eyes.	
	Jesu Maria, what a deal of brine	
	Hath washed thy sallow cheeks for Rosaline!	70
	How much salt water thrown away in waste	
	To season love, that of it doth not taste!	
	The sun not yet thy sighs from heaven clears,	
	Thy old groans ring yet in mine ancient ears;	
	Lo, here upon thy cheek the stain doth sit	
	Of an old tear that is not washed off yet.	
	If e'er thou wast thyself, and these woes thine,	
	Thou and these woes were all for Rosaline.	
	And art thou changed? Pronounce this sentence, then –	
	Women may fall, when there's no strength in men.	80
ROMEO	Thou chid'st me oft for loving Rosaline.	
FRIAR	For doting, not for loving, pupil mine.	
ROMEO	And bad'st me bury love.	
FRIAR	Not in a grave	
	To lay one in, another out to have.	
ROMEO	I pray thee chide me not. Her I love now	
	Doth grace for grace and love for love allow:	
	The other did not so.	
FRIAR	O, she knew well	
	Thy love did read by rote, that could not spell.	

But come, young waverer, come go with me;
In one respect I'll thy assistant be: 90
For this alliance may so happy prove
To turn your households' rancour to pure love.

ROMEO   O let us hence! I stand on sudden haste.

FRIAR   Wisely and slow. They stumble that run fast.   [*they go*

SCENE 4

A public place

'Enter BENVOLIO *and* MERCUTIO*'*

MERCUTIO Where the devil should this Romeo be? Came he not
          home tonight?

BENVOLIO Not to his father's; I spoke with his man.

MERCUTIO Why, that same pale hard-hearted wench, that Rosaline,
          Torments him so, that he will sure run mad.

BENVOLIO Tybalt, the kinsman to old Capulet,
          Hath sent a letter to his father's house.

MERCUTIO A challenge, on my life.

BENVOLIO Romeo will answer it.

MERCUTIO Any man that can write may answer a letter.   10

BENVOLIO Nay, he will answer the letter's master, how he dares
          being dared.

MERCUTIO Alas, poor Romeo, he is already dead – stabbed with a
          white wench's black eye, run through the ear with a
          love-song, the very pin of his heart cleft with the blind
          bow-boy's butt-shaft; and is he a man to encounter
          Tybalt?

BENVOLIO Why, what is Tybalt?

MERCUTIO More than Prince of Cats. O, he's the courageous cap-
          tain of compliments. He fights as you sing pricksong – 20
          keeps time, distance, and proportion; he rests his minim
          rests – one, two, and the third in your bosom. The very
          butcher of a silk button, a duellist, a duellist, a gentle-
          man of the very first house, of the first and second cause!
          Ah, the immortal passado, the punto reverso, the hai!

BENVOLIO The what?

MERCUTIO The pox of such antic, lisping, affecting fantasticoes, these new tuners of accent! 'By Jesu, a very good blade! a very tall man! a very good whore!' Why, is not this a lamentable thing, grandsire, that we should 30 be thus afflicted with these strange flies, these fashion-mongers, these pardon-me's, who stand so much on the new form that they cannot sit at ease on the old bench? O, their bones, their bones!

'*Enter* ROMEO'

BENVOLIO Here comes Romeo, here comes Romeo!

MERCUTIO Without his roe, like a dried herring. O flesh, flesh, how art thou fishified! Now is he for the numbers that Petrarch flowed in. Laura to his lady was a kitchen wench – marry, she had a better love to be-rhyme her! – Dido a dowdy, Cleopatra a gipsy, Helen and 40 Hero hildings and harlots, Thisbe a gray eye or so, but not to the purpose. Signior Romeo, bon jour! There's a French salutation to your French slop. You gave us the counterfeit fairly last night.

ROMEO Good morrow to you both. What counterfeit did I give you?

MERCUTIO The slip, sir, the slip. Can you not conceive?

ROMEO Pardon, good Mercutio. My business was great, and in such a case as mine a man may strain courtesy.

MERCUTIO That's as much as to say, such a case as yours constrains 50 a man to bow in the hams.

ROMEO Meaning to curtsy?

MERCUTIO Thou hast most kindly hit it.

ROMEO A most courteous exposition.

MERCUTIO Nay, I am the very pink of courtesy.

ROMEO Pink for flower?

MERCUTIO Right.

ROMEO Why, then is my pump well flowered.

MERCUTIO Sure wit! Follow me this jest now till thou hast worn out thy pump, that, when the single sole of it is worn, 60 the jest may remain, after the wearing, solely singular.

ROMEO O single-soled jest, solely singular for the singleness!

MERCUTIO Come between us, good Benvolio; my wits faints.

ROMEO   Switch and spurs, switch and spurs; or I'll cry a match.

MERCUTIO   Nay, if our wits run the wild-goose chase, I am done:
           for thou hast more of the wild goose in one of thy wits
           than, I am sure, I have in my whole five. Was I with
           you there for the goose?

ROMEO   Thou wast never with me for anything when thou
           wast not there for the goose.   70

MERCUTIO   I will bite thee by the ear for that jest.

ROMEO   Nay, good goose, bite not.

MERCUTIO   Thy wit is a very bitter sweeting; it is a most sharp
           sauce.

ROMEO   And is it not then well served in to a sweet goose?

MERCUTIO   O, here's a wit of cheveril, that stretches from an inch
           narrow to an ell broad.

ROMEO   I stretch it out for that word 'broad', which, added to
           the goose, proves thee far and wide a broad goose.

MERCUTIO   Why, is not this better now than groaning for love?   80
           Now art thou sociable, now art thou Romeo: now art
           thou what thou art, by art as well as by nature. For this
           drivelling love is like a great natural that runs lolling up
           and down to hide his bauble in a hole.

BENVOLIO   Stop there, stop there!

MERCUTIO   Thou desirest me to stop in my tale, against the hair?

BENVOLIO   Thou wouldst else have made thy tale large.

MERCUTIO   O, thou art deceived! I would have made it short, for I
           was come to the whole depth of my tale, and meant
           indeed to occupy the argument no longer.   90

The NURSE *in her best array is seen approaching with her man* PETER

ROMEO   Here's goodly gear! A sail, a sail!

MERCUTIO   Two, two! a shirt and a smock.

NURSE   Peter!

PETER   Anon.

NURSE   My fan, Peter.

MERCUTIO   Good Peter, to hide her face; for her fan's the fairer
           face.

NURSE   God ye good morrow, gentlemen.

MERCUTIO   God ye good-den, fair gentlewoman.

NURSE   Is it good-den?   10

MERCUTIO 'Tis no less, I tell ye; for the bawdy hand of the dial is now upon the prick of noon.

NURSE Out upon you! What a man are you?

ROMEO One, gentlewoman, that God hath made, himself to mar.

NURSE By my troth, it is well said. 'For himself to mar,' quoth 'a? Gentlemen, can any of you tell me where I may find the young Romeo?

ROMEO I can tell you; but young Romeo will be older when you have found him than he was when you sought him. 110 I am the youngest of that name, for fault of a worse.

NURSE You say well.

MERCUTIO Yea, is the worst well? Very well took, i' faith! Wisely, wisely!

NURSE If you be he, sir, I desire some confidence with you.

BENVOLIO She will indite him to some supper.

MERCUTIO A bawd, a bawd, a bawd! So ho!

ROMEO What, hast thou found?

MERCUTIO No hare, sir; unless a hare, sir, in a lenten pie, that is something stale and hoar ere it be spent. 120

'He walks by them and sings'

> An old hare hoar
> And an old hare hoar
> Is very good meat in Lent.
> But a hare that is hoar
> Is too much for a score
> When it hoars ere it be spent.

Romeo, will you come to your father's? We'll to dinner thither.

ROMEO I will follow you.

MERCUTIO Farewell, ancient lady; farewell, [*singing*] 'lady, lady, lady'.   [*Mercutio and Benvolio go off* 130

NURSE I pray you, sir, what saucy merchant was this that was so full of his ropery?

ROMEO A gentleman, Nurse, that loves to hear himself talk, and will speak more in a minute than he will stand to in a month.

NURSE And 'a speak anything against me, I'll take him down

and 'a were lustier than he is, and twenty such Jacks: and if I cannot, I'll find those that shall. Scurvy knave! I am none of his flirt-gills, I am none of his skains-mates. [*To Peter*] And thou must stand by too, and suffer every knave to use me at his pleasure! 140

PETER   I saw no man use you at his pleasure. If I had, my weapon should quickly have been out. I warrant you I dare draw as soon as another man, if I see occasion in a good quarrel, and the law on my side.

NURSE   Now afore God, I am so vexed that every part about me quivers. Scurvy knave! Pray you, sir, a word. And as I told you, my young lady bid me enquire you out. What she bid me say I will keep to myself: but first let me tell ye, if ye should lead her in a fool's paradise, as 150 they say, it were a very gross kind of behaviour, as they say: for the gentlewoman is young; and therefore, if you should deal double with her, truly it were an ill thing to be offered to any gentlewoman, and very weak dealing.

ROMEO   Nurse, commend me to thy lady and mistress. I protest unto thee –

NURSE   Good heart! and i' faith I will tell her as much. Lord, Lord! she will be a joyful woman.

ROMEO   What wilt thou tell her, Nurse? Thou dost not mark me! 160

NURSE   I will tell her, sir, that you do protest, which, as I take it, is a gentlemanlike offer.

ROMEO   Bid her devise
Some means to come to shrift this afternoon,
And there she shall at Friar Lawrence' cell
Be shrived and married. Here is for thy pains.

NURSE   No, truly, sir; not a penny.

ROMEO   Go to, I say you shall.

NURSE   This afternoon, sir; well, she shall be there.

ROMEO   And stay, good Nurse, behind the abbey wall. 170
Within this hour my man shall be with thee
And bring thee cords made like a tackled stair,
Which to the high topgallant of my joy
Must be my convoy in the secret night.
Farewell. Be trusty, and I'll quit thy pains.

Farewell. Commend me to thy mistress.

NURSE Now God in heaven bless thee! Hark you, sir.

ROMEO What sayst thou, my dear Nurse?

NURSE Is your man secret? Did you ne'er hear say,
  'Two may keep counsel, putting one away'? 180

ROMEO I warrant thee my man's as true as steel.

NURSE Well, sir, my mistress is the sweetest lady. Lord, Lord!
  when 'twas a little prating thing – O, there is a nobleman in town, one Paris, that would fain lay knife
  aboard: but she, good soul, had as lief see a toad, a very
  toad, as see him. I anger her sometimes, and tell her
  that Paris is the properer man; but I'll warrant you,
  when I say so, she looks as pale as any clout in the
  versal world. Doth not rosemary and Romeo begin
  both with a letter? 190

ROMEO Ay, Nurse; what of that? Both with an R.

NURSE Ah, mocker, that's the dog-name; R is for the – No; I
  know it begins with some other letter; and she hath
  the prettiest sententious of it, of you and rosemary,
  that it would do you good to hear it.

ROMEO Commend me to thy lady.

NURSE Ay, a thousand times. [*Romeo goes*] Peter!

PETER Anon.

NURSE Before and apace.   [*they go*

SCENE 5

Capulet's orchard

'Enter JULIET*'*

JULIET The clock struck nine when I did send the Nurse;
  In half an hour she promised to return.
  Perchance she cannot meet him. That's not so.
  O, she is lame! Love's heralds should be thoughts,
  Which ten times faster glides than the sun's beams
  Driving back shadows over louring hills.
  Therefore do nimble-pinioned doves draw Love,
  And therefore hath the wind-swift Cupid wings.
  Now is the sun upon the highmost hill

Of this day's journey, and from nine till twelve   10
Is three long hours; yet she is not come.
Had she affections and warm youthful blood,
She would be swift in motion as a ball;
My words would bandy her to my sweet love,
And his to me.
But old folks, many feign as they were dead –
Unwieldy, slow, heavy, and pale as lead.

'Enter NURSE*', with* PETER

O God, she comes! O honey Nurse, what news?
Hast thou met with him? Send thy man away.

NURSE	Peter, stay at the gate. [*Peter withdraws* 20
JULIET	Now good sweet Nurse – O Lord, why look'st thou sad?
	Though news be sad, yet tell them merrily;
	If good, thou shamest the music of sweet news
	By playing it to me with so sour a face.
NURSE	I am aweary, give me leave a while.
	Fie, how my bones ache! What a jaunce have I!
JULIET	I would thou hadst my bones, and I thy news:
	Nay, come, I pray thee speak; good, good Nurse, speak.
NURSE	Jesu, what haste! Can you not stay awhile?
	Do you not see that I am out of breath? 30
JULIET	How art thou out of breath when thou hast breath
	To say to me that thou art out of breath?
	The excuse that thou dost make in this delay
	Is longer than the tale thou dost excuse.
	Is thy news good or bad? Answer to that.
	Say either, and I'll stay the circumstance.
	Let me be satisfied; is't good or bad?
NURSE	Well, you have made a simple choice; you know not
	how to choose a man. Romeo? No, not he. Though
	his face be better than any man's, yet his leg excels all 40
	men's; and for a hand and a foot and a body, though
	they be not to be talked on, yet they are past compare.
	He is not the flower of courtesy, but, I'll warrant him,
	as gentle as a lamb. Go thy ways, wench; serve God.
	What, have you dined at home?
JULIET	No, no. But all this did I know before.
	What says he of our marriage, what of that?

NURSE   Lord, how my head aches! what a head have I!
         It beats as it would fall in twenty pieces.
         My back o' t'other side; ah, my back, my back!   50
         Beshrew your heart for sending me about
         To catch my death with jauncing up and down.
JULIET   I' faith, I am sorry that thou art not well.
         Sweet, sweet, sweet Nurse, tell me, what says my love?
NURSE   Your love says, like an honest gentleman, and a cour-
         teous, and a kind, and a handsome, and, I warrant, a
         virtuous – Where is your mother?
JULIET   Where is my mother? Why, she is within.
         Where should she be? How oddly thou repliest:
         'Your love says, like an honest gentleman,   60
         "Where is your mother?" '
NURSE   O God's Lady dear!
         Are you so hot? Marry come up, I trow!
         Is this the poultice for my aching bones?
         Henceforward do your messages yourself.
JULIET   Here's such a coil! Come, what says Romeo?
NURSE   Have you got leave to go to shrift today?
JULIET   I have.
NURSE   Then hie you hence to Friar Lawrence' cell;
         There stays a husband to make you a wife.
         Now comes the wanton blood up in your cheeks;   70
         They'll be in scarlet straight at any news.
         Hie you to church; I must another way,
         To fetch a ladder, by the which your love
         Must climb a bird's nest soon when it is dark.
         I am the drudge, and toil in your delight:
         But you shall bear the burden soon at night.
         Go; I'll to dinner; hie you to the cell.
JULIET   Hie to high fortune! Honest Nurse, farewell.   [they go

SCENE 6

Friar Lawrence's cell

'Enter FRIAR *and* ROMEO

FRIAR   So smile the heavens upon this holy act
           That after-hours with sorrow chide us not.
ROMEO   Amen, amen. But come what sorrow can,
           It cannot countervail the exchange of joy
           That one short minute gives me in her sight.
           Do thou but close our hands with holy words,
           Then love-devouring death do what he dare;
           It is enough I may but call her mine.
FRIAR   These violent delights have violent ends,
           And in their triumph die like fire and powder   10
           Which, as they kiss, consume. The sweetest honey
           Is loathsome in his own deliciousness,
           And in the taste confounds the appetite.
           Therefore love moderately; long love doth so:
           Too swift arrives as tardy as too slow.
           Here comes the lady.

'Enter JULIET*'*

                    O, so light a foot
           Will ne'er wear out the everlasting flint!
           A lover may bestride the gossamers
           That idles in the wanton summer air,
           And yet not fall; so light is vanity.   20
JULIET   Good even to my ghostly confessor.
FRIAR   Romeo shall thank thee, daughter, for us both.
JULIET   As much to him, else is his thanks too much.
                                                [*they embrace*
ROMEO   Ah, Juliet, if the measure of thy joy
           Be heaped like mine, and that thy skill be more
           To blazon it, then sweeten with thy breath
           This neighbour air, and let rich music's tongue
           Unfold the imagined happiness that both
           Receive in either by this dear encounter.

JULIET   Conceit, more rich in matter than in words,   30
          Brags of his substance, not of ornament.
          They are but beggars that can count their worth;
          But my true love is grown to such excess
          I cannot sum up sum of half my wealth.
FRIAR   Come, come with me, and we will make short work;
          For, by your leaves, you shall not stay alone
          Till Holy Church incorporate two in one.   [they go

ACT 3 SCENE I

A public place

'Enter MERCUTIO, BENVOLIO, *and men'*

BENVOLIO I pray thee, good Mercutio, let's retire;
The day is hot, the Capels are abroad:
And if we meet we shall not scape a brawl,
For now, these hot days, is the mad blood stirring.

MERCUTIO Thou art like one of these fellows that, when he enters
the confines of a tavern, claps me his sword upon the
table and says 'God send me no need of thee'; and, by
the operation of the second cup, draws him on the
drawer, when indeed there is no need.

BENVOLIO Am I like such a fellow?   10

MERCUTIO Come, come, thou art as hot a Jack in thy mood as any
in Italy; and as soon moved to be moody, and as soon
moody to be moved.

BENVOLIO And what to?

MERCUTIO Nay, an there were two such, we should have none
shortly, for one would kill the other. Thou? Why,
thou wilt quarrel with a man that hath a hair more or a
hair less in his beard than thou hast. Thou wilt quarrel
with a man for cracking nuts, having no other reason
but because thou hast hazel eyes. What eye but such   20
an eye would spy out such a quarrel? Thy head is as
full of quarrels as an egg is full of meat, and yet thy
head hath been beaten as addle as an egg for quarrelling. Thou hast quarrelled with a man for coughing in
the street, because he hath wakened thy dog that hath
lain asleep in the sun. Didst thou not fall out with a
tailor for wearing his new doublet before Easter? With
another for tying his new shoes with old riband? And
yet thou wilt tutor me from quarrelling?

BENVOLIO An I were so apt to quarrel as thou art, any man should 30
buy the fee-simple of my life for an hour and a
quarter.

MERCUTIO The fee-simple? O simple!

'Enter TYBALT*', 'and others'*

BENVOLIO	By my head, here comes the Capulets.
MERCUTIO	By my heel, I care not.
TYBALT	Follow me close, for I will speak to them.
	Gentlemen, good-den: a word with one of you.
MERCUTIO	And but one word with one of us? Couple it with
	something; make it a word and a blow.
TYBALT	You shall find me apt enough to that, sir, an you will 40
	give me occasion.
MERCUTIO	Could you not take some occasion without giving?
TYBALT	Mercutio, thou consort'st with Romeo –
MERCUTIO	Consort? What, dost thou make us minstrels? An thou
	make minstrels of us, look to hear nothing but
	discords. Here's my fiddlestick; here's that shall make
	you dance. Zounds, consort!
BENVOLIO	We talk here in the public haunt of men.
	Either withdraw unto some private place
	And reason coldly of your grievances, 50
	Or else depart: here all eyes gaze on us.
MERCUTIO	Men's eyes were made to look, and let them gaze.
	I will not budge for no man's pleasure, I.

'Enter ROMEO*'*

TYBALT	Well, peace be with you, sir; here comes my man.
MERCUTIO	But I'll be hanged, sir, if he wears your livery.
	Marry, go before to field, he'll be your follower!
	Your worship in that sense may call him man.
TYBALT	Romeo, the love I bear thee can afford
	No better term than this: thou art a villain.
ROMEO	Tybalt, the reason that I have to love thee 60
	Doth much excuse the appertaining rage
	To such a greeting. Villain am I none –
	Therefore farewell; I see thou knowest me not.
TYBALT	Boy, this shall not excuse the injuries
	That thou hast done me; therefore turn and draw.
ROMEO	I do protest I never injured thee,
	But love thee better than thou canst devise
	Till thou shalt know the reason of my love:
	And so, good Capulet, which name I tender

As dearly as mine own, be satisfied.   70
MERCUTIO O calm, dishonourable, vile submission!
'Alla stoccata' carries it away.   [draws
Tybalt, you rat-catcher, will you walk?
TYBALT   What wouldst thou have with me?
MERCUTIO Good King of Cats, nothing but one of your nine lives
that I mean to make bold withal and, as you shall use
me hereafter, dry-beat the rest of the eight. Will you
pluck your sword out of his pilcher by the ears? Make
haste, lest mine be about your ears ere it be out.
TYBALT   I am for you.   [draws 80
ROMEO   Gentle Mercutio, put thy rapier up.
MERCUTIO Come, sir, your passado.   [they fight
ROMEO   Draw, Benvolio; beat down their weapons.
Gentlemen, for shame forbear this outrage.
Tybalt, Mercutio, the prince expressly hath
Forbid this bandying in Verona streets.
Hold, Tybalt! good Mercutio!

'Tybalt under Romeo's arm thrusts Mercutio in and flies'

MERCUTIO   I am hurt.
A plague o' both your houses! I am sped.
Is he gone and hath nothing?
BENVOLIO   What, art thou hurt?   90
MERCUTIO Ay, ay, a scratch, a scratch; marry, 'tis enough.
Where is my page? Go, villain, fetch a surgeon.
[Page goes
ROMEO   Courage, man; the hurt cannot be much.
MERCUTIO No, 'tis not so deep as a well, nor so wide as a church
door, but 'tis enough, 'twill serve. Ask for me tomor-
row and you shall find me a grave man. I am peppered,
I warrant, for this world. A plague o' both your
houses! Zounds! A dog, a rat, a mouse, a cat, to scratch
a man to death! A braggart, a rogue, a villain, that
fights by the book of arithmetic! Why the devil came 100
you between us? I was hurt under your arm.
ROMEO   I thought all for the best.
MERCUTIO Help me into some house, Benvolio,
Or I shall faint. A plague o' both your houses!

They have made worms' meat of me. I have it,
And soundly too. Your houses!

                        [*Benvolio helps him away*

ROMEO   This gentleman, the prince's near ally,
My very friend, hath got this mortal hurt
In my behalf, my reputation stained
With Tybalt's slander – Tybalt that an hour   110
Hath been my cousin. O sweet Juliet,
Thy beauty hath made me effeminate,
And in my temper softened valour's steel!

BENVOLIO *returns*

BENVOLIO   O Romeo, Romeo, brave Mercutio's dead.
That gallant spirit hath aspired the clouds,
Which too untimely here did scorn the earth.

ROMEO   This day's black fate on moe days doth depend;
This but begins the woe others must end.

TYBALT *returns*

BENVOLIO   Here comes the furious Tybalt back again.

ROMEO   Again! in triumph, and Mercutio slain!   120
Away to heaven, respective lenity,
And fire-eyed fury be my conduct now!
Now, Tybalt, take the 'villain' back again
That late thou gavest me, for Mercutio's soul
Is but a little way above our heads,
Staying for thine to keep him company.
Either thou or I, or both, must go with him.

TYBALT   Thou wretched boy that didst consort him here
Shalt with him hence.

ROMEO   This shall determine that.

                 [*'they fight, Tybalt falls'*

BENVOLIO   Romeo, away, be gone!   130
The citizens are up, and Tybalt slain.
Stand not amazed. The prince will doom thee death
If thou art taken. Hence, be gone, away!

ROMEO   O, I am Fortune's fool.

BENVOLIO   Why dost thou stay?

                           [*Romeo goes*

'Enter Citizens'

A CITIZEN Which way ran he that killed Mercutio?
          Tybalt, that murderer, which way ran he?
BENVOLIO There lies that Tybalt.
A CITIZEN   Up, sir, go with me:
          I charge thee in the prince's name obey.

'Enter PRINCE, *old* MONTAGUE, CAPULET, *their wives and all'*

PRINCE   Where are the vile beginners of this fray?
BENVOLIO O noble Prince, I can discover all   140
          The unlucky manage of this fatal brawl.
          There lies the man, slain by young Romeo,
          That slew thy kinsman, brave Mercutio.
LADY CAP. Tybalt, my cousin, O my brother's child!
          O prince! O husband! O, the blood is spilled
          Of my dear kinsman. Prince, as thou art true,
          For blood of ours shed blood of Montague.
          O cousin, cousin!
PRINCE   Benvolio, who began this bloody fray?
BENVOLIO Tybalt, here slain, whom Romeo's hand did slay.   150
          Romeo, that spoke him fair, bid him bethink
          How nice the quarrel was, and urged withal
          Your high displeasure. All this – utteréd
          With gentle breath, calm look, knees humbly bowed –
          Could not take truce with the unruly spleen
          Of Tybalt deaf to peace, but that he tilts
          With piercing steel at bold Mercutio's breast,
          Who, all as hot, turns deadly point to point,
          And, with a martial scorn, with one hand beats
          Cold death aside and with the other sends   160
          It back to Tybalt, whose dexterity
          Retorts it. Romeo he cries aloud,
          'Hold, friends! friends, part!' and, swifter than his
                                                        tongue,
          His agile arm beats down their fatal points,
          And 'twixt them rushes; underneath whose arm
          An envious thrust from Tybalt hit the life
          Of stout Mercutio, and then Tybalt fled,
          But by and by comes back to Romeo

Who had but newly entertained revenge,
And to 't they go like lightning; for, ere I   170
Could draw to part them, was stout Tybalt slain,
And, as he fell, did Romeo turn and fly:
This is the truth, or let Benvolio die.

LADY CAP. He is a kinsman to the Montague;
Affection makes him false, he speaks not true.
Some twenty of them fought in this black strife,
And all those twenty could but kill one life.
I beg for justice, which thou, Prince, must give:
Romeo slew Tybalt; Romeo must not live.

PRINCE   Romeo slew him; he slew Mercutio.   180
Who now the price of his dear blood doth owe?

MONTAG.   Not Romeo, Prince; he was Mercutio's friend;
His fault concludes but what the law should end –
The life of Tybalt.

PRINCE   And for that offence
Immediately we do exile him hence.
I have an interest in your hearts' proceeding:
My blood for your rude brawls doth lie a-bleeding.
But I'll amerce you with so strong a fine
That you shall all repent the loss of mine.
I will be deaf to pleading and excuses;   190
Nor tears nor prayers shall purchase out abuses.
Therefore use none. Let Romeo hence in haste,
Else, when he is found, that hour is his last.
Bear hence this body, and attend our will.
Mercy but murders, pardoning those that kill.

                                        [*they go*

SCENE 2

Capulet's house

'Enter JULIET *alone'*

JULIET   Gallop apace, you fiery-footed steeds,
Towards Phoebus' lodging! Such a waggoner
As Phaëton would whip you to the west
And bring in cloudy night immediately.

Spread thy close curtain, love-performing night,
That runaways' eyes may wink, and Romeo
Leap to these arms untalked of and unseen.
Lovers can see to do their amorous rites
By their own beauties; or, if love be blind,
It best agrees with night. Come, civil Night,   10
Thou sober-suited matron all in black,
And learn me how to lose a winning match,
Played for a pair of stainless maidenhoods.
Hood my unmanned blood, bating in my cheeks,
With thy black mantle till strange love, grown bold,
Think true love acted simple modesty.
Come, Night! Come, Romeo! Come, thou day in night;
For thou wilt lie upon the wings of night
Whiter than snow upon a raven's back.
Come, gentle Night; come, loving, black-browed
                                        Night: 20
Give me my Romeo; and, when he shall die,
Take him and cut him out in little stars,
And he will make the face of heaven so fine
That all the world will be in love with night
And pay no worship to the garish sun.
O, I have bought the mansion of a love,
But not possessed it; and though I am sold,
Not yet enjoyed. So tedious is this day
As is the night before some festival
To an impatient child that hath new robes   30
And may not wear them. O, here comes my nurse,

                'Enter NURSE with cords'

And she brings news; and every tongue that speaks
But Romeo's name speaks heavenly eloquence.
Now, Nurse, what news? What hast thou there?
                                        The cords
That Romeo bid thee fetch?

NURSE   Ay, ay, the cords.
                                        [*throws them down*

JULIET   Ay me, what news? Why dost thou wring thy hands?
NURSE   Ah, weraday! He's dead, he's dead, he's dead!
We are undone, lady, we are undone.

	Alack the day, he's gone, he's killed, he's dead!
JULIET	Can heaven be so envious?
NURSE	Romeo can, 40

Though heaven cannot. O Romeo, Romeo!
Who ever would have thought it? Romeo!

JULIET   What devil art thou that dost torment me thus?
This torture should be roared in dismal hell.
Hath Romeo slain himself? Say thou but 'ay',
And that bare vowel 'I' shall poison more
Than the death-darting eye of cockatrice.
I am not I if there be such an 'I',
Or those eyes shut that makes thee answer 'ay'.
If he be slain, say 'ay', or, if not, 'no'.   50
Brief sounds determine of my weal or woe.

NURSE   I saw the wound, I saw it with mine eyes,
(God save the mark!) here on his manly breast.
A piteous corse, a bloody piteous corse,
Pale, pale as ashes, all bedaubed in blood,
All in gore blood; I swounded at the sight.

JULIET   O break, my heart! Poor bankrout, break at once!
To prison, eyes; ne'er look on liberty.
Vile earth, to earth resign, end motion here,
And thou and Romeo press one heavy bier!   60

NURSE   O Tybalt, Tybalt, the best friend I had!
O courteous Tybalt, honest gentleman,
That ever I should live to see thee dead!

JULIET   What storm is this that blows so contrary?
Is Romeo slaught'red? And is Tybalt dead?
My dearest cousin, and my dearer lord?
Then, dreadful trumpet, sound the general doom;
For who is living if those two are gone?

NURSE   Tybalt is gone and Romeo banishéd;
Romeo that killed him, he is banishéd.   70

JULIET   O God! did Romeo's hand shed Tybalt's blood?

NURSE   It did, it did! alas the day, it did!

JULIET   O serpent heart, hid with a flowering face!
Did ever dragon keep so fair a cave?
Beautiful tyrant, fiend angelical,
Dove-feathered raven, wolvish-ravening lamb!

Despiséd substance of divinest show,
Just opposite to what thou justly seemst –
A damnéd saint, an honourable villain!
O nature, what hadst thou to do in hell   80
When thou didst bower the spirit of a fiend
In mortal paradise of such sweet flesh?
Was ever book containing such vile matter
So fairly bound? O that deceit should dwell
In such a gorgeous palace!

NURSE   There's no trust,
No faith, no honesty in men; all perjured,
All forsworn, all naught, all dissemblers.
Ah, where's my man? Give me some aqua vitae.
These griefs, these woes, these sorrows make me old.
Shame come to Romeo!

JULIET   Blistered be thy tongue   90
For such a wish! He was not born to shame.
Upon his brow shame is ashamed to sit:
For 'tis a throne where honour may be crowned
Sole monarch of the universal earth.
O what a beast was I to chide at him!

NURSE   Will you speak well of him that killed your cousin?
JULIET   Shall I speak ill of him that is my husband?
Ah, poor my lord, what tongue shall smooth thy name
When I, thy three-hours wife, have mangled it?
But wherefore, villain, didst thou kill my cousin?   100
That villain cousin would have killed my husband.
Back, foolish tears, back to your native spring!
Your tributary drops belong to woe
Which you, mistaking, offer up to joy.
My husband lives, that Tybalt would have slain,
And Tybalt's dead that would have slain my husband:
All this is comfort; wherefore weep I then?
Some word there was, worser than Tybalt's death,
That murd'red me. I would forget it fain,
But oh, it presses to my memory   110
Like damnéd guilty deeds to sinners' minds –
'Tybalt is dead and Romeo banishéd'.
That 'banishéd', that one word 'banishéd',

Hath slain ten thousand Tybalts. Tybalt's death
Was woe enough if it had ended there:
Or, if sour woe delights in fellowship
And needly will be ranked with other griefs,
Why followed not, when she said 'Tybalt's dead',
'Thy father', or 'thy mother', nay, or both,
Which modern lamentation might have moved?   120
But, with a rearward following Tybalt's death,
'Romeo is banishéd'! To speak that word
Is father, mother, Tybalt, Romeo, Juliet,
All slain, all dead: 'Romeo is banishéd'!
There is no end, no limit, measure, bound,
In that word's death; no words can that woe sound.
Where is my father and my mother, Nurse?

NURSE   Weeping and wailing over Tybalt's corse.
Will you go to them? I will bring you thither.

JULIET   Wash they his wounds with tears? Mine shall be
                                        spent,   130
When theirs are dry, for Romeo's banishment.
Take up those cords. Poor ropes, you are beguiled,
Both you and I, for Romeo is exiled.
He made you for a highway to my bed,
But I, a maid, die maiden-widowéd.
Come, cords; come, Nurse: I'll to my wedding bed,
And death, not Romeo, take my maidenhead!

NURSE   Hie to your chamber. I'll find Romeo
To comfort you: I wot well where he is.
Hark ye, your Romeo will be here at night: 140
I'll to him; he is hid at Lawrence' cell.

JULIET   O find him! Give this ring to my true knight
And bid him come to take his last farewell.

                                        [they go

SCENE 3

Friar Lawrence's cell with his study at the back

Enter FRIAR

FRIAR   Romeo, come forth; come forth, thou fearful man.
             Affliction is enamoured of thy parts,
             And thou art wedded to calamity.

Enter ROMEO *from the study*

ROMEO   Father, what news? What is the prince's doom?
             What sorrow craves acquaintance at my hand
             That I yet know not?

FRIAR   Too familiar
             Is my dear son with such sour company!
             I bring thee tidings of the prince's doom.

ROMEO   What less than doomsday is the prince's doom?

FRIAR   A gentler judgment vanished from his lips;   10
             Not body's death, but body's banishment.

ROMEO   Ha, banishment? Be merciful, say 'death':
             For exile hath more terror in his look,
             Much more than death: do not say 'banishment'.

FRIAR   Hence from Verona art thou banishéd.
             Be patient, for the world is broad and wide.

ROMEO   There is no world without Verona walls,
             But purgatory, torture, hell itself:
             Hence banishéd is banished from the world,
             And world's exile is death. Then 'banishéd'   20
             Is death mis-termed. Calling death 'banishéd',
             Thou cut'st my head off with a golden axe,
             And smilest upon the stroke that murders me.

FRIAR   O deadly sin! O rude unthankfulness!
             Thy fault our law calls death, but the kind Prince,
             Taking thy part, hath rushed aside the law,
             And turned that black word 'death' to 'banishment'.
             This is dear mercy, and thou seest it not.

ROMEO   'Tis torture and not mercy. Heaven is here
             Where Juliet lives, and every cat and dog   30

And little mouse, every unworthy thing,
Live here in heaven and may look on her,
But Romeo may not. More validity,
More honourable state, more courtship, lives
In carrion flies than Romeo: they may seize
On the white wonder of dear Juliet's hand,
And steal immortal blessing from her lips,
Who even in pure and vestal modesty
Still blush, as thinking their own kisses sin;
This may flies do, when I from this must fly;   40
And say'st thou yet that exile is not death?
But Romeo may not – he is banishéd.
Flies may do this, but I from this must fly:
They are free men, but I am banishéd.
Hadst thou no poison mixed, no sharp-ground knife,
No sudden mean of death, though ne'er so mean,
But 'banishéd' to kill me? 'Banishéd'!
O friar, the damnéd use that word in hell:
Howling attends it. How hast thou the heart,
Being a divine, a ghostly confessor,   50
A sin-absolver, and my friend professed,
To mangle me with that word 'banishéd'?

FRIAR   Thou fond mad man, hear me a little speak.
ROMEO   O thou wilt speak again of banishment.
FRIAR   I'll give thee armour to keep off that word –
         Adversity's sweet milk, philosophy,
         To comfort thee though thou art banishéd.
ROMEO   Yet 'banishéd'? Hang up philosophy!
         Unless philosophy can make a Juliet,
         Displant a town, reverse a prince's doom,   60
         It helps not, it prevails not; talk no more.
FRIAR   O then I see that madmen have no ears.
ROMEO   How should they, when that wise men have no eyes?
FRIAR   Let me dispute with thee of thy estate.
ROMEO   Thou canst not speak of that thou dost not feel.
         Wert thou as young as I, Juliet thy love,
         An hour but married, Tybalt murderéd,
         Doting like me, and like me banishéd,

Then mightst thou speak, then mightst thou tear
                                        thy hair,
And fall upon the ground as I do now,   70
Taking the measure of an unmade grave.
                              [*knocking without*

FRIAR   Arise; one knocks. Good Romeo, hide thyself.

ROMEO   Not I, unless the breath of heartsick groans
           Mist-like infold me from the search of eyes.
                              [*knocking again*

FRIAR   Hark, how they knock! – Who's there? – Romeo, arise;
           Thou wilt be taken. – Stay awhile! – Stand up;
                              [*louder knocking*
           Run to my study. – By and by! – God's will,
           What simpleness is this? – I come, I come.
                              [*knocking yet again*
           Who knocks so hard? Whence come you? What's
                                        your will?

NURSE   [*from without*]
           Let me come in and you shall know my errand   80
           I come from Lady Juliet.

FRIAR   Welcome then.

                        '*Enter* NURSE'

NURSE   O holy friar, O tell me, holy friar,
           Where is my lady's lord? Where's Romeo?

FRIAR   There on the ground, with his own tears made drunk.

NURSE   O he is even in my mistress' case,
           Just in her case.

FRIAR   O woeful sympathy:
           Piteous predicament!

NURSE   Even so lies she,
           Blubbering and weeping, weeping and blubbering.
           Stand up, stand up! Stand an you be a man;
           For Juliet's sake, for her sake rise and stand   90
           Why should you fall into so deep an O?

ROMEO   [*rising*] Nurse!

NURSE   Ah sir, ah sir, death's the end of all.

ROMEO   Spakest thou of Juliet? How is it with her?
           Doth not she think me an old murderer,
           Now I have stained the childhood of our joy

With blood removed but little from her own?
Where is she? And how doth she? And what says
My concealed lady to our cancelled love?

NURSE   O she says nothing, sir, but weeps and weeps,
And now falls on her bed, and then starts up,   100
And Tybalt calls, and then on Romeo cries,
And then down falls again.

ROMEO   As if that name,
Shot from the deadly level of a gun,
Did murder her, as that name's curséd hand
Murdered her kinsman. O tell me, friar, tell me,
In what vile part of this anatomy
Doth my name lodge? Tell me, that I may sack
The hateful mansion.   ['he offers to stab himself,
                              and Nurse snatches the dagger away'

FRIAR   Hold thy desperate hand!
Art thou a man? Thy form cries out thou art:
Thy tears are womanish, thy wild acts denote   110
The unreasonable fury of a beast.
Unseemly woman in a seeming man,
And ill-beseeming beast in seeming both!
Thou hast amazed me. By my holy order,
I thought thy disposition better tempered.
Hast thou slain Tybalt? Wilt thou slay thyself?
And slay thy lady, that in thy life lives,
By doing damnéd hate upon thyself?
Why rail'st thou on thy birth, the heaven, and earth,
Since birth, and heaven, and earth, all three do meet   120
In thee at once, which thou at once wouldst lose?
Fie, fie! thou sham'st thy shape, thy love, thy wit,
Which like a usurer abound'st in all,
And usest none in that true use indeed
Which should bedeck thy shape, thy love, thy wit.
Thy noble shape is but a form of wax,
Digressing from the valour of a man;
Thy dear love sworn but hollow perjury,
Killing that love which thou hast vowed to cherish;
Thy wit, that ornament to shape and love,   130
Misshapen in the conduct of them both,

Like powder in a skilless soldier's flask
Is set afire by thine own ignorance,
And thou dismembered with thine own defence.
What, rouse thee, man! Thy Juliet is alive,
For whose dear sake thou wast but lately dead.
There art thou happy. Tybalt would kill thee,
But thou slewest Tybalt. There art thou happy.
The law that threatened death becomes thy friend,
And turns it to exile. There art thou happy too.   140
A pack of blessings light upon thy back;
Happiness courts thee in her best array;
But, like a misbehaved and sullen wench,
Thou pouts upon thy fortune and thy love.
Take heed, take heed, for such die miserable.
Go get thee to thy love, as was decreed;
Ascend her chamber; hence and comfort her.
But look thou stay not till the watch be set,
For then thou canst not pass to Mantua,
Where thou shalt live till we can find a time   150
To blaze your marriage, reconcile your friends,
Beg pardon of the prince, and call thee back
With twenty hundred thousand times more joy
Than thou wentst forth in lamentation.
Go before, Nurse. Commend me to thy lady,
And bid her hasten all the house to bed,
Which heavy sorrow makes them apt unto.
Romeo is coming.

NURSE   O Lord, I could have stayed here all the night
To hear good counsel; O what learning is!   160
My lord, I'll tell my lady you will come.

ROMEO   Do so, and bid my sweet prepare to chide.

                    'Nurse offers to go in and turns again'

NURSE   Here, sir, a ring she bid me give you, sir.
Hie you, make haste, for it grows very late.   [*she goes*

ROMEO   How well my comfort is revived by this.

FRIAR   Go hence; goodnight; and here stands all your state:
Either be gone before the watch be set,
Or by the break of day disguised from hence.
Sojourn in Mantua. I'll find out your man,

And he shall signify from time to time   170
Every good hap to you that chances here.
Give me thy hand. 'Tis late; farewell, goodnight.

ROMEO   But that a joy past joy calls out on me,
It were a grief so brief to part with thee.
Farewell.   [*they go*

SCENE 4

Capulet's house

'Enter old CAPULET, *his wife, and* PARIS'

CAPULET   Things have fall'n out, sir, so unluckily
That we have had no time to move our daughter.
Look you, she loved her kinsman Tybalt dearly,
And so did I. Well, we were born to die.
'Tis very late; she'll not come down tonight.
I promise you, but for your company,
I would have been abed an hour ago.

PARIS   These times of woe afford no times to woo.
Madam, goodnight; commend me to your daughter.

LADY CAP. I will, and know her mind early tomorrow;   10
Tonight she's mewed up to her heaviness.

Paris offers to go; Capulet calls him again

CAPULET   Sir Paris, I will make a desperate tender
Of my child's love: I think she will be ruled
In all respects by me: nay more, I doubt it not.
Wife, go you to her ere you go to bed;
Acquaint her ear of my son Paris' love,
And bid her, mark you me, on Wednesday next –
But soft, what day is this?

PARIS   Monday, my lord.

CAPULET: Monday, ha, ha; well, Wednesday is too soon;
O' Thursday let it be – O' Thursday, tell her,   20
She shall be married to this noble earl –
Will you be ready? Do you like this haste?
We'll keep no great ado; a friend or two:
For hark you, Tybalt being slain so late,

It may be thought we held him carelessly,
Being our kinsman, if we revel much:
Therefore we'll have some half a dozen friends,
And there an end. But what say you to Thursday?

PARIS   My lord, I would that Thursday were tomorrow.

CAPULET Well, get you gone. O' Thursday be it then.   30
Go you to Juliet ere you go to bed;
Prepare her, wife, against this wedding day.
Farewell, my lord. Light to my chamber, ho!
Afore me, 'tis so very late, that we
May call it early by and by. Goodnight.   *[they go*

SCENE 5

*Juliet's bedroom: to one side the window above
the orchard; to the other a door*

ROMEO *and* JULIET *stand by the window*

JULIET   Wilt thou be gone? It is not yet near day.
It was the nightingale, and not the lark,
That pierced the fearful hollow of thine ear.
Nightly she sings on yond pomegranate tree.
Believe me, love, it was the nightingale.

ROMEO   It was the lark, the herald of the morn;
No nightingale. Look, love, what envious streaks
Do lace the severing clouds in yonder east.
Night's candles are burnt out, and jocund day
Stands tiptoe on the misty mountain tops.   10
I must be gone and live, or stay and die.

JULIET   Yond light is not daylight; I know it, I:
It is some meteor that the sun exhaled
To be to thee this night a torchbearer
And light thee on thy way to Mantua.
Therefore stay yet; thou needst not to be gone.

ROMEO   Let me be ta'en, let me be put to death;
I am content, so thou wilt have it so.
I'll say yon gray is not the morning's eye,
'Tis but the pale reflex of Cynthia's brow;   20
Nor that is not the lark whose notes do beat

The vaulty heaven so high above our heads.
I have more care to stay than will to go:
Come, death, and welcome! Juliet wills it so.
How is't, my soul? Let's talk; it is not day.

JULIET   It is, it is! Hie hence, be gone, away!
It is the lark that sings so out of tune,
Straining harsh discords and unpleasing sharps.
Some say the lark makes sweet division:
This doth not so, for she divideth us.   30
Some say the lark and loathéd toad changed eyes;
O now I would they had changed voices too,
Since arm from arm that voice doth us affray,
Hunting thee hence with hunt's-up to the day.
O now be gone! More light and light it grows.

ROMEO   More light and light, more dark and dark our woes.

                        'Enter NURSE hastily'

NURSE   Madam!
JULIET   Nurse?
NURSE   Your lady mother is coming to your chamber.
The day is broke; be wary, look about.   40
                              [*she goes; Juliet bolts the door*
JULIET   Then, window, let day in and let life out.
ROMEO   Farewell, farewell; one kiss, and I'll descend.
                              [*he lowers the ladder and descends*
JULIET   Art thou gone so, love, lord, ay husband, friend?
I must hear from thee every day in the hour,
For in a minute there are many days.
O, by this count I shall be much in years
Ere I again behold my Romeo.

ROMEO   [*from the orchard*] Farewell!
I will omit no opportunity
That may convey my greetings, love, to thee.   50

JULIET   O, think'st thou we shall ever meet again?
ROMEO   I doubt it not; and all these woes shall serve
For sweet discourses in our times to come.
JULIET   O God, I have an ill-divining soul!
Methinks I see thee, now thou art so low,
As one dead in the bottom of a tomb.
Either my eyesight fails or thou look'st pale.

ROMEO   And trust me, love, in my eye so do you.
           Dry sorrow drinks our blood. Adieu, adieu!
                                                        [*he goes*

JULIET   O Fortune, Fortune, all men call thee fickle;   60
           If thou art fickle, what dost thou with him
           That is renowned for faith? Be fickle, Fortune:
           For then I hope thou wilt not keep him long,
           But send him back.

LADY CAP. [*without the door*]   Ho, daughter, are you up?

JULIET   [*pulls up and conceals the ladder*]
           Who is't that calls? It is my lady mother.
           Is she not down so late, or up so early?
           What unaccustomed cause procures her hither?
                                              [*she unlocks the door*

                    Enter LADY CAPULET

LADY CAP. Why, how now, Juliet?

JULIET   Madam, I am not well.

LADY CAP. Evermore weeping for your cousin's death?
           What, wilt thou wash him from his grave with tears?   70
           An if thou couldst, thou couldst not make him live:
           Therefore have done – some grief shows much of love,
           But much of grief shows still some want of wit.

JULIET   Yet let me weep for such a feeling loss.

LADY CAP. So shall you feel the loss, but not the friend
           Which you weep for.

JULIET   Feeling so the loss,
           I cannot choose but ever weep the friend.

LADY CAP. Well, girl, thou weep'st not so much for his death,
           As that the villain lives which slaughtered him.

JULIET   What villain, madam?

LADY CAP.   That same villain Romeo,   80

JULIET   Villain and he be many miles asunder.
           [*aloud*] God pardon him; I do, with all my heart:
           And yet no man like he doth grieve my heart.

LADY CAP. That is because the traitor murderer lives.

JULIET   Ay, madam, from the reach of these my hands.
           Would none but I might venge my cousin's death!

LADY CAP. We will have vengeance for it, fear thou not.
           Then weep no more. I'll send to one in Mantua,

Where that same banished runagate doth live,
Shall give him such an unaccustomed dram   90
That he shall soon keep Tybalt company;
And then I hope thou wilt be satisfied.

JULIET   Indeed I never shall be satisfied
With Romeo till I behold him – dead –
Is my poor heart so for a kinsman vexed.
Madam, if you could find out but a man
To bear a poison, I would temper it
That Romeo should upon receipt thereof
Soon sleep in quiet. O how my heart abhors
To hear him named and cannot come to him   100
To wreak the love I bore my cousin
Upon his body that hath slaughtered him.

LADY CAP. Find thou the means and I'll find such a man.
But now I'll tell thee joyful tidings, girl.

JULIET   And joy comes well in such a needy time.
What are they, I beseech your ladyship?

LADY CAP. Well, well, thou hast a careful father, child;
One who, to put thee from thy heaviness,
Hath sorted out a sudden day of joy
That thou expects not, nor I looked not for.   110

JULIET   Madam, in happy time! What day is that?

LADY CAP. Marry, my child, early next Thursday morn
The gallant, young, and noble gentleman,
The County Paris, at Saint Peter's Church
Shall happily make thee there a joyful bride.

JULIET   Now by Saint Peter's Church, and Peter too,
He shall not make me there a joyful bride.
I wonder at this haste, that I must wed
Ere he that should be husband comes to woo.
I pray you tell my lord and father, madam,   120
I will not marry yet; and when I do, I swear
It shall be Romeo, whom you know I hate,
Rather than Paris. These are news indeed!

LADY CAP. Here comes your father; tell him so yourself,
And see how he will take it at your hands.

'Enter CAPULET and NURSE'

CAPULET   When the sun sets, the air doth drizzle dew;

But for the sunset of my brother's son
It rains downright.
How now, a conduit, girl? What, still in tears?
Evermore showering? In one little body   130
Thou counterfeits a bark, a sea, a wind:
For still thy eyes, which I may call the sea,
Do ebb and flow with tears; the bark thy body is,
Sailing in this salt flood; the winds thy sighs,
Who raging with thy tears, and they with them,
Without a sudden calm will overset
Thy tempest-tossèd body. How now, wife?
Have you delivered to her our decree?

LADY CAP. Ay, sir; but she will none, she gives you thanks.
I would the fool were married to her grave!   140

CAPULET Soft, take me with you, take me with you, wife.
How? Will she none? Doth she not give us thanks?
Is she not proud? Doth she not count her blest,
Unworthy as she is, that we have wrought
So worthy a gentleman to be her bride?

JULIET   Not proud you have, but thankful that you have.
Proud can I never be of what I hate,
But thankful even for hate that is meant love.

CAPULET How how! how how, chop-logic! What is this?
'Proud', and 'I thank you', and 'I thank you not',   150
And yet 'not proud', mistress minion you?
Thank me no thankings nor proud me no prouds,
But fettle your fine joints 'gainst Thursday next
To go with Paris to Saint Peter's Church,
Or I will drag thee on a hurdle thither.
Out, you green-sickness carrion! Out, you baggage!
You tallow-face!

LADY CAP.   Fie, fie! what, are you mad?

JULIET   [kneeling] Good father, I beseech you on my knees,
Hear me with patience but to speak a word.

CAPULET Hang thee, young baggage! disobedient wretch!   160
I tell thee what; get thee to church o' Thursday,
Or never after look me in the face.
Speak not, reply not, do not answer me!
My fingers itch. Wife, we scarce thought us blest

That God had lent us but this only child;
But now I see this one is one too much,
And that we have a curse in having her.
Out on her, hilding!

NURSE   God in heaven bless her!
You are to blame, my lord, to rate her so.

CAPULET And why, my Lady Wisdom? Hold your tongue,   170
Good Prudence. Smatter with your gossips, go!

NURSE   I speak no treason.

CAPULET   O Godigoden!

NURSE   May not one speak?

CAPULET   Peace, you mumbling fool!
Utter your gravity o'er a gossip's bowl,
For here we need it not.

LADY CAP.   You are too hot.

CAPULET God's bread! It makes me mad. Day, night, work, play,
Alone, in company, still my care hath been
To have her matched; and having now provided
A gentleman of noble parentage,
Of fair demesnes, youthful and nobly trained,   180
Stuffed, as they say, with honourable parts,
Proportioned as one's thought would wish a man –
And then to have a wretched puling fool,
A whining mammet, in her fortune's tender,
To answer 'I'll not wed, I cannot love;
I am too young, I pray you pardon me.'
But, an you will not wed, I'll pardon you –
Graze where you will; you shall not house with me.
Look to't, think on't; I do not use to jest.
Thursday is near. Lay hand on heart; advise.   190
An you be mine, I'll give you to my friend;
An you be not, hang, beg, starve, die in the streets,
For by my soul I'll ne'er acknowledge thee,
Nor what is mine shall never do thee good:
Trust to't; bethink you; I'll not be forsworn.
                                        [he goes

JULIET   Is there no pity sitting in the clouds
That sees into the bottom of my grief?
O sweet my mother, cast me not away!

Delay this marriage for a month, a week;
Or, if you do not, make the bridal bed   200
In that dim monument where Tybalt lies.

LADY CAP. Talk not to me, for I'll not speak a word;
Do as thou wilt, for I have done with thee.   [*she goes*

JULIET   O God! — O nurse, how shall this be prevented?
My husband is on earth, my faith in heaven;
How shall that faith return again to earth,
Unless that husband send it me from heaven
By leaving earth? Comfort me, counsel me.
Alack, alack, that heaven should practise stratagems
Upon so soft a subject as myself!   210
What sayst thou? Hast thou not a word of joy?
Some comfort, nurse.

NURSE   Faith, here it is. Romeo
Is banishèd; and all the world to nothing
That he dares ne'er come back to challenge you;
Or, if he do, it needs must be by stealth.
Then, since the case so stands as now it doth,
I think it best you married with the County.
O, he's a lovely gentleman!
Romeo's a dishclout to him. An eagle, madam,
Hath not so green, so quick, so fair an eye   220
As Paris hath. Beshrew my very heart,
I think you are happy in this second match,
For it excels your first; or, if it did not,
Your first is dead — or 'twere as good he were
As living here and you no use of him.

JULIET   Speakst thou from thy heart?

NURSE   And from my soul too; else beshrew them both.

JULIET   Amen!

NURSE   What?

JULIET   Well, thou hast comforted me marvellous much.   230
Go in and tell my lady I am gone,
Having displeased my father, to Lawrence' cell
To make confession and to be absolved.

NURSE   Marry, I will; and this is wisely done.   [*she goes*

JULIET   Ancient damnation! O most wicked fiend!
Is it more sin to wish me thus forsworn,

Or to dispraise my lord with that same tongue
Which she hath praised him with above compare
So many thousand times? Go, counsellor!
Thou and my bosom henceforth shall be twain.   240
I'll to the friar to know his remedy.
If all else fail, myself have power to die.   [*she goes*

ACT 4 SCENE I

Friar Lawrence's cell

'Enter FRIAR *and County* PARIS*'*

FRIAR	On Thursday, sir? The time is very short.
PARIS	My father Capulet will have it so,
	And I am nothing slow to slack his haste.
FRIAR	You say you do not know the lady's mind?
	Uneven is the course; I like it not.
PARIS	Immoderately she weeps for Tybalt's death,
	And therefore have I little talked of love,
	For Venus smiles not in a house of tears.
	Now, sir, her father counts it dangerous
	That she do give her sorrow so much sway, 10
	And in his wisdom hastes our marriage
	To stop the inundation of her tears,
	Which, too much minded by herself alone,
	May be put from her by society.
	Now do you know the reason of this haste.
FRIAR	I would I knew not why it should be slowed –
	Look, sir, here comes the lady toward my cell.

'Enter JULIET*'*

PARIS	Happily met, my lady and my wife!
JULIET	That may be, sir, when I may be a wife.
PARIS	That 'may be' must be, love, on Thursday next. 20
JULIET	What must be shall be.
FRIAR	That's a certain text.
PARIS	Come you to make confession to this father?
JULIET	To answer that, I should confess to you.
PARIS	Do not deny to him that you love me.
JULIET	I will confess to you that I love him.
PARIS	So will ye, I am sure, that you love me.
JULIET	If I do so, it will be of more price,
	Being spoke behind your back, than to your face.
PARIS	Poor soul, thy face is much abused with tears.
JULIET	The tears have got small victory by that, 30

	For it was bad enough before their spite.
PARIS	Thou wrong'st it more than tears with that report.
JULIET	That is no slander, sir, which is a truth;
	And what I spake, I spake it to my face.
PARIS	Thy face is mine, and thou hast sland'red it.
JULIET	It may be so, for it is not mine own. –
	Are you at leisure, holy father, now,
	Or shall I come to you at evening mass?
FRIAR	My leisure serves me, pensive daughter, now.
	My lord, we must entreat the time alone. 40
PARIS	God shield I should disturb devotion!
	Juliet, on Thursday early will I rouse ye;
	Till then adieu, and keep this holy kiss.

[kisses her, and departs

JULIET	O shut the door, and, when thou hast done so,
	Come weep with me – past hope, past cure, past help.
FRIAR	O Juliet, I already know thy grief;
	It strains me past the compass of my wits.
	I hear thou must, and nothing may prorogue it,
	On Thursday next be married to this County.
JULIET	Tell me not, friar, that thou hearest of this, 50
	Unless thou tell me how I may prevent it.
	If in thy wisdom thou canst give no help,
	Do thou but call my resolution wise
	And with this knife I'll help it presently.
	God joined my heart and Romeo's, thou our hands;
	And ere this hand, by thee to Romeo's sealed,
	Shall be the label to another deed,
	Or my true heart with treacherous revolt
	Turn to another, this shall slay them both:
	Therefore, out of thy long-experienced time, 60
	Give me some present counsel; or, behold,
	'Twixt my extremes and me this bloody knife
	Shall play the umpire, arbitrating that
	Which the commission of thy years and art
	Could to no issue of true honour bring.
	Be not so long to speak: I long to die
	If what thou speak'st speak not of remedy.
FRIAR	Hold, daughter. I do spy a kind of hope,

Which craves as desperate an execution
As that is desperate which we would prevent.
If, rather than to marry County Paris,
Thou hast the strength of will to slay thyself,
Then is it likely thou wilt undertake
A thing like death to chide away this shame,
That copest with death himself to scape from it;
And, if thou darest, I'll give thee remedy.

JULIET   O bid me leap, rather than marry Paris,
From off the battlements of any tower,
Or walk in thievish ways, or bid me lurk
Where serpents are; chain me with roaring bears,   80
Or hide me nightly in a charnel house,
O'ercovered quite with dead men's rattling bones,
With reeky shanks and yellow chapless skulls;
Or bid me go into a new-made grave
And lay me with a dead man in his shroud –
Things that, to hear them told, have made me
                                        tremble –
And I will do it without fear or doubt,
To live an unstained wife to my sweet love.

FRIAR   Hold, then. Go home, be merry, give consent
To marry Paris. Wednesday is tomorrow.   90
Tomorrow night look that thou lie alone;
Let not the nurse lie with thee in thy chamber.
Take thou this vial, being then in bed,
And this distilléd liquor drink thou off,
When presently through all thy veins shall run
A cold and drowsy humour, for no pulse
Shall keep his native progress, but surcease;
No warmth, no breath, shall testify thou livest;
The roses in thy lips and cheeks shall fade
To wanny ashes, thy eyes' windows fall   10
Like death when he shuts up the day of life.
Each part, deprived of supple government,
Shall stiff and stark and cold appear like death;
And in this borrowed likeness of shrunk death
Thou shalt continue two and forty hours,
And then awake as from a pleasant sleep.

Now, when the bridegroom in the morning comes
To rouse thee from thy bed, there art thou dead.
Then, as the manner of our country is,
In thy best robes, uncovered on the bier,   110
Thou shalt be borne to that same ancient vault
Where all the kindred of the Capulets lie.
In the meantime, against thou shalt awake,
Shall Romeo by my letters know our drift,
And hither shall he come; and he and I
Will watch thy waking, and that very night
Shall Romeo bear thee hence to Mantua.
And this shall free thee from this present shame,
If no inconstant toy nor womanish fear
Abate thy valour in the acting it.   120

JULIET   Give me, give me! O tell not me of fear!

FRIAR   Hold, get you gone! Be strong and prosperous
In this resolve. I'll send a friar with speed
To Mantua with my letters to thy lord.

JULIET   Love give me strength! And strength shall help afford.
Farewell, dear father.   [*they go*

SCENE 2

Capulet's house

Enter CAPULET, LADY CAPULET, NURSE
and two or three Servingmen

CAPULET   [*giving a paper*]
So many guests invite as here are writ.
                  [*Servingman goes out with it*
[*to another*] Sirrah, go hire me twenty cunning cooks.

SERV'MAN   You shall have none ill, sir; for I'll try if they can lick
their fingers.

CAPULET   How canst thou try them so?

SERV'MAN   Marry, sir, 'tis an ill cook that cannot lick his own
fingers: therefore he that cannot lick his fingers goes
not with me.

CAPULET   Go, be gone.   [*he goes*
We shall be much unfurnished for this time.   10

What, is my daughter gone to Friar Lawrence?

NURSE   Ay, forsooth.

CAPULET   Well, he may chance to do some good on her.
A peevish self-willed harlotry it is.

'Enter JULIET*'*

NURSE   See where she comes from shrift with merry look.

CAPULET   How now, my headstrong? Where have you been
                                                                    gadding?

JULIET   Where I have learned me to repent the sin
Of disobedient opposition
To you and your behests, and am enjoined
By holy Lawrence to fall prostrate here   20
To beg your pardon. [*abasing herself*] Pardon,
                                                        I beseech you!
Henceforward I am ever ruled by you.

CAPULET   Send for the County: go tell him of this.
I'll have this knot knit up tomorrow morning.

JULIET   I met the youthful lord at Lawrence' cell
And gave him what becoméd love I might,
Not stepping o'er the bounds of modesty.

CAPULET   Why, I am glad on't; this is well. Stand up.
This is as 't should be. Let me see, the County:
Ay, marry, go, I say, and fetch him hither.   30
Now, afore God, this reverend holy friar,
All our whole city is much bound to him.

JULIET   Nurse, will you go with me into my closet
To help me sort such needful ornaments
As you think fit to furnish me tomorrow?

LADY CAP. No, not till Thursday; there is time enough.

CAPULET   Go, nurse, go with her; we'll to church tomorrow.
                                        [*Nurse departs with Juliet*

LADY CAP. We shall be short in our provision;
'Tis now near night.

CAPULET   Tush, I will stir about,
And all things shall be well, I warrant thee, wife.   40
Go thou to Juliet; help to deck up her.
I'll not to bed tonight. Let me alone;
I'll play the housewife for this once. What, ho!
They are all forth; well, I will walk myself

To County Paris, to prepare up him
Against tomorrow. My heart is wondrous light
Since this same wayward girl is so reclaimed.   [*they go*

SCENE 3

Juliet's chamber; at the back a bed with curtains

'*Enter* JULIET *and* NURSE'

JULIET   Ay, those attires are best. But, gentle nurse,
            I pray thee leave me to myself tonight:
            For I have need of many orisons
            To move the heavens to smile upon my state,
            Which well thou knowest is cross and full of sin.

Enter LADY CAPULET

LADY CAP.   What, are you busy, ho? Need you my help?
JULIET   No, madam, we have culled such necessaries
            As are behoveful for our state tomorrow.
            So please you, let me now be left alone,
            And let the nurse this night sit up with you,   10
            For I am sure you have your hands full all
            In this so sudden business.
LADY CAP.   Good night.
            Get thee to bed and rest, for thou hast need.
                              [*she departs with the Nurse*
JULIET   Farewell! God knows when we shall meet again.
            I have a faint cold fear thrills through my veins
            That almost freezes up the heat of life.
            I'll call them back again to comfort me.
            Nurse! – What should she do here?
            My dismal scene I needs must act alone.
            Come, vial!   20
            What if this mixture do not work at all?
            Shall I be married then tomorrow morning?
            No, no! This shall forbid it. Lie thou there.
                              [*laying down her knife*
            What if it be a poison which the friar
            Subtly hath minist'red to have me dead,

Lest in this marriage he should be dishonoured
Because he married me before to Romeo?
I fear it is; and yet methinks it should not,
For he hath still been tried a holy man.
How if, when I am laid into the tomb,   30
I wake before the time that Romeo
Come to redeem me? There's a fearful point!
Shall I not then be stifled in the vault,
To whose foul mouth no healthsome air breathes in,
And there die strangled ere my Romeo comes?
Or, if I live, is it not very like
The horrible conceit of death and night,
Together with the terror of the place –
As in a vault, an ancient receptacle
Where for this many hundred years the bones   40
Of all my buried ancestors are packed;
Where bloody Tybalt, yet but green in earth,
Lies festering in his shroud; where, as they say,
At some hours in the night spirits resort –
Alack, alack, is it not like that I,
So early waking – what with loathsome smells,
And shrieks like mandrakes' torn out of the earth,
That living mortals, hearing them, run mad –
O, if I wake, shall I not be distraught,
Environéd with all these hideous fears,   50
And madly play with my forefathers' joints,
And pluck the mangled Tybalt from his shroud,
And, in this rage, with some great kinsman's bone,
As with a club, dash out my desp'rate brains?
O, look! Methinks I see my cousin's ghost
Seeking out Romeo, that did spit his body
Upon a rapier's point. Stay, Tybalt, stay!
Romeo, I come! This do I drink to thee.

                    ['*she falls upon her bed within the curtains*'

SCENE 4

Hall in Capulet's house

Enter LADY CAPULET *and* 'NURSE, *with herbs'*

LADY CAP. Hold, take these keys and fetch more spices, nurse.

NURSE   They call for dates and quinces in the pastry.

'Enter old CAPULET*'*

CAPULET   Come, stir, stir, stir! The second cock hath crowed:
The curfew bell hath rung, 'tis three o'clock.
Look to the baked meats, good Angelica;
Spare not for cost.

NURSE   Go, you cot-quean, go,
Get you to bed. Faith, you'll be sick tomorrow
For this night's watching.

CAPULET   No, not a whit. What, I have watched ere now
All night for lesser cause, and ne'er been sick.   10

LADY CAP. Ay, you have been a mouse-hunt in your time,
But I will watch you from such watching now.

                    [*she hurries out with Nurse*

CAPULET   A jealous hood, a jealous hood!

'Enter three or four with spits and logs and baskets'

                 Now, fellow, what is there?

1 SER'MAN Things for the cook, sir; but I know not what.

CAPULET   Make haste, make haste.   [*1 Servingman goes*]
                  Sirrah, fetch drier logs.
Call Peter; he will show thee where they are.

2 SER'MAN I have a head, sir, that will find out logs
And never trouble Peter for the matter.

CAPULET   Mass, and well said; a merry whoreson, ha!
Thou shalt be loggerhead.   [*2 Servingman goes*]
                  Good faith, 'tis day!   20
The County will be here with music straight,
For so he said he would. [*music*] I hear him near.
Nurse! Wife! What, ho! What, nurse, I say!

'*Enter* NURSE'

Go waken Juliet; go and trim her up.
I'll go and chat with Paris. Hie, make haste,
Make haste! The bridegroom he is come already:
Make haste, I say.   [*they go*

SCENE 5

Juliet's chamber; the curtains closed about the bed

Enter NURSE

NURSE   Mistress! What, mistress! Juliet! Fast, I warrant her, she.
Why, lamb! why, lady! Fie, you slug-a-bed!
Why, love, I say! madam! sweetheart! why, bride!
What, not a word? You take your pennyworths now!
Sleep for a week; for the next night, I warrant,
The County Paris hath set up his rest
That you shall rest but little. God forgive me!
Marry, and amen! How sound is she asleep!
I needs must wake her. Madam, madam, madam!
Ay, let the County take you in your bed,   10
He'll fright you up, i'faith! Will it not be?
                              [*draws back the curtains*
What, dressed, and in your clothes, and down again?
I must needs wake you. Lady, lady, lady!   [*shakes her*
Alas, alas! Help, help! My lady's dead!
O weraday that ever I was born!
Some aqua vitae, ho! My lord! My lady!

Enter LADY CAPULET

LADY CAP. What noise is here?
NURSE   O lamentable day!
LADY CAP. What is the matter?
NURSE   Look, look! O heavy day!
LADY CAP. O me, O me! My child, my only life!
Revive, look up, or I will die with thee!   20
Help, help! Call help.

Enter CAPULET

CAPULET   For shame, bring Juliet forth; her lord is come.
NURSE   She's dead, deceased: she's dead, alack the day!
LADY CAP. Alack the day, she's dead, she's dead, she's dead!
CAPULET   Ha, let me see her. Out, alas! She's cold,
          Her blood is settled, and her joints are stiff:
          Life and these lips have long been separated;
          Death lies on her like an untimely frost
          Upon the sweetest flower of all the field.
NURSE   O lamentable day!
LADY CAP.   O woeful time!   30
CAPULET   Death, that hath ta'en her hence to make me wail,
          Ties up my tongue and will not let me speak.

          'Enter FRIAR *and the* COUNTY*' with Musicians*

FRIAR   Come, is the bride ready to go to church?
CAPULET   Ready to go, but never to return.
          O son, the night before thy wedding day
          Hath Death lain with thy wife. There she lies,
          Flower as she was, defloweréd by him.
          Death is my son-in-law, Death is my heir;
          My daughter he hath wedded! I will die
          And leave him all; life, living, all is Death's.   40
PARIS   Have I thought long to see this morning's face,
          And doth it give me such a sight as this?
LADY CAP. Accursed, unhappy, wretched, hateful day!
          Most miserable hour that e'er time saw
          In lasting labour of his pilgrimage!
          But one, poor one, one poor and loving child,
          But one thing to rejoice and solace in,
          And cruel Death hath catched it from my sight!
NURSE   O woe! O woeful, woeful, woeful day!
          Most lamentable day, most woeful day   50
          That ever, ever I did yet behold!
          O day, O day, O day, O hateful day!
          Never was seen so black a day as this.
          O woeful day, O woeful day!
PARIS   Beguiled, divorcéd, wrongéd, spited, slain!
          Most detestable Death, by thee beguiled,

By cruel, cruel thee quite overthrown!
O love! O life! Not life, but love in death!

CAPULET   Despised, distressèd, hated, martyred, killed!
Uncomfortable time, why cam'st thou now   60
To murder, murder our solemnity?
O child, O child! My soul, and not my child!
Dead art thou. Alack, my child is dead,
And with my child my joys are burièd!

FRIAR   Peace, ho, for shame! Confusion's cure lives not
In these confusions. Heaven and yourself
Had part in this fair maid; now heaven hath all,
And all the better is it for the maid.
Your part in her you could not keep from death,
But heaven keeps his part in eternal life.   70
The most you sought was her promotion,
For 'twas your heaven she should be advanced;
And weep ye now, seeing she is advanced
Above the clouds as high as heaven itself?
O, in this love you love your child so ill
That you run mad, seeing that she is well.
She's not well married that lives married long,
But she's best married that dies married young.
Dry up your tears and stick your rosemary
On this fair corse, and as the custom is,   80
All in her best array, bear her to church:
For though fond nature bids us all lament,
Yet nature's tears are reason's merriment.

CAPULET   All things that we ordainèd festival
Turn from their office to black funeral,
Our instruments to melancholy bells,
Our wedding cheer to a sad burial feast;
Our solemn hymns to sullen dirges change,
Our bridal flowers serve for a buried corse,
And all things change them to the contrary.   90

FRIAR   Sir, go you in; and, madam, go with him;
And go, Sir Paris. Everyone prepare
To follow this fair corse unto her grave.
The heavens do lour upon you for some ill;
Move them no more by crossing their high will.

[*'all but the Nurse' and the Musicians 'go forth, casting
rosemary upon her and shutting the curtains'*

1 MUSIC'N Faith, we may put up our pipes and be gone.

NURSE Honest good fellows, ah, put up, put up!
For well you know this is a pitiful case.

1 MUSIC'N Ay, by my troth, the case may be amended.

[*Nurse goes*

Enter PETER

PETER Musicians, O musicians, 'Heart's ease', 'Heart's ease'! 100
O, an you will have me live, play 'Heart's ease'.

1 MUSIC'N Why 'Heart's ease'?

PETER O musicians, because my heart itself plays 'My heart is
full of woe'. O play me some merry dump to comfort
me.

1 MUSIC'N Not a dump we! 'Tis no time to play now.

PETER You will not then?

1 MUSIC'N No.

PETER I will then give it you soundly.

1 MUSIC'N What will you give us? 110

PETER No money, on my faith, but the gleek. I will give you
the minstrel.

1 MUSIC'N Then will I give you the serving-creature.

PETER Then will I lay the serving-creature's dagger on your
pate. I will carry no crotchets. I'll re you, I'll fa you.
Do you note me?

1 MUSIC'N An you re us and fa us, you note us.

2 MUSIC'N Pray you put up your dagger, and put out your wit.

PETER Then have at you with my wit! I will dry-beat you
with an iron wit, and put up my iron dagger. Answer 120
me like men:

'When griping grief the heart doth wound,
And doleful dumps the mind oppress,
Then music with her silver sound – '

Why 'silver sound'? Why 'music with her silver
sound'? What say you, Simon Catling?

1 MUSIC'N Marry, sir, because silver hath a sweet sound.

PETER Pretty! What say you, Hugh Rebeck?

2 MUSIC'N I say 'silver sound', because musicians sound for silver.

PETER   Pretty too! What say you, James Soundpost?   13

3 MUSIC'N Faith, I know not what to say.

PETER   O, I cry you mercy! You are the singer. I will say for
          you. It is 'music with her silver sound', because music-
          ians have no gold for sounding.
                    'Then music with her silver sound
                    With speedy help doth lend redress.'

                                                              [*he goes*

1 MUSIC'N What a pestilent knave is this same!

2 MUSIC'N Hang him, Jack! Come, we'll in here, tarry for the
          mourners, and stay dinner.

                                                       [*they go also*

ACT 5 SCENE I

Mantua. A street with shops

'*Enter* ROMEO'

ROMEO   If I may trust the flattering truth of sleep,
My dreams presage some joyful news at hand.
My bosom's lord sits lightly in his throne,
And all this day an unaccustomed spirit
Lifts me above the ground with cheerful thoughts.
I dreamt my lady came and found me dead –
Strange dream that gives a dead man leave to think! –
And breathed such life with kisses in my lips
That I revived and was an emperor.
Ah me! How sweet is love itself possessed,   10
When but love's shadows are so rich in joy!

Enter BALTHASAR, *Romeo's man, booted*

News from Verona! How now, Balthasar?
Dost thou not bring me letters from the friar?
How doth my lady? Is my father well?
How fares my Juliet? That I ask again,
For nothing can be ill if she be well.

BALTH'SAR Then she is well, and nothing can be ill.
Her body sleeps in Capel's monument,
And her immortal part with angels lives.
I saw her laid low in her kindred's vault,   20
And presently took post to tell it you.
O pardon me for bringing these ill news,
Since you did leave it for my office, sir.

ROMEO   Is it e'en so? Then I defy you, stars!
Thou know'st my lodging. Get me ink and paper,
And hire post-horses; I will hence tonight.

BALTH'SAR I do beseech you, sir, have patience.
Your looks are pale and wild and do import
Some misadventure.

ROMEO   Tush, thou art deceived.
Leave me, and do the thing I bid thee do.   30

Hast thou no letters to me from the friar?
BALTH'SAR No, my good lord.
ROMEO   No matter. Get thee gone,
And hire those horses; I'll be with thee straight.

                                        [*Balthasar goes*

Well, Juliet, I will lie with thee tonight.
Let's see for means. O mischief, thou art swift
To enter in the thoughts of desperate men!
I do remember an apothecary,
And hereabouts 'a dwells, which late I noted
In tatt'red weeds, with overwhelming brows,
Culling of simples. Meagre were his looks;   40
Sharp misery had worn him to the bones:
And in his needy shop a tortoise hung,
An alligator stuffed, and other skins
Of ill-shaped fishes; and about his shelves
A beggarly account of empty boxes,
Green earthen pots, bladders, and musty seeds,
Remnants of packthread, and old cakes of roses
Were thinly scattered, to make up a show.
Noting this penury, to myself I said,
'An if a man did need a poison now,   50
Whose sale is present death in Mantua,
Here lives a caitiff wretch would sell it him.'
O, this same thought did but forerun my need,
And this same needy man must sell it me.
As I remember, this should be the house.
Being holiday, the beggar's shop is shut.
What ho, apothecary!

                    Enter APOTHECARY

APOTH'ARY   Who calls so loud?
ROMEO   Come hither, man. I see that thou art poor.
Hold, there is forty ducats; let me have
A dram of poison, such soon-speeding gear   60
As will disperse itself through all the veins
That the life-weary taker may fall dead,
And that the trunk may be discharged of breath
As violently as hasty powder fired
Doth hurry from the fatal cannon's womb.

APOTH'ARY Such mortal drugs I have, but Mantua's law
          Is death to any he that utters them.
ROMEO   Art thou so bare and full of wretchedness
          And fear'st to die? Famine is in thy cheeks,
          Need and oppression starveth in thy eyes,   70
          Contempt and beggary hangs upon thy back:
          The world is not thy friend, nor the world's law;
          The world affords no law to make thee rich:
          Then be not poor, but break it and take this.
APOTH'ARY My poverty but not my will consents.
ROMEO   I pay thy poverty and not thy will.
APOTH'ARY [giving a phial] Put this in any liquid thing you will
          And drink it off, and if you had the strength
          Of twenty men it would dispatch you straight.
ROMEO   There is thy gold – worse poison to men's souls,   80
          Doing more murder in this loathsome world,
          Than these poor compounds that thou mayst not sell.
          I sell thee poison; thou hast sold me none.
          Farewell; buy food and get thyself in flesh.
                                        [Apothecary goes in
          Come, cordial and not poison, go with me
          To Juliet's grave, for there must I use thee.
                                            [he passes on

SCENE 2

Verona. Friar Lawrence's cell

Enter FRIAR JOHN

FRIAR J. Holy Franciscan friar, brother, ho!

Enter FRIAR LAWRENCE

FRIAR L. This same should be the voice of Friar John.
          Welcome from Mantua. What says Romeo?
          Or, if his mind be writ, give me his letter.
FRIAR J. Going to find a barefoot brother out,
          One of our order, to associate me,
          Here in this city visiting the sick,
          And finding him, the searchers of the town,

Suspecting that we both were in a house
Where the infectious pestilence did reign,   10
Sealed up the doors, and would not let us forth,
So that my speed to Mantua there was stayed.

FRIAR L. Who bare my letter then to Romeo?

FRIAR J. I could not send it – here it is again –
Nor get a messenger to bring it thee,
So fearful were they of infection.

FRIAR L. Unhappy fortune! By my brotherhood,
The letter was not nice, but full of charge,
Of dear import; and the neglecting it
May do much danger. Friar John, go hence,   20
Get me an iron crow and bring it straight
Unto my cell.

FRIAR J. Brother, I'll go and bring it thee.   [goes

FRIAR L. Now must I to the monument alone.
Within this three hours will fair Juliet wake.
She will beshrew me much that Romeo
Hath had no notice of these accidents;
But I will write again to Mantua,
And keep her at my cell till Romeo come.
Poor living corse, closed in a dead man's tomb!   30
                                                    [he goes

SCENE 3

Verona. A churchyard; in it the monument of the Capulets

'*Enter* PARIS *and his* PAGE', *bearing flowers and a torch*

PARIS   Give me thy torch, boy. Hence, and stand aloof.
Yet put it out, for I would not be seen.
Under yond yew-trees lay thee all along,
Holding thine ear close to the hollow ground;
So shall no foot upon the churchyard tread,
Being loose, unfirm with digging up of graves,
But thou shalt hear it. Whistle then to me
As signal that thou hear'st some thing approach.
Give me those flowers. Do as I bid thee; go.

PAGE   I am almost afraid to stand alone   10

| | Here in the churchyard, yet I will adventure.   [*retires* |
| PARIS | Sweet flower, with flowers thy bridal bed I strew – |

PARIS
  Here in the churchyard, yet I will adventure.   [*retires*
  Sweet flower, with flowers thy bridal bed I strew –
  O woe, thy canopy is dust and stones! –
  Which with sweet water nightly I will dew,
  Or, wanting that, with tears distilled by moans.
  The obsequies that I for thee will keep
  Nightly shall be to strew thy grave and weep.

                                        [*Page whistles*

  The boy gives warning something doth approach.
  What curséd foot wanders this way tonight
  To cross my obsequies and true love's rite?   20
  What, with a torch? Muffle me, night, awhile.   [*retires*

     'Enter ROMEO *and* BALTHASAR, *with a torch,*
       a mattock, and a crow of iron'

ROMEO
  Give me that mattock and the wrenching iron.
  Hold, take this letter. Early in the morning
  See thou deliver it to my lord and father.
  Give me the light. Upon thy life I charge thee,
  Whate'er thou hear'st or seest, stand all aloof
  And do not interrupt me in my course.
  Why I descend into this bed of death
  Is partly to behold my lady's face,
  But chiefly to take thence from her dead finger   30
  A precious ring, a ring that I must use
  In dear employment. Therefore hence, be gone.
  But if thou, jealous, dost return to pry
  In what I farther shall intend to do,
  By heaven, I will tear thee joint by joint
  And strew this hungry churchyard with thy limbs.
  The time and my intents are savage-wild,
  More fierce and more inexorable far
  Than empty tigers or the roaring sea.

BALTH'SAR I will be gone, sir, and not trouble ye.   40

ROMEO
  So shalt thou show me friendship. Take thou that;
                                  [*gives money*
  Live and be prosperous; and farewell, good fellow.

BALTH'SAR For all this same, I'll hide me hereabout.
  His looks I fear, and his intents I doubt.   [*retires*

ROMEO   Thou detestable maw, thou womb of death,
         Gorged with the dearest morsel of the earth,
         Thus I enforce thy rotten jaws to open,
                              [*begins to open the tomb*
         And in despite I'll cram thee with more food.

PARIS   This is that banished haughty Montague
         That murd'red my love's cousin – with which grief   50
         It is supposéd the fair creature died –
         And here is come to do some villainous shame
         To the dead bodies: I will apprehend him. –
                              [*comes forward*
         Stop thy unhallowed toil, vile Montague!
         Can vengeance be pursued further than death?
         Condemnéd villain, I do apprehend thee.
         Obey, and go with me, for thou must die.

ROMEO   I must indeed, and therefore came I hither.
         Good gentle youth, tempt not a desp'rate man.
         Fly hence and leave me. Think upon these gone;   60
         Let them affright thee. I beseech thee, youth,
         Put not another sin upon my head
         By urging me to fury. O be gone!
         By heaven, I love thee better than myself,
         For I come hither armed against myself.
         Stay not, be gone. Live, and hereafter say
         A madman's mercy bid thee run away.

PARIS   I do defy thy conjuration,
         And apprehend thee for a felon here.

ROMEO   Wilt thou provoke me? Then have at thee, boy!   70
                              [*they fight*
PAGE   O Lord, they fight! I will go call the watch.   [*runs off*
PARIS   O, I am slain! [*falls*] If thou be merciful,
         Open the tomb, lay me with Juliet.   [*dies*
ROMEO   In faith, I will. Let me peruse this face.
         Mercutio's kinsman, noble County Paris!
         What said my man when my betosséd soul
         Did not attend him as we rode? I think
         He told me Paris should have married Juliet.
         Said he not so? Or did I dream it so?
         Or am I mad, hearing him talk of Juliet,   8

To think it was so? O give me thy hand,
One writ with me in sour misfortune's book!
I'll bury thee in a triumphant grave.
A grave? O no! – a lanthorn, slaught'red youth:
For here lies Juliet, and her beauty makes
This vault a feasting presence full of light.
Dead, lie thou there, by a dead man interred.

                [lays Paris within the tomb

How oft when men are at the point of death
Have they been merry, which their keepers call
A light'ning before death! O how may I   90
Call this a light'ning? O my love, my wife!
Death, that hath sucked the honey of thy breath,
Hath had no power yet upon thy beauty.
Thou art not conquered; beauty's ensign yet
Is crimson in thy lips and in thy cheeks,
And death's pale flag is not advancéd there.
Tybalt, liest thou there in thy bloody sheet?
O, what more favour can I do to thee
Than with that hand that cut thy youth in twain
To sunder his that was thine enemy?   100
Forgive me, cousin! Ah, dear Juliet,
Why art thou yet so fair? Shall I believe
That unsubstantial Death is amorous,
And that the lean abhorréd monster keeps
Thee here in dark to be his paramour?
For fear of that I still will stay with thee,
And never from this palace of dim night
Depart again. Here, here will I remain
With worms that are thy chambermaids. O, here
Will I set up my everlasting rest,   110
And shake the yoke of inauspicious stars
From this world-wearied flesh. Eyes, look your last!
Arms, take your last embrace! And lips, O you,
The doors of breath, seal with a righteous kiss
A dateless bargain to engrossing Death!
Come, bitter conduct; come, unsavoury guide!
Thou desperate pilot, now at once run on
The dashing rocks thy seasick weary bark!

Here's to my love! [*drinks*] O true apothecary!
Thy drugs are quick. Thus with a kiss I die.   [*dies*

'*Enter Friar*' LAWRENCE '*with lanthorn, crow, and spade*'

FRIAR   Saint Francis be my speed! how oft tonight
               Have my old feet stumbled at graves! Who's there?
BALTH'SAR Here's one, a friend, and one that knows you well.
FRIAR   Bliss be upon you! Tell me, good my friend,
               What torch is yond that vainly lends his light
               To grubs and eyeless skulls? As I discern,
               It burneth in the Capels' monument.
BALTH'SAR It doth so, holy sir; and there's my master,
               One that you love.
FRIAR   Who is it?
BALTH'SAR   Romeo.
FRIAR   How long hath he been there?
BALTH'SAR   Full half an hour.   130
FRIAR   Go with me to the vault.
BALTH'SAR   I dare not, sir.
               My master knows not but I am gone hence,
               And fearfully did menace me with death
               If I did stay to look on his intents.
FRIAR   Stay then; I'll go alone. Fear comes upon me.
               O, much I fear some ill unthrifty thing.
BALTH'SAR As I did sleep under this yew-tree here,
               I dreamt my master and another fought,
               And that my master slew him.
FRIAR   Romeo!   [*advances*
               Alack, alack, what blood is this which stains   140
               The stony entrance of this sepulchre?
               What mean these masterless and gory swords
               To lie discoloured by this place of peace?
                                                  [*enters the tomb*
               Romeo! O, pale! Who else? What, Paris too?
               And steeped in blood? Ah, what an unkind hour
               Is guilty of this lamentable chance!
               The lady stirs.   [*Juliet wakes*
JULIET   O comfortable friar, where is my lord?
               I do remember well where I should be,
               And there I am. Where is my Romeo?   [*voices afar off* 150

FRIAR   I hear some noise, lady. Come from that nest
            Of death, contagion, and unnatural sleep.
            A greater power than we can contradict
            Hath thwarted our intents. Come, come away.
            Thy husband in thy bosom there lies dead:
            And Paris too. Come, I'll dispose of thee
            Among a sisterhood of holy nuns.
            Stay not to question, for the watch is coming.
            Come, go, good Juliet; I dare no longer stay.

JULIET   Go, get thee hence, for I will not away.   [he goes 160
            What's here? A cup, closed in my true love's hand?
            Poison, I see, hath been his timeless end,
            O churl! Drunk all, and left no friendly drop
            To help me after? I will kiss thy lips.
            Haply some poison yet doth hang on them
            To make me die with a restorative.   [kisses him
            Thy lips are warm!

            The Page of Paris enters the graveyard with Watchmen

1 WATCH   Lead, boy. Which way?
JULIET   Yea, noise? Then I'll be brief. O happy dagger,
                                        [snatching Romeo's dagger
            This is thy sheath [stabs herself]; there rest, and let me die.   170
                                        [falls on Romeo's body and dies
PAGE   This is the place, there where the torch doth burn.
1 WATCH   The ground is bloody. Search about the churchyard.
            Go, some of you; whoe'er you find attach.
                                        [some Watchmen depart
            Pitiful sight! Here lies the County slain:
            And Juliet bleeding, warm and newly dead,
            Who here hath lain this two days buriéd.
            Go tell the Prince; run to the Capulets;
            Raise up the Montagues; some others search.
                                        [other Watchmen depart
            We see the ground whereon these woes do lie,
            But the true ground of all these piteous woes   180
            We cannot without circumstance descry.

            Re-enter some of the Watch, with BALTHASAR

2 WATCH   Here's Romeo's man; we found him in the churchyard.

1 WATCH: Hold him in safety till the Prince come hither.

Re-enter another Watchman, with FRIAR LAWRENCE

3 WATCH   Here is a friar that trembles, sighs, and weeps.
            We took this mattock and this spade from him
            As he was coming from this churchyard's side.

1 WATCH   A great suspicion! Stay the friar too.

'Enter the Prince' and attendants

PRINCE   What misadventure is so early up,
            That calls our person from our morning rest?

Enter CAPULET *and his wife*

CAPULET   What should it be that is so shrieked abroad?   190

LADY CAP. O, the people in the street cry 'Romeo',
            Some 'Juliet', and some 'Paris', and all run
            With open outcry toward our monument.

PRINCE   What fear is this which startles in our ears?

1 WATCH   Sovereign, here lies the County Paris slain;
            And Romeo dead; and Juliet, dead before,
            Warm and new killed.

PRINCE   Search, seek, and know how this foul murder comes.

1 WATCH   Here is a friar, and slaughtered Romeo's man,
            With instruments upon them fit to open   200
            These dead men's tombs.

CAPULET   O heaven! O wife, look how our daughter bleeds!
            This dagger hath mista'en, for, lo, his house
            Is empty on the back of Montague,
            And it mis-sheathéd in my daughter's bosom.

LADY CAP. O me! this sight of death is as a bell
            That warns my old age to a sepulchre.

'Enter MONTAGUE*'*

PRINCE   Come Montague; for thou art early up
            To see thy son and heir more early down.

MONTAG.   Alas, my liege, my wife is dead tonight;   210
            Grief of my son's exile hath stopped her breath.
            What further woe conspires against mine age?

PRINCE   Look and thou shalt see.

MONTAG.   O thou untaught! what manners is in this,
            To press before thy father to a grave?

PRINCE   Seal up the mouth of outrage for a while,
Till we can clear these ambiguities,
And know their spring, their head, their true descent;
And then will I be general of your woes,
And lead you even to death. Meantime forbear,   220
And let mischance be slave to patience.
Bring forth the parties of suspicion.

                  [*Watchmen bring forward Friar Lawrence
                                    and Balthasar*

FRIAR   I am the greatest; able to do least,
Yet most suspected, as the time and place
Doth make against me, of this direful murder:
And here I stand both to impeach and purge
Myself condemnéd and myself excused.

PRINCE   Then say at once what thou dost know in this.

FRIAR   I will be brief, for my short date of breath
Is not so long as is a tedious tale.   230
Romeo there dead was husband to that Juliet;
And she, there dead, that Romeo's faithful wife.
I married them; and their stol'n marriage day
Was Tybalt's doomsday, whose untimely death
Banished the new-made bridegroom from this city;
For whom, and not for Tybalt, Juliet pined.
You, to remove that siege of grief from her,
Betrothed and would have married her perforce
To County Paris. Then comes she to me,
And with wild looks bid me devise some mean   240
To rid her from this second marriage,
Or in my cell there would she kill herself.
Then gave I her (so tutored by my art)
A sleeping potion; which so took effect
As I intended, for it wrought on her
The form of death. Meantime I writ to Romeo
That he should hither come as this dire night
To help to take her from her borrowed grave,
Being the time the potion's force should cease.
But he which bore my letter, Friar John,   250
Was stayed by accident, and yesternight
Returned my letter back. Then all alone

At the prefixéd hour of her waking
Came I to take her from her kindred's vault,
Meaning to keep her closely at my cell
Till I conveniently could send to Romeo.
But when I came, some minute ere the time
Of her awakening, here untimely lay
The noble Paris and true Romeo dead.
She wakes; and I entreated her come forth,   260
And bear this work of heaven with patience;
But then a noise did scare me from the tomb,
And she, too desperate, would not go with me,
But, as it seems, did violence on herself.
All this I know; and to the marriage
Her nurse is privy: and if aught in this
Miscarried by my fault, let my old life
Be sacrificed, some hour before his time,
Unto the rigour of severest law.

PRINCE   We still have known thee for a holy man.   270
            Where's Romeo's man? What can he say to this?

BALTH'SAR I brought my master news of Juliet's death,
          And then in post he came from Mantua
          To this same place, to this same monument.
          This letter he early bid me give his father,
          And threat'ned me with death, going in the vault,
          If I departed not and left him there.

PRINCE   Give me the letter; I will look on it.
            Where is the County's page, that raised the watch?
                                    [Page comes forward
            Sirrah, what made your master in this place?   28c

PAGE   He came with flowers to strew his lady's grave,
            And bid me stand aloof, and so I did.
            Anon comes one with light to ope the tomb,
            And by and by my master drew on him,
            And then I ran away to call the watch.

PRINCE   This letter doth make good the friar's words,
            Their course of love, the tidings of her death;
            And here he writes that he did buy a poison
            Of a poor pothecary, and therewithal
            Came to this vault to die, and lie with Juliet.   29c

Where be these enemies? Capulet, Montague?
See what a scourge is laid upon your hate,
That heaven finds means to kill your joys with love!
And I, for winking at your discords too,
Have lost a brace of kinsmen. All are punished.

CAPULET   O brother Montague, give me thy hand.
This is my daughter's jointure, for no more
Can I demand.

MONTAG.   But I can give thee more;
For I will raise her statue in pure gold,
That, whiles Verona by that name is known,   300
There shall no figure at such rate be set
As that of true and faithful Juliet.

CAPULET   As rich shall Romeo's by his lady's lie —
Poor sacrifices of our enmity!

PRINCE   A glooming peace this morning with it brings;
The sun for sorrow will not show his head.
Go hence, to have more talk of these sad things.
Some shall be pardoned, and some punishéd;
For never was a story of more woe
Than this of Juliet and her Romeo.   310

[they go

HAMLET

INTRODUCTION

Putting a date to *Hamlet* is complicated by the existence of conflicting evidence and three distinct printed versions of the play. There may have been a Hamlet play before Shakespeare's, which belongs to the period of around 1600, although this, like much else in the play, has been the subject of endless scholarly debate. *Hamlet* is at once familiar – the moody prince addressing a skull, or 'To be or not to be' (3.1.56) – and yet opaque and intractable, requiring explanation and amplification. The fragments are well-known, but the whole is elusive. A standard critical work on the play has the title 'What happens in *Hamlet*' (J. Dover Wilson, first published in 1935 and still in print in the U.K.), attesting to both the necessity and the difficulty of paraphrase. Laurence Olivier's 1948 film of the play took as a prologue Hamlet's speech beginning 'So, oft it chances in particular men, That for some vicious mole in nature in them' (1.4.23–24) and constructed the play rather reductively as 'the tragedy of a man who could not make up his mind'. Horatio's attempt to tell the story in the final scene is marked by a similar inadequacy, as he reduces the play we have just read or watched to an inventory of 'carnal, bloody and unnatural acts, Of accidental judgments, casual slaughters, Of deaths put on by cunning and forced cause' (5.2.368–70). The play may have been these things but it is also ineffably more than their melodramatic sum. The challenge of 'pluck[ing] out the heart of [its] mystery' (3.2.354) has contributed to its central and profoundly influential position in western culture.

The play tells the story of Hamlet, Prince of Denmark, who is mourning the death of his father and his mother's remarriage to his uncle, Claudius. The ghost of Hamlet's father appears to his son and tells him that he was murdered by Claudius and must be avenged. When some travelling actors visit the Danish court, Hamlet gets them to perform a play about the murder of a king by his brother, in order to test Claudius's reaction. Later, Hamlet has the chance to murder Claudius, but refrains because his uncle is praying. Visiting his mother Gertrude in her chamber, Hamlet kills the old courtier Polonius, whose daughter Ophelia, with whom Hamlet may have been in love, runs mad and also dies. Polonius' son Laertes returns to Denmark to avenge these deaths. Claudius attempts to get rid of Hamlet by sending him to England with secret orders that he be murdered, but Hamlet escapes. He fights a duel with Laertes, whose foil has been tipped with poison by Claudius. Both die, as do Claudius and Gertrude. Into the scene of carnage marches the army of the Norwegian prince Fortinbras who has been advancing on Denmark, and in his dying speech, Hamlet prophesies Fortinbras's appointment as next Danish king.

An early reference to the play in 1602 gives it an interestingly extended title. Modern editors of the tragedies have tended to standardise their titles as single (or occasionally double) names, and thus to lose certain nuances of the plays' early reception. *The Revenge of Hamlet Prince [of] Denmark* identifies Shakespeare's play within the popular dramatic genre of revenge tragedy, inaugurated by Thomas Kyd's *The Spanish Tragedy* (1592). Revenge plays focused on an injured individual – in Kyd's play the main revenger is Hieronimo, whose son Horatio has been murdered – who must gain redress, often urged on by a ghost, outside a legal system which is frequently implicated in the original crime. The revenge process is rarely neatly accomplished, however, and there are usually supernumerary casualties swept up in its bloody path. The ethics of revenge were then, as now, complex, and it is hard to reconstruct the attitudes of contemporary audiences to the bloodletting represented in plays of the genre. What is clear from the plays is that revenge tragedies themselves began to debate the right and wrongs of private revenge, in relation both to judicial and divine punishment. All revenge plays had a kind of sympathy for their hero but could not countenance his survival after taking his revenge, invariably including him in the final tableau of bloody bodies. Hamlet's conscience, therefore, may be dissected in extreme detail by Shakespeare, but he is by no means the first play hero caught between impulses towards revenge and away from violence. Nor is he the first revenger to delay. Revenge tragedy was dependent on delay for its dramatic form and tension, for if a wrong were immediately avenged, the play would, of necessity, be a very short one. Like other revenge plays including Kyd's, revenge in *Hamlet* is not confined to one individual. Hamlet is charged to 'revenge his [father's] foul and most unnatural murder' (1.5.25), and Laertes is spurred on by the deaths of his father and sister. Their final fatal duel is the clash of two revengers who must die. Hamlet is both revenger and villain – the injured and the injuring party. Even Fortinbras could be seen to be on a kind of revenge quest, another son putting right the wrongs done to a father by pressing for 'the surrender of those lands Lost by his father' (1.2.23–24). Revenge, like bloodshed, multiplies in the play until it consumes the whole Danish court.

The play's double-figure death count may sit awkwardly with the impression of *Hamlet* as a philosophical play of words rather than action. In fact, the play is both. Hamlet himself shifts from the bloody and excessive rhetoric of the stage-revenger in his 'now could I drink hot blood, And do such bitter business as the day Would quake to look on' (3.2.378–80) to the contemplative metaphysics of 'What a piece of work is a man, how noble in reason, how infinite in faculties [. . .] how like a god: the beauty of the world [. . .] and yet to me, what is this quintessence of dust?' (2.2.298–303). In asking Laertes' forgiveness at the last, Hamlet solidifies a view of himself as a divided personality, and is thus able to deny culpability for his actions, blaming them on 'his madness'. He distances himself through the repeated use of the third person: 'Was't Hamlet wronged Laertes? Never Hamlet. If Hamlet from himself be ta'en away, And when he's not himself does wrong Laertes, Then Hamlet does it not.' (5.2.219–22) Despite this denial, Hamlet is both bloodthirsty and contemplative, impulsive and havering. His is a play about action, and about the psychological and cultural impediments to action; Hamlet seems paralysed by the gap between the senses of acting as doing something and acting as pretending to do something, and the implications of these contradictory meanings become most evident in conversation with the troupe of players.

The players and their play 'The Murder of Gonzago' force

Hamlet, and *Hamlet*, into highly self-conscious musings on the differences between appearance and reality, art and life. All these reflections are infinitely complicated by the material fact of the artistry, the artificiality, of the play *Hamlet*. Hamlet berates himself for not showing his true grief to the extent of the Player King's 'dream of passion': 'what would he do, Had he the motive and the cue for passion That I have?' (2.2.543–45). But the characteristic self-consciousness of the early modern stage must impinge on Hamlet's theatrical assertion of his own 'reality' within a play, a 'fiction'. Throughout Hamlet, appearance and reality, superficiality and depth, are contrasted, but often their distinctness is blurred. Take Hamlet's first appearance, for example, in the second scene of the play, dressed ostentatiously in black. 'Why seems it so particular with thee?' his mother asks, referring to the death of the old king, and Hamlet immediately questions her use of the word 'seems'. He then reviles outer appearances – 'customary suits of solemn black', 'fruitful river in the eye', 'dejected haviour of the visage' – as, in suitably theatrical terminology, 'actions that a man might play'. He himself, however, announces that he is not playing at grief. He has 'that within which passes show', in the first assertion of his own secret inner self which he reiterates later in the play. Hamlet seems to need to believe that there is more to him than his exterior appearances, yet he is a skilful operator of those appearances, such that we do not and cannot know whether, for example, he 'feigns' madness or 'is' mad, nor, indeed, whether these two states are ever distinct. Despite his concern for a private subjectivity, Hamlet is not averse to the visible gestures which manifest these hidden depths. Here, Hamlet's 'that within which passes show' is implicitly identical with the show itself. Inside he is feeling what the outside denotes: the grief which expresses itself in black clothes, tears, and gloomy looks. Appearance and reality turn out to be the same, rather slippery, thing. At his first entry in the play, Hamlet has made a conscious decision to look like he feels, or to imply his feelings through his looks. Clearly, however, his adoption of dark clothes in the festive post-wedding celebrations of Claudius and Gertrude is not the involuntary result of the continuum of inner and outer, but an intentional and premeditated public reproach. (Such a reading of the scene is beautifully rendered in Kenneth Branagh's 1996 film of the play, in which

Hamlet is depicted as an immature spoilsport determined to wreck the celebrations.) Hamlet has used his appearance theatrically, to great visual and verbal effect, while simultaneously admitting that others in less pain might also do this – but not he. His manipulation of the dramatic situation and our perceptions is consummate: he must have been a very sharp student at Wittenburg university, known to play audiences since Christopher Marlowe's *Dr Faustus* (1592) as the *alma mater* of those rather too clever for their own good.

While the character of Hamlet holds the stage throughout, as Shakespeare's longest and most demanding role, the play is not simply an individual tragedy. In twentieth-century performances, however, there has been a tendency to focus on the central character to the exclusion of all else, and this narrowness has frequently been achieved through cutting the more political aspects of the play, especially the role of Fortinbras, whose 'promised march' (4.4.3) over Denmark is in the background for much of the play and takes centre stage in its final moments. When Marcellus states that 'something is rotten in the state of Denmark' (1.4.90), this extends the tragedy into the public sphere. Ultimately the price of Claudius' actions is the loss of Denmark itself, as the advance of the Norwegian army is counterpoised with the events at court. The early modern idea that the body of the monarch symbolised the body of the country meant that an ailing or wicked king affected, even infected, the kingdom. This analogy is highlighted by the use of 'Denmark' as a title for old Hamlet (1.1.48) and then for Claudius (1.2.69). Alongside Hamlet's personal tragedy is the tragedy of state, as Denmark itself is destroyed in the violence bred in its royal house. There are also other individual tragedies which the extraordinary power of Hamlet's ego can obscure. Gertrude, for example, is often harshly treated by critics of the play, who unfairly load much of the blame for events on her shoulders. Given, however, that there is no evidence that she suspects her new husband, her remarriage may be a pragmatic survival technique, both for herself and her son. Claudius seems to have the whole court in his pocket; it is hard to see what resistance Gertrude might have made, nor what her life would have been worth had she not married the ambitious new king. Ophelia, too, is a tragic character, and her relationship with Hamlet is an early casualty of the prince's obsession with his mother's remarriage. Denmark – arguably like Shakespeare's tragedies in general – seems a place inhospitable to women, and Gertrude and Ophelia are isolated figures – pawns of male politicking and victims of male opprobrium. It would be interesting to look at tragic events of the play from their perspective, in order to recentre them in a play determined to push them to its margins. Ultimately, however, the play is crowded by the force of Hamlet's personality, until the other characters seem merely the ciphers to his story. 'The rest is silence' (5.2.345), says the dying Prince; but as the fascination with the story of *Hamlet* shows no sign of abating, such quiet seems indefinitely postponed.

The Scene: Denmark

CHARACTERS IN THE PLAY

CLAUDIUS, *King of Denmark*
HAMLET, *Prince of Denmark, son to the late, and nephew to the present king*
POLONIUS, *Principal Secretary of State*
HORATIO, *friend to Hamlet*
LAERTES, *son to Polonius*
VALTEMAND
CORNELIUS } *ambassadors to Norway*
ROSENCRANTZ
GUILDENSTERN } *formerly fellow-students with Hamlet*
OSRIC, *a fantastic fop*
A Gentleman
A Doctor of Divinity
MARCELLUS
BARNARDO } *Gentlemen of the Guard*
FRANCISCO
REYNALDO, *servant to Polonius*
Four or five Players
Two Grave-diggers
FORTINBRAS, *Prince of Norway*
A Norwegian Captain
English Ambassadors

GERTRUDE, *Queen of Denmark, mother to Hamlet*
OPHELIA, *daughter to Polonius*

Lords, Ladies, Soldiers, Sailors, Messenger, and Attendants

The GHOST *of Hamlet's father*

THE TRAGEDY OF HAMLET PRINCE OF DENMARK

ACT I SCENE I

The castle at Elsinore. A narrow platform upon the battlements;
turret-doors to right and left. Starlight, very cold

FRANCISCO, a sentinel armed with a partisan, paces to and fro.
A bell tolls twelve. Presently BARNARDO, *another sentinel*
likewise armed, comes from the castle; he starts, hearing
Francisco's tread in the darkness

BARNARDO Who's there?

FRANCISCO Nay, answer me. Stand and unfold yourself.

BARNARDO Long live the King!

FRANCISCO Barnardo?

BARNARDO He.

FRANCISCO You come most carefully upon your hour.

BARNARDO 'Tis now struck twelve, get thee to bed, Francisco.

FRANCISCO For this relief much thanks, 'tis bitter cold,
      And I am sick at heart.

BARNARDO Have you had quiet guard?

FRANCISCO   Not a mouse stirring.   10

BARNARDO Well, good night:
      If you do meet Horatio and Marcellus,
      The rivals of my watch, bid them make haste.

        HORATIO *and* MARCELLUS *come forth*

FRANCISCO [*listens*] I think I hear them. Stand ho, who is there?

HORATIO   Friends to this ground.

MARCEL.   And liegemen to the Dane.

FRANCISCO Give you good night.

MARCEL.   O, farewell honest soldier,
      Who hath relieved you?

FRANCISCO   Barnardo hath my place;
      Give you good night.   [*Francisco goes*

MARCEL.   Holla, Barnardo!

BARNARDO   Say,
      What, is Horatio there?

HORATIO   A piece of him.

BARNARDO Welcome Horatio, welcome good Marcellus.   20
HORATIO   What, has this thing appeared again tonight?
BARNARDO I have seen nothing.
MARCEL.   Horatio says 'tis but our fantasy,
          And will not let belief take hold of him
          Touching this dreaded sight twice seen of us,
          Therefore I have entreated him along
          With us to watch the minutes of this night,
          That if again this apparition come,
          He may approve our eyes and speak to it.
HORATIO   Tush, tush, 'twill not appear.
BARNARDO   Sit down awhile,   30
          And let us once again assail your ears,
          That are so fortified against our story,
          What we have two nights seen.
HORATIO   Well, sit we down,
          And let us hear Barnardo speak of this.
BARNARDO Last night of all,
          When yon same star that's westward from the pole
          Had made his course t' illume that part of heaven
          Where now it burns, Marcellus and myself,
          The bell then beating one –

          A GHOST *appears; it is clad in armour from head to foot,
          and bears a marshal's truncheon*

MARCEL.   Peace, break thee off, look where it comes again!   40
BARNARDO In the same figure like the King that's dead.
MARCEL.   Thou art a scholar, speak to it, Horatio.
BARNARDO Looks 'a not like the King? Mark it, Horatio.
HORATIO   Most like, it harrows me with fear and wonder.
BARNARDO It would be spoke to.
MARCEL.   Question it, Horatio.
HORATIO   What art thou that usurp'st this time of night,
          Together with that fair and warlike form
          In which the majesty of buried Denmark
          Did sometimes march? by heaven I charge thee speak.
MARCEL.   It is offended.
BARNARDO   See, it stalks away.   50
HORATIO   Stay, speak, speak, I charge thee speak.
                                        [*the Ghost vanishes*

MARCEL.	'Tis gone and will not answer.
BARNARDO	How now Horatio, you tremble and look pale,
	Is not this something more than fantasy?
	What think you on't?
HORATIO	Before my God, I might not this believe
	Without the sensible and true avouch
	Of mine own eyes.
MARCEL.	Is it not like the King?
HORATIO	As thou art to thyself.

Such was the very armour be had on,   60
When he the ambitious Norway combated,
So frowned he once, when in an angry parle
He smote the sledded Polacks on the ice.
'Tis strange.

MARCEL.   Thus twice before, and jump at the dead hour,
With martial stalk hath he gone by our watch.

HORATIO   In what particular thought to work I know not,
But in the gross and scope of mine opinion,
This bodes some strange eruption to our state.

MARCEL.   Good now sit down, and tell me he that knows,   70
Why this same strict and most observant watch
So nightly toils the subject of the land,
And why such daily cast of brazen cannon
And foreign mart for implements of war,
Why such impress of shipwrights, whose sore task
Does not divide the Sunday from the week,
What might be toward that this sweaty haste
Doth make the night joint-labourer with the day,
Who is't that can inform me?

HORATIO   That can I,
At least the whisper goes so; our last king,   80
Whose image even but now appeared to us,
Was as you know by Fortinbras of Norway,
Thereto pricked on by a most emulate pride,
Dared to the combat; in which our valiant Hamlet
(For so this side of our known world esteemed him)
Did say this Fortinbras, who by a sealed compact,
Well ratified by law and heraldry,
Did forfeit (with his life) all those his lands

Which he stood seized of, to the conqueror,
Against the which a moiety competent   90
Was gagéd by our king, which had returned
To the inheritance of Fortinbras,
Had he been vanquisher; as by the same co-mart,
And carriage of the article designed,
His fell to Hamlet; now sir, young Fortinbras,
Of unimprovéd mettle hot and full,
Hath in the skirts of Norway here and there
Sharked up a list of lawless resolutes
For food and diet to some enterprise
That hath a stomach in't, which is no other,   100
As it doth well appear unto our state,
But to recover of us by strong hand
And terms compulsatory, those foresaid lands
So by his father lost; and this, I take it,
Is the main motive of our preparations,
The source of this our watch, and the chief head
Of this post-haste and romage in the land.

BARNARDO I think it be no other but e'en so;
Well may it sort that this portentous figure
Comes arméd through our watch so like the king   110
That was and is the question of these wars.

HORATIO A mote it is to trouble the mind's eye:
In the most high and palmy state of Rome,
A little ere the mightiest Julius fell,
The graves stood tenantless, and the sheeted dead
Did squeak and gibber in the Roman streets,
And even the like precurse of fierce events,
As harbingers preceding still the fates
And prologue to the omen coming on,
Have heaven and earth together demonstrated   120
Unto our climatures and countrymen,
As stars with trains of fire and dews of blood,
Disasters in the sun; and the moist star,
Upon whose influence Neptune's empire stands,
Was sick almost to doomsday with eclipse.

The GHOST *reappears*

But soft, behold, lo where it comes again!

I'll cross it though it blast me.   [*he 'spreads his arms'*
                              Stay, illusion!
If thou hast any sound or use of voice,
Speak to me.
If there be any good thing to be done   130
That may to thee do ease, and grace to me,
Speak to me.
If thou art privy to thy country's fate
Which happily foreknowing may avoid,
O, speak!
Or if thou hast uphoarded in thy life
Extorted treasure in the womb of earth,
For which they say you spirits oft walk in death,
                                        [*a cock crows*
Speak of it – stay and speak – stop it, Marcellus!

MARCEL.   Shall I strike at it with my partisan?   140
HORATIO   Do if it will not stand.
BARNARDO   'Tis here!
HORATIO   'Tis here!
MARCEL.   'Tis gone!   [*the Ghost vanishes*
            We do it wrong being so majestical
            To offer it the show of violence,
            For it is as the air, invulnerable,
            And our vain blows malicious mockery.
BARNARDO It was about to speak when the cock crew.
HORATIO   And then it started like a guilty thing,
            Upon a fearful summons; I have heard
            The cock that is the trumpet to the morn   150
            Doth with his lofty and shrill-sounding throat
            Awake the god of day, and at his warning
            Whether in sea or fire, in earth or air,
            Th'extravagant and erring spirit hies
            To his confine, and of the truth herein
            This present object made probation.
MARCEL.   It faded on the crowing of the cock.
            Some say that ever 'gainst that season comes
            Wherein our Saviour's birth is celebrated
            This bird of dawning singeth all night long,   160
            And then they say no spirit dare stir abroad,

The nights are wholesome, then no planets strike,
No fairy takes, nor witch hath power to charm,
So hallowed, and so gracious is that time.

HORATIO   So have I heard and do in part believe it.
But look, the morn in russet mantle clad
Walks o'er the dew of yon high eastward hill.
Break we our watch up and by my advice
Let us impart what we have seen tonight
Unto young Hamlet, for upon my life   17
This spirit, dumb to us, will speak to him:
Do you consent we shall acquaint him with it,
As needful in our loves, fitting our duty?

MARCEL.   Let's do't, I pray, and I this morning know
Where we shall find him most convenient.   *[they go*

SCENE 2

The Council Chamber in the castle

A 'flourish' of trumpets. 'Enter CLAUDIUS *King of Denmark,*
GERTRUDE *the Queen, Councillors,* POLONIUS *and his son* LAERTES',
VALTEMAND *and* CORNELIUS, *all clad in gay apparel, as from the*
coronation; and last of all Prince HAMLET *in black, with downcast eyes.*
The King and Queen ascend steps to the thrones

KING   Though yet of Hamlet our dear brother's death
The memory be green, and that it us befitted
To bear our hearts in grief, and our whole kingdom
To be contracted in one brow of woe,
Yet so far hath discretion fought with nature,
That we with wisest sorrow think on him
Together with remembrance of ourselves:
Therefore our sometime sister, now our queen,
Th'imperial jointress to this warlike state,
Have we as 'twere with a defeated joy,   10
With an auspicious, and a dropping eye,
With mirth in funeral, and with dirge in marriage,
In equal scale weighing delight and dole,
Taken to wife: nor have we herein barred

Your better wisdoms, which have freely gone
With this affair along – for all, our thanks.
Now follows that you know, young Fortinbras,
Holding a weak supposal of our worth,
Or thinking by our late dear brother's death
Our state to be disjoint and out of frame,   20
Colleaguéd with this dream of his advantage,
He hath not failed to pester us with message
Importing the surrender of those lands
Lost by his father, with all bands of law,
To our most valiant brother – so much for him:
Now for ourself, and for this time of meeting,
Thus much the business is. We have here writ
To Norway, uncle of young Fortinbras –
Who impotent and bed-rid scarcely hears
Of this his nephew's purpose – to suppress   30
His further gait herein, in that the levies,
The lists, and full proportions, are all made
Out of his subject. And we here dispatch
You good Cornelius, and you Valtemand,
For bearers of this greeting to old Norway,
Giving to you no further personal power
To business with the king, more than the scope
Of these delated articles allow:
Farewell, and let your haste commend your duty.

CORNEL.,
VALTEM'D   In that, and all things, will we show our duty.   40
KING   We doubt it nothing, heartily farewell.
                    [*Valtemand and Cornelius bow, and depart*
            And now, Laertes, what's the news with you?
            You told us of some suit, what is't, Laertes?
            You cannot speak of reason to the Dane,
            And lose your voice; what wouldst thou beg, Laertes,
            That shall not be my offer, not thy asking?
            The head is not more native to the heart,
            The hand more instrumental to the mouth,
            Than is the throne of Denmark to thy father.
            What wouldst thou have, Laertes?

LAERTES   My dread lord,   50

Your leave and favour to return to France,
From whence though willingly I came to Denmark,
To show my duty in your coronation;
Yet now I must confess, that duty done,
My thoughts and wishes bend again toward France,
And bow them to your gracious leave and pardon.

KING   Have you your father's leave? What says Polonius?

POLONIUS He hath my lord, wrung from me my slow leave
          By laboursome petition, and at last
          Upon his will I sealed my hard consent.   60
          I do beseech you give him leave to go.

KING   Take thy fair hour, Laertes, time be thine,
          And thy best graces spend it at thy will.
          But now my cousin Hamlet, and my son –

HAMLET   A little more than kin, and less than kind.

KING   How is it that the clouds still hang on you?

HAMLET   Not so, my lord, I am too much in the sun.

QUEEN   Good Hamlet, cast thy nighted colour off,
          And let thine eye look like a friend on Denmark;
          Do not for ever with thy vailéd lids   70
          Seek for thy noble father in the dust;
          Thou know'st 'tis common, all that lives must die,
          Passing through nature to eternity.

HAMLET   Ay, madam, it is common.

QUEEN   If it be,
          Why seems it so particular with thee?

HAMLET   Seems, madam! Nay it is, I know not 'seems'.
          'Tis not alone my inky cloak, good mother,
          Nor customary suits of solemn black,
          Nor windy suspiration of forced breath,
          No, nor the fruitful river in the eye,   80
          Nor the dejected haviour of the visage,
          Together with all forms, motes, shapes of grief,
          That can denote me truly. These indeed seem,
          For they are actions that a man might play,
          But I have that within which passes show,
          These but the trappings and the suits of woe.

KING   'Tis sweet and commendable in your nature, Hamlet,
          To give these mourning duties to your father,

But you must know your father lost a father,
That father lost, lost his, and the survivor bound   90
In filial obligation for some term
To do obsequious sorrow. But to persever
In obstinate condolement is a course
Of impious stubbornness, 'tis unmanly grief,
It shows a will most incorrect to heaven,
A heart unfortified, a mind impatient,
An understanding simple and unschooled.
For what we know must be and is as common
As any the most vulgar thing to sense,
Why should we in our peevish opposition   100
Take it to heart? Fie, 'tis a fault to heaven,
A fault against the dead, a fault to nature,
To reason most absurd, whose common theme
Is death of fathers, and who still hath cried,
From the first corse till he that died today,
'This must be so'. We pray you throw to earth
This unprevailing woe, and think of us
As of a father, for let the world take note
You are the most immediate to our throne,
And with no less nobility of love   110
Than that which dearest father bears his son,
Do I impart toward you. For your intent
In going back to school in Wittenberg,
It is most retrograde to our desire,
And we beseech you, bend you to remain
Here in the cheer and comfort of our eye,
Our chiefest courtier, cousin, and our son.

QUEEN   Let not thy mother lose her prayers, Hamlet;
I pray thee stay with us, go not to Wittenberg.

HAMLET   I shall in all my best obey you, madam.   120

KING   Why, 'tis a loving and a fair reply,
Be as ourself in Denmark. Madam, come.
This gentle and unforced accord of Hamlet,
Sits smiling to my heart, in grace whereof,
No jocund health that Denmark drinks today,
But the great cannon to the clouds shall tell,
And the king's rouse the heaven shall bruit again,

Re-speaking earthly thunder; come away.

['Flourish. Exeunt all but Hamlet'

HAMLET   O, that this too too solid flesh would melt,

Thaw and resolve itself into a dew,   130

Or that the Everlasting had not fixed

His canon 'gainst self-slaughter. O God, God,

How weary, stale, flat, and unprofitable

Seem to me all the uses of this world!

Fie on't, ah fie, 'tis an unweeded garden

That grows to seed, things rank and gross in nature

Possess it merely. That it should come to this,

But two months dead, nay not so much, not two,

So excellent a king, that was to this

Hyperion to a satyr, so loving to my mother,   140

That he might not beteem the winds of heaven

Visit her face too roughly – heaven and earth,

Must I remember? Why, she would hang on him

As if increase of appetite had grown

By what it fed on, and yet within a month,

Let me not think on't. Frailty, thy name is woman!

A little month or ere those shoes were old

With which she followed my poor father's body,

Like Niobe all tears, why she, even she –

O God, a beast that wants discourse of reason   150

Would have mourned longer – married with my uncle,

My father's brother, but no more like my father

Than I to Hercules, within a month,

Ere yet the salt of most unrighteous tears

Had left the flushing in her gallèd eyes

She married. O most wicked speed, to post

With such dexterity to incestuous sheets!

It is not, nor it cannot come to good,

But break my heart, for I must hold my tongue.

     HORATIO, MARCELLUS *and* BARNARDO *enter*

HORATIO   Hail to your lordship!

HAMLET   I am glad to see you well;   160

Horatio – or I do forget myself!

HORATIO   The same, my lord, and your poor servant ever.

HAMLET Sir, my good friend, I'll change that name with you.
                                      [*they clasp hands*
        And what make you from Wittenberg, Horatio?
        Marcellus.   [*he gives his hand*
MARCEL. My good lord!
HAMLET I am very glad to see you – good even, sir.
                                      [*he bows to Barnardo*
        But what in faith make you from Wittenberg?
                                      [*he draws Horatio apart*
HORATIO A truant disposition, good my lord.
HAMLET I would not hear your enemy say so,   170
        Nor shall you do mine ear that violence
        To make it truster of your own report
        Against yourself. I know you are no truant,
        But what is your affair in Elsinore?
        We'll teach you to drink deep ere you depart.
HORATIO My lord, I came to see your father's funeral.
HAMLET I prithee do not mock me, fellow-student,
        I think it was to see my mother's wedding.
HORATIO Indeed, my lord, it followed hard upon.
HAMLET Thrift, thrift, Horatio, the funeral baked meats   180
        Did coldly furnish forth the marriage tables.
        Would I had met my dearest foe in heaven
        Or ever I had seen that day, Horatio –
        My father, methinks I see my father.
HORATIO Where, my lord?
HAMLET   In my mind's eye, Horatio.
HORATIO I saw him once, 'a was a goodly king –
HAMLET 'A was a man, take him for all in all,
        I shall not look upon his like again.
HORATIO My lord, I think I saw him yesternight.
HAMLET Saw, who?   190
HORATIO My lord, the king your father.
HAMLET   The king my father!
HORATIO Season your admiration for a while
        With an attent ear till I may deliver
        Upon the witness of these gentlemen
        This marvel to you.
                          [*he turns to Marcellus and Barnardo*

HAMLET   For God's love let me hear!
HORATIO Two nights together had these gentlemen,
         Marcellus and Barnardo, on their watch
         In the dead waste and middle of the night,
         Been thus encountered. A figure like your father,
         Arméd at point exactly, cap-a-pe,   200
         Appears before them, and with solemn march,
         Goes slow and stately by them; thrice he walked
         By their oppressed and fear-surprised eyes
         Within his truncheon's length, whilst they distilled
         Almost to jelly with the act of fear,
         Stand dumb and speak not to him; this to me
         In dreadful secrecy impart they did,
         And I with them the third night kept the watch,
         Where, as they had delivered, both in time,
         Form of the thing, each word made true and good,   210
         The apparition comes: I knew your father,
         These hands are not more like.
HAMLET   But where was this?
MARCEL. My lord, upon the platform where we watch.
HAMLET   Did you not speak to it?
HORATIO   My lord, I did,
         But answer made it none, yet once methought
         It lifted up it head, and did address
         Itself to motion like as it would speak:
         But even then the morning cock crew loud,
         And at the sound it shrunk in haste away
         And vanished from our sight.
HAMLET   'Tis very strange.   220
HORATIO As I do live, my honoured lord, 'tis true,
         And we did think it writ down in our duty
         To let you know of it.
HAMLET   Indeed, indeed, sirs, but this troubles me.
         Hold you the watch tonight?
ALL   We do, my lord.
HAMLET   Armed, say you?
ALL   Armed, my lord.
HAMLET   From top to toe?
ALL   My lord, from head to foot.

HAMLET	Then saw you not his face.
HORATIO	O yes, my lord, he wore his beaver up.

HAMLET   What, looked he frowningly?

HORATIO   A countenance more in sorrow than in anger.

HAMLET   Pale, or red?

HORATIO   Nay, very pale.

HAMLET   And fixed his eyes upon you?

HORATIO   Most constantly.

HAMLET   I would I had been there.

HORATIO   It would have much amazed you.

HAMLET   Very like, very like. Stayed it long?

HORATIO   While one with moderate haste might tell a hundred.

MARCEL., BARN. Longer, longer.

HORATIO   Not when I saw't.

HAMLET   His beard was grizzled, no?   240

HORATIO   It was as I have seen it in his life,
            A sable silvered.

HAMLET   I will watch tonight,
            Perchance 'twill walk again.

HORATIO   I war'nt it win.

HAMLET   If it assume my noble father's person,
            I'll speak to it though hell itself should gape
            And bid me hold my peace; I pray you all
            If you have hitherto concealed this sight,
            Let it be tenable in your silence still,
            And whatsomever else shall hap tonight,
            Give it an understanding but no tongue.   250
            I will requite your loves, so fare you well:
            Upon the platform 'twixt eleven and twelve
            I'll visit you.

ALL   Our duty to your honour.

HAMLET   Your loves, as mine to you. Farewell.

                                        [*they bow and depart*
            My father's spirit (in arms!); all is not well,
            I doubt some foul play. Would the night were come;
            Till then sit still my soul, foul deeds will rise,
            Though all the earth o'erwhelm them, to men's eyes.
                                        [*he goes*

SCENE 3

A room in the house of Polonius

'Enter LAERTES *and* OPHELIA *his sister'*

LAERTES My necessaries are embarked, farewell,
And sister, as the winds give benefit
And convoy is assistant, do not sleep,
But let me hear from you.

OPHELIA   Do you doubt that?

LAERTES For Hamlet, and the trifling of his favour,
Hold it a fashion, and a toy in blood,
A violet in the youth of primy nature,
Forward, not permanent, sweet, not lasting,
The perfume and suppliance of a minute,
No more.

OPHELIA   No more but so?

LAERTES   Think it no more.   10
For nature crescent does not grow alone
In thews and bulk, but as this temple waxes
The inward service of the mind and soul
Grows wide withal. Perhaps he loves you now,
And now no soil nor cautel doth besmirch
The virtue of his will. But you must fear,
His greatness weighed, his will is not his own,
For he himself is subject to his birth.
He may not, as unvalued persons do,
Carve for himself, for on his choice depends   20
The sanity and health of this whole state,
And therefore must his choice be circumscribed
Unto the voice and yielding of that body
Whereof he is the head. Then if he says he loves you,
It fits your wisdom so far to believe it
As he in his particular act and place
May give his saying deed, which is no further
Than the main voice of Denmark goes withal.
Then weigh what loss your honour may sustain
If with too credent ear you list his songs,   30

Or lose your heart, or your chaste treasure open
To his unmast'red importunity.
Fear it Ophelia, fear it my dear sister,
And keep you in the rear of your affection,
Out of the shot and danger of desire.
'The chariest maid is prodigal enough
If she unmask her beauty to the moon.'
'Virtue itself 'scapes not calumnious strokes.'
'The canker galls the infants of the spring
Too oft before their buttons be disclosed,   40
And in the morn and liquid dew of youth
Contagious blastments are most imminent.'
Be wary then – best safety lies in fear,
Youth to itself rebels, though none else near.

OPHELIA   I shall the effect of this good lesson keep
As watchman to my heart. But good my brother,
Do not, as some ungracious pastors do,
Show me the steep and thorny way to heaven,
Whiles like a puffed and reckless libertine
Himself the primrose path of dalliance treads,   50
And recks not his own rede.

POLONIUS enters

LAERTES   O fear me not;
I stay too long – but here my father comes.
A double blessing is a double grace,   [he kneels
Occasion smiles upon a second leave.

POLONIUS Yet here, Laertes? Aboard, aboard for shame!
The wind sits in the shoulder of your sail,
And you are stayed for. There – my blessing with thee,
            [he lays his hand on Laertes' head
And these few precepts in thy memory
Look thou character. Give thy thoughts no tongue,
Nor any unproportioned thought his act.   60
Be thou familiar, but by no means vulgar;
Those friends thou hast, and their adoption tried,
Grapple them unto thy soul with hoops of steel,
But do not dull thy palm with entertainment
Of each new-hatched unfledged courage. Beware
Of entrance to a quarrel, but being in,

Bear't that th'opposéd may beware of thee.
Give every man thy ear, but few thy voice;
Take each man's censure, but reserve thy judgment.
Costly thy habit as thy purse can buy,   7⟨0⟩
But not expressed in fancy; rich not gaudy.
For the apparel oft proclaims the man,
And they in France of the best rank and station,
Or of a most select and generous, chief in that.
Neither a borrower nor a lender be,
For loan oft loses both itself and friend,
And borrowing dulls the edge of husbandry;
This above all, to thine own self be true
And it must follow as the night the day
Thou canst not then be false to any man.   8⟨0⟩
Farewell – my blessing season this in thee.

LAERTES   Most humbly do I take my leave, my lord.

POLONIUS The time invites you, go, your servants tend.

LAERTES   [rises] Farewell, Ophelia, and remember well
What I have said to you.

OPHELIA   'Tis in my memory locked,
And you yourself shall keep the key of it. [they embrace

LAERTES   Farewell.   [he goes

POLONIUS What is't, Ophelia, he hath said to you?

OPHELIA   So please you, something touching the Lord Hamlet.

POLONIUS Marry, well bethought.   9⟨0⟩
'Tis told me he hath very oft of late
Given private time to you, and you yourself
Have of your audience been most free and bounteous.
If it be so – as so 'tis put on me,
And that in way of caution – I must tell you,
You do not understand yourself so clearly
As it behoves my daughter and your honour.
What is between you? Give me up the truth.

OPHELIA   He hath, my lord, of late made many tenders
Of his affection to me.   1⟨00⟩

POLONIUS Affection, pooh! You speak like a green girl
Unsifted in such perilous circumstance.
Do you believe his tenders, as you call them?

OPHELIA   I do not know, my lord, what I should think.

POLONIUS   Marry, I will teach you – think yourself a baby
That you have ta'en these tenders for true pay
Which are not sterling. Tender yourself more dearly,
Or (not to crack the wind of the poor phrase,
Running it thus) you'll tender me a fool.

OPHELIA   My lord, he hath importuned me with love   110
In honourable fashion.

POLONIUS   Ay, fashion you may call it, go to, go to.

OPHELIA   And hath given countenance to his speech, my lord,
With almost all the holy vows of heaven.

POLONIUS   Ay, springes to catch woodcocks. I do know
When the blood burns, how prodigal the soul
Lends the tongue vows. These blazes, daughter,
Giving more light than heat, extinct in both,
Even in their promise, as it is a-making,
You must not take for fire. From this time   120
Be something scanter of your maiden presence,
Set your entreatments at a higher rate
Than a command to parle; for Lord Hamlet,
Believe so much in him that he is young,
And with a larger tether may he walk
Than may be given you: in few, Ophelia,
Do not believe his vows, for they are brokers
Not of that dye which their investments show,
But mere implorators of unholy suits,
Breathing like sanctified and pious bonds   130
The better to beguile. This is for all,
I would not in plain terms from this time forth
Have you so slander any moment leisure
As to give words or talk with the Lord Hamlet.
Look to't, I charge you, come your ways.

OPHELIA   I shall obey, my lord.   [they go

SCENE 4

The platform on the battlements

HAMLET, HORATIO *and* MARCELLUS *come from one of the turrets*

HAMLET   The air bites shrewdly, it is very cold.
HORATIO   It is a nipping and an eager air.
HAMLET   What hour now?
HORATIO   I think it lacks of twelve.
MARCEL.   No, it is struck.
HORATIO   Indeed? I heard it not – it then draws near the season,
          Wherein the spirit held his wont to walk.
                    ['*a flourish of trumpets', and ordnance shot off*
          What does this mean, my lord?
HAMLET   The King doth wake tonight and takes his rouse,
          Keeps wassail and the swagg'ring upspring reels:
          And as he drains his draughts of Rhenish down,   1
          The kettle-drum and trumpet thus bray out
          The triumph of his pledge.
HORATIO   Is it a custom?
HAMLET   Ay marry is't,
          But to my mind, though I am native here
          And to the manner born, it is a custom
          More honoured in the breach than the observance.
          This heavy-headed revel east and west
          Makes us traduced and taxed of other nations.
          They clepe us drunkards, and with swinish phrase
          Soil our addition, and indeed it takes   2
          From our achievements, though performed at height,
          The pith and marrow of our attribute.
          So, oft it chances in particular men,
          That for some vicious mole of nature in them,
          As in their birth, wherein they are not guilty
          (Since nature cannot choose his origin),
          By the o'ergrowth of some complexion,
          Oft breaking down the pales and forts of reason,
          Or by some habit, that too much o'er-leavens

The form of plausive manners – that these men,   30
Carrying I say the stamp of one defect,
Being nature's livery, or fortune's star,
His virtues else be they as pure as grace,
As infinite as man may undergo,
Shall in the general censure take corruption
From that particular fault: the dram of evil
Doth all the noble substance of a doubt,
To his own scandal.

The GHOST appears

HORATIO   Look, my lord, it comes!

HAMLET   Angels and ministers of grace defend us!
Be thou a spirit of health, or goblin damned,   40
Bring with thee airs from heaven, or blasts from hell,
Be thy intents wicked, or charitable,
Thou com'st in such a questionable shape,
That I will speak to thee. I'll call thee Hamlet,
King, father, royal Dane. O, answer me!
Let me not burst in ignorance, but tell
Why thy canonized bones hearsèd in death
Have burst their cerements? Why the sepulchre,
Wherein we saw thee quietly inurned,
Hath oped his ponderous and marble jaws   50
To cast thee up again? What may this mean
That thou, dead corse, again in complete steel
Revisits thus the glimpses of the moon,
Making night hideous, and we fools of nature
So horridly to shake our disposition
With thoughts beyond the reaches of our souls?
Say why is this? Wherefore? What should we do?

[the Ghost 'beckons'

HORATIO   It beckons you to go away with it,
As if it some impartment did desire
To you alone.

MARCEL.   Look with what courteous action   60
It wares you to a more removèd ground,
But do not go with it.

HORATIO   No, by no means.

HAMLET   It will not speak, then I will follow it.

HORATIO   Do not my lord.

HAMLET   Why, what should be the fear?
I do not set my life at a pin's fee,
And for my soul, what can it do to that
Being a thing immortal as itself;
It waves me forth again, I'll follow it.

HORATIO   What if it tempt you toward the flood, my lord,
Or to the dreadful summit of the cliff   70
That beetles o'er his base into the sea,
And there assume some other horrible form,
Which might deprive your sovereignty of reason,
And draw you into madness? Think of it –
The very place puts toys of desperation,
Without more motive, into every brain
That looks so many fathoms to the sea
And hears it roar beneath.

HAMLET   It waves me still.
Go on, I'll follow thee.

MARCEL.   You shall not go, my lord.

HAMLET   Hold off your hands.   80

HORATIO   Be ruled, you shall not go.

HAMLET   My fate cries out,
And makes each petty artere in this body
As hardy as the Nemean lion's nerve;
Still am I called, unhand me gentlemen,
          [*he breaks from them, drawing his sword*
By heaven, I'll make a ghost of him that lets me!
I say, away! Go on, I'll follow thee.
       [*the Ghost passes into one of the turrets, Hamlet following*

HORATIO   He waxes desperate with imagination.

MARCEL.   Lets follow, 'tis not fit thus to obey him.

HORATIO   Have after – to what issue will this come?

MARCEL.   Something is rotten in the state of Denmark.   90

HORATIO   Heaven will direct it.

MARCEL.   Nay, let's follow him.
                             [*they follow*

SCENE 5

An open space at the foot of the castle wall

A door in the wall opens; the GHOST *comes forth and* HAMLET
after, the hilt of his drawn sword held crosswise before him

HAMLET Whither wilt thou lead me? speak, I'll go no further.
GHOST [*turns*] Mark me.
HAMLET   I will.
GHOST   My hour is almost come,
  When I to sulph'rous and tormenting flames
  Must render up myself.
HAMLET   Alas, poor ghost!
GHOST Pity me not, but lend thy serious hearing
  To what I shall unfold.
HAMLET   Speak, I am bound to hear.
GHOST So art thou to revenge, when thou shalt hear.
HAMLET What?
GHOST I am thy father's spirit,
  Doomed for a certain term to walk the night,   10
  And for the day confined to fast in fires,
  Till the foul crimes done in my days of nature
  Are burnt and purged away: but that I am forbid
  To tell the secrets of my prison-house,
  I could a tale unfold whose lightest word
  Would harrow up thy soul, freeze thy young blood,
  Make thy two eyes like stars start from their spheres,
  Thy knotted and combinéd locks to part,
  And each particular hair to stand an end,
  Like quills upon the fretful porpentine.   20
  But this eternal blazon must not be
  To ears of flesh and blood. List, list, O list!
  If thou didst ever thy dear father love –
HAMLET O God!
GHOST Revenge his foul and most unnatural murder.
HAMLET Murder!
GHOST Murder most foul, as in the best it is,
  But this most foul, strange and unnatural.

HAMLET   Haste me to know't, that I with wings as swift
As meditation or the thoughts of love,   30
May sweep to my revenge.

GHOST   I find thee apt,
And duller shouldst thou be than the fat weed
That rots itself in ease on Lethe wharf,
Wouldst thou not stir in this; now Hamlet hear,
'Tis given out, that sleeping in my orchard,
A serpent stung me, so the whole ear of Denmark
Is by a forgéd process of my death
Rankly abused: but know, thou noble youth,
The serpent that did sting thy father's life
Now wears his crown.

HAMLET   O, my prophetic soul!   40
My uncle?

GHOST   Ay, that incestuous, that adulterate beast,
With witchcraft of his wit, with traitorous gifts,
O wicked wit and gifts, that have the power
So to seduce; won to his shameful lust
The will of my most seeming-virtuous queen;
O Hamlet, what a falling-off was there!
From me whose love was of that dignity,
That it went hand in hand even with the vow
I made to her in marriage, and to decline   50
Upon a wretch whose natural gifts were poor
To those of mine;
But virtue, as it never will be moved,
Though lewdness court it in a shape of heaven,
So lust, though to a radiant angel linked,
Will sate itself in a celestial bed
And prey on garbage.
But soft, methinks I scent the morning air,
Brief let me be; sleeping within my orchard,
My custom always of the afternoon,   60
Upon my secure hour thy uncle stole
With juice of cursed hebona in a vial,
And in the porches of my ears did pour
The leperous distilment, whose effect
Holds such an enmity with blood of man,

That swift as quicksilver it courses through
The natural gates and alleys of the body,
And with a sudden vigour it doth posset
And curd, like eager droppings into milk,
The thin and wholesome blood; so did it mine,   70
And a most instant tetter barked about
Most lazar-like with vile and loathsome crust
All my smooth body.
Thus was I sleeping by a brother's hand,
Of life, of crown, of queen at once dispatched,
Cut off even in the blossoms of my sin,
Unhouseled, disappointed, unaneled,
No reck'ning made, but sent to my account
With all my imperfections on my head.
O, horrible! O, horrible! Most horrible !   80
If thou hast nature in thee bear it not,
Let not the royal bed of Denmark be
A couch for luxury and damnéd incest.
But howsomever thou pursues this act,
Taint not thy mind, nor let thy soul contrive
Against thy mother aught – leave her to heaven,
And to those thorns that in her bosom lodge
To prick and sting her. Fare thee well at once,
The glow-worm shows the matin to be near,
And 'gins to pale his uneffectual fire.   90
Adieu, adieu, adieu, remember me.

[the Ghost vanishes into the ground; Hamlet
falls distraught upon his knees

HAMLET   O all you host of heaven! O earth! What else?
And shall I couple hell? O fie! Hold, hold, my heart,
And you, my sinews, grow not instant old,
But bear me stiffly up. [*he rises*] Remember thee?
Ay thou poor ghost, whiles memory holds a seat
In this distracted globe. Remember thee?
Yea, from the table of my memory
I'll wipe away all trivial fond records,
All saws of books, all forms, all pressures past   100
That youth and observation copied there,
And thy commandment all alone shall live

Within the book and volume of my brain,
Unmixed with baser matter – yes by heaven!
O most pernicious woman!
O villain, villain, smiling damnéd villain!
My tables, meet it is I set it down　　　　　*[he writes*
That one may smile, and smile, and be a villain,
At least I am sure it may be so in Denmark.
So, uncle, there you are. Now, to my word,　　　　110
It is 'Adieu, adieu, remember me.'

　　　　[he kneels and lays his hand upon the hilt of his sword
I have sworn't.　　　　　　　　　　　　*[he prays*

　　　HORATIO *and* MARCELLUS *come from the castle,*
　　　　　　　calling in the darkness

HORATIO	My lord, my lord!
HAMLET	Lord Hamlet!
HORATIO	Heaven secure him!
HAMLET	So be it!　　　　　　　　　　*[he rises*
MARCEL.	Illo, ho, ho, my lord!
HAMLET	Hillo, ho, ho, boy! Come, bird, come.

　　　　　　　　　　　　　　　　[they see Hamlet

MARCEL.	How is't, my noble lord?
HORATIO	What news, my lord?
HAMLET	O, wonderful!
HORATIO	Good my lord, tell it.
HAMLET	No, you will reveal it.
HORATIO	Not I, my lord, by heaven.
MARCEL.	Nor I, my lord.　　　120
HAMLET	How say you then, would heart of man once think it? But you'll be secret?
HORATIO, MARCEL.	Ay, by heaven, my lord.
HAMLET	There's ne'er a villain dwelling in all Denmark But he's an arrant knave.
HORATIO	There needs no ghost, my lord, come from the grave, To tell us this.
HAMLET	Why right, you are in the right, And so without more circumstance at all I hold it fit that we shake hands and part, You, as your business and desire shall point you,

	For every man hath business and desire	130
	Such as it is, and for my own poor part,	
	Look you, I will go pray.	
HORATIO	These are but wild and whirling words, my lord.	
HAMLET	I am sorry they offend you, heartily,	
	Yes, faith, heartily.	
HORATIO	There's no offence, my lord.	
HAMLET	[to Horatio] Yes, by Saint Patrick, but there is, Horatio,	
	And much offence too – touching this vision here,	
	It is an honest ghost, that let me tell you –	
	For your desire to know what is between us,	
	O'ermaster't as you may.	
	[to both] And now, good friends,	140
	As you are friends, scholars, and soldiers,	
	Give me one poor request.	
HORATIO	What is't, my lord? We will.	
HAMLET	Never make known what you have seen tonight.	
BOTH	My lord, we will not.	
HAMLET	Nay, but swear't.	
HORATIO	In faith,	
	My lord, not I.	
MARCEL.	Nor I, my lord, in faith.	
HAMLET	[draws] Upon my sword.	
MARCEL.	We have sworn, my lord, already.	
HAMLET	Indeed, upon my sword, indeed.	
GHOST	[beneath] Swear.	
HAMLET	Ha, ha, boy! Say'st thou so? Art thou there, truepenny?	150
	Come on, you hear this fellow in the cellarage,	
	Consent to swear.	
HORATIO	Propose the oath, my lord.	
HAMLET	Never to speak of this that you have seen,	
	Swear by my sword.	
	[they lay their hands upon the hilt	
GHOST	[beneath] Swear.	
HAMLET	Hic et ubique? Then we'll shift our ground:	
	Come hither gentlemen,	
	And lay your hands again upon my sword.	
	Swear by my sword,	
	Never to speak of this that you have heard.	160

GHOST   [*beneath*] Swear by his sword.
HAMLET   Well said, old mole! Canst work i'th'earth so fast?
                                              [*they swear again in silence*
            A worthy pioneer! Once more remove, good friends.
HORATIO   O day and night, but this is wondrous strange!
HAMLET   And therefore as a stranger give it welcome.
            There are more things in heaven and earth, Horatio,
            Than are dreamt of in your philosophy.
            But come –
            Here as before, never, so help you mercy
            (How strange or odd some'er I bear myself;   17
            As I perchance hereafter shall think meet
            To put an antic disposition on)
            That you at such times seeing me, never shall
            With arms encumbered thus, or this head-shake,
            Or by pronouncing of some doubtful phrase,
            As 'Well, well, we know', or 'We could an if we
                                                      would',
            Or 'If we list to speak', or 'There be an if they might',
            Or such ambiguous giving out, to note
            That you know aught of me – this do swear,
            So grace and mercy at your most need help you!   18
GHOST   [*beneath*] Swear.
HAMLET   Rest, rest, perturbéd spirit! [*they swear a third time*]
                                    So, gentlemen,
            With all my love I do commend me to you,
            And what so poor a man as Hamlet is
            May do t'express his love and friending to you
            God willing shall not lack. Let us go in together,
            And still your fingers on your lips I pray.
            The time is out of joint, O curséd spite,
            That ever I was born to set it right!
            Nay come, let's go together.   [*they enter the castle* 19

                      [*Some weeks pass*]

ACT 2 SCENE 1

A room in the house of Polonius

POLONIUS *and* REYNALDO

POLONIUS Give him this money, and these notes, Reynaldo,
REYNALDO I will, my lord.
POLONIUS You shall do marvellous wisely, good Reynaldo,
           Before you visit him, to make inquire
           Of his behaviour.
REYNALDO: My lord, I did intend it.
POLONIUS Marry, well said, very well said; look you sir,
           Inquire me first what Danskers are in Paris,
           And how, and who, what means, and where they keep,
           What company, at what expense, and finding
           By this encompassment and drift of question   10
           That they do know my son, come you more nearer
           Than your particular demands will touch it,
           Take you as 'twere some distant knowledge of him,
           As thus, 'I know his father, and his friends,
           And in part him' – do you mark this, Reynaldo?
REYNALDO Ay, very well, my lord.
POLONIUS 'And in part him, but,' you may say, 'not well,
           But if't be he I mean, he's very wild,
           Addicted so and so.' And there put on him
           What forgeries you please, marry none so rank   20
           As may dishonour him, take heed of that,
           But sir such wanton, wild, and usual slips
           As are companions noted and most known
           To youth and liberty.
REYNALDO   As gaming, my lord.
POLONIUS Ay, or drinking, fencing, swearing, quarrelling,
           Drabbing – you may go so far.
REYNALDO My lord, that would dishonour him.
POLONIUS Faith no, as you may season it in the charge.
           You must not put another scandal on him,
           That he is open to incontinency,   30

That's not my meaning, but breathe his faults so quaintly
That they may seem the taints of liberty,
The flash and outbreak of a fiery mind,
A savageness in unreclaimed blood,
Of general assault.

REYNALDO   But, my good lord –
POLONIUS Wherefore should you do this?
REYNALDO   Ay my lord,
I would know that.
POLONIUS   Marry sir, here's my drift,
And I believe it is a fetch of warrant,
You laying these slight sullies on my son,
As 'twere a thing a little soiled i'th' working,   40
Mark you, your party in converse, him you would
                                                 sound,
Having ever seen in the prenominate crimes
The youth you breathe of guilty, be assured
He closes with you in this consequence,
'Good sir', or so, or 'friend', or 'gentleman',
According to the phrase, or the addition
Of man and country.

REYNALDO   Very good, my lord.
POLONIUS And then sir, does 'a this, 'a does, what was I about
                                                 to say?
By the mass I was about to say something.
Where did I leave?
REYNALDO   At 'closes in the consequence',   50
At 'friend, or so, and gentleman'.
POLONIUS At 'closes in the consequence'. Ay marry –
He closes thus, 'I know the gentleman,
I saw him yesterday, or th'other day,
Or then, or then, with such or such, and as you say,
There was 'a gaming, there o'ertook in's rouse,
There falling out at tennis', or perchance,
'I saw him enter such a house of sale',
Videlicet, a brothel, or so forth. See you now,
Your bait of falsehood takes this carp of truth,   60
And thus do we of wisdom, and of reach,
With windlasses, and with assays of bias,

By indirections find directions out,
So by my former lecture and advice
Shall you my son; you have me, have you not?

REYNALDO My lord, I have.

POLONIUS   God bye ye, fare ye well.

REYNALDO Good, my lord.

POLONIUS Observe his inclination in yourself.

REYNALDO I shall, my lord.

POLONIUS And let him ply his music.

REYNALDO   Well, my lord.   [*he goes* 70

POLONIUS Farewell.

OPHELIA *enters in perturbation*

                    How now Ophelia, what's the matter?

OPHELIA O my lord, my lord, I have been so affrighted!

POLONIUS With what, i'th'name of God?

OPHELIA My lord, as I was sewing in my closet,
Lord Hamlet with his doublet all unbraced,
No hat upon his head, his stockings fouled,
Ungart'red, and down-gyvéd to his ankle,
Pale as his shirt, his knees knocking each other,
And with a look so piteous in purport
As if he had been looséd out of hell   80
To speak of horrors – he comes before me.

POLONIUS Mad for thy love?

OPHELIA   My lord, I do not know,
But truly I do fear it.

POLONIUS   What said he?

OPHELIA He took me by the wrist, and held me hard,
Then goes he to the length of all his arm,
And with his other hand thus o'er his brow,
He falls to such perusal of my face
As 'a would draw it. Long stayed he so,
At last, a little shaking of mine arm,
And thrice his head thus waving up and down,   90
He raised a sigh so piteous and profound
As it did seem to shatter all his bulk,
And end his being; that done, he lets me go,
And with his head over his shoulder turned
He seemed to find his way without his eyes,

                    For out adoors he went without their helps,
                    And to the last bended their light on me.
POLONIUS Come, go with me. I will go seek the king.
                    This is the very ecstasy of love,
                    Whose violent property fordoes itself,   10
                    And leads the will to desperate undertakings,
                    As oft as any passion under heaven
                    That does afflict our natures: I am sorry —
                    What, have you given him any hard words of late?
OPHELIA   No, my good lord, but as you did command
                    I did repel his letters, and denied
                    His access to me.
POLONIUS   That hath made him mad.
                    I am sorry that with better heed and judgment
                    I had not quoted him. I feared he did but trifle
                    And meant to wreck thee, but beshrew my jealousy   11
                    By heaven, it is as proper to our age
                    To cast beyond ourselves in our opinions,
                    As it is common for the younger sort
                    To lack discretion; come, go we to the king.
                    This must be known, which, being kept close,
                                                                  might move
                    More grief to hide, than hate to utter love.
                    Come.   [they go

SCENE 2

*An audience chamber in the castle; at the back a lobby, with curtains
to left and right of the entry and a door to the rear within*

A flourish of trumpets. The KING *and* QUEEN *enter followed by*
ROSENCRANTZ, GUILDENSTERN, *and attendants*

KING   Welcome, dear Rosencrantz and Guildenstern!
                    Moreover that we much did long to see you,
                    The need we have to use you did provoke
                    Our hasty sending. Something have you heard
                    Of Hamlet's transformation — so call it,
                    Sith nor th'exterior nor the inward man
                    Resembles that it was. What it should be,

More than his father's death, that thus hath put him
So much from th'understanding of himself,
I cannot dream of: I entreat you both,   10
That being of so young days brought up with him,
And sith so neighboured to his youth and haviour,
That you vouchsafe your rest here in our court
Some little time, so by your companies
To draw him on to pleasures, and to gather
So much as from occasion you may glean
Whether aught to us unknown afflicts him thus,
That opened lies within our remedy.

QUEEN   Good gentlemen, he hath much talked of you,
And sure I am two men there are not living   20
To whom he more adheres. If it will please you
To show us so much gentry and good will
As to expend your time with us awhile,
For the supply and profit of our hope,
Your visitation shall receive such thanks
As fits a king's remembrance.

ROSENC'Z   Both your majesties
Might by the sovereign power you have of us,
Put your dread pleasures more into command
Than to entreaty.

GUILD'RN   But we both obey,
And here give up ourselves in the full bent,   30
To lay our service freely at your feet
To be commanded.

KING   Thanks Rosencrantz, and gentle Guildenstern.

QUEEN   Thanks Guildenstern, and gentle Rosencrantz,
And I beseech you instantly to visit
My too much changéd son. Go some of you
And bring these gentlemen where Hamlet is.

GUILD'RN   Heavens make our presence and our practices
Pleasant and helpful to him!

QUEEN   Ay, amen!

[Rosencrantz and Guildenstern bow and depart

POLONIUS *enters, and speaks with the King apart*

POLONIUS   The ambassadors from Norway, my good lord,   40
Are joyfully returned.

KING   Thou still hast been the father of good news.
POLONIUS   Have I, my lord? Assure you, my good liege,
            I hold my duty as I hold my soul,
            Both to my God and to my gracious king;
            And I do think, or else this brain of mine
            Hunts not the trail of policy so sure
            As it hath used to do, that I have found
            The very cause of Hamlet's lunacy.
KING   O speak of that, that do I long to hear.   50
POLONIUS   Give first admittance to th'ambassadors.
            My news shall be the fruit to that great feast.
KING   Thyself do grace to them, and bring them in.
                                            [*Polonius goes out*
            He tells me, my dear Gertrude, he hath found
            The head and source of all your son's distemper.
QUEEN   I doubt it is no other but the main,
            His father's death and our o'erhasty marriage.
KING   Well, we shall sift him.

            POLONIUS *returns with* VALTEMAND *and* CORNELIUS

                            Welcome, my good friends!
            Say Valtemand, what from our brother Norway?
VALTEM'D   Most fair return of greetings and desires;   [*they bow* 60
            Upon our first, he sent out to suppress
            His nephew's levies, which to him appeared
            To be a preparation 'gainst the Polack,
            But better looked into, he truly found
            It was against your highness, whereat grieved
            That so his sickness, age and impotence
            Was falsely borne in hand, sends out arrests
            On Fortinbras, which he in brief obeys,
            Receives rebuke from Norway, and in fine,
            Makes vow before his uncle never more   70
            To give th'assay of arms against your majesty:
            Whereon old Norway, overcome with joy,
            Gives him threescore thousand crowns in annual fee,
            And his commission to employ those soldiers,
            So levied, as before, against the Polack,
            With an entreaty, herein further shown,
            That it might please you to give quiet pass

Through your dominions for this enterprise,
On such regards of safety and allowance
As therein are set down.   *[he proffers a paper*

KING   *[takes it]* It likes us well,   80
And at our more considered time, we'll read,
Answer, and think upon this business:
Meantime, we thank you for your well-took labour.
Go to your rest, at night we'll feast together.
Most welcome home!
          [Valtemand and Cornelius bow and depart

POLONIUS   This business is well ended.
My liege and madam, to expostulate
What majesty should be, what duty is,
Why day is day, night night, and time is time,
Were nothing but to waste night, day and time.
Therefore since brevity is the soul of wit,   90
And tediousness the limbs and outward flourishes,
I will be brief – your noble son is mad:
Mad call I it, for to define true madness,
What is't but to be nothing else but mad?
But let that go.

QUEEN   More matter, with less art.

POLONIUS Madam, I swear I use no art at all.
That he is mad 'tis true, 'tis true, 'tis pity,
And pity 'tis 'tis true – a foolish figure,
But farewell it, for I will use no art.
Mad let us grant him then, and now remains   100
That we find out the cause of this effect,
Or rather say, the cause of this defect,
For this effect defective comes by cause:
Thus it remains, and the remainder thus.
Perpend.   *[he takes papers from his doublet*
I have a daughter, have while she is mine,
Who in her duty and obedience, mark,
Hath given me this, now gather and surmise. *[he reads]*
'To the celestial, and my soul's idol, the most beautified
Ophelia,' –   110
That's an ill phrase, a vile phrase, 'beautified' is a vile
phrase, but you shall hear. Thus: *[he reads]*

        'In her excellent white bosom, these, etc.' –

QUEEN   Came this from Hamlet to her?

POLONIUS Good madam, stay awhile, I will be faithful – [*he reads*]

        'Doubt thou the stars are fire,

          Doubt that the sun doth move,

        Doubt truth to be a liar,

          But never doubt I love.

O dear Ophelia, I am ill at these numbers, I have not art 12
to reckon my groans, but that I love thee best, O most
best, believe it. Adieu.

        Thine evermore, most dear lady, whilst
        this machine is to him, Hamlet.'

This in obedience hath my daughter shown me,
And more above hath his solicitings,
As they fell out by time, by means, and place,
All given to mine ear.

KING   But how hath she
Received his love?

POLONIUS   What do you think of me ?

KING   As of a man faithful and honourable.   13

POLONIUS I would fain prove so. But what might you think
When I had seen this hot love on the wing,
As I perceived it (I must tell you that)
Before my daughter told me, what might you,
Or my dear majesty your queen here think,
If I had played the desk or table-book,
Or given my heart a working mute and dumb,
Or looked upon this love with idle sight,
What might you think? No, I went round to work,
And my young mistress thus I did bespeak –   14
'Lord Hamlet is a prince out of thy star,
This must not be': and then I prescripts gave her
That she should lock herself from his resort,
Admit no messengers, receive no tokens.
Which done, she took the fruits of my advice:
And he repelléd, a short tale to make,
Fell into a sadness, then into a fast,
Thence to a watch, thence into a weakness,
Thence to a lightness, and by this declension,

       Into the madness wherein now he raves,   150
       And all we mourn for.

KING   Do you think 'tis this?

QUEEN   It may be, very like.

POLONIUS   Hath there been such a time, I would fain know that,
       That I have positively said ' 'Tis so',
       When it proved otherwise?

KING   Not that I know.

POLONIUS   Take this from this, if this be otherwise;

            [he points to his head and shoulder
       If circumstances lead me, I will find
       Where truth is hid, though it were hid indeed
       Within the centre.

    HAMLET, *disorderly attired and reading a book, enters the lobby*
     by the door at the back; he hears voices from the chamber and
      pauses a moment beside one of the curtains, unobserved

KING   How may we try it further?

POLONIUS   You know sometimes he walks four hours together   160
       Here in the lobby.

QUEEN   So he does, indeed.

POLONIUS   At such a time I'll loose my daughter to him.
       Be you and I behind an arras then;
       Mark the encounter, if he love her not,
       And be not from his reason fall'n thereon,
       Let me be no assistant for a state,
       But keep a farm and carters.

KING   We will try it.

     HAMLET *comes forward, his eyes on the book*

QUEEN   But look where sadly the poor wretch comes reading.

POLONIUS   Away, I do beseech you both away,
       I'll board him presently, O give me leave.   170
            [the King and Queen hurry forth
       How does my good Lord Hamlet?

HAMLET   Well, God-a-mercy.

POLONIUS   Do you know me, my lord?

HAMLET   Excellent well, you are a fishmonger.

POLONIUS   Not I, my lord.

HAMLET   Then I would you were so honest a man.

POLONIUS   Honest, my lord?

HAMLET   Ay sir, to be honest as this world goes, is to be one
man picked out of ten thousand.

POLONIUS   That's very true, my lord.   180

HAMLET   For if the sun breed maggots in a dead dog, being a
good kissing carrion. Have you a daughter?

POLONIUS   I have, my lord.

HAMLET   Let her not walk i'th'sun. Conception is a blessing, but
as your daughter may conceive, friend look to't.

                                              [*he reads again*

POLONIUS   How say you by that? Still harping on my daughter, yet
he knew me not at first, 'a said I was a fishmonger. 'A is
far gone, far gone, and truly in my youth I suffered
much extremity for love, very near this. I'll speak to
him again – What do you read, my lord?   190

HAMLET   Words, words, words.

POLONIUS   What is the matter, my lord?

HAMLET   Between who?

POLONIUS   I mean the matter that you read, my lord.

HAMLET   [*bears down upon him, Polonius retreating backwards*]
Slanders, sir; for the satirical rogue says here that old
men have grey beards, that their faces are wrinkled,
their eyes purging thick amber and plum-tree gum,
and that they have a plentiful lack of wit, together
with most weak hams – all which, sir, though I most
powerfully and potently believe, yet I hold it not hon-   200
esty to have it thus set down, for yourself, sir, shall
grow old as I am, if like a crab you could go backward.

                                              [*he reads again*

POLONIUS   Though this be madness, yet there is method in't.
Will you walk out of the air, my lord?

HAMLET   Into my grave.

POLONIUS   Indeed, that's out of the air; how pregnant sometimes
his replies are! A happiness that often madness hits on,
which reason and sanity could not so prosperously be
delivered of. I will leave him, and suddenly contrive
the means of meeting between him and my daughter. –   210
My honourable lord, I will most humbly take my leave
of you.

HAMLET	You cannot, sir, take from me anything that I will more willingly part withal: except my life, except my life, except my life.
POLONIUS	Fare you well, my lord. *[he bows low*
HAMLET	These tedious old fools! *[he returns to his book*

ROSENCRANTZ *and* GUILDENSTERN *enter*

POLONIUS	You go to seek the Lord Hamlet, there he is.	
ROSENC'Z	*[to Polonius]* God save you, sir! *[Polonius goes out*	
GUILD'RN	My honoured lord!	220
ROSENC'Z	My most dear lord!	
HAMLET	*[looks up]* My excellent good friends! How dost thou, Guildenstern? *[putting up the book* Ah, Rosencrantz! Good lads, how do you both?	
ROSENC'Z	As the indifferent children of the earth.	
GUILD'RN	Happy, in that we are not over-happy, On Fortune's cap we are not the very button.	
HAMLET	Nor the soles of her shoe?	
ROSENC'Z	Neither, my lord.	
HAMLET	Then you live about her waist or in the middle of her favours?	230
GUILD'RN	Faith, her privates we.	
HAMLET	In the secret parts of fortune? O most true, she is a strumpet. What's the news?	
ROSENC'Z	None, my lord, but that the world's grown honest.	
HAMLET	Then is doomsday near. But your news is not true. Let me question more in particular: what have you, my good friends, deserved at the hands of Fortune, that she sends you to prison hither?	
GUILD'RN	Prison, my lord!	240
HAMLET	Denmark's a prison.	
ROSENC'Z	Then is the world one.	
HAMLET	A goodly one, in which there are many confines, wards and dungeons; Denmark being one o'th'worst.	
ROSENC'Z	We think not so, my lord.	
HAMLET	Why, then 'tis none to you; for there is nothing either good or bad, but thinking makes it so: to me it is a prison.	
ROSENC'Z	Why, then your ambition makes it one: 'tis too narrow for your mind.	
HAMLET	O God! I could be bounded in a nut-shell, and count	250

myself a king of infinite space; were it not that I have
bad dreams.

GUILD'RN　Which dreams, indeed, are ambition: for the very substance of the ambitious is merely the shadow of a
dream.

HAMLET　A dream itself is but a shadow.

ROSENC'Z　Truly, and I hold ambition of so airy and light a
quality, that it is but a shadow's shadow.

HAMLET　Then are our beggars bodies, and our monarchs and
outstretched heroes the beggars' shadows. Shall we to　260
th' court? For, by my fay, I cannot reason.

ROSENC'Z, GUILD'RN　We'll wait upon you.

HAMLET　No such matter: I will not sort you with the rest of my
servants; for to speak to you like an honest man, I am
most dreadfully attended. But, in the beaten way of
friendship, what make you at Elsinore?

ROSENC'Z　To visit you, my lord, no other occasion.

HAMLET　Beggar that I am, I am even poor in thanks, but I
thank you – and sure, dear friends, my thanks are too
dear a halfpenny: were you not sent for? Is it your own　270
inclining? Is it a free visitation? Come, come, deal
justly with me, come, come, nay speak.

GUILD'RN　What should we say, my lord?

HAMLET　Why, anything but to th'purpose. You were sent for,
and there is a kind of confession in your looks, which
your modesties have not craft enough to colour – I
know the good king and queen have sent for you.

ROSENC'Z　To what end, my lord?

HAMLET　That you must teach me: but let me conjure you, by
the rights of our fellowship, by the consonancy of our　280
youth, by the obligation of our ever-preserved love,
and by what more dear a better proposer can charge
you withal, be even and direct with me whether you
were sent for or no?

ROSENC'Z　What say you?　　　　　　　　　　[to Guildenstern

HAMLET　Nay then, I have an eye of you!
[aloud] If you love me, hold not off.

GUILD'RN　My lord, we were sent for.

HAMLET　I will tell you why, so shall my anticipation prevent

your discovery, and your secrecy to the king and queen 290
moult no feather. I have of late, but wherefore I know
not, lost all my mirth, forgone all custom of exercises:
and indeed it goes so heavily with my disposition, that
this goodly frame the earth, seems to me a sterile prom-
ontory, this most excellent canopy the air, look you, this
brave o'erhanging firmament, this majestical roof fretted
with golden fire, why it appeareth nothing to me but a
foul and pestilent congregation of vapours. What a piece
of work is a man, how noble in reason, how infinite in
faculties, in form and moving, how express and admira- 300
ble in action, how like an angel in apprehension, how
like a god: the beauty of the world; the paragon of
animals; and yet to me, what is this quintessence of dust?
man delights not me, no, nor woman neither, though
by your smiling you seem to say so.

ROSENC'Z   My lord, there was no such stuff in my thoughts.

HAMLET   Why did ye laugh then, when I said 'man delights not
me'?

ROSENC'Z   To think, my lord, if you delight not in man, what
lenten entertainment the players shall receive from 310
you. We coted them on the way, and hither are they
coming to offer you service.

HAMLET   He that plays the King shall be welcome, his majesty
shall have tribute on me, the adventurous Knight shall
use his foil and target, the Lover shall not sigh gratis, the
Humorous Man shall end his part in peace, the Clown
shall make those laugh whose lungs are tickle o'th'sere,
and the Lady shall say her mind freely – or the blank
verse shall halt for't. What players are they?

ROSENC'Z   Even those you were wont to take such delight in, the 320
tragedians of the city.

HAMLET   How chances it they travel? Their residence both in
reputation and profit was better both ways.

ROSENC'Z   I think their inhibition comes by the means of the late
innovation.

HAMLET   Do they hold the same estimation they did when I was
in the city? Are they so followed?

ROSENC'Z   No, indeed, are they not.

HAMLET   How comes it? do they grow rusty?

ROSENC'Z   Nay, their endeavour keeps in the wonted pace; but   33
            there is, sir, an eyrie of children, little eyases, that cry
            out on the top of question, and are most tyrannically
            clapped for't: these are now the fashion, and so berattle
            the common stages (so they call them) that many
            wearing rapiers are afraid of goose-quills, and dare
            scarce come thither.

HAMLET   What, are they children? Who maintains 'em? How are
            they escoted? Will they pursue the quality no longer
            than they can sing? will they not say afterwards if they
            should grow themselves to common players (as it is like   34
            most will if their means are not better) their writers do
            them wrong, to make them exclaim against their own
            succession?

ROSENC'Z   Faith, there has been much to-do on both sides: and
            the nation holds it no sin to tarre them to controversy.
            There was, for a while, no money bid for argument,
            unless the Poet and the Player went to cuffs in the
            question.

HAMLET   Is't possible?

GUILD'RN   O, there has been much throwing about of brains.   35

HAMLET   Do the boys carry it away?

ROSENC'Z   Ay, that they do my lord, Hercules and his load too.

HAMLET   It is not very strange, for my uncle is king of Denmark,
            and those that would make mows at him while my
            father lived, give twenty, forty, fifty, a hundred ducats
            apiece for his picture in little. 'Sblood, there is some-
            thing in this more than natural, if philosophy could
            find it out.   [*'A flourish' of trumpets heard*

GUILD'RN   There are the players.

HAMLET   Gentlemen, you are welcome to Elsinore. [*he bows*]   36
            Your hands? Come then, th'appurtenance of welcome
            is fashion and ceremony; let me comply with you in
            this garb [*he takes their hands*], lest my extent to the
            players, which I tell you must show fairly outwards,
            should more appear like entertainment than yours.
            You are welcome: but my uncle-father, and aunt-
            mother, are deceived.

GUILD'RN   In what, my dear lord?

HAMLET   I am but mad north-north-west; when the wind is
southerly, I know a hawk from a handsaw.   370

POLONIUS enters

POLONIUS   Well be with you, gentlemen!

HAMLET   Hark you Guildenstern, and you too, at each ear a
hearer – that great baby you see there is not yet out of
his swaddling-clouts.

ROSENC'Z   Happily he is the second time come to them, for they
say an old man is twice a child.

HAMLET   I will prophesy, he comes to tell me of the players,
mark it. [*raises his voice*] You say right sir, a Monday
morning, 'twas then indeed.

POLONIUS   My lord, I have news to tell you.   380

HAMLET   My lord, I have news to tell you. When Roscius was
an actor in Rome –

POLONIUS   The actors are come hither, my lord.

HAMLET   Buz, buz!

POLONIUS   Upon my honour –

HAMLET   'Then came each actor on his ass' –

POLONIUS   The best actors in the world, either for tragedy,
comedy, history, pastoral, pastoral-comical, historical-
pastoral, tragical-historical, tragical-comical-historical-
pastoral, scene individable, or poem unlimited. Seneca   390
cannot be too heavy nor Plautus too light. For the law
of writ and the liberty, these are the only men.

HAMLET   O Jephthah, judge of Israel, what a treasure hadst thou!

POLONIUS   What a treasure had he, my lord?

HAMLET   Why,

> 'One fair daughter, and no more,
>   The which he lovéd passing well.'

POLONIUS   Still on my daughter.

HAMLET   Am I not i'th' right, old Jephthah?

POLONIUS   If you call me Jephthah, my lord, I have a daughter   400
that I love passing well.

HAMLET   Nay, that follows not.

POLONIUS   What follows then, my lord?

HAMLET   Why,

'As by lot, God wot',
and then you know
'It came to pass, as most like it was.'
The first row of the pious chanson will show you
more, for look where my abridgement comes.

'Enter four or five Players'

You are welcome masters, welcome all – I am glad to 4>
see thee well – Welcome, good friends – O, my old
friend! Why, thy face is valanced since I saw thee last,
com'st thou to beard me in Denmark? – What, my
young lady and mistress! By'r lady, your ladyship is
nearer to heaven than when I saw you last by the
altitude of a chopine. Pray God your voice, like a
piece of uncurrent gold, be not cracked within the
ring. Masters, you are all welcome. We'll e'en to't like
French falconers, fly at anything we see, we'll have a
speech straight. [*to the First Player*] Come give us a taste 42
of your quality, come, a passionate speech.

I PLAYER What speech, my good lord?

HAMLET I heard thee speak me a speech once, but it was never
acted, or if it was, not above once, for the play I
remember pleased not the million, 'twas caviary to the
general, but it was – as I received it, and others, whose
judgments in such matters cried in the top of mine – an
excellent play, well digested in the scenes, set down
with as much modesty as cunning. I remember one said
there were no sallets in the lines, to make the matter 43
savoury, nor no matter in the phrase that might indict
the author of affection, but called it an honest method,
as wholesome as sweet, and by very much more handsome than fine: one speech in't I chiefly loved, 'twas
Aeneas' tale to Dido, and thereabout of it especially
where he speaks of Priam's slaughter. If it live in your
memory begin at this line, let me see, let me see –
'The rugged Pyrrhus, like th'Hyrcanian beast' –
'tis not so, it begins with Pyrrhus –
'The rugged Pyrrhus, he whose sable arms,   44
Black as his purpose, did the night resemble
When he lay couchéd in th'ominous horse,

Hath now this dread and black complexion smeared
With heraldry more dismal: head to foot
Now is he total gules, horridly tricked
With blood of fathers, mothers, daughters, sons,
Baked and impasted with the parching streets,
That lend a tyrannous and a damnéd light
To their lord's murder. Roasted in wrath and fire,
And thus o'er-sizéd with coagulate gore,   450
With eyes like carbuncles, the hellish Pyrrhus
Old grandsire Priam seeks.'
So proceed you.

POLONIUS 'Fore God, my lord, well spoken, with good accent and
good discretion.

I PLAYER   'Anon he finds him
Striking too short at Greeks; his antique sword,
Rebellious to his arm, lies where it falls,
Repugnant to command; unequal matched,
Pyrrhus at Priam drives, in rage strikes wide,
But with the whiff and wind of his fell sword   460
Th'unnervéd father falls: then senseless Ilium,
Seeming to feel this blow, with flaming top
Stoops to his base; and with a hideous crash
Takes prisoner Pyrrhus' ear. For lo! his sword,
Which was declining on the milky head
Of reverend Priam, seemed i'th'air to stick,
So as a painted tyrant Pyrrhus stood,
And like a neutral to his will and matter,
Did nothing:
But as we often see, against some storm,   470
A silence in the heavens, the rack stand still,
The bold winds speechless, and the orb below
As hush as death, anon the dreadful thunder
Doth rend the region, so after Pyrrhus' pause,
A rouséd vengeance sets him new awork,
And never did the Cyclops' hammers fall
On Mars's armour, forged for proof eterne,
With less remorse than Pyrrhus' bleeding sword
Now falls on Priam.
Out, out, thou strumpet Fortune! All you gods,   480

In general synod take away her power,
Break all the spokes and fellies from her wheel,
And bowl the round nave down the hill of heaven
As low as to the fiends.'

POLONIUS This is too long.

HAMLET It shall to the barber's with your beard; prithee say on
– he's for a jig, or a tale of bawdry, or he sleeps – say
on, come to Hecuba.

1 PLAYER 'But who, ah woe! had seen the mobled queen – '

HAMLET 'The mobled queen'?   490

POLONIUS That's good, 'mobled queen' is good.

1 PLAYER 'Run barefoot up and down, threat'ning the flames
With bisson rheum, a clout upon that head
Where late the diadem stood, and for a robe,
About her lank and all o'er-teeméd loins,
A blanket in the alarm of fear caught up –
Who this had seen, with tongue in venom steeped,
'Gainst Fortune's state would treason have pronounced;
But if the gods themselves did see her then,
When she saw Pyrrhus make malicious sport   500
In mincing with his sword her husband's limbs,
The instant burst of clamour that she made,
Unless things mortal move them not at all,
Would have made milch the burning eyes of heaven,
And passion in the gods.'

POLONIUS Look whe'r he has not turned his colour, and has tears
in's eyes – prithee no more.

HAMLET 'Tis well, I'll have thee speak out the rest of this soon.
Good my lord, will you see the players well bestowed;
do you hear, let them be well used, for they are the 510
abstracts and brief chronicles of the time; after your
death you were better have a bad epitaph than their ill
report while you live.

POLONIUS My lord, I will use them according to their desert.

HAMLET God's bodkin, man, much better! Use every man after
his desert, and who shall 'scape whipping? Use them
after your own honour and dignity – the less they deserve the more merit is in your bounty. Take them in.

POLONIUS Come, sirs.   [he goes to the door

HAMLET   Follow him, friends, we'll hear a play tomorrow. [*he*   520
          stops the First Player] Dost thou hear me, old friend, can
          you play The Murder of Gonzago?
I PLAYER Ay, my lord.
HAMLET   We'll ha't tomorrow night. You could for a need
          study a speech of some dozen or sixteen lines, which I
          would set down and insert in't, could you not?
I PLAYER Ay, my lord.   [*Polonius and the Players go out*
HAMLET   Very well. Follow that lord, and look you mock him
          not. [*to Rosencrantz and Guildenstern*] My good friends,
          I'll leave you till night. You are welcome to Elsinore.   530
ROSENC'Z Good my lord.   [*they take their leave*
HAMLET   Ay, so, God bye to you! Now I am alone.
          O, what a rogue and peasant slave am I!
          Is it not monstrous that this player here,
          But in a fiction, in a dream of passion,
          Could force his soul so to his own conceit
          That from her working all his visage wanned,
          Tears in his eyes, distraction in his aspect,
          A broken voice, and his whole function suiting
          With forms to his conceit; and all for nothing!   540
          For Hecuba!
          What's Hecuba to him, or he to Hecuba,
          That he should weep for her? What would he do,
          Had he the motive and the cue for passion
          That I have? He would drown the stage with tears,
          And cleave the general ear with horrid speech,
          Make mad the guilty and appal the free,
          Confound the ignorant, and amaze indeed
          The very faculties of eyes and ears; yet I,
          A dull and muddy-mettled rascal, peak   550
          Like John-a-dreams, unpregnant of my cause,
          And can say nothing; no, not for a king,
          Upon whose property and most dear life
          A damned defeat was made: am I a coward?
          Who calls me villain, breaks my pate across,
          Plucks off my beard and blows it in my face
          Tweaks me by the nose, gives me the lie i'th'throat
          As deep as to the lungs – who does me this,

Ha, 'swounds, I should take it: for it cannot be
But I am pigeon-livered, and lack gall   560
To make oppression bitter, or ere this
I should ha' fatted all the region kites
With this slave's offal. Bloody, bawdy villain!
Remorseless, treacherous, lecherous, kindless villain!
O, vengeance!
Why, what an ass am I. This is most brave,
That I, the son of a dear father murdered,
Prompted to my revenge by heaven and hell,
Must like a whore unpack my heart with words,
And fall a-cursing like a very drab;   570
A stallion! Fie upon't! Foh!
About, my brains; hum, I have heard
That guilty creatures sitting at a play
Have by the very cunning of the scene
Been struck so to the soul, that presently
They have proclaimed their malefactions:
For murder, though it have no tongue, will speak
With most miraculous organ: I'll have these players
Play something like the murder of my father
Before mine uncle, I'll observe his looks,   580
I'll tent him to the quick; if 'a do blench
I know my course. The spirit that I have seen
May be a devil, and the devil hath power
T'assume a pleasing shape, yea, and perhaps
Out of my weakness and my melancholy,
As he is very potent with such spirits,
Abuses me to damn me; I'll have grounds
More relative than this — the play's the thing
Wherein I'll catch the conscience of the king. [*he goes*

[*a day passes*]

ACT 3 SCENE I

The lobby of the audience chamber, the walls hung with arras;
a table in the midst; to one side a faldstool with a crucifix

The KING *and the* QUEEN *enter with* POLONIUS,
ROSENCRANTZ, and GUILDENSTERN;
OPHELIA follows a little behind

KING	And can you by no drift of conference
	Get from him why he puts on this confusion,
	Grating so harshly all his days of quiet
	With turbulent and dangerous lunacy?
ROSENC'Z	He does confess he feels himself distracted,
	But from what cause 'a will by no means speak.
GUILD'RN	Nor do we find him forward to be sounded,
	But with a crafty madness keeps aloof
	When we would bring him on to some confession
	Of his true state.
QUEEN	Did he receive you well?
ROSENC'Z	Most like a gentleman.
GUILD'RN	But with much forcing of his disposition.
ROSENC'Z	Niggard of question, but of our demands
	Most free in his reply.
QUEEN	Did you assay him
	To any pastime?
ROSENC'Z	Madam, it so fell out that certain players
	We o'er-raught on the way. Of these we told him,
	And there did seem in him a kind of joy
	To hear of it: they are here about the court,
	And as I think, they have already order
	This night to play before him.
POLONIUS	'Tis most true,
	And he beseeched me to entreat your majesties
	To hear and see the matter.
KING	With all my heart, and it doth much content me
	To hear him so inclined.
	Good gentlemen, give him a further edge,

10

20

And drive his purpose into these delights.

ROSENC'Z   We shall, my lord.

                              [*Rosencrantz and Guildenstern go out*

KING   Sweet Gertrude, leave us too,
For we have closely sent for Hamlet hither,
That he, as 'twere by accident, may here   30
Affront Ophelia;
Her father and myself, lawful espials,
Will so bestow ourselves, that seeing unseen,
We may of their encounter frankly judge,
And gather by him as he is behaved,
If't be th'affliction of his love or no
That thus he suffers for.

QUEEN   I shall obey you –
And for your part, Ophelia, I do wish
That your good beauties be the happy cause
Of Hamlet's wildness, so shall I hope your virtues   40
Will bring him to his wonted way again,
To both your honours.

OPHELIA   Madam, I wish it may.

                              [*the Queen goes*

POLONIUS   Ophelia, walk you here. Gracious, so please you,
We will bestow ourselves. Read on this book,

                  [*he takes a book from the faldstool*

That show of such an exercise may colour
Your loneliness; we are oft to blame in this,
'Tis too much proved, that with devotion's visage
And pious action we do sugar o'er
The devil himself.

KING   O, 'tis too true,
How smart a lash that speech doth give my conscience.   50
The harlot's cheek, beautied with plast'ring art,
Is not more ugly to the thing that helps it,
Than is my deed to my most painted word:
O heavy burden!

POLONIUS   I hear him coming, let's withdraw, my lord.

                  [*they bestow themselves behind the arras;*
                  Ophelia kneels at the faldstool

HAMLET *enters*

HAMLET   To be, or not to be, that is the question,
         Whether 'tis nobler in the mind to suffer
         The slings and arrows of outrageous fortune,
         Or to take arms against a sea of troubles,
         And by opposing, end them. To die, to sleep –   60
         No more, and by a sleep to say we end
         The heart-ache, and the thousand natural shocks
         That flesh is heir to; 'tis a consummation
         Devoutly to be wished to die to sleep!
         To sleep, perchance to dream, ay there's the rub,
         For in that sleep of death what dreams may come
         When we have shuffled off this mortal coil
         Must give us pause – there's the respect
         That makes calamity of so long life:
         For who would bear the whips and scorns of time,   70
         Th'oppressor's wrong, the proud man's contumely,
         The pangs of disprized love, the law's delay,
         The insolence of office, and the spurns
         That patient merit of th'unworthy takes,
         When he himself might his quietus make
         With a bare bodkin; who would fardels bear,
         To grunt and sweat under a weary life,
         But that the dread of something after death,
         The undiscovered country, from whose bourn
         No traveller returns, puzzles the will,   80
         And makes us rather bear those ills we have,
         Than fly to others that we know not of?
         Thus conscience does make cowards of us all,
         And thus the native hue of resolution
         Is sicklied o'er with the pale cast of thought,
         And enterprises of great pitch and moment
         With this regard their currents turn awry,
         And lose the name of action. Soft you now,
         The fair Ophelia – Nymph, in thy orisons
         Be all my sins remembered.
OPHELIA   [*rises*] Good my lord,   90
         How does your honour for this many a day?

HAMLET   I humbly thank you, well, well, well.

OPHELIA   My lord, I have remembrances of yours,
            That I have longéd long to re-deliver.
            I pray you now receive them.

HAMLET   No, not I,
            I never gave you aught.

OPHELIA   My honoured lord, you know right well you did,
            And with them words of so sweet breath composed
            As made the things more rich. Their perfume lost,
            Take these again, for to the noble mind   100
            Rich gifts wax poor when givers prove unkind.
            There, my lord.   [she takes jewels from her bosom and
                                        places them on the table before him

HAMLET   [remembers the plot] Ha, ha! Are you honest?

OPHELIA   My lord?

HAMLET   Are you fair?

OPHELIA   What means your lordship?

HAMLET   That if you be honest and fair, your honesty should
            admit no discourse to your beauty.

OPHELIA   Could beauty, my lord, have better commerce than
            with honesty?   110

HAMLET   Ay truly, for the power of beauty will sooner trans-
            form honesty from what it is to a bawd, than the force
            of honesty can translate beauty into his likeness. This
            was sometime a paradox, but now the time gives it
            proof. I did love you once.

OPHELIA   Indeed, my lord, you made me believe so.

HAMLET   You should not have believed me, for virtue cannot so
            inoculate our old stock, but we shall relish of it – I
            loved you not.

OPHELIA   I was the more deceived.   120

HAMLET   [points to the faldstool] Get thee to a nunnery, why
            wouldst thou be a breeder of sinners? I am myself
            indifferent honest, but yet I could accuse me of such
            things, that it were better my mother had not borne
            me: I am very proud, revengeful, ambitious, with more
            offences at my beck, than I have thoughts to put them
            in, imagination to give them shape, or time to act them
            in: what should such fellows as I do crawling between

earth and heaven? We are arrant knaves all, believe
none of us – go thy ways to a nunnery. [*suddenly*] 130
Where's your father?

OPHELIA At home, my lord.

HAMLET Let the doors be shut upon him, that he may play the
fool nowhere but in's own house. Farewell.

[*he goes out*

OPHELIA [*kneels before the crucifix*] O help him, you sweet heavens!

HAMLET [*returns, distraught*] If thou dost marry, I'll give thee this
plague for thy dowry – be thou as chaste as ice, as pure
as snow, thou shalt not escape calumny; get thee to a
nunnery, go, farewell. [*he paces to and fro*] Or if thou
wilt needs marry, marry a fool, for wise men know 140
well enough what monsters you make of them: to a
nunnery, go, and quickly too, farewell.   [*he rushes out*

OPHELIA O heavenly powers, restore him!

HAMLET [*once more returning*] I have heard of your paintings too,
well enough. God hath given you one face and you
make yourselves another, you jig, you amble, and you
lisp, you nickname God's creatures, and make your
wantonness your ignorance; go to, I'll no more on't,
it hath made me mad. I say we will have no mo
marriage – those that are married already, all but one, 150
shall live, the rest shall keep as they are: to a nunnery,
go.   [*he departs again*

OPHELIA O, what a noble mind is here o'erthrown!
The courtier's, soldier's, scholar's, eye, tongue, sword,
Th'expectancy and rose of the fair state,
The glass of fashion, and the mould of form,
Th'observed of all observers, quite quite down,
And I of ladies most deject and wretched,
That sucked the honey of his music vows,
Now see that noble and most sovereign reason 160
Like sweet bells jangled, out of tune and harsh,
That unmatched form and feature of blown youth,
Blasted with ecstasy! O, woe is me!
T'have seen what I have seen, see what I see!

[*she prays*

The KING *and* POLONIUS *steal forth from behind the arras*

KING Love! his affections do not that way tend,
    Nor what he spake, though it lacked form a little,
    Was not like madness – there's something in his soul
    O'er which his melancholy sits on brood,
    And I do doubt the hatch and the disclose
    Will be some danger; which for to prevent,   170
    I have in quick determination
    Thus set it down: he shall with speed to England,
    For the demand of our neglected tribute.
    Haply the seas, and countries different,
    With variable objects, shall expel
    This something-settled matter in his heart,
    Whereon his brains still beating puts him thus
    From fashion of himself. What think you on't?
            [*Ophelia comes forward*

POLONIUS It shall do well. But yet do I believe
    The origin and commencement of his grief   180
    Sprung from neglected love. How now, Ophelia?
    You need not tell us what Lord Hamlet said,
    We heard it all. My lord, do as you please,
    But if you hold it fit, after the play,
    Let his queen-mother all alone entreat him
    To show his grief, let her be round with him,
    And I'll be placed (so please you) in the ear
    Of all their conference. If she find him not,
    To England send him; or confine him where
    Your wisdom best shall think.

KING   It shall be so, 190
    Madness in great ones must not unwatched go.
                [*they depart*

SCENE 2

*The hall of the castle, with seats set to both sides as for a spectacle;
at the back a dais with curtains concealing an inner stage*

'HAMLET, *and three of the Players' come from behind the curtains*

HAMLET   [*to the First Player*] Speak the speech I pray you as I
pronounced it to you, trippingly on the tongue, but if
you mouth it as many of your players do, I had as lief
the town-crier spoke my lines. Nor do not saw the air
too much with your hand thus, but use all gently, for in
the very torrent, tempest, and as I may say whirlwind of
your passion, you must acquire and beget a temperance
that may give it smoothness. O, it offends me to the
soul, to hear a robustious periwig-pated fellow tear a
passion to tatters, to very rags, to split the ears of the   10
groundlings, who for the most part are capable of
nothing but inexplicable dumb-shows and noise: I
would have such a fellow whipped for o'erdoing
Termagant, it out-herods Herod, pray you avoid it.

1 PLAYER   I warrant your honour.

HAMLET   Be not too tame neither, but let your own discretion
be your tutor, suit the action to the word, the word
to the action, with this special observance, that you
o'erstep not the modesty of nature: for anything so
o'erdone is from the purpose of playing, whose end   20
both at the first, and now, was and is, to hold as
'twere the mirror up to nature, to show virtue her
own feature, scorn her own image, and the very age
and body of the time his form and pressure. Now this
overdone, or come tardy off, though it make the
unskilful laugh, cannot but make the judicious grieve,
the censure of the which one must in your allowance
o'erweigh a whole theatre of others. O there be players that I have seen play – and heard others praise, and
that highly – not to speak it profanely, that neither   30
having th'accent of Christians, nor the gait of Christian, pagan, nor man, have so strutted and bellowed,

that I have thought some of nature's journeymen had
made men, and not made them well, they imitated
humanity so abominably.

I PLAYER   I hope we have reformed that indifferently with us, sir.

HAMLET   O reform it altogether, and let those that play your
clowns speak no more than is set down for them, for
there be of them that will themselves laugh, to set on
some quantity of barren spectators to laugh too,   40
though in the mean time some necessary question of
the play be then to be considered. That's villainous,
and shows a most pitiful ambition in the fool that uses
it. Go, make you ready.

                                    [*the Players retire behind the curtains*

POLONIUS *enters with* ROSENCRANTZ *and* GUILDENSTERN

How now, my lord? Will the king hear this piece of
work?

POLONIUS   And the queen too, and that presently.

HAMLET   Bid the players make haste.

                                        [*Polonius bows and departs*

Will you two help to hasten them?

ROSENC'Z   Ay, my lord.   50

                        [*Rosencrantz and Guildenstern follow Polonius*

HAMLET   What, ho! Horatio!

HORATIO *comes in*

HORATIO   Here, sweet lord, at your service.

HAMLET   Horatio, thou art e'en as just a man
As e'er my conversation coped withal.

HORATIO   O, my dear lord, –

HAMLET   Nay, do not think I flatter,
For what advancement may I hope from thee,
That no revenue hast but thy good spirits
To feed and clothe thee? Why should the poor be
                                                    flattered?
No, let the candied tongue lick absurd pomp,
And crook the pregnant hinges of the knee   60
Where thrift may follow fawning. Dost thou hear?
Since my dear soul was mistress of her choice,
And could of men distinguish her election,

Sh' hath sealed thee for herself, for thou hast been
As one in suff'ring all that suffers nothing,
A man that Fortune's buffets and rewards
Hast ta'en with equal thanks; and blest are those
Whose blood and judgment are so well co-meddled,
That they are not a pipe for Fortune's finger
To sound what stop she please: give me that man 70
That is not passion's slave, and I will wear him
In my heart's core, ay in my heart of heart,
As I do thee. Something too much of this –
There is a play tonight before the king,
One scene of it comes near the circumstance
Which I have told thee of my father's death.
I prithee when thou seest that act afoot,
Even with the very comment of thy soul
Observe my uncle – if his occulted guilt
Do not itself unkennel in one speech, 80
It is a damnéd ghost that we have seen,
And my imaginations are as foul
As Vulcan's stithy; give him heedful note,
For I mine eyes will rivet to his face,
And after we will both our judgments join
In censure of his seeming.

HORATIO   Well, my lord,
If 'a steal aught the whilst this play is playing,
And 'scape detecting, I will pay the theft.

         [trumpets and kettle-drums heard

HAMLET They are coming to the play. I must be idle. Get you a
    place.   90

The KING *and* QUEEN *enter, followed by* POLONIUS, OPHELIA,
ROSENCRANTZ, GUILDENSTERN, *and other courtiers; they sit,*
the King, the Queen and Polonius on this side, Ophelia and
Horatio and others on that

KING How fares our cousin Hamlet?
HAMLET Excellent i'faith, of the chameleon's dish, I eat the air,
    promise-crammed – you cannot feed capons so.
KING I have nothing with this answer, Hamlet. These words
    are not mine.

HAMLET	No, nor mine now. [*to Polonius*] My lord, you played once i'th'university, you say?
POLONIUS	That did I, my lord, and was accounted a good actor.
HAMLET	What did you enact?
POLONIUS	I did enact Julius Caesar. I was killed i'th'Capitol, 100 Brutus killed me.
HAMLET	It was a brute part of him to kill so capital a calf there. Be the players ready?
ROSENC'Z	Ay, my lord, they stay upon your patience.
QUEEN	Come hither, my dear Hamlet, sit by me.
HAMLET	No, good mother, here's metal more attractive.

[*he turns towards Ophelia*

POLONIUS [*to the King*] O ho! Do you mark that?

[*they whisper together, watching Hamlet*

HAMLET	Lady, shall I lie in your lap?
OPHELIA	No, my lord.
HAMLET	I mean, my head upon your lap? 110
OPHELIA	Ay, my lord. [*he lies at her feet*
HAMLET	Do you think I meant country matters?
OPHELIA	I think nothing, my lord.
HAMLET	That's a fair thought to lie between maids' legs.
OPHELIA	What is, my lord?
HAMLET	Nothing.
OPHELIA	You are merry, my lord.
HAMLET	Who, I?
OPHELIA	Ay, my lord.
HAMLET	O God, your only jig-maker. What should a man do 120 but be merry, for look you how cheerfully my mother looks, and my father died within's two hours.

[*the Queen turns away and whispers
with the King and Polonius*

OPHELIA	Nay, 'tis twice two months, my lord.
HAMLET	So long? Nay, then let the devil wear black, for I'll have a suit of sables; O heavens, die two months ago, and not forgotten yet? Then there's hope a great man's memory may outlive his life half a year, but by'r lady 'a must build churches then, or else shall 'a suffer not thinking on, with the hobby-horse, whose epitaph is 'For O! for O! the hobby-horse is forgot.' 130

'The trumpets sound', the curtains are drawn aside, discovering
the inner stage, and a Dumb-Show is performed thereon

The Dumb-Show

'Enter a King and a Queen, very lovingly, the Queen embracing him
and he her, she kneels and makes show of protestation unto him, he takes
her up and declines his head open her neck, he lies him down upon a
bank of flowers, she seeing him asleep leaves him: anon comes in another
man, takes off his crown, kisses it, and pours poison in the sleeper's ears
and leaves him: the Queen returns, finds the King dead, and makes
passionate action: the poisoner with some three or four mutes comes in
again, seeming to condole with her: the dead body is carried away: the
poisoner woos the Queen with gifts, she seems harsh awhile, but in the
end accepts his love'   [*the curtains are closed*

Hamlet seems troubled and casts glances at the King and Queen as the
show goes forward; they continue in talk with Polonius throughout

OPHELIA   What means this, my lord?
HAMLET   Marry, this is miching mallecho, it means mischief.
OPHELIA   Belike this show imports the argument of the play.

Enter a player before the curtains, the King and Queen turn to listen

HAMLET   We shall know by this fellow. The players cannot keep
            counsel, they'll tell all.
OPHELIA   Will 'a tell us what this show meant?
HAMLET   [*savagely*] Ay, or any show that you will show him – be
            not you ashamed to show, he'll not shame to tell you
            what it means.
OPHELIA   You are naught, you are naught, I'll mark the play.   140
PLAYER   For us and for our tragedy,
            Here stooping to your clemency,
            We beg your hearing patiently.   [*exit*
HAMLET   Is this a prologue, or the posy of a ring?
OPHELIA   'Tis brief, my lord.
HAMLET   As woman's love.

Enter on the dais two Players, a King and a Queen

PL. KING   Full thirty times hath Phoebus' cart gone round
            Neptune's salt wash, and Tellus' orbèd ground,
            And thirty dozen moons with borrowed sheen
            About the world have times twelve thirties been,   150

Since love our hearts and Hymen did our hands
Unite commutual in most sacred bands.

PL. QUEEN So many journeys may the sun and moon
Make us again count o'er ere love be done!
But woe is me, you are so sick of late,
So far from cheer, and from your former state,
That I distrust you. Yet though I distrust,
Discomfort you, my lord, it nothing must,
For women fear too much, even as they love,
And women's fear and love hold quantity,   160
In neither aught, or in extremity.
Now what my love is proof hath made you know,
And as my love is sized, my fear is so.
Where love is great, the littlest doubts are fear,
Where little fears grow great, great love grows there.

PL. KING Faith, I must leave thee, love, and shortly too.
My operant powers their functions leave to do,
And thou shalt live in this fair world behind,
Honoured, beloved, and haply one as kind
For husband shalt thou —

PL. QUEEN   O, confound the rest!   170
Such love must needs be treason in my breast,
In second husband let me be accurst,
None wed the second, but who killed the first.

HAMLET   That's wormwood, wormwood.

PL. QUEEN The instances that second marriage move
Are base respects of thrift, but none of love.
A second time I kill my husband dead,
When second husband kisses me in bed.

PL. KING I do believe you think what now you speak,
But what we do determine, oft we break.   180
Purpose is but the slave to memory,
Of violent birth but poor validity,
Which now like fruit unripe sticks on the tree,
But fall unshaken when they mellow be.
Most necessary 'tis that we forget
To pay ourselves what to ourselves is debt.
What to ourselves in passion we propose,
The passion ending, doth the purpose lose.

    The violence of either grief or joy
    Their own enactures with themselves destroy,   190
    Where joy most revels, grief doth most lament,
    Grief joys, joy grieves, on slender accident.
    This world is not for aye, nor 'tis not strange
    That even our loves should with our fortunes change:
    For 'tis a question left us, yet to prove,
    Whether love lead fortune, or else fortune love.
    The great man down, you mark his favourite flies,
    The poor advanced makes friends of enemies,
    And hitherto doth love on fortune tend,
    For who not needs shall never lack a friend,   200
    And who in want a hollow friend doth try,
    Directly seasons him his enemy.
    But orderly to end where I begun,
    Our wills and fates do so contrary run,
    That our devices still are overthrown,
    Our thoughts are ours, their ends none of our own —
    So think thou wilt no second husband wed,
    But die thy thoughts when thy first lord is dead.

PL. QUEEN Nor earth to me give food nor heaven light,
    Sport and repose lock from me day and night,   210
    To desperation turn my trust and hope,
    An anchor's cheere in prison be my scope,
    Each opposite that blanks the face of joy
    Meet what I would have well and it destroy,
    Both here and hence pursue me lasting strife,
    If once a widow, ever I be wife!

HAMLET   If she should break it now!

PL. KING   'Tis deeply sworn. Sweet, leave me here awhile,
    My spirits grow dull, and fain I would beguile
    The tedious day with sleep.   *[he 'sleeps'*

PL. QUEEN   Sleep rock thy brain,   220
    And never come mischance between us twain!   *[exit*

HAMLET   Madam, how like you this play?

QUEEN   The lady doth protest too much, methinks.

HAMLET   O, but she'll keep her word.

KING   Have you heard the argument? Is there no offence
    in't?

HAMLET   No, no, they do but jest, poison in jest, no offence
            i'th'world.

KING   What do you call the play?

HAMLET   The Mouse-trap. Marry, how? – tropically. This play is   230
            the image of a murder done in Vienna. Gonzago is the
            duke's name, his wife Baptista, you shall see anon, 'tis a
            knavish piece of work, but what of that? Your majesty,
            and we that have free souls, it touches us not – let the
            galled jade wince, our withers are unwrung.

            Enter First Player for LUCIANUS, *clad in a black doublet and
            with a vial in his hand; he struts towards the sleeping King
                    making mouths and threatening gestures*

            This is one Lucianus, nephew to the king.

OPHELIA   You are as good as a chorus, my lord.

HAMLET   I could interpret between you and your love, if I could
            see the puppets dallying.

OPHELIA   You are keen, my lord, you are keen.   240

HAMLET   It would cost you a groaning to take off mine edge.

OPHELIA   Still better and worse.

HAMLET   So you mis-take your husbands. [*he looks up*] Begin,
            murderer. Pox! Leave thy damnable faces and begin!
            Come – 'the croaking raven doth bellow for revenge.'

LUCIANUS   Thoughts black, hands apt, drugs fit, and time agreeing,
            Confederate season, else no creature seeing,
            Thou mixture rank, of midnight weeds collected,
            With Hecate's ban thrice blasted, thrice infected,
            Thy natural magic and dire property   250
            On wholesome life usurps immediately.
                                      [*'pours the poison in his ears'*

HAMLET   'A poisons him i'th'garden for's estate, his name's
            Gonzago, the story is extant, and written in very choice
            Italian, you shall see anon how the murderer gets the
            love of Gonzago's wife.
                            [*the King, very pale, totters to his feet*

OPHELIA   The king rises.

HAMLET   What, frighted with false fire!

QUEEN   How fares my lord?

POLONIUS   Give o'er the play.

KING　　　Give me some light – away!　　　*[he rushes from the hall* 260
POLONIUS Lights, lights, lights!

　　　　　　　　　　　　　　[all but Hamlet and Horatio depart

HAMLET　　Why, let the stricken deer go weep,
　　　　　　　　The hart ungallèd play,
　　　　　　　For some must watch while some must sleep,
　　　　　　　　Thus runs the world away.
　　　　　　Would not this, sir, and a forest of feathers, if the rest of
　　　　　　my fortunes turn Turk with me, with two Provincial
　　　　　　roses on my razed shoes, get me a fellowship in a cry of
　　　　　　players, sir?
HORATIO　Half a share. 270
HAMLET　　A whole one, I.
　　　　　　　For thou dost know, O Damon dear,
　　　　　　　　This realm dismantled was
　　　　　　　Of Jove himself, and now reigns here
　　　　　　　　A very, very – peacock.
HORATIO　You might have rhymed.
HAMLET　　O good Horatio, I'll take the ghost's word for a thousand
　　　　　　pound. Didst perceive?
HORATIO　Very well, my lord.
HAMLET　　Upon the talk of the poisoning? 280
HORATIO　I did very well note him.

　　　　　ROSENCRANTZ *and* GUILDENSTERN *return*

HAMLET　　Ah, ha! *[turns his back upon them]* Come, some music!
　　　　　　Come, the recorders!
　　　　　　　For if the king like not the comedy,
　　　　　　　Why then, belike, – he likes it not, perdy.
　　　　　　Come, some music!
GUILD'RN　Good my lord, vouchsafe me a word with you.
HAMLET　　Sir, a whole history.
GUILD'RN　The king, sir, –
HAMLET　　Ay, sir, what of him? 290
GUILD'RN　Is in his retirement marvellous distempered.
HAMLET　　With drink, sir?
GUILD'RN　No my lord, rather with choler.
HAMLET　　Your wisdom should show itself more richer to signify
　　　　　　this to the doctor. For, for me to put him to his

purgation, would perhaps plunge him into more choler.

GUILD'RN   Good my lord, put your discourse into some frame,
and start not so wildly from my affair.

HAMLET   I am tame, sir – pronounce.

GUILD'RN   The queen your mother, in most great affliction of   300
spirit, hath sent me to you.

HAMLET   You are welcome.

GUILD'RN   Nay, good my lord, this courtesy is not of the right
breed. If it shall please you to make me a wholesome
answer, I will do your mother's commandment. If not,
your pardon and my return shall be the end of my
business.   [he bows and turns away

HAMLET   Sir, I cannot.

ROSENC'Z   What, my lord?

HAMLET   Make you a wholesome answer – my wit's diseased.   310
But, sir, such answer as I can make, you shall command,
or rather as you say, my mother. Therefore no more,
but to the matter – my mother, you say –

ROSENC'Z   Then thus she says, your behaviour hath struck her
into amazement and admiration.

HAMLET   O wonderful son that can so stonish a mother! But is
there no sequel at the heels of this mother's admiration?
Impart.

ROSENC'Z   She desires to speak with you in her closet ere you go
to bed.   320

HAMLET   We shall obey, were she ten times our mother. Have
you any further trade with us?

ROSENC'Z   My lord, you once did love me.

HAMLET   And do still, by these pickers and stealers.

ROSENC'Z   Good my lord, what is your cause of distemper? You
do surely bar the door upon your own liberty, if you
deny your griefs to your friend.

HAMLET   Sir, I lack advancement.

ROSENC'Z   How can that be, when you have the voice of the king
himself for your succession in Denmark?   330

HAMLET   Ay, sir, but 'While the grass grows' – the proverb is
something musty.

Players bring in recorders

O, the recorders, let me see one. [*he takes a recorder and leads Guildenstern aside*] To withdraw with you, why do you go about to recover the wind of me, as if you would drive me into a toil?

GUILD'RN   O, my lord, if my duty be too bold, my love is too unmannerly.

HAMLET   I do not well understand that – will you play upon this pipe?   340

GUILD'RN   My lord, I cannot.

HAMLET   I pray you.

GUILD'RN   Believe me, I cannot.

HAMLET   I do beseech you.

GUILD'RN   I know no touch of it, my lord.

HAMLET   It is as easy as lying; govern these ventages with your fingers and thumb, give it breath with your mouth, and it will discourse most eloquent music – look you, these are the stops.

GUILD'RN   But these cannot I command to any utt'rance of har-   350
mony, I have not the skill.

HAMLET   Why, look you now, how unworthy a thing you make of me! You would play upon me, you would seem to know my stops, you would pluck out the heart of my mystery, you would sound me from my lowest note to the top of my compass – and there is much music, excellent voice, in this little organ, yet cannot you make it speak. 'Sblood, do you think I am easier to be played on than a pipe? Call me what instrument you will, though you can fret me, you cannot play upon me.   360

POLONIUS *enters*

God bless you, sir!

POLONIUS   My lord, the queen would speak with you, and presently.

HAMLET   Do you see yonder cloud that's almost in shape of a camel?

POLONIUS   By th'mass and 'tis, like a camel indeed.

HAMLET   Methinks it is like a weasel.

POLONIUS   It is backed like a weasel.

HAMLET   Or, like a whale?

POLONIUS   Very like a whale.

HAMLET	Then I will come to my mother by and by. [*aside*] 37
	They fool me to the top of my bent – I will come by
	and by.
POLONIUS	I will say so.

                [*Polonius, Rosencrantz and Guildenstern depart*

HAMLET 'By and by' is easily said.

        Leave me, friends.   [*the rest go*

        'Tis now the very witching time of night,

        When churchyards yawn, and hell itself breathes out

        Contagion to this world: now could I drink hot blood,

        And do such bitter business as the day

        Would quake to look on: soft, now to my mother –   38

        O heart, lose not thy nature, let not ever

        The soul of Nero enter this firm bosom,

        Let me be cruel not unnatural.

        I will speak daggers to her, but use none.

        My tongue and soul in this be hypocrites,

        How in my words somever she be shent,

        To give them seals never, my soul, consent!   [*he goes*

SCENE 3

The lobby, with the faldstool as before; the audience chamber without

The KING, ROSENCRANTZ *and* GUILDENSTERN

KING   I like him not, nor stands it safe with us

        To let his madness range. Therefore prepare you,

        I your commission will forthwith dispatch,

        And he to England shall along with you.

        The terms of our estate may not endure

        Hazard so near's as doth hourly grow

        Out of his brows.

GUILD'RN   We will ourselves provide.

        Most holy and religious fear it is

        To keep those many many bodies safe

        That live and feed upon your majesty.   10

ROSENC'Z The single and peculiar life is bound

        With all the strength and armour of the mind

        To keep itself from noyance, but much more

That spirit upon whose weal depends and rests
The lives of many. The cess of majesty
Dies not alone; but like a gulf doth draw
What's near it with it. O, 'tis a massy wheel
Fixed on the summit of the highest mount,
To whose huge spokes ten thousand lesser things
Are mortised and adjoined, which when it falls,   20
Each small annexment, petty consequence,
Attends the boist'rous ruin. Never alone
Did the king sigh, but with a general groan.

GUILD'RN Arm you, I pray you, to this speedy voyage,
For we will fetters put about this fear,
Which now goes too free-footed.

ROSENC'Z   We will haste us.   [they go

POLONIUS enters

POLONIUS My lord, he's going to his mother's closet —
Behind the arras I'll convey myself
To hear the process — I'll warrant she'll tax him home,
And as you said, and wisely was it said,   30
'Tis meet that some more audience than a mother,
Since nature makes them partial, should o'erhear
The speech of vantage; fare you well, my liege,
I'll call upon you ere you go to bed,
And tell you what I know.

KING   Thanks, dear my lord.
                [Polonius goes; the King paces to and fro
O, my offence is rank, it smells to heaven,
It hath the primal eldest curse upon't,
A brother's murder! Pray can I not,
Though inclination be as sharp as will.
My stronger guilt defeats my strong intent,   40
And like a man to double business bound,
I stand in pause where I shall first begin,
And both neglect. What if this cursèd hand
Were thicker than itself with brother's blood,
Is there not rain enough in the sweet heavens
To wash it white as snow? Whereto serves mercy
But to confront the visage of offence?
And what's in prayer but this twofold force,

To be forestalléd ere we come to fall,
Or pardoned being down? Then I'll look up.   50
My fault is past, but O, what form of prayer
Can serve my turn? 'Forgive me my foul murder'?
That cannot be since I am still possessed
Of those effects for which I did the murder;
My crown, mine own ambition, and my queen;
May one be pardoned and retain th'offence?
In the corrupted currents of this world
Offence's gilded hand may shove by justice,
And oft 'tis seen the wicked prize itself
Buys out the law. But 'tis not so above,   60
There is no shuffling, there the action lies
In his true nature, and we ourselves compelled
Even to the teeth and forehead of our faults
To give in evidence. What then? What rests?
Try what repentance can – what can it not?
Yet what can it, when one can not repent?
O wretched state! O bosom black as death!
O liméd soul, that struggling to be free,
Art more engaged; help, angels! Make assay,
Bow stubborn knees, and heart, with strings of steel,   70
Be soft as sinews of the new-born babe –
All may be well.   [*he kneels*

HAMLET *enters the audience chamber and pauses, seeing the King*

HAMLET   [*approaches the entry to the lobby*]
Now might I do it pat, now 'a is a-praying –
And now I'll do't, [*he draws his sword*] and so a' goes
                                                    to heaven,
And so am I revenged. That would be scanned:
A villain kills my father, and for that
I his sole son do this same villain send
To heaven.
Why, this is bait and salary, not revenge.
'A took my father grossly, full of bread,   80
With all his crimes broad blown, as flush as May,
And how his audit stands who knows save heaven?
But in our circumstance and course of thought,
'Tis heavy with him: and am I then revenged

To take him in the purging of his soul,
When he is fit and seasoned for his passage?
No.　　　　　　　　　　　　　*[he sheathes his sword*
Up, sword, and know thou a more horrid hent,
When he is drunk asleep, or in his rage,
Or in th'incestuous pleasure of his bed,　　　　　　　90
At game, a-swearing, or about some act
That has no relish of salvation in't,
Then trip him that his heels may kick at heaven,
And that his soul may be as damned and black
As hell whereto it goes; my mother stays,
This physic but prolongs thy sickly days.　　*[he passes on*

KING　　*[rises]* My words fly up, my thoughts remain below.
Words without thoughts never to heaven go.　　*[he goes*

SCENE 4

The QUEEN *and* POLONIUS

> *The Queen's closet hung with arras, and with portraits of*
> *King Hamlet and Claudius upon one wall; seats and a couch*

POLONIUS　'A will come straight. Look you lay home to him,
Tell him his pranks have been too broad to bear with,
And that your grace hath screened and stood between
Much heat and him. I'll silence me even here –
Pray you be round with him.

HAMLET　*[without]* Mother, mother, mother!

QUEEN　　　　　　　　　　　　　I'll war'nt you,
Fear me not. Withdraw, I hear him coming.
　　　　　　　　　[Polonius hides behind the arras

HAMLET *enters*

HAMLET　Now, mother, what's the matter?

QUEEN　Hamlet, thou hast thy father much offended.

HAMLET　Mother, you have my father much offended.　　10

QUEEN　Come, come, you answer with an idle tongue.

HAMLET　Go, go, you question with a wicked tongue.

QUEEN　Why, how now, Hamlet?

HAMLET　　　　　　　　　What's the matter now?

QUEEN	Have you forgot me?
HAMLET	No, by the rood not so,

You are the queen, your husband's brother's wife,
And would it were not so, you are my mother.

QUEEN   Nay then, I'll set those to you that can speak.   *[going*

HAMLET   *[seizes her arm]*

Come, come, and sit you down, you shall not budge,
You go not till I set you up a glass
Where you may see the inmost part of you.   20

QUEEN   What wilt thou do? thou wilt not murder me?
Help, help, ho!

POLONIUS   *[behind the arras]* What, ho! help, help, help!

HAMLET   *[draws]* How now! A rat? Dead, for a ducat, dead.
        [he makes a pass through the arras

POLONIUS   *[falls]* O, I am slain!

QUEEN   O me, what hast thou done?

HAMLET   Nay, I know not,
Is it the king?
    [he lifts up the arras and discovers Polonius, dead

QUEEN   O what a rash and bloody deed is this!

HAMLET   A bloody deed – almost as bad, good mother,
As kill a king, and marry with his brother.

QUEEN   As kill a king!

HAMLET   Ay, lady, it was my word.   30
[to Polonius] Thou wretched, rash, intruding fool,
               farewell!
I took thee for thy better, take thy fortune,
Thou find'st to be too busy is some danger.
    [he turns back, dropping the arras
Leave wringing of your hands, peace, sit you down,
And let me wring your heart, for so I shall
If it be made of penetrable stuff,
If damnéd custom have not brassed it so,
That it be proof and bulwark against sense.

QUEEN   What have I done, that thou dar'st wag thy tongue
In noise so rude against me?

HAMLET   Such an act   40
That blurs the grace and blush of modesty,
Calls virtue hypocrite, takes off the rose

From the fair forehead of an innocent love
And sets a blister there, makes marriage vows
As false as dicers' oaths, O such a deed
As from the body of contraction plucks
The very soul, and sweet religion makes
A rhapsody of words; heaven's face does glow,
And this solidity and compound mass
With heated visage, as against the doom,   50
Is thought-sick at the act.

QUEEN   Ay me, what act,
That roars so loud, and thunders in the index?

HAMLET   [*leads her to the portraits on the wall*]
Look here, upon this picture, and on this,
The counterfeit presentment of two brothers.
See what a grace was seated on this brow —
Hyperion's curls, the front of Jove himself,
An eye like Mars to threaten and command,
A station like the herald Mercury,
New-lighted on a heaven-kissing hill,
A combination and a form indeed,   60
Where every god did seem to set his seal
To give the world assurance of a man.
This was your husband — Look you now what follows.
Here is your husband, like a mildewed ear,
Blasting his wholesome brother. Have you eyes?
Could you on this fair mountain leave to feed,
And batten on this moor? Ha! Have you eyes?
You cannot call it love, for at your age
The heyday in the blood is tame, it's humble,
And waits upon the judgment, and what judgment   70
Would step from this to this? Sense sure you have
Else could you not have motion, but sure that sense
Is apoplexed, for madness would not err,
Nor sense to ecstasy was ne'er so thralled,
But it reserved some quantity of choice
To serve in such a difference. What devil was't
That thus hath cozened you at hoodman-blind?
Eyes without feeling, feeling without sight,
Ears without hands or eyes, smelling sans all,

| | Or but a sickly part of one true sense | 80 |

Or but a sickly part of one true sense

Could not so mope: O shame, where is thy blush?

Rebellious hell,

If thou canst mutine in a matron's bones,

To flaming youth let virtue be as wax

And melt in her own fire. Proclaim no shame

When the compulsive ardour gives the charge,

Since frost itself as actively doth burn,

And reason pandars will.

QUEEN   O Hamlet, speak no more.

Thou turn'st my eyes into my very soul,

And there I see such black and grainéd spots   90

As will not leave their tinct.

HAMLET   Nay, but to live

In the rank sweat of an enseaméd bed

Stewed in corruption, honeying and making love

Over the nasty sty –

QUEEN   O speak to me no more,

These words like daggers enter in mine ears,

No more, sweet Hamlet.

HAMLET   A murderer and a villain,

A slave that is not twentieth part the tithe

Of your precedent lord, a vice of kings,

A cutpurse of the empire and the rule,

That from a shelf the precious diadem stole   100

And put it in his pocket –

QUEEN   No more.

HAMLET   A king of shreds and patches –

'Enter the GHOST in his night-gown'

Save me and hover o'er me with your wings,

You heavenly guards! – What would your gracious

figure?

QUEEN   Alas, he's mad.

HAMLET   Do you not come your tardy son to chide,

That lapsed in time and passion lets go by

Th'important acting of your dread command?

O, say!

GHOST   Do not forget! this visitation   110

Is but to whet thy almost blunted purpose –

But look, amazement on thy mother sits,
O step between her and her fighting soul;
Conceit in weakest bodies strongest works,
Speak to her, Hamlet.

HAMLET   How is it with you, lady?

QUEEN   Alas, how is't with you,
That you do bend your eye on vacancy,
And with th'incorporal air do hold discourse?
Forth at your eyes your spirits wildly peep,
And as the sleeping soldiers in th'alarm,   120
Your bedded hairs like life in excrements
Start up and stand an end. O gentle son,
Upon the heat and flame of thy distemper
Sprinkle cool patience. Whereon do you look?

HAMLET   On him! on him! Look you, how pale he glares!
His form and cause conjoined, preaching to stones,
Would make them capable. Do not look upon me,
Lest with this piteous action you convert
My stern effects, then what I have to do
Will want true colour, tears perchance for blood.   130

QUEEN   To whom do you speak this?

HAMLET   Do you see nothing there?

QUEEN   Nothing at all, yet all that is I see.

HAMLET   Nor did you nothing hear?

QUEEN   No, nothing but ourselves.

HAMLET   Why, look you there! Look how it steals away!
My father in his habit as he lived,
Look where he goes, even now, out at the portal.
                                    [the Ghost vanishes

QUEEN   This is the very coinage of your brain!
This bodiless creation ecstasy
Is very cunning in.

HAMLET   Ecstasy!
My pulse as yours doth temperately keep time,   140
And makes as healthful music – it is not madness
That I have uttered; bring me to the test
And I the matter will re-word, which madness
Would gambol from. Mother, for love of grace,
Lay not that flattering unction to your soul,

That not your trespass but my madness speaks,
It will but skin and film the ulcerous place,
Whiles rank corruption mining all within
Infects unseen. Confess yourself to heaven,
Repent what's past, avoid what is to come,   150
And do not spread the compost on the weeds
To make them ranker. Forgive me this my virtue,
For in the fatness of these pursy times
Virtue itself of vice must pardon beg,
Yea curb and woo for leave to do him good.

QUEEN   O Hamlet, thou hast cleft my heart in twain.

HAMLET   O throw away the worser part of it,
And live the purer with the other half.
Good night, but go not to my uncle's bed,
Assume a virtue if you have it not.   160
That monster custom, who all sense doth eat
Of habits evil, is angel yet in this,
That to the use of actions fair and good
He likewise gives a frock or livery
That aptly is put on. Refrain tonight,
And that shall lend a kind of easiness
To the next abstinence, the next more easy:
For use almost can change the stamp of nature,
And either . . . the devil, or throw him out,
With wondrous potency: once more, good night,   170
And when you are desirous to be blessed,
I'll blessing beg of you. For this same lord,
                           [pointing to Polonius
I do repent; but heaven hath pleased it so,
To punish me with this, and this with me,
That I must be their scourge and minister.
I will bestow him and will answer well
The death I gave him; so, again, good night.
I must be cruel only to be kind.
This bad begins, and worse remains behind.
                           [he makes to go, but returns
One word more, good lady.

QUEEN   What shall I do?   180

HAMLET   Not this by no means that I bid you do –

Let the bloat king tempt you again to bed,
Pinch wanton on your cheek, call you his mouse,
And let him for a pair of reechy kisses,
Or paddling in your neck with his damned fingers,
Make you to ravel all this matter out
That I essentially am not in madness,
But mad in craft. 'Twere good you let him know,
For who that's but a queen, fair, sober, wise,
Would from a paddock, from a bat, a gib, 190
Such dear concernings hide? Who would do so?
No, in despite of sense and secrecy,
Unpeg the basket on the house's top,
Let the birds fly, and like the famous ape,
To try conclusions in the basket creep,
And break your own neck down.

QUEEN   Be thou assured, if words be made of breath,
And breath of life, I have no life to breathe
What thou hast said to me.

HAMLET   I must to England, you know that?

QUEEN   Alack, 200
I had forgot, 'tis so concluded on.

HAMLET   There's letters sealed, and my two school-fellows,
Whom I will trust as I will adders fanged,
They bear the mandate — they must sweep my way
And marshal me to knavery: let it work,
For 'tis the sport to have the engineer
Hoist with his own petar, and't shall go hard
But I will delve one yard below their mines,
And blow them at the moon: O, 'tis most sweet
When in one line two crafts directly meet. 210
This man shall set me packing,
I'll lug the guts into the neighbour room;
Mother, good night in deed. This counsellor
Is now most still, most secret, and most grave,
Who was in life a foolish prating knave.
Come, sir, to draw toward an end with you.
Good night, mother.

                    [he drags the body from the room; the Queen
                    casts herself sobbing upon the couch

ACT 4 SCENE I

After a short while the KING *enters with* ROSENCRANTZ *and*
GUILDENSTERN

KING   [*raises her*] There's matter in these sighs, these
                                              profound heaves,
          You must translate, 'tis fit we understand them.
          Where is your son?
QUEEN   Bestow this place on us a little while.
                              [*Rosencrantz and Guildenstern depart*
          Ah, mine own lord, what have I seen tonight!
KING   What, Gertrude? How does Hamlet?
QUEEN   Mad as the sea and wind when both contend
          Which is the mightier — in his lawless fit,
          Behind the arras hearing something stir,
          Whips out his rapier, cries 'A rat, a rat!'
          And in this brainish apprehension kills   10
          The unseen good old man.
KING   O heavy deed!
          It had been so with us had we been there.
          His liberty is full of threats to all,
          To you yourself, to us, to everyone.
          Alas, how shall this bloody deed be answered?
          It will be laid to us, whose providence
          Should have kept short, restrained, and out of haunt
          This mad young man; but so much was our love,
          We would not understand what was most fit,
          But like the owner of a foul disease,   20
          To keep it from divulging, let it feed
          Even on the pith of life: where is he gone?
QUEEN   To draw apart the body he hath killed,
          O'er whom his very madness, like some ore
          Among a mineral of metals base,
          Shows itself pure — 'a weeps for what is done.
KING   O, Gertrude, come away!
          The sun no sooner shall the mountains touch,
          But we will ship him hence, and this vile deed

We must with all our majesty and skill   30
Both countenance and excuse. Ho! Guildenstern!

ROSENCRANTZ *and* GUILDENSTERN *return*

Friends both, go join you with some further aid –
Hamlet in madness hath Polonius slain,
And from his mother's closet hath he dragged him –
Go, seek him out, speak fair, and bring the body
Into the chapel; I pray you, haste in this.   [*they go*
Come, Gertrude, we'll call up our wisest friends,
And let them know both what we mean to do
And what's untimely done: [so haply slander,]
Whose whisper o'er the world's diameter,   40
As level as the cannon to his blank
Transports his poisoned shot, may miss our name,
And hit the woundless air. O, come away!
My soul is full of discord and dismay.   [*they go*

SCENE 2

Another room of the castle

HAMLET *enters*

HAMLET   Safely stowed.
CALLING WITHOUT   Hamlet! Lord Hamlet!
HAMLET   But soft, what noise, who calls on Hamlet?
                O, here they come!

ROSENCRANTZ *and* GUILDENSTERN *enter in haste, with a guard*

ROSENC'Z   What have you done, my lord, with the dead body?
HAMLET   Compounded it with dust whereto 'tis kin.
ROSENC'Z   Tell us where 'tis that we may take it thence,
           And bear it to the chapel.
HAMLET   Do not believe it.
ROSENC'Z   Believe what?
HAMLET   That I can keep your counsel and not mine own. 10
           Besides, to be demanded of a sponge, what replication
           should be made by the son of a king?
ROSENC'Z   Take you me for a sponge, my lord?

HAMLET   Ay, sir, that soaks up the king's countenance, his re-
            wards, his authorities. But such officers do the king
            best service in the end, he keeps them like an apple, in
            the corner of his jaw, first mouthed to be last swal-
            lowed – when he needs what you have gleaned, it is
            but squeezing you, and, sponge, you shall be dry again. 20

ROSENC'Z   I understand you not, my lord.

HAMLET   I am glad of it – a knavish speech sleeps in a foolish ear.

ROSENC'Z   My lord, you must tell us where the body is, and go
            with us to the king.

HAMLET   The body is with the king, but the king is not with the
            body. The king is a thing –

GUILD'RN   A thing, my lord!

HAMLET   Of nothing, bring me to him. Hide fox, and all after.

                           [*he runs out; they pursue with the guard*

SCENE 3

The hall of the castle, as before

The KING *seated at a table on the dais with
'two or three' councillors of state*

KING   I have sent to seek him, and to find the body.
            How dangerous is it that this man goes loose!
            Yet must not we put the strong law on him,
            He's loved of the distracted multitude,
            Who like not in their judgment but their eyes,
            And where 'tis so, th'offender's scourge is weighed
            But never the offence: to bear all smooth and even,
            This sudden sending him away must seem
            Deliberate pause. Diseases desperate grown
            By desperate appliance are relieved,   10
            Or not at all.

            ROSENCRANTZ, GUILDENSTERN *and others enter*

                           How now! what hath befallen?

ROSENC'Z   Where the dead body is bestowed, my lord,
            We cannot get from him.

KING   But where is he?

ROSENC'Z	Without, my lord, guarded, to know your pleasure.
KING	Bring him before us.
ROSENC'Z	Ho! bring in the lord.

HAMLET *enters guarded by soldiers*

KING	Now, Hamlet, where's Polonius?
HAMLET	At supper.
KING	At supper? Where?
HAMLET	Not where he eats, but where 'a is eaten – a certain convocation of politic worms are e'en at him: your worm is your only emperor for diet, we fat all creatures else to fat us, and we fat ourselves for maggots. Your fat king and your lean beggar is but variable service, two dishes, but to one table – that's the end.
KING	Alas, alas!
HAMLET	A man may fish with the worm that hath eat of a king, and eat of the fish that hath fed of that worm.
KING	What dost thou mean by this?
HAMLET	Nothing but to show you how a king may go a progress through the guts of a beggar.
KING	Where is Polonius?
HAMLET	In heaven – send thither to see, if your messenger find him not there, seek him i'th'other place yourself. But if indeed you find him not within this month, you shall nose him as you go up the stairs into the lobby.
KING	[*to attendants*] Go seek him there.
HAMLET	'A will stay till you come. [*they depart*
KING	Hamlet, this deed, for thine especial safety, Which we do tender, as we dearly grieve For that which thou hast done, must send thee hence With fiery quickness. Therefore prepare thyself, The bark is ready, and the wind at help, Th'associates tend, and everything is bent For England.
HAMLET	For England.
KING	Ay, Hamlet.
HAMLET	Good.
KING	So is it if thou knew'st our purposes.
HAMLET	I see a cherub that sees them. But, come, for England! [*he bows*] Farewell, dear mother.

20

30

40

KING   Thy loving father, Hamlet.

HAMLET   My mother – father and mother is man and wife, man
            and wife is one flesh, and so my mother: [*he turns to his* 50
            guards] come, for England!   [*they go*

KING   [*to Rosencrantz and Guildenstern*]
            Follow him at foot, tempt him with speed aboard,
            Delay it not, I'll have him hence tonight.
            Away! for everything is sealed and done
            That else leans on th'affair – pray you, make haste.
                                        [*all depart save the King*
            And, England, if my love thou hold'st at aught –
            As my great power thereof may give thee sense,
            Since yet thy cicatrice looks raw and red
            After the Danish sword, and thy free awe
            Pays homage to us – thou mayst not coldly set   60
            Our sovereign process, which imports at full
            By letters congruing to that effect,
            The present death of Hamlet. Do it, England,
            For like the hectic in my blood he rages,
            And thou must cure me; till I know 'tis done,
            Howe'er my haps, my joys were ne'er begun. [*he goes*

                                SCENE 4

                    A plain near to a port in Denmark

                Prince FORTINBRAS, *with his army on the march*

FORT'BRAS   Go, captain, from me greet the Danish king,
            Tell him that by his licence Fortinbras
            Craves the conveyance of a promised march
            Over his kingdom. You know the rendezvous.
            If that his majesty would aught with us,
            We shall express our duty in his eye,
            And let him know so.

CAPTAIN   I will do't, my lord.
                                        [*he turns one way*

FORT'BRAS   [*to the troops*] Go softly on.
                    [*Fortinbras and the army go forward another way*

The Captain meets HAMLET, ROSENCRANTZ, GUILDENSTERN
and the guard on their road to port

HAMLET	Good sir, whose powers are these?
CAPTAIN	They are of Norway, sir.
HAMLET	How purposed, sir, I pray you?
CAPTAIN	Against some part of Poland.

10

HAMLET	Who commands them, sir?
CAPTAIN	The nephew to old Norway, Fortinbras.
HAMLET	Goes it against the main of Poland, sir,
	Or for some frontier?
CAPTAIN	Truly to speak, and with no addition,
	We go to gain a little patch of ground
	That hath in it no profit but the name.
	To pay five ducats, five, I would not farm it;
	Nor will it yield to Norway or the Pole
	A ranker rate should it be sold in fee.

20

HAMLET	Why, then the Polack never will defend it.
CAPTAIN	Yes, 'tis already garrisoned.
HAMLET	Two thousand souls and twenty thousand ducats
	Will not debate the question of this straw!
	This is th'imposthume of much wealth and peace,
	That inward breaks, and shows no cause without
	Why the man dies. I humbly thank you, sir.
CAPTAIN	God bye you, sir. [*he goes*
ROSENC'Z	Will't please you go, my lord?
HAMLET	I'll be with you straight, go a little before.

            [*Rosencrantz, Guildenstern and the rest pass on* 30

How all occasions do inform against me,
And spur my dull revenge! What is a man,
If his chief good and market of his time
Be but to sleep and feed? A beast, no more:
Sure he that made us with such large discourse,
Looking before and after, gave us not
That capability and god-like reason
To fust in us unused. Now, whether it be
Bestial oblivion, or some craven scruple
Of thinking too precisely on th'event –
A thought which quartered hath but one part wisdom,   40

And ever three parts coward – I do not know
Why yet I live to say 'This thing's to do',
Sith I have cause, and will, and strength, and means,
To do't. Examples gross as earth exhort me.
Witness this army of such mass and charge,
Led by a delicate and tender prince,
Whose spirit with divine ambition puffed
Makes mouths at the invisible event,
Exposing what is mortal and unsure
To all that fortune, death and danger dare,   50
Even for an egg-shell. Rightly to be great
Is not to stir without great argument,
But greatly to find quarrel in a straw
When honour's at the stake. How stand I then,
That have a father killed, a mother stained,
Excitements of my reason and my blood,
And let all sleep? While to my shame I see
The imminent death of twenty thousand men,
That for a fantasy and trick of fame
Go to their graves like beds, fight for a plot   60
Whereon the numbers cannot try the cause,
Which is not tomb enough and continent
To hide the slain? O, from this time forth,
My thoughts be bloody, or be nothing worth!

[he follows on

[*Some weeks pass*]

SCENE 5

A room in the castle of Elsinore

The QUEEN *with her ladies,* HORATIO *and a gentleman*

QUEEN   I will not speak with her.
GENT'MAN   She is importunate, indeed distract,
            Her mood will needs be pitied.
QUEEN   What would she have?
GENT'MAN   She speaks much of her father, says she hears
            There's tricks i'th'world, and hems, and beats her heart,

Spurns enviously at straws, speaks things in doubt
That carry but half sense. Her speech is nothing,
Yet the unshapéd use of it doth move
The hearers to collection – they aim at it,
And botch the words up fit to their own thoughts,   10
Which as her winks and nods and gestures yield them,
Indeed would make one think there might be thought,
Though nothing sure, yet much unhappily.

HORATIO 'Twere good she were spoken with, for she may strew
Dangerous conjectures in ill-breeding minds.

QUEEN Let her come in.   [the gentleman goes out
[aside] To my sick soul, as sin's true nature is,
Each toy seems prologue to some great amiss,
So full of artless jealousy is guilt,
It spills itself, in fearing to be spilt.   20

The gentleman returns with OPHELIA, *distracted, a lute*
in her hands and her hair about her shoulders

OPHELIA Where is the beauteous majesty of Denmark?
QUEEN How now, Ophelia?
OPHELIA [sings] How should I your true love know
                    From another one?
                    By his cockle hat and staff,
                    And his sandal shoon.
QUEEN Alas, sweet lady, what imports this song?
OPHELIA Say you? Nay, pray you mark.
         [sings] He is dead and gone, lady,
                    He is dead and gone,   30
                    At his head a grass-green turf,
                    At his heels a stone.
         O, ho!
QUEEN   Nay, but Ophelia –
OPHELIA   Pray you mark.
         [sings] White his shroud as the mountain snow –

The KING *enters*

QUEEN Alas, look here, my lord.
OPHELIA [sings]   Larded all with sweet flowers,
                    Which bewept to the grave did not go,
                    With true-love showers.

KING   How do you, pretty lady?

OPHELIA   Well, God dild you! They say the owl was a baker's 40
            daughter. Lord, we know what we are, but know not
            what we may be. God be at your table!

KING   Conceit upon her father.

OPHELIA   Pray you let's have no words of this, but when they
            ask you what it means, say you this.
            [*sings*] Tomorrow is Saint Valentine's day,
                        All in the morning betime,
                        And I a maid at your window
                          To be your Valentine.
                        Then up he rose, and donned his clo'es,   50
                          And dupped the chamber door,
                        Let in the maid, that out a maid
                          Never departed more.

KING   Pretty Ophelia!

OPHELIA   Indeed, la, without an oath, I'll make an end on't –
            [*sings*]   By Gis and by Saint Charity,
                          Alack and fie for shame!
                        Young men will do't, if they come to't,
                          By Cock, they are to blame.
                        Quoth she, Before you tumbled me,   60
                          You promised me to wed.
            he answers
                        So would I ha' done, by yonder sun,
                          An thou hadst not come to my bed.

KING   How long hath she been thus?

OPHELIA   I hope all will be well. We must be patient, but I
            cannot choose but weep to think they would lay him
            i'th'cold ground. My brother shall know of it, and so I
            thank you for your good counsel. Come, my coach!
            Good night, ladies, good night. Sweet ladies, good
            night, good night.   [*she goes* 70

KING   Follow her close, give her good watch, I pray you.
                        [*Horatio and the gentleman follow her*
            O, this is the poison of deep grief, it springs
            All from her father's death – and now behold!
            O Gertrude, Gertrude,
            When sorrows come, they come not single spies,

But in battalions: first her father slain,
Next your son gone, and he most violent author
Of his own just remove, the people muddied,
Thick and unwholesome in their thoughts and whispers
For good Polonius' death – and we have done but
                                greenly,   80
In hugger-mugger to inter him – poor Ophelia
Divided from herself and her fair judgment,
Without the which we are pictures or mere beasts,
Last, and as much containing as all these,
Her brother is in secret come from France,
Feeds on his wonder, keeps himself in clouds,
And wants not buzzers to infect his ear
With pestilent speeches of his father's death,
Wherein necessity, of matter beggared,
Will nothing stick our person to arraign   90
In ear and ear: O my dear Gertrude, this
Like to a murdering-piece in many places
Gives me superfluous death!   [*a tumult without*

QUEEN   Alack! what noise is this?

KING   [*calls*] Attend!   [*an attendant enters*
Where are my Switzers? let them guard the door.
What is the matter?

ATTENDANT   Save yourself, my lord!
The ocean, overpeering of his list,
Eats not the flats with more impiteous haste
Than young Laertes in a riotous head   100
O'erbears your officers: the rabble call him lord,
And as the world were now but to begin,
Antiquity forgot, custom not known,
The ratifiers and props of every word,
They cry 'Choose we, Laertes shall be king!'
Caps, hands, and tongues applaud it to the clouds,
'Laertes shall be king, Laertes king!'
                        [*the shouts grow louder*

QUEEN   How cheerfully on the false trail they cry!
O, this is counter, you false Danish dogs!

KING   The doors are broke.   110

LAERTES, armed, bursts into the room with Danes following

LAERTES   Where is this king? Sirs, stand you all without.

DANES   No, let's come in.

LAERTES   I pray you, give me leave.

DANES   We will, we will.

                        [they retire without the door

LAERTES   I thank you, keep the door. O thou vile king,
           Give me my father.

QUEEN   Calmly, good Laertes.

LAERTES   That drop of blood that's calm proclaims me bastard,
           Cries cuckold to my father, brands the harlot,
           Even here, between the chaste unsmirchéd brows
           Of my true mother.   *[he advances upon them; the Queen*
                                           throws herself in his path

KING   What is the cause, Laertes,
           That thy rebellion looks so giant-like?   120
           Let him go, Gertrude, do not fear our person,
           There's such divinity doth hedge a king,
           That treason can but peep to what it would,
           Acts little of his will. Tell me, Laertes,
           Why thou art thus incensed – let him go, Gertrude –
           Speak, man.

LAERTES   Where is my father?

KING   Dead.

QUEEN   But not by him.

KING   Let him demand his fill.

LAERTES   How came he dead? I'll not be juggled with.
           To hell allegiance, vows to the blackest devil,   130
           Conscience and grace to the profoundest pit!
           I dare damnation. To this point I stand,
           That both the worlds I give to negligence,
           Let come what comes, only I'll be revenged
           Most throughly for my father.

KING   Who shall stay you.

LAERTES   My will, not all the world's:
           And for my means, I'll husband them so well,
           They shall go far with little.

KING   Good Laertes,
           If you desire to know the certainty

	Of your dear father, is't writ in your revenge,	140
	That, sweepstake, you will draw both friend and foe,	
	Winner and loser?	
LAERTES	None but his enemies.	
KING	Will you know them then?	
LAERTES	To his good friends thus wide I'll ope my arms,	
	And like the kind life-rend'ring pelican,	
	Repast them with my blood.	
KING	Why, now you speak	
	Like a good child and a true gentleman.	
	That I am guiltless of your father's death,	
	And am most sensibly in grief for it,	
	It shall as level to your judgment 'pear,	150
	As day does to your eye.	
SHOUTING WITHOUT	Let her come in.	
LAERTES	How now! What noise is that?	

OPHELIA *re-enters with flowers in her hand*

> O heat, dry up my brains, tears seven times salt,
> Burn out the sense and virtue of mine eye!
> By heaven, thy madness shall be paid with weight,
> Till our scale turn the beam. O rose of May,
> Dear maid, kind sister, sweet Ophelia!
> O heavens, is't possible a young maid's wits
> Should be as mortal as an old man's life?
> Nature is fine in love, and where 'tis fine,   160
> It sends some precious instance of itself
> After the thing it loves.

OPHELIA	[*sings*] They bore him barefaced on the bier,
	Hey non nonny, nonny, hey nonny,
	And in his grave rained many a tear –
	Fare you well, my dove!
LAERTES	Hadst thou thy wits, and didst persuade revenge,
	It could not move thus.
OPHELIA	You must sing 'Adown adown', an you call him
	adown-a. O, how the wheel becomes it! It is the false 170
	steward that stole his master's daughter.
LAERTES	This nothing's more than matter.
OPHELIA	[*to Laertes*] There's rosemary, that's for remembrance –

pray you, love, remember – and there is pansies, that's
for thoughts.

LAERTES   A document in madness, thoughts and remembrance
fitted.

OPHELIA   [*to the King*] There's fennel for you, and columbines.
[*to the Queen*] There's rue for you, and here's some for
me, we may call it herb of grace o'Sundays – O, you   18o
must wear your rue with a difference. There's a daisy.
I would give you some violets, but they withered all,
when my father died – they say 'a made a good end –
[*sings*] For bonny sweet Robin is all my joy –

LAERTES   Thought and affliction, passion, hell itself,
She turns to favour and to prettiness.

OPHELIA   [*sings*] And will 'a not come again?
And will 'a not come again?
No, no, he is dead,
Go to thy death-bed,
He never will come again.   19o

His beard was as white as snow,
All flaxen was his poll,
He is gone, he is gone,
And we cast away moan,
God ha' mercy on his soul! –

And of all Christian souls I pray God. God bye you.
[*she goes*

LAERTES   Do you see this, O God?

KING   Laertes, I must commune with your grief,
Or you deny me right. Go but apart,   20o
Make choice of whom your wisest friends you will
And they shall hear and judge 'twixt you and me.
If by direct or by collateral hand
They find us touched, we will our kingdom give,
Our crown, our life, and all that we call ours,
To you in satisfaction; but if not,
Be you content to lend your patience to us,
And we shall jointly labour with your soul
To give it due content.

LAERTES   Let this be so.

His means of death, his obscure funeral,   210
No trophy, sword, nor hatchment o'er his bones,
No noble rite, nor formal ostentation,
Cry to be heard as 'twere from heaven to earth,
That I must call't in question.
KING   So you shall,
And where th'offence is let the great axe fall.
I pray you, go with me.   [they go

SCENE 6

'HORATIO and others' enter

HORATIO What are they that would speak with me?
GENT'MAN Seafaring men, sir. They say they have letters for you.
HORATIO Let them come in.   [an attendant goes out
         [aside] I do not know from what part of the world
         I should be greeted, if not from Lord Hamlet.

The attendant brings in sailors

1 SAILOR God bless you, sir.
HORATIO Let him bless thee too.
1 SAILOR 'A shall, sir, an't please him. There's a letter for you,
         sir, it came from th'ambassador that was bound for
         England, if your name be Horatio, as I am let to know 10
         it is.
HORATIO [turns aside and reads] 'Horatio, when thou shalt have
         overlooked this, give these fellows some means to the
         king, they have letters for him. Ere we were two days
         old at sea, a pirate of very warlike appointment gave us
         chase. Finding ourselves too slow of sail, we put on a
         compelled valour, and in the grapple I boarded them.
         On the instant they got clear of our ship, so I alone
         became their prisoner. They have dealt with me like
         thieves of mercy, but they knew what they did; I am to 20
         do a good turn for them. Let the king have the letters I
         have sent, and repair thou to me with as much speed as
         thou wouldest fly death. I have words to speak in thine
         ear will make thee dumb, yet are they much too light

for the bore of the matter. These good fellows will bring
thee where I am. Rosencrantz and Guildenstern hold
their course for England – of them I have much to tell
thee. Farewell.
     He that thou knowest thine, HAMLET.'
Come, I will give you way for these your letters,   30
And do't the speedier that you may direct me
To him from whom you brought them.   *[they go*

SCENE 7

The KING *and* LAERTES *return*

KING   Now must your conscience my acquittance seal,
    And you must put me in your heart for friend,
    Sith you have heard and with a knowing ear
    That he which hath your noble father slain
    Pursued my life.
LAERTES   It well appears: but tell me,
    Why you proceeded not against these feats,
    So crimeful and so capital in nature,
    As by your safety, greatness, wisdom, all things else,
    You mainly were stirred up.
KING   O, for two special reasons,
    Which may to you perhaps seem much unsinewed,   10
    But yet to me they're strong. The queen his mother
    Lives almost by his looks, and for myself,
    My virtue or my plague, be it either which,
    She is so conjunctive to my life and soul,
    That as the star moves not but in his sphere
    I could not but by her. The other motive,
    Why to a public count I might not go,
    Is the great love the general gender bear him,
    Who dipping all his faults in their affection,
    Would like the spring that turneth wood to stone,   20
    Convert his gyves to graces, o that my arrows,
    Too slightly timbered for so loud a wind,
    Would have reverted to my bow again,
    And not where I had aimed them.
LAERTES And so have I a noble father lost,

A sister driven into desperate terms,
Whose worth, if praises may go back again,
Stood challenger on mount of all the age
For her perfections. But my revenge will come.

KING   Break not your sleeps for that, you must not think 30
That we are made of stuff so flat and dull,
That we can let our beard be shook with danger
And think it pastime. You shortly shall hear more.
I loved your father, and we love ourself,
And that I hope will teach you to imagine –

     'Enter a MESSENGER *with letters'*

How now! what news?

MESSENGER   Letters, my lord, from Hamlet.
These to your majesty, these to the queen.

KING   From Hamlet! who brought them?

MESSENGER Sailors, my lord, they say, I saw them not.
They were given me by Claudio, he received them 40
Of him that brought them.

KING   Laertes, you shall hear them.
Leave us.   *[the Messenger goes*
[*reads*] 'High and mighty, you shall know I am set
naked on your kingdom. Tomorrow shall I beg leave
to see your kingly eyes, when I shall, first asking your
pardon thereunto, recount the occasion of my sudden
and more strange return.   HAMLET.'
What should this mean? Are all the rest come back?
Or is it some abuse, and no such thing?

LAERTES Know you the hand?   50

KING   'Tis Hamlet's character. 'Naked' –
And in a postscript here he says 'alone'.
Can you devise me?

LAERTES I am lost in it, my lord, but let him come!
It warms the very sickness in my heart
That I shall live and tell him to his teeth
'Thus diest thou.'

KING   If it be so, Laertes, –
As how should it be so? How otherwise? –
Will you be ruled by me?

LAERTES   Ay, my lord,

So you will not o'errule me to a peace.   6(

KING   To thine own peace. If he be now returned,
As checking at his voyage, and that he means
No more to undertake it, I will work him
To an exploit, now ripe in my device,
Under the which he shall not choose but fall:
And for his death no wind of blame shall breathe,
But even his mother shall uncharge the practice,
And call it accident.

LAERTES   My lord, I will be ruled,
The rather if you could devise it so
That I might be the organ.

KING   It falls right.   7(
You have been talked of since your travel much,
And that in Hamlet's hearing, for a quality
Wherein they say you shine. Your sum of parts
Did not together pluck such envy from him,
As did that one, and that in my regard
Of the unworthiest siege.

LAERTES   What part is that, my lord?

KING   A very riband in the cap of youth,
Yet needful too, for youth no less becomes
The light and careless livery that it wears,
Than settled age his sables and his weeds   8(
Importing health and graveness; two months since,
Here was a gentleman of Normandy –
I have seen myself, and served against, the French,
And they can well on horseback – but this gallant
Had witchcraft in't, he grew unto his seat,
And to such wondrous doing brought his horse,
As had he been incorpsed and demi-natured
 With the brave beast. So far he topped my thought,
That I in forgery of shapes and tricks
Come short of what he did.

LAERTES   A Norman, was't?   9(

KING   A Norman.

LAERTES Upon my life, Lamord.

KING   The very same.

LAERTES I know him well, he is the brooch indeed

And gem of all the nation.

KING   He made confession of you,
And gave you such a masterly report
For art and exercise in your defence,
And for your rapier most especial,
That he cried out 'twould be a sight indeed
If one could match you; the scrimers of their nation   100
He swore had neither motion, guard, nor eye,
If you opposed them; sir, this report of his
Did Hamlet so envenom with his envy,
That he could nothing do but wish and beg
Your sudden coming o'er to play with him.
Now, out of this –

LAERTES   What out of this, my lord?

KING   Laertes, was your father dear to you?
Or are you like the painting of a sorrow,
A face without a heart?

LAERTES   Why ask you this?

KING   Not that I think you did not love your father,   110
But that I know love is begun by time,
And that I see in passages of proof
Time qualifies the spark and fire of it.
There lives within the very flame of love
A kind of wick or snuff that will abate it,
And nothing is at a like goodness still,
For goodness, growing to a pleurisy,
Dies in his own too much. That we would do
We should do when we would: for this 'would'
                                        changes,
And hath abatements and delays as many   120
As there are tongues, are hands, are accidents,
And then this 'should' is like a spendthrift sigh,
That hurts by easing; but to the quick o'th'ulcer –
Hamlet comes back, what would you undertake
To show yourself your father's son in deed
More than in words?

LAERTES   To cut his throat i'th'church.

KING   No place indeed should murder sanctuarize,
Revenge should have no bounds: but, good Laertes,

Will you do this, keep close within your chamber.
Hamlet returned shall know you are come home.   130
We'll put on those shall praise your excellence,
And set a double varnish on the fame
The Frenchman gave you, bring you in fine together,
And wager on your heads; he being remiss,
Most generous, and free from all contriving,
Will not peruse the foils, so that with ease,
Or with a little shuffling, you may choose
A sword unbated, and in a pass of practice
Requite him for your father.

LAERTES   I will do't,
And, for the purpose, I'll anoint my sword.   140
I bought an unction of a mountebank,
So mortal, that but dip a knife in it,
Where it draws blood, no cataplasm so rare,
Collected from all simples that have virtue
Under the moon, can save the thing from death
That is but scratched withal. I'll touch my point
With this contagion, that if I gall him slightly,
It may be death.

KING   Let's further think of this,
Weigh what convenience both of time and means
May fit us to our shape. If this should fail,   150
And that our drift look through our bad performance,
'Twere better not assayed. Therefore this project
Should have a back or second that might hold,
If this did blast in proof; soft, let me see,
We'll make a solemn wager on your cunnings –
I ha't!
When in your motion you are hot and dry,
As make your bouts more violent to that end,
And that he calls for drink, I'll have preferred him
A chalice for the nonce, whereon but sipping,   160
If he by chance escape your venomed stuck,
Our purpose may hold there. But stay, what noise?

The QUEEN enters weeping

QUEEN   One woe doth tread upon another's heel,

           So fast they follow; your sister's drowned, Laertes.

LAERTES   Drowned! O, where?

QUEEN   There is a willow grows askant the brook,
           That shows his hoar leaves in the glassy stream,
           Therewith fantastic garlands did she make
           Of crow-flowers, nettles, daisies, and long purples
           That liberal shepherds give a grosser name,   170
           But our cold maids do dead men's fingers call them.
           There on the pendent boughs her crownet weeds
           Clamb'ring to hang, an envious sliver broke,
           When down her weedy trophies and herself
           Fell in the weeping brook. Her clothes spread wide,
           And mermaid-like awhile they bore her up,
           Which time she chanted snatches of old lauds,
           As one incapable of her own distress,
           Or like a creature native and indued
           Unto that element. But long it could not be   180
           Till that her garments, heavy with their drink,
           Pulled the poor wretch from her melodious lay
           To muddy death.

LAERTES   Alas then, she is drowned?

QUEEN   Drowned, drowned.

LAERTES   Too much of water hast thou, poor Ophelia,
           And therefore I forbid my tears; but yet
           It is our trick, nature her custom holds,
           Let shame say what it will – when these are gone,
           The woman will be out. Adieu, my lord!
           I have a speech o' fire that fain would blaze,   190
           But that this folly douts it.   [he goes

KING   Let's follow, Gertrude.
           How much I had to do to calm his rage!
           Now fear I this will give it start again,
           Therefore let's follow.   [they follow

ACT 5 SCENE I

A graveyard, with a newly opened grave; yew-trees, and a gate

*Two clowns (a sexton and his mate) enter with spades
and mattocks; they make them ready to dig*

1 CLOWN   Is she to be buried in Christian burial when she wilfully seeks her own salvation?

2 CLOWN   I tell thee she is, therefore make her grave straight.
The crowner hath sat on her, and finds it Christian
burial.

1 CLOWN   How can that be, unless she drowned herself in her
own defence?

2 CLOWN   Why, 'tis found so.

1 CLOWN   It must be 'se offendendo', it cannot be else. For here
lies the point, if I drown myself wittingly, it argues an   10
act, and an act hath three branches, it is to act, to do,
and to perform – argal, she drowned herself wittingly.

2 CLOWN   Nay, but hear you, goodman delver.

1 CLOWN   Give me leave. Here lies the water – good. Here
stands the man – good. If the man go to this water and
drown himself, it is, will he nill he, he goes, mark you
that. But if the water come to him, and drown him, he
drowns not himself – argal, he that is not guilty of his
own death, shortens not his own life.

2 CLOWN   But is this law?   20

1 CLOWN   Ay, marry is't, crowner's quest law.

2 CLOWN   Will you ha' the truth an't? If this had not been a
gentlewoman, she should have been buried out a
Christian burial.

1 CLOWN   Why, there thou say'st, and the more pity that great
folk should have countenance in this world to drown
or hang themselves more than their even-Christen.
Come, my spade! there is no ancient gentlemen but
gardeners, ditchers and grave-makers – they hold up
Adam's profession.   30

[he goes down into the open grave

2 CLOWN   Was he a gentleman?

1 CLOWN   'A was the first that ever bore arms.

2 CLOWN   Why, he had none.

1 CLOWN   What, art a heathen? How dost thou understand the Scripture? the Scripture says Adam digged; could he dig without arms? I'll put another question to thee. If thou answerest me not to the purpose, confess thyself –

2 CLOWN   Go to.

1 CLOWN   What is he that builds stronger than either the mason, the shipwright, or the carpenter?   40

2 CLOWN   The gallows-maker, for that frame outlives a thousand tenants.

1 CLOWN   I like thy wit well in good faith, the gallows does well – but how does it well? It does well to those that do ill. Now thou dost ill to say the gallows is built stronger than the church – argal, the gallows may do well to thee. To't again, come.

2 CLOWN   'Who builds stronger than a mason, a shipwright, or a carpenter?'

1 CLOWN   Ay, tell me that, and unyoke.   50

2 CLOWN   Marry, now I can tell.

1 CLOWN   To't.

2 CLOWN   Mass, I cannot tell.

1 CLOWN   Cudgel thy brains no more about it, for your dull ass will not mend his pace with beating. And when you are asked this question next, say 'a grave-maker'. The houses he makes lasts till doomsday. Go, get thee to Yaughan, and fetch me a stoup of liquor.

                                       [Second Clown goes

        HAMLET *(clad in sailor's garb)* and HORATIO *are seen*
                     entering the graveyard

                 First Clown digs and sings

          In youth when I did love, did love,
            Methought it was very sweet,
         To contract o' the time for a my behove,   60
            O, methought there a was nothing a meet.

HAMLET   Has this fellow no feeling of his business that 'a sings in grave-making?

HORATIO   Custom hath made it in him a property of easiness.

HAMLET   'Tis e'en so, the hand of little employment hath the
            daintier sense.

1 CLOWN   [*sings*] But age with his stealing steps
                            Hath clawed me in his clutch,
                            And hath shipped me intil the land,   70
                            As if I had never been such.

                                        [*he throws up a skull*]

HAMLET   That skull had a tongue in it, and could sing once!
            How the knave jowls it to the ground, as if 'twere
            Cain's jaw-bone, that did the first murder! This might
            be the pate of a politician, which this ass now o'er-
            reaches; one that would circumvent God, might it
            not?

HORATIO   It might, my lord.

HAMLET   Or of a courtier, which could say 'Good morrow,
            sweet lord! How dost thou, good lord?' This might be 80
            my lord such-a-one, that praised my lord such a-one's
            horse, when 'a meant to beg it, might it not?

HORATIO   Ay, my lord.

HAMLET   Why, e'en so, and now my Lady Worm's, chopless
            and knocked about the mazzard with a sexton's spade;
            here's fine revolution an we had the trick to see't! Did
            these bones cost no more the breeding, but to play at
            loggats with them? Mine ache to think on't.

1 CLOWN   [*sings*] A pick-axe, and a spade, a spade,
                            For and a shrouding sheet,   90
                            O, a pit of clay for to be made
                            For such a guest is meet.

                                        [*he throws up a second skull*

HAMLET   There's another. Why may not that be the skull of a
            lawyer? Where be his quiddities now, his quillities, his
            cases, his tenures, and his tricks? Why does he suffer
            this rude knave now to knock him about the sconce
            with a dirty shovel, and will not tell him of his action
            of battery? [*he takes up the skull*] Hum! This fellow
            might be in's time a great buyer of land, with his
            statutes, his recognizances, his fines, his double vouch- 100
            ers, his recoveries: is this the fine of his fines, and the
            recovery of his recoveries, to have his fine pate full of

fine dirt? Will his vouchers vouch him no more of his purchases, and double ones too, than the length and breadth of a pair of indentures? The very conveyances of his lands will scarcely lie in this box [*he taps the skull*], and must th'inheritor himself have no more, ha?

HORATIO   Not a jot more, my lord.

HAMLET   Is not parchment made of sheep-skins?

HORATIO   Ay, my lord, and of calves'-skins too.   110

HAMLET   They are sheep and calves which seek out assurance in that. I will speak to this fellow. [*they go forward*] Whose grave's this, sirrah?

I CLOWN   Mine, sir – [*sings*]
              O, a pit of clay for to be made
                For such a guest is meet.

HAMLET   I think it be thine, indeed, for thou liest in't.

I CLOWN   You lie out on't sir, and therefore 'tis not yours; for my part I do not lie in't, and yet it is mine.

HAMLET   Thou dost lie in't, to be in't and say it is thine. 'Tis for   120 the dead, not for the quick – therefore thou liest.

I CLOWN   'Tis a quick lie, sir, 'twill away again from me to you.

HAMLET   What man dost thou dig it for?

I CLOWN   For no man, sir.

HAMLET   What woman then?

I CLOWN   For none neither.

HAMLET   Who is to be buried in't?

I CLOWN   One that was a woman, sir, but rest her soul she's dead.

HAMLET   How absolute the knave is! We must speak by the card or equivocation will undo us. By the Lord, Horatio,   130 this three years I have took note of it, the age is grown so picked, that the toe of the peasant comes so near the heel of the courtier he galls his kibe. How long hast thou been grave-maker?

I CLOWN   Of all the days i'th'year I came to't that day that our last king Hamlet overcame Fortinbras.

HAMLET   How long is that since?

I CLOWN   Cannot you tell that? Every fool can tell that. It was that very day that young Hamlet was born: he that is mad and sent into England.   140

HAMLET	Ay, marry, why was he sent into England?
1 CLOWN	Why, because 'a was mad: 'a shall recover his wits there, or if 'a do not, 'tis no great matter there.
HAMLET	Why?
1 CLOWN	'Twill not be seen in him there, there the men are as mad as he.
HAMLET	How came he mad?
1 CLOWN	Very strangely, they say.
HAMLET	How strangely?
1 CLOWN	Faith, e'en with losing his wits.
HAMLET	Upon what ground?
1 CLOWN	Why, here in Denmark: I have been sexton here man and boy thirty years.
HAMLET	How long will a man lie i'th'earth ere he rot?
1 CLOWN	Faith, if 'a be not rotten before 'a die, as we have many pocky corses nowadays that will scarce hold the laying in, 'a will last you some eight year, or nine year. A tanner will last you nine year.
HAMLET	Why he more than another?
1 CLOWN	Why sir, his hide is so tanned with his trade, that 'a will keep out water a great while; and your water is a sore decayer of your whoreson dead body Here's a skull now: this skull hath lien you i'th'earth three-and-twenty years.
HAMLET	Whose was it?
1 CLOWN	A whoreson mad fellow's it was, whose do you think it was?
HAMLET	Nay, I know not.
1 CLOWN	A pestilence on him for a mad rogue! 'A poured a flagon of Rhenish on my head once; this same skull, sir, was, sir, Yorick's skull, the king's jester.
HAMLET	This?
1 CLOWN	E'en that.
HAMLET	Let me see. [he takes the skull] Alas, poor Yorick! I knew him, Horatio – a fellow of infinite jest, of most excellent fancy. He hath borne me on his back a thousand times, and now how abhorred in my imagination it is! My gorge rises at it. Here hung those lips that I have kissed I know not how oft. Where be your gibes

150

160

170

now? Your gambols, your songs, your flashes of merri- 180
ment, that were wont to set the table on a roar? Not
one now to mock your own grinning? Quite chop
fallen? Now get you to my lady's chamber, and tell her,
let her paint an inch thick, to this favour she must
come. Make her laugh at that. Prithee, Horatio, tell me
one thing.

HORATIO What's that, my lord.

HAMLET Dost thou think Alexander looked o' this fashion i'th'
earth?

HORATIO E'en so.   190

HAMLET And smelt so? Pah!   *[he sets down the skull*

HORATIO E'en so, my lord.

HAMLET To what base uses we may return, Horatio! Why may
not imagination trace the noble dust of Alexander, till
'a find it stopping a bung-hole?

HORATIO 'Twere to consider too curiously, to consider so.

HAMLET No, faith, not a jot, but to follow him thither with
modesty enough, and likelihood to lead it; as thus –
Alexander died, Alexander was buried, Alexander
returneth to dust, the dust is earth, of earth we make 200
loam, and why of that loam whereto he was converted
might they not stop a beer-barrel?

> Imperious Caesar, dead and turned to clay,
> Might stop a hole to keep the wind away.
> O, that that earth, which kept the world in awe,
> Should patch a wall t'expel the winter's flaw!

But soft, but soft, awhile – here comes the king,
The queen, the courtiers.

A procession enters the graveyard: the corpse of OPHELIA *in an open
coffin, with* LAERTES, *the* KING, *the* QUEEN, *courtiers and a Doctor of
Divinity in cassock and gown following*

                                        Who is this they follow?
And with such maiméd rites? This doth betoken
The corse they follow did with desperate hand   210
Fordo it own life. 'Twas of some estate.
Couch we awhile, and mark.   *[they sit under a yew*

LAERTES What ceremony else?

HAMLET   That is Laertes,
            A very noble youth – mark.

LAERTES   What ceremony else?

DOCTOR   Her obsequies have been as far enlarged
            As we have warranty. Her death was doubtful,
            And but that great command o'ersways the order,
            She should in ground unsanctified have lodged
            Till the last trumpet: for charitable prayers,   220
            Shards, flints and pebbles should be thrown on her:
            Yet here she is allowed her virgin crants,
            Her maiden strewments, and the bringing home
            Of bell and burial.

LAERTES   Must there no more be done?

DOCTOR   No more be done!
            We should profane the service of the dead
            To sing sage requiem and such rest to her
            As to peace-parted souls.

LAERTES   Lay her i'th'earth,
            And from her fair and unpolluted flesh
            May violets spring!   [*the coffin is laid within the grave*]
                              I tell thee, churlish priest,   230
            A minist'ring angel shall my sister be,
            When thou liest howling.

HAMLET   What, the fair Ophelia!

QUEEN   [*scattering flowers*] Sweets to the sweet. Farewell!
            I hoped thou shouldst have been my Hamlet's wife:
            I thought thy bride-bed to have decked, sweet maid,
            And not have strewed thy grave.

LAERTES   O, treble woe
            Fall ten times treble on that curséd head
            Whose wicked deed thy most ingenious sense
            Deprived thee of! Hold off the earth awhile,
            Till I have caught her once more in mine arms;   240
                              [*'leaps in the grave'*
            Now pile your dust upon the quick and dead,
            Till of this flat a mountain you have made
            T'o'ertop old Pelion, or the skyish head
            Of blue Olympus.

HAMLET   [*comes forward*]   What is he whose grief

Bears such an emphasis? whose phrase of sorrow
Conjures the wand'ring stars, and makes them stand
Like wonder-wounded hearers? This is I,
Hamlet the Dane.   ['*leaps in after Laertes*'

LAERTES   [*grappling with him*] The devil take thy soul!

HAMLET   Thou pray'st not well.
           I prithee take thy fingers from my throat,   250
           For though I am not splenitive and rash,
           Yet have I in me something dangerous,
           Which let thy wiseness fear; hold off thy hand.

KING   Pluck them asunder.

QUEEN   Hamlet, Hamlet!

ALL   Gentlemen!

HORATIO   Good my lord, be quiet.
                           [*Attendants part them, and they
                                come up out of the grave*

HAMLET   Why, I will fight with him upon this theme
           Until my eyelids will no longer wag.

QUEEN   O my son, what theme?

HAMLET   I loved Ophelia, forty thousand brothers
           Could not with all their quantity of love   260
           Make up my sum. What wilt thou do for her?

KING   O he is mad, Laertes.

QUEEN   For love of God, forbear him.

HAMLET   'Swounds, show me what thou't do:
           Woo't weep? Woo't fight? Woo't fast? Woo't
                                                 tear thyself?
           Woo't drink up eisel? Eat a crocodile?
           I'll do't. Dost thou come here to whine?
           To outface me with leaping in her grave?
           Be buried quick with her, and so will I.
           And if thou prate of mountains, let them throw   270
           Millions of acres on us, till our ground,
           Singeing his pate against the burning zone,
           Make Ossa like a wart! Nay, an thou'lt mouth,
           I'll rant as well as thou.

QUEEN   This is mere madness,
           And thus awhile the fit will work on him.
           Anon as patient as the female dove

When that her golden couplets are disclosed
His silence will sit drooping.

HAMLET   Hear you, sir,
What is the reason that you use me thus?
I loved you ever, but it is no matter,   280
Let Hercules himself do what he may,
The cat will mew, and dog will have his day.   [*he goes*
KING   I pray thee, good Horatio, wait upon him.
[*Horatio follows*

[*aside to Laertes*]
Strengthen your patience in our last night's speech,
We'll put the matter to the present push.
Good Gertrude, set some watch over your son.
This grave shall have a living monument;
An hour of quiet shortly shall we see,
Till then, in patience our proceeding be.   [*they go*

SCENE 2

The hall of the castle; chairs of state, benches, tables, etc.

HAMLET *and* HORATIO *enter talking*

HAMLET   So much for this, sir, now shall you see the other –
You do remember all the circumstance?
HORATIO   Remember it, my lord!
HAMLET   Sir, in my heart there was a kind of fighting
That would not let me sleep – methought I lay
Worse than the mutines in the bilboes. Rashly,
And praised be rashness for it. Let us know
Our indiscretion sometime serves us well,
When our deep plots do pall, and that should learn us
There's a divinity that shapes our ends,   10
Rough-hew them how we will –
HORATIO   That is most certain.
HAMLET   Up from my cabin,
My sea-gown scarfed about me, in the dark
Groped I to find out them, had my desire,
Fingered their packet, and in fine withdrew

To mine own room again, making so bold,
My fears forgetting manners, to unseal
Their grand commission; where I found, Horatio –
Ah, royal knavery! – an exact command,
Larded with many several sorts of reasons,   20
Importing Denmark's health and England's too,
With, ho! such bugs and goblins in my life,
That on the supervise, no leisure bated,
No, not to stay the grinding of the axe,
My head should be struck off.

HORATIO   Is't possible?

HAMLET   Here's the commission, read it at more leisure.
But wilt thou hear now how I did proceed?

HORATIO   I beseech you.

HAMLET   Being thus be-netted round with villainies –
Or I could make a prologue to my brains   30
They had begun the play. I sat me down,
Devised a new commission, wrote it fair –
I once did hold it, as our statists do,
A baseness to write fair, and laboured much
How to forget that learning, but, sir, now
It did me yeoman's service. Wilt thou know
Th'effect of what I wrote?

HORATIO   Ay, good my lord.

HAMLET   An earnest conjuration from the king,
As England was his faithful tributary,
As love between them like the palm might flourish,   40
As peace should still her wheaten garland wear
And stand a comma 'tween their amities,
And many such like 'as'es' of great charge,
That on the view and knowing of these contents
Without debatement further, more or less,
He should those bearers put to sudden death,
Not shriving-time allowed.

HORATIO   How was this sealed?

HAMLET   Why, even in that was heaven ordinant,
I had my father's signet in my purse,
Which was the model of that Danish seal,   50
Folded the writ up in the form of th'other,

Subscribed it, gave't th'impression, placed it safely,
The changeling never known: now, the next day
Was our sea-fight, and what to this was sequent
Thou knowest already.

HORATIO   So Guildenstern and Rosencrantz go to't.

HAMLET   Why, man, they did make love to this employment,
They are not near my conscience, their defeat
Does by their own insinuation grow.
'Tis dangerous when the baser nature comes   60
Between the pass and fell incensèd points
Of mighty opposites.

HORATIO   Why, what a king is this!

HAMLET   Does it not, think thee, stand me now upon –
He that hath killed my king, and whored my mother,
Popped in between th'election and my hopes,
Thrown out his angle for my proper life,
And with such cozenage – is't not perfect conscience
To quit him with this arm? And is't not to be damned,
To let this canker of our nature come
In further evil?   70

HORATIO   It must be shortly known to him from England
What is the issue of the business there.

HAMLET   It will be short, the interim is mine,
And a man's life's no more than to say 'one'.
But I am very sorry, good Horatio,
That to Laertes I forgot myself;
For by the image of my cause I see
The portraiture of his; I'll court his favours:
But sure the bravery of his grief did put me
Into a towering passion.

HORATIO   Peace, who comes here?   80

OSRIC, *a diminutive and fantastical courtier, enters the hall,*
wearing a winged doublet and a hat of latest fashion

OSRIC   [*doffs his hat and bows low*] Your lordship is right welcome
back to Denmark.

HAMLET   I humbly thank you, sir. [*aside*] Dost know this water-fly?

HORATIO   No, my good lord.

HAMLET   Thy state is the more gracious, for 'tis a vice to know

him. He hath much land, and fertile: let a beast be lord
of beasts, and his crib shall stand at the king's mess. 'Tis
a chough, but, as I say, spacious in the possession of dirt.

OSRIC   [*bows again*] Sweet lord, if your lordship were at leisure,
I should impart a thing to you from his majesty.   90

HAMLET   I will receive it, sir, with all diligence of spirit. [*Osric
continues bowing and waving his hat to and fro*] Put your
bonnet to his right use, 'tis for the head.

OSRIC   I thank your lordship, it is very hot.

HAMLET   No, believe me, 'tis very cold, the wind is northerly.

OSRIC   It is indifferent cold, my lord, indeed.

HAMLET   But yet, methinks, it is very sultry and hot for my
complexion.

OSRIC   Exceedingly, my lord, it is very sultry — as 'twere — I
cannot tell how. But, my lord, his majesty bade me   100
signify to you that 'a has laid a great wager on your
head. Sir, this is the matter, —

HAMLET   [*again moves him to put on his hat*]
I beseech you remember —

OSRIC   Nay, good my lord, for mine ease, in good faith. Sir,
here is newly come to court Laertes — believe me, an
absolute gentleman, full of most excellent differences,
of very soft society, and great showing: indeed, to
speak sellingly of him, he is the card or calendar of
gentry; for you shall find in him the continent of what
parts a gentleman would see.   110

HAMLET   Sir, his definement suffers no perdition in you, though
I know to divide him inventorially would dizzy
th'arithmetic of memory, and yet but yaw neither in
respect of his quick sail, but in the verity of extolment
I take him to be a soul of great article, and his infusion
of such dearth and rareness, as to make true diction of
him, his semblable is his mirror, and who else would
trace him? — his umbrage, nothing more.

OSRIC   Your lordship speaks most infallibly of him.

HAMLET   The concernancy, sir? Why do we wrap the gentleman 120
in our more rawer breath?

OSRIC   Sir?

HORATIO   Is't not possible to understand in another tongue? You will to't, sir, really.

HAMLET   What imports the nomination of this gentleman?

OSRIC   Of Laertes?

HORATIO   His purse is empty already, all's golden words are spent.

HAMLET   Of him, sir.

OSRIC   I know you are not ignorant —

hamlet   I would you did, sir, yet in faith if you did, it would   130
not much approve me. Well, sir?

OSRIC   You are not ignorant of what excellence Laertes is —

HAMLET   I dare not confess that, lest I should compare with him
in excellence, but to know a man well were to know
himself.

OSRIC   I mean, sir, for his weapon, but in the imputation laid
on him by them in his meed, he's unfellowed.

HAMLET   What's his weapon?

OSRIC   Rapier and dagger.

HAMLET   That's two of his weapons — but, well.   140

OSRIC   The king, sir, hath wagered with him six Barbary
horses, against the which he has impawned, as I take it,
six French rapiers and poniards, with their assigns, as
girdle, hangers, and so. Three of the carriages in faith
are very dear to fancy, very responsive to the hilts,
most delicate carriages, and of very liberal conceit.

HAMLET   What call you the carriages?

HORATIO   I knew you must be edified by the margent ere you
had done.

OSRIC   The carriages, sir, are the hangers.   150

HAMLET   The phrase would be more germane to the matter, if
we could carry a cannon by our sides — I would it
might be hangers till then. But on! Six Barbary horses
against six French swords, their assigns, and three lib-
eral-conceited carriages — that's the French bet against
the Danish. Why is this all 'impawned' as you call it?

OSRIC   The king, sir, hath laid, sir, that in a dozen passes
between yourself and him he shall not exceed you
three hits. He hath laid on twelve for nine. And it
would come to immediate trial, if your lordship would   160
vouchsafe the answer.

HAMLET   How if I answer 'no'?

OSRIC   I mean, my lord, the opposition of your person in trial.

HAMLET   Sir, I will walk here in the hall, if it please his majesty.
It is the breathing time of day with me. Let the foils be
brought, the gentleman willing, and the king hold his
purpose, I will win for him an I can, if not I will gain
nothing but my shame and the odd hits.

OSRIC   Shall I re-deliver you e'en so?

HAMLET   To this effect, sir, after what flourish your nature will.   170

OSRIC   [*bows*] I commend my duty to your lordship.

HAMLET   Yours, yours.   [*after another deep bow, Osric*
                                  dons his hat and trips forth
He does well to commend it himself, there are no
tongues else for's turn.

HORATIO   This lapwing runs away with the shell on his head.

HAMLET   'A did comply, sir, with his dug before 'a sucked it.
Thus has he and many more of the same bevy that I
know the drossy age dotes on – only got the tune of the
time and, out of an habit of encounter, a kind of yeasty
collection, which carries them through and through the   180
most profound and winnowed opinions, and do but
blow them to their trial, the bubbles are out.

A lord enters

LORD   My lord, his majesty commended him to you by young
Osric, who brings back to him that you attend him in
the hall. He sends to know if your pleasure hold to play
with Laertes, or that you will take longer time.

HAMLET   I am constant to my purposes, they follow the king's
pleasure. If his fitness speaks, mine is ready; now or
whensoever, provided I be so able as now.

LORD   The king, and queen, and all are coming down.   190

HAMLET   In happy time.

LORD   The queen desires you to use some gentle entertainment to Laertes before you fall to play.

HAMLET   She well instructs me.   [*the lord departs*

HORATIO   You will lose this wager, my lord.

HAMLET   I do not think so. Since he went into France, I have
been in continual practice. I shall win at the odds; but
thou wouldst not think how ill all's here about my
heart – but it is no matter.

HORATIO   Nay, good my lord –   200
HAMLET   It is but foolery, but it is such a kind of gain-giving as
          would perhaps trouble a woman.
HORATIO   If your mind dislike anything, obey it. I will forestall
          their repair hither, and say you are not fit.
HAMLET   Not a whit, we defy augury. There is special provid-
          ence in the fall of a sparrow. If it be now, 'tis not to
          come – if it be not to come, it will be now – if it be
          not now, yet it will come – the readiness is all. Since
          no man, of aught he leaves, knows what is't to leave
          betimes, let be.   210

Attendants enter to set benches and carry in cushions for the spectators;
next follow trumpeters and drummers with kettle-drums, the KING, *the*
QUEEN and all the court, OSRIC *and another lord, as judges, bearing*
foils and daggers which are placed upon a table near the walls, and last
of all LAERTES *dressed for the fence*

KING   Come, Hamlet, come and take this hand from me.
                    [*he puts the hand of Laertes into the hand of Hamlet;*
                              and after leads the Queen to the chairs of state
HAMLET   Give me your pardon, sir. I have done you wrong,
          But pardon't, as you are a gentleman.
          This presence knows, and you must needs have heard,
          How I am punished with a sore distraction.
          What I have done
          That might your nature, honour and exception
          Roughly awake, I here proclaim was madness.
          Was't Hamlet wronged Laertes? Never Hamlet.
          If Hamlet from himself be ta'en away,   220
          And when he's not himself does wrong Laertes,
          Then Hamlet does it not, Hamlet denies it.
          Who does it then? His madness. If't be so,
          Hamlet is of the faction that is wronged,
          His madness is poor Hamlet's enemy.
          Sir, in this audience,
          Let my disclaiming from a purposed evil
          Free me so far in your most generous thoughts,
          That I have shot my arrow o'er the house,
          And hurt my brother.

LAERTES	I am satisfied in nature, 230
	Whose motive in this case should stir me most
	To my revenge, but in my terms of honour
	I stand aloof, and will no reconcilement,
	Till by some elder masters of known honour
	I have a voice and precedent of peace,
	To keep my name ungored: but till that time,
	I do receive your offered love like love,
	And will not wrong it.
HAMLET	I embrace it freely,
	And will this brother's wager frankly play.
	Give us the foils, come on.
LAERTES	Come, one for me. 240
HAMLET	I'll be your foil, Laertes. In mine ignorance
	Your skill shall like a star i'th'darkest night
	Stick fiery off indeed.
LAERTES	You mock me, sir.
HAMLET	No, by, this hand.
KING	Give them the foils, young Osric.

> [Osric brings forward some four or five foils;
> Laertes takes one and makes a pass or two

	Cousin Hamlet,
	You know the wager?
HAMLET	Very well, my lord.
	Your grace has hid the odds o'th'weaker side.
KING	I do not fear it, I have seen you both –
	But since he is bettered, we have therefore odds.
LAERTES	This is too heavy: let me see another. 250

> [he goes to the table and brings from it
> the poisoned and unbated rapier

HAMLET	[takes a foil from Osric]
	This likes me well. These foils have all a length?
OSRIC	Ay, my good lord.

*The judges and attendants prepare the floor for the fence; Hamlet makes
ready; other servants bear in flagons of wine with cups*

KING	Set me the stoups of wine upon that table.
	If Hamlet give the first or second hit,
	Or quit in answer of the third exchange,

Let all the battlements their ordnance fire.
The king shall drink to Hamlet's better breath,
And in the cup an union shall he throw,
Richer than that which four successive kings
In Denmark's crown have worn: give me the cups,   26
And let the kettle to the trumpet speak,
The trumpet to the cannoneer without,
The cannons to the heavens, the heaven to earth,
'Now the king drinks to Hamlet.' Come, begin,
And you, the judges, bear a wary eye.

The cups are set at his side; trumpets sound;
Hamlet and Laertes take their stations

HAMLET   Come on, sir.
LAERTES   Come, my lord,

They play

HAMLET   One!
LAERTES   No.
HAMLET   Judgment?
OSRIC   A hit, a very palpable hit.
                    [they break off; the kettle-drum sounds, the trumpets blow,
                                        and a cannon-shot is heard without
LAERTES   Well, again.
KING   Stay, give me drink. Hamlet, this pearl is thine.
            Here's to thy health!   *[he drinks and then seems to cast*
                                                        the pearl into the cup
                            Give him the cup.   27
HAMLET   I'll play this bout first, set it by a while.
                            [the servant sets it on a table behind him
            Come.   *[they play again*
                    Another hit! What say you?
LAERTES   A touch, a touch, I do confess't.   *[they break off*
KING   Our son shall win.
QUEEN   He's fat, and scant of breath.
            Here, Hamlet, take my napkin, rub thy brows.
                            [she gives it him, and going to the table
                                        takes up his cup of wine
            The queen carouses to thy fortune, Hamlet.

HAMLET	Good madam!
KING	Gertrude, do not drink.
QUEEN	I will, my lord, I pray you pardon me.

[she drinks and offers the cup to Hamlet

KING	It is the poisoned cup, it is too late!
HAMLET	I dare not drink yet, madam – by and by. 280
QUEEN	Come, let me wipe thy face. *[she does so*
LAERTES	*[to the King]* My lord, I'll hit him now.
KING	I do not think't.
LAERTES	And yet 'tis almost 'gainst my conscience.
HAMLET	Come, for the third, Laertes. You do but dally,
	I pray you pass with your best violence.
	I am afeard you make a wanton of me.
LAERTES	Say you so? Come on.

They play the third bout

OSRIC	Nothing neither way. *[they break off*
LAERTES	*[suddenly]* Have at you now!

*[he takes Hamlet off his guard and wounds
him slightly; Hamlet enraged closes with
him, and 'in scuffling they change rapiers'*

KING	Part them, they are incensed.
HAMLET	*[attacks]* Nay, come again. *[the Queen falls*
OSRIC	Look to the queen there, ho! 290

[Hamlet wounds Laertes deeply

HORATIO	They bleed on both sides! – how is it, my lord?

[Laertes falls

OSRIC	*[tending him]* How is't, Laertes?
LAERTES	Why, as a woodcock to my own springe, Osric!
	I am justly killed with mine own treachery.
HAMLET	How does the queen?
KING	She swoons to see them bleed.
QUEEN	No, no, the drink, the drink – O my dear Hamlet –
	The drink, the drink! I am poisoned! *[she dies*
HAMLET	O villainy! Ho! Let the door be locked –
	Treachery! Seek it out.
LAERTES	It is here, Hamlet. Hamlet, thou art slain, 300
	No medicine in the world can do thee good,
	In thee there is not half an hour of life,

The treacherous instrument is in thy hand,
Unbated and envenomed. The foul practice
Hath turned itself on me, lo, here I lie,
Never to rise again – thy mother's poisoned –
I can no more – the king, the king's to blame.

HAMLET   The point envenomed too! –
Then, venom, to thy work.   [*he stabs the King*

ALL   Treason! treason!   3

KING   O, yet defend me, friends, I am but hurt.

HAMLET   Here, thou incestuous, murderous, damnéd Dane,
                                        [*he forces him to drink*
Drink off this potion. Is thy union here?
Follow my mother.   [*the King dies*

LAERTES   He is justly served,
It is a poison tempered by himself.
Exchange forgiveness with me, noble Hamlet,
Mine and my father's death come not upon thee,
Nor thine on me!   [*he dies*

HAMLET   Heaven make thee free of it! I follow thee.   [*he falls*
I am dead, Horatio. Wretched queen, adieu!   32
You that look pale and tremble at this chance,
That are but mutes or audience to this act,
Had I but time, as this fell sergeant, Death,
Is strict in his arrest, O, I could tell you –
But let it be; Horatio, I am dead,
Thou livest, report me and my cause aright
To the unsatisfied.

HORATIO   Never believe it;
I am more an antique Roman than a Dane –
Here's yet some liquor left.   [*he seizes the cup*

HAMLET   [*rises*]   As thou'rt a man,
Give me the cup, let go, by heaven I'll ha't!   3
                    [*he dashes the cup to the ground and falls back*
O God, Horatio, what a wounded name,
Things standing thus unknown, shall live behind me!
If thou didst ever hold me in thy heart,
Absent thee from felicity awhile,
And in this harsh world draw thy breath in pain,
To tell my story.

[*the tread of soldiers marching heard afar off,*
and later a shot; Osric goes out

What warlike noise is this?

OSRIC   [*returning*] Young Fortinbras, with conquest come
                                   from Poland,
    To th'ambassadors of England gives
    This warlike volley.

HAMLET   O, I die, Horatio,
    The potent poison quite o'er-crows my spirit,   340
    I cannot live to hear the news from England,
    But I do prophesy th'election lights
    On Fortinbras, he has my dying voice.
    So tell him, with th'occurrents more and less
    Which have solicited – the rest is silence.   [*he dies*

HORATIO   Now cracks a noble heart. Good night, sweet prince,
    And flights of angels sing thee to thy rest!
    Why does the drum come hither?

Prince FORTINBRAS, *the English ambassadors, and others enter*

FORT'BRAS Where is this sight?

HORATIO   What is it you would see?
    If aught of woe or wonder cease your search   350

FORT'BRAS This quarry cries on havoc. O proud death,
    What feast is toward in thine eternal cell,
    That thou so many princes at a shot
    So bloodily hast struck?

I AMBASS.   The sight is dismal,
    And our affairs from England come too late.
    The ears are senseless that should give us hearing,
    To tell him his commandment is fulfilled,
    That Rosencrantz and Guildenstern are dead.
    Where should we have our thanks?

HORATIO   Not from his mouth
    Had it th'ability of life to thank you;   360
    He never gave commandment for their death;
    But since, so jump upon this bloody question,
    You from the Polack wars, and you from England,
    Are here arrived, give order that these bodies
    High on a stage be placéd to the view,

And let me speak to th'yet unknowing world
How these things came about; so shall you hear
Of carnal, bloody and unnatural acts,
Of accidental judgments, casual slaughters,
Of deaths put on by cunning and forced cause,   3
And, in this upshot, purposes mistook
Fall'n on th'inventors' heads: all this can I
Truly deliver.

FORT'BRAS   Let us haste to hear it,
And call the noblest to the audience.
For me, with sorrow I embrace my fortune.
I have some rights of memory in this kingdom,
Which now to claim my vantage doth invite me.

HORATIO   Of that I shall have also cause to speak,
And from his mouth whose voice will draw on more.
But let this same be presently performed,   3
Even while men's minds are wild, lest more mischance
On plots and errors happen.

FORT'BRAS   Let four captains
Bear Hamlet like a soldier to the stage,
For he was likely, had he been put on,
To have proved most royal; and for his passage,
The soldiers' music and the rite of war
Speak loudly for him:
Take up the bodies – such a sight as this
Becomes the field, but here shows much amiss.
Go, bid the soldiers shoot.   3

The soldiers bear away the bodies, the while a dead march is heard;
'after the which a peal of ordnance is shot off'

OTHELLO

INTRODUCTION

The outline story of *Othello* is taken from the works of an Italian prose writer, Giambattista Cinthio Geraldi, published in 1564. Shakespeare also used Cinthio as his source for *Measure for Measure*, written at about the same time as *Othello*, around 1604. In Cinthio's story, an unnamed 'Moor', 'ensign' and 'corporal' stand for Othello, Iago and Cassio, although Desdemona is named. From this rather two-dimensional narrative, Shakespeare develops a complicated psychological portrait of jealousy and its effects, first performed at court before James I.

The play is the story of Othello, a black general in Venice who is renowned for his bravery and service to the state. Against her father's will, he marries Desdemona, and she immediately accompanies him to Cyprus, where it is feared the Turks are about to attack. Iago, Othello's companion, is passed over when the general makes Cassio his lieutenant. He engineers the downfall of Othello and Cassio by planting the seeds of suspicion about Desdemona's fidelity in Othello's fertile mind. Othello believes Desdemona has been unfaithful to him with Cassio, and the evidence, arranged by Iago with the inadvertent help of his wife Emilia, Desdemona's maid, seems to confirm his error. Othello smothers Desdemona, and then kills himself when he realises his mistake. Cassio becomes governor of Cyprus, and is left to decide the unrepentant Iago's punishment.

The most significant element of *Othello*, in literary-historical and plot terms, and in terms of its ongoing reception, is the blackness of its central character. On the stage, this fact cannot be overlooked, although it is possible to lose sight of it in reading the play. The cultural representation of blackness on which Shakespeare could draw dealt entirely in negative moral polarities: blackness was the property of the devil, the savage, the uncivilised. It was associated with sin, death, and villainy – and Shakespeare had not been averse to calling up these stereotypical associations in his characterisation of Aaron in *Titus Andronicus* (*c.*1593). Othello, however, offers a more complicated representation. Making a black man a hero was an intrepid development of the tragic form. The significance of Othello's colour cannot be overestimated, but its precise meanings are notoriously difficult to pin down. Certainly the play articulates, and seems to subvert, a conventional moral vocabulary which associated blackness with evil. As the Duke tells Brabantio, Desdemona's father, whose opposition to the match is entirely on racial grounds, 'your son-in-law is far more fair than black' (1.3.290), although for Brabantio, Othello is a 'sooty bosom' who has used 'foul charms' to ensnare his 'tender, fair, and happy' daughter and keep her from suitors 'of our nation' (1.2.66–71). Iago, Roderigo and Brabantio all voice their prejudices against Othello in racial terms, but the object of these remarks, Othello himself, is the representative of Venice in Cyprus, its loyal and decorated defender. Even Iago recognises Othello's 'free and open nature' (1.3.394) and uses this to plot his downfall. By contrast, it is Iago who is associated, particularly when his plotting is discovered, with the kind of qualities conventionally allied with and attributed to blackness: he is 'heathenish' (5.2.315) and 'hellish' (370). Clearly his terrible and destructive scheming is driven by a malevolence out of scale with his perceived slight by Othello over Cassio's promotion, even if his casual remark that ''twixt my sheets He's done my office' (1.3.382–83) is added to the supposed charges. In the representation of Othello and Iago, Shakespeare might be seen to have reversed stereotypical expectations that white equals good, black bad.

In another way, though, it seems that the stereotype is fulfilled. While Iago is single-minded in provoking Othello's jealousy, perhaps Othello must bear some of the responsibility also. Ultimately, he does kill his wife, at which Emilia calls him 'the blacker devil' (5.2.134). The justice of his own final self-exculpation is questionable: 'one that loved not wisely but too well' (5.2.346). Is Othello a stereotypical barbarian whose savagery is only thinly covered by Venetian manners, and whose excessive and uncontrollable jealousy prompts him to murder his innocent wife? Or is he an outsider, the black man grudgingly accepted for his military usefulness but under such personal pressure from a prejudiced society that he is particularly and tragically susceptible to Iago's provocation? Either way, the play seems to endorse the concept of blackness – as stereotypical moral inferiority, or as oppressed and brutalised minority – as crucial to any interpretation. For many modern readers, Othello emerges as the victim of prejudice, a representative sacrifice to the self-contained Venetian society whose agent is Iago. Shakespeare's Venice in *Othello*, as in *The Merchant of Venice*, is a seemingly cosmopolitan society policed by complex rules of incorporation and exclusion. Like Shylock, Othello is, ultimately, an outsider. It is likely that Venice functioned, on one level, as a kind of surrogate London in the dramatic geography of the late Elizabethan period, and, after reading *Othello*, it is no surprise to discover that, a couple of years before its first performances, Elizabeth I had formally banished from England all 'negars and blackamoors'. The play's representation of race has proved strikingly modern, and has tended to address contemporary racial concerns and attitudes. When the black actor Paul Robeson played the title role in a London production of the play in the 1930s, for example, he was not admitted to the hotel where the rest of the cast were celebrating. In the publicity for a 1995 film of the play (directed by Oliver Parker), parallels were drawn with the contemporaneous and public trial of the black American sportsman O. J. Simpson for the murder of his white girlfriend. One of the most interesting aspects of the play has to be its continued relevance to ongoing prejudices and racial politics.

Black and white are not the only polarities in the play, however, and not necessarily those which would have been most significant to its first audiences. The opposition between Christian Venice and Muslim ('infidel') Turkey is a crucial dynamic, and this geopolitical context extends the action beyond the claustrophobic, essentially domestic world of much of *Othello*. As long as Venice has Turkey as an external enemy against which it can unite, everything goes well enough. But the Turkish threat evaporates, thanks to a convenient storm, and the troops on Cyprus engage in drinking and mischief. 'Are we turned Turks?' thunders Othello, disturbed from the marital bed by his drunken soldiers. 'For Christian shame, put by this barbarous brawl' (2.3.157–59). It is cruelly apt that the *Oxford English Dictionary* includes among its definitions of the phrase 'to turn Turk' both anyone 'behaving as a barbarian or savage' and 'one who treats his wife hardly'. Suddenly barbarity is a threat from within, not without. Instead of being an externalised menace, it is insidiously ever-present. Iago personifies the enemy working within, but it is Othello himself who switches sides most startlingly. His final speech exemplifies the complex web of allegiances and social and cultural identities in which he is trapped. He likens himself to 'the base Indian' and then in a complex gesture of self-inscription and substitution, imagines his suicide as the act of the state's defender killing its enemy: 'in Aleppo once, Where a malignant and a turbaned Turk Beat a Venetian and traduced the state, I took by th'throat the circumcised dog And smote him – thus' (5.2.354–58). In this final act, Othello is the enemy and the victim within.

The play's insistence on reversals and revelations, on turning tables as well as Turks, rests on Iago, who speaks with uncanny skill to weaknesses and insecurities in those around him. Much psychologising about the play has focused on Iago's character, following Coleridge's influential statement of his 'motiveless malignity'. Iago's belief in his ruthless control over himself and others marks him as a distinctly modern dramatic subject. He asserts his own autonomy outside the structures of belief and hierarchy in which he refuses to be situated. Like gardeners, he argues, we each have responsibility for what grows in the soil of our character, for it is 'in ourselves that we are thus or thus' as 'the power and corrigible authority of this lies in our wills' (1.3.319–25). Iago is charismatic, and Cassio, Roderigo, and Othello himself, are all willing to respond to his force of personality. Othello's is a rather distant character, formal, unreachable, whereas Iago's tone is confiding, implicating, speaking in asides and soliloquies to the audience. In his asides, Iago operates both as a dramatic villain, like Richard III, or Edmund in *King Lear*, while his habit of soliloquising also links him with dramatic heroes like Hamlet or Macbeth. Othello, on the other hand, seems to be acted upon, rather than active. He takes the bait from Iago's hook, and all his actions, from his first appearance when he is summoned before the Duke's nocturnal council of war, seem to be dictated by others. Not until his suicide does he act autonomously, and even then, as has been seen, his sense of self is chronically fractured. Othello reacts; Iago acts. Othello's language is removed and oratorical; Iago soliloquises. Othello is a creature of the middle-stage, apparently unaware of his audience; Iago comes forward to fix us with an unsettlingly conspiratorial stare. For all Othello's tragic centrality in the plot, audience interest is largely located in Iago. Because we are given access to Iago's machiavellian plotting, we may lose sympathy with Othello's blind faith in his ensign, his unquestioning belief in 'honest Iago' and his willingness to accept the calumny against his new bride. He won Desdemona with his storytelling, and he commissions his own story, like so many tragic protagonists, in his dying speech. Othello is insistently self-dramatising but curiously uncertain of his own image. He recounts how he wooed Desdemona through his stories of himself, but he is then haunted by the fear that she loves an exotic idea of him rather than himself. His uncertainties make a gap into which Iago is able to insinuate his plots. Iago never voices any such self-doubt, and even when his role is discovered, he is unrepentant and unbroken.

Othello looks back and forward among Shakespeare's tragedies. Like *Romeo and Juliet*, it begins as a love story against a backdrop of a divided and sectarian society, and like that play, there is some hope that all may be well. (Shakespeare's apparent interest in this shift from comedy to tragedy is tellingly reversed in his revisiting of elements of the *Othello* story in *The Winter's Tale* (1611)). Like *Hamlet*, *Othello* has an element of the revenge tragedy, as Iago claims he is redressing wrongs done him by the Moor. The play looks forward, however, to the concerns of *King Lear* and *Macbeth* in its representation of the breakdown of its central personality. Othello undergoes a kind of mental collapse as all his worst fears seem to be realised, and he becomes his own destroyer. The extent to which he is a tragic victim, and the extent to which he is at least a partial architect of his downfall, are held in tension by the play and by critical reactions to it. *Othello* thus develops an idea of the tragic trajectory compelled by a destructive coalition of external and internal forces and agents: the external motor of *Romeo and Juliet* and the internal dynamic of *Hamlet* have been yoked together, as they will be again in *King Lear* and *Macbeth*.

The Scene: Venice; Cyprus

CHARACTERS IN THE PLAY

DUKE OF VENICE
BRABANTIO, *a senator, father to Desdemona*
Other Senators
GRATIANO, *brother to Brabantio*
LODOVICO, *kinsman to Brabantio*
OTHELLO, *a noble Moor in the service of the
    Venetian state*
CASSIO, *his lieutenant*
IAGO, *his ancient*
RODERIGO, *a Venetian gentleman*
MONTANO, *Othello's predecessor as governor
    of Cyprus*
Clown, servant to Othello

DESDEMONA, *daughter to Brabantio and wife
    to Othello*
EMILIA, *wife to Iago*
BIANCA, *mistress to Cassio*

*Sailor, Messenger, Herald, Officers, Gentlemen,
Musicians, and Attendants*

OTHELLO

ACT I SCENE I

Venice. A street

Enter RODERIGO *and* IAGO

RODERIGO Tush, never tell me; I take it much unkindly
That thou, Iago, who hast had my purse
As if the strings were thine, shouldst know of this.

IAGO 'Sblood, but you'll not hear me.
If ever I did dream of such a matter,
Abhor me.

RODERIGO Thou told'st me thou didst hold him in thy hate.

IAGO Despise me if I do not. Three great ones of the city,
In personal suit to make me his lieutenant,
Off-capped to him; and, by the faith of man,   10
I know my price: I am worth no worse a place.
But he, as loving his own pride and purposes,
Evades them with a bombast circumstance
Horribly stuffed with epithets of war;
And, in conclusion,
Nonsuits my mediators: for, 'Certes,' says he,
'I have already chose my officer.'
And what was he?
Forsooth, a great arithmetician,
One Michael Cassio, a Florentine,   20
A fellow almost damned in a fair wife,
That never set a squadron in the field,
Nor the division of a battle knows
More than a spinster – unless the bookish theoric,
Wherein the togéd consuls can propose
As masterly as he; mere prattle without practice
Is all his soldiership. But he, sir, had th'election;
And I, of whom his eyes had seen the proof
At Rhodes, at Cyprus, and on other grounds
Christian and heathen, must be be-lee'd and calmed   30
By debitor-and-creditor: this counter-caster,
He, in good time, must his lieutenant be,

	And I – God bless the mark! – His Moorship's ancient.
RODERIGO	By heaven, I rather would have been his hangman.
IAGO	Why, there's no remedy: 'tis the curse of service;
	Preferment goes by letter and affection,
	And not by old gradation, where each second
	Stood heir to th'first. Now, sir, be judge yourself
	Whether I in any just term am affined
	To love the Moor.
RODERIGO	I would not follow him then. 40
IAGO	O, sir, content you.
	I follow him to serve my turn upon him.
	We cannot all be masters, nor all masters
	Cannot be truly followed. You shall mark
	Many a duteous and knee-crooking knave
	That, doting on his own obsequious bondage,
	Wears out his time, much like his master's ass,
	For nought but provender, and, when he's old, cashiered.
	Whip me such honest knaves. Others there are
	Who, trimmed in forms and visages of duty, 50
	Keep yet their hearts attending on themselves;
	And, throwing but shows of service on their lords,
	Do well thrive by them; and, when they've lined
	their coats,
	Do themselves homage. These fellows have some soul,
	And such a one do I profess myself:
	For sir,
	It is as sure as you are Roderigo,
	Were I the Moor, I would not be Iago;
	In following him, I follow but myself;
	Heaven is my judge, not I for love and duty, 60
	But seeming so, for my peculiar end;
	For when my outward action doth demonstrate
	The native act and figure of my heart
	In compliment extern, 'tis not long after
	But I will wear my heart upon my sleeve
	For daws to peck at – I am not what I am.
RODERIGO	What a full fortune does the thick-lips owe,
	If he can carry't thus!
IAGO	Call up her father,

Rouse him, make after him, poison his delight,
Proclaim him in the streets, incense her kinsmen, 70
And, though he in a fertile climate dwell,
Plague him with flies; though that his joy be joy,
Yet throw such changes of vexation on't
As it may lose some colour.

RODERIGO Here is her father's house; I'll call aloud.

IAGO Do; with like timorous accent and dire yell
As when, by night and negligence, the fire
Is spied in populous cities.

RODERIGO What, ho, Brabantio! Signior Brabantio, ho!

IAGO Awake! What, ho, Brabantio! Thieves! Thieves! Thieves! 80
Look to your house, your daughter, and your bags!
Thieves! Thieves!

BRABANTIO *appears above, at a window*

BRABANTIO What is the reason of this terrible summons?
What is the matter there?

RODERIGO Signior, is all your family within?

IAGO Are your doors locked?

BRABANTIO   Why, wherefore ask you this?

IAGO 'Zounds, sir, you're robbed; for shame, put on
                                your gown;
Your heart is burst; you have lost half your soul;
Even now, now, very now, an old black ram
Is tupping your white ewe. Arise, arise; 90
Awake the snorting citizens with the bell,
Or else the devil will make a grandsire of you.
Arise, I say.

BRABANTIO   What, have you lost your wits?

RODERIGO Most reverend signior, do you know my voice?

BRABANTIO Not I; what are you?

RODERIGO My name is Roderigo.

BRABANTIO   The worser welcome:
I have charged thee not to haunt about my doors;
In honest plainness thou hast heard me say
My daughter is not for thee; and now, in madness,
Being full of supper and distempering draughts, 100
Upon malicious knavery dost thou come
To start my quiet.

RODERIGO Sir, sir, sir —

BRABANTIO   But thou must needs be sure
My spirit and my place have in them power
To make this bitter to thee.

RODERIGO   Patience, good sir.

BRABANTIO What tell'st thou me of robbing? This is Venice:
My house is not a grange.

RODERIGO   Most grave Brabantio,
In simple and pure soul I come to you.

IAGO 'Zounds, sir, you are one of those that will not serve
God, if the devil bid you. Because we come to do you 11
service and you think we are ruffians, you'll have your
daughter covered with a Barbary horse; you'll have
your nephews neigh to you; you'll have coursers for
cousins, and jennets for germans.

BRABANTIO What profane wretch art thou?

IAGO I am one, sir, that comes to tell you your daughter and
the Moor are now making the beast with two backs.

BRABANTIO Thou art a villain.

IAGO   You are a senator.

BRABANTIO This thou shalt answer; I know thee, Roderigo. 12

RODERIGO Sir, I will answer anything. But I beseech you,
If't be your pleasure and most wise consent,
As partly I find it is, that your fair daughter,
At this odd-even and dull watch o' th'night,
Transported with no worse nor better guard
But with a knave of common hire, a gondolier,
To the gross clasps of a lascivious Moor —
If this be known to you, and your allowance,
We then have done you bold and saucy wrong;
But if you know not this, my manners tell me 1.
We have your wrong rebuke. Do not believe
That, from the sense of all civility,
I thus would play and trifle with your reverence.
Your daughter, if you have not given her leave,
I say again, hath made a gross revolt,
Tying her duty, beauty, wit, and fortunes
In an extravagant and wheeling stranger
Of here and everywhere. Straight satisfy yourself.

If she be in her chamber or your house,
Let loose on me the justice of the state   140
For thus deluding you.

BRABANTIO   Strike on the tinder, ho!
Give me a taper! Call up all my people!
This accident is not unlike my dream;
Belief of it oppresses me already.
Light, I say! Light!   [he goes in

IAGO   Farewell, for I must leave you:
It seems not meet nor wholesome to my place
To be produced — as, if I stay, I shall —
Against the Moor; for I do know the state,
However this may gall him with some check,
Cannot with safety cast him; for he's embarked   150
With such loud reason to the Cyprus wars,
Which even now stand in act, that, for their souls,
Another of his fathom they have none
To lead their business: in which regard,
Though I do hate him as I do hell-pains,
Yet, for necessity of present life,
I must show out a flag and sign of love,
Which is indeed but sign. That you shall surely find him,
Lead to the Sagittary the raiséd search,
And there will I be with him. So farewell.   [he goes 160

Enter, below, BRABANTIO, *and Servants with torches*

BRABANTIO It is too true an evil: gone she is;
And what's to come of my despiséd time
Is nought but bitterness. Now, Roderigo,
Where didst thou see her? O unhappy girl!
With the Moor, say'st thou? Who would be a father!
How didst thou know 'twas she? O, she deceives me
Past thought! What said she to you? Get more tapers.
Raise all my kindred. Are they married, think you?
RODERIGO Truly, I think they are.
BRABANTIO O heaven! How got she out? O treason of the blood!   170
Fathers, from hence trust not your daughters' minds
By what you see them act! Is there not charms
By which the property of youth and maidhood
May be abused? Have you not read, Roderigo,

                    Of some such thing?
RODERIGO   Yes, sir, I have indeed.
BRABANTIO Call up my brother. O, that you had had her!
                    Some one way, some another. Do you know
                    Where we may apprehend her and the Moor?
RODERIGO I think I can discover him, if you please
                    To get good guard and go along with me.   180
BRABANTIO Pray you, lead on. At every house I'll call;
                    I may command at most. Get weapons, ho!
                    And raise some special officers of night.
                    On, good Roderigo; I'll deserve your pains.   [*they go*

SCENE 2

Another street

Enter OTHELLO, IAGO, *and Attendants with torches*

IAGO   Though in the trade of war I have slain men,
                    Yet do I hold it very stuff o'th'conscience
                    To do no contrived murder. I lack iniquity
                    Sometimes to do me service. Nine or ten times
                    I had thought t'have jerked him here under the ribs.
OTHELLO 'Tis better as it is.
IAGO   Nay, but he prated,
                    And spoke such scurvy and provoking terms
                    Against your honour
                    That, with the little godliness I have,
                    I did full hard forbear him. But I pray, sir,   10
                    Are you fast married? For be sure of this,
                    That the magnifico is much beloved,
                    And hath in his effect a voice potential
                    As double as the duke's. He will divorce you,
                    Or put upon you what restraint and grievance
                    The law, with all his might to enforce it on,
                    Will give him cable.
OTHELLO   Let him do his spite;
                    My services which I have done the signiory
                    Shall out-tongue his complaints. 'Tis yet to know –
                    Which, when I know that boasting is an honour,   20

I shall promulgate – I fetch my life and being
From men of royal siege; and my demerits
May speak unbonneted to as proud a fortune
As this that I have reached. For know, Iago,
But that I love the gentle Desdemona,
I would not my unhouséd free condition
Put into circumscription and confine
For the sea's worth. But look what lights come yond!

IAGO   Those are the raiséd father and his friends.
You were best go in.

OTHELLO   Not I; I must be found.   30
My parts, my title, and my perfect soul,
Shall manifest me rightly. Is it they?

IAGO   By Janus, I think no.

Enter CASSIO, *and certain Officers with torches*

OTHELLO   The servants of the duke, and my lieutenant!
The goodness of the night upon you, friends!
What is the news?

CASSIO   The duke does greet you, general,
And he requires your haste-post-haste appearance
Even on the instant.

OTHELLO   What is the matter, think you?

CASSIO   Something from Cyprus, as I may divine.
It is a business of some heat: the galleys   40
Have sent a dozen sequent messengers
This very night at one another's heels;
And many of the consuls, raised and met,
Are at the duke's already. You have been hotly
                               called for;
When, being not at your lodging to be found,
The senate hath sent about three several quests
To search you out.

OTHELLO   'Tis well I am found by you.
I will but spend a word here in the house,
And go with you.   [*he goes in*

CASSIO   Ancient, what makes he here?

IAGO   Faith, he tonight hath boarded a land carack;   50
If it prove lawful prize, he's made for ever.

CASSIO	I do not understand.
IAGO	He's married.
CASSIO	To who?

Re-enter OTHELLO

IAGO	Marry, to – Come, captain, will you go?
OTHELLO	Have with you.
CASSIO	Here comes another troop to seek for you.
IAGO	It is Brabantio. General, be advised;
	He comes to bad intent.

Enter BRABANTIO, RODERIGO, and Officers with torches and weapons

OTHELLO	Holla! Stand there!
RODERIGO	Signior, it is the Moor.
BRABANTIO	Down with him, thief!

[they draw on both sides

IAGO   You, Roderigo! Come sir, I am for you.

OTHELLO   Keep up your bright swords, for the dew will rust
                                                    them.
          Good signior, you shall more command with years   60
          Than with your weapons.

BRABANTIO O thou foul thief, where hast thou stowed my daughter?
          Damned as thou art, thou hast enchanted her.
          For I'll refer me to all things of sense,
          If she in chains of magic were not bound,
          Whether a maid so tender, fair, and happy,
          So opposite to marriage that she shunned
          The wealthy curléd darlings of our nation,
          Would ever have, t'incur a general mock,
          Run from her guardage to the sooty bosom   70
          Of such a thing as thou – to fear, not to delight.
          Judge me the world, if 'tis not gross in sense
          That thou hast practised on her with foul charms,
          Abused her delicate youth with drugs or minerals
          That weaken motion: I'll have't disputed on;
          'Tis probable and palpable to thinking.
          I therefore apprehend and do attach thee
          For an abuser of the world, a practiser
          Of arts inhibited and out of warrant.
          Lay hold upon him. If he do resist,   80

Subdue him at his peril.

OTHELLO   Hold your hands,
Both you of my inclining and the rest:
Were it my cue to fight, I should have known it
Without a prompter. Where will you that I go
To answer this your charge?

BRABANTIO   To prison, till fit time
Of law and course of direct session
Call thee to answer.

OTHELLO   What if I do obey?
How may the duke be therewith satisfied,
Whose messengers are here about my side,
Upon some present business of the state   90
To bring me to him?

I OFFICER   'Tis true, most worthy signior;
The duke's in council, and your noble self,
I am sure, is sent for.

BRABANTIO   How! The duke in council!
In this time of the night! Bring him away.
Mine's not an idle cause: the duke himself,
Or any of my brothers of the state,
Cannot but feel this wrong as 'twere their own;
For if such actions may have passage free,
Bond-slaves and pagans shall our statesmen be.

                            [they go

SCENE 3

A council-chamber

The DUKE *and Senators sitting at a table; Officers attending*

DUKE   There is no composition in these news
That gives them credit.

I SENATOR   Indeed they are disproportioned:
My letters say a hundred and seven galleys.

DUKE   And mine, a hundred and forty.

2 SENATOR   And mine, two hundred;
But though they jump not on a just account —
As in these cases where the aim reports

'Tis oft with difference – yet do they all confirm
A Turkish fleet, and bearing up to Cyprus.

DUKE Nay, it is possible enough to judgment;
I do not so secure me in the error,   10
But the main article I do approve
In fearful sense.

SAILOR [*without*]   What, ho! What, ho! What, ho!
1 OFFICER A messenger from the galleys.

Enter Sailor

DUKE   Now, what's the business?
SAILOR The Turkish preparation makes for Rhodes;
So was I bid report here to the state
By Signior Angelo.

DUKE How say you by this change?
1 SENATOR   This cannot be,
By no assay of reason; 'tis a pageant
To keep us in false gaze. When we consider
Th'importancy of Cyprus to the Turk,   20
And let ourselves again but understand
That, as it more concerns the Turk than Rhodes,
So may he with more facile question bear it,
For that it stands not in such warlike brace,
But altogether lacks th'abilities
That Rhodes is dressed in – if we make thought of this,
We must not think the Turk is so unskilful
To leave that latest which concerns him first,
Neglecting an attempt of ease and gain
To wake and wage a danger profitless.   30

DUKE Nay, in all confidence, he's not for Rhodes.
1 OFFICER Here is more news.

Enter a Messenger

MESSENGER The Ottomites, reverend and gracious,
Steering with due course toward the isle of Rhodes,
Have there injointed with an after fleet.

1 SENATOR Ay, so I thought. How many, as you guess?
MESSENGER Of thirty sail; and now they do re-stem
Their backward course, bearing with frank appearance
Their purposes toward Cyprus. Signior Montano,

Your trusty and most valiant servitor,   40
With his free duty recommends you thus,
And prays you to relieve him.

DUKE   'Tis certain then for Cyprus.
Marcus Luccicos, is not he in town?

I SENATOR He's now in Florence.

DUKE   Write from us to him; post-post-haste dispatch.

I SENATOR Here comes Brabantio and the valiant Moor.

Enter BRABANTIO, OTHELLO, IAGO, RODERIGO, *and Officers*

DUKE   Valiant Othello, we must straight employ you
Against the general enemy Ottoman.
[*to Brabantio*]
I did not see you; welcome, gentle signior;   50
We lacked your counsel and your help tonight.

BRABANTIO So did I yours. Good your grace, pardon me:
Neither my place nor aught I heard of business
Hath raised me from my bed, nor doth the general care
Take hold on me; for my particular grief
Is of so flood-gate and o'erbearing nature
That it engluts and swallows other sorrows,
And yet is still itself.

DUKE   Why, what's the matter?

BRABANTIO My daughter! O, my daughter!

ALL   Dead?

BRABANTIO   Ay, to me:
She is abused, stolen from me and corrupted   60
By spells and medicines bought of mountebanks;
For nature so preposterously to err,
Being not deficient, blind, or lame of sense,
Sans witchcraft could not.

DUKE   Whoe'er he be that in this foul proceeding
Hath thus beguiled your daughter of herself,
And you of her, the bloody book of law
You shall yourself read in the bitter letter
After your own sense, yea, though our proper son
Stood in your action.

BRABANTIO   Humbly I thank your grace.   70
Here is the man: this Moor, whom now, it seems,
Your special mandate for the state affairs

        Hath hither brought.

ALL   We are very sorry for't.

DUKE   [to Othello]
        What in your own part can you say to this?

BRABANTIO Nothing, but this is so.

OTHELLO Most potent, grave, and reverend signiors,
        My very noble and approved good masters,
        That I have ta'en away this old man's daughter,
        It is most true; true, I have married her:
        The very head and front of my offending   80
        Hath this extent, no more. Rude am I in my speech,
        And little blest with the soft phrase of peace:
        For since these arms of mine had seven years' pith
        Till now some nine moons wasted, they have used
        Their dearest action in the tented field;
        And little of this great world can I speak
        More than pertains to feats of broil and battle;
        And therefore little shall I grace my cause
        In speaking for myself. Yet, by your patience,
        I will a round unvarnished tale deliver   90
        Of my whole course of love: what drugs, what charms,
        What conjuration, and what mighty magic –
        For such proceedings I am charged withal –
        I won his daughter.

BRABANTIO   A maiden never bold;
        Of spirit so still and quiet that her motion
        Blushed at herself; and she – in spite of nature,
        Of years, of country, credit, everything –
        To fall in love with what she feared to look on!
        It is a judgment maimed and most imperfect
        That will confess perfection so could err   10
        Against all rules of nature, and must be driven
        To find out practices of cunning hell
        Why this should be. I therefore vouch again
        That with some mixtures powerful o'er the blood,
        Or with some dram conjured to this effect,
        He wrought upon her.

DUKE   To vouch this is no proof,
    Without more wider and more overt test

Than these thin habits and poor likelihoods
Of modern seeming do prefer against him.

I SENATOR But, Othello, speak: 110
Did you by indirect and forcéd courses
Subdue and poison this young maid's affections?
Or came it by request and such fair question
As soul to soul affordeth?

OTHELLO   I beseech you,
Send for the lady to the Sagittary,
And let her speak of me before her father;
If you do find me foul in her report,
The trust, the office I do hold of you,
Not only take away, but let your sentence
Even fall upon my life.

DUKE   Fetch Desdemona hither.   120

OTHELLO Ancient, conduct them; you best know the place.

                    [*Iago departs with attendants*

And till she come, as truly as to heaven
I do confess the vices of my blood,
So justly to your grave ears I'll present
How I did thrive in this fair lady's love,
And she in mine.

DUKE Say it, Othello.

OTHELLO Her father loved me, oft invited me,
Still questioned me the story of my life
From year to year – the battles, sieges, fortunes,   130
That I have passed.
I ran it through, even from my boyish days
To th' very moment that he bade me tell it:
Wherein I spake of most disastrous chances,
Of moving accidents by flood and field,
Of hair-breadth scapes i'th'imminent deadly breach,
Of being taken by the insolent foe,
And sold to slavery; of my redemption thence,
And portance in my travels' history:
Wherein of antres vast and deserts idle,   140
Rough quarries, rocks, and hills whose heads touch
                         heaven,
It was my hint to speak – such was the process;

And of the Cannibals that each other eat,
The Anthropophagi, and men whose heads
Do grow beneath their shoulders. This to hear
Would Desdemona seriously incline;
But still the house affairs would draw her thence,
Which ever as she could with haste dispatch
She'ld come again, and with a greedy ear
Devour up my discourse; which I observing,   15
Took once a pliant hour, and found good means
To draw from her a prayer of earnest heart
That I would all my pilgrimage dilate,
Whereof by parcels she had something heard,
But not intentively. I did consent,
And often did beguile her of her tears
When I did speak of some distressful stroke
That my youth suffered. My story being done,
She gave me for my pains a world of sighs:
She swore, in faith 'twas strange, 'twas passing strange;   160
'Twas pitiful, 'twas wondrous pitiful;
She wished she had not heard it, yet she wished
That heaven had made her such a man; she thanked me,
And bade me, if I had a friend that loved her,
I should but teach him how to tell my story,
And that would woo her. Upon this hint I spake;
She loved me for the dangers I had passed,
And I loved her that she did pity them.
This only is the witchcraft I have used.
Here comes the lady; let her witness it.   17

Enter DESDEMONA, IAGO, *and Attendants*

DUKE   I think this tale would win my daughter too.
            Good Brabantio,
            Take up this mangled matter at the best:
            Men do their broken weapons rather use
            Than their bare hands.

BRABANTIO   I pray you, hear her speak.
            If she confess that she was half the wooer,
            Destruction on my head, if my bad blame
            Light on the man! Come hither, gentle mistress:
            Do you perceive in all this company

Where most you owe obedience?

DESDEM.   My noble father,   180
I do perceive here a divided duty.
To you I am bound for life and education;
My life and education both do learn me
How to respect you. You are the lord of duty;
I am hitherto your daughter. But here's my husband;
And so much duty as my mother showed
To you, preferring you before her father,
So much I challenge that I may profess
Due to the Moor my lord.

BRABANTIO   God bu'y! I've done.
Please it your grace, on to the state affairs.   190
I had rather to adopt a child than get it.
Come hither, Moor:
I here do give thee that with all my heart,
Which, but thou hast already, with all my heart
I would keep from thee. For your sake, jewel,
I am glad at soul I have no other child;
For thy escape would teach me tyranny,
To hang clogs on them. I have done, my Lord.

DUKE   Let me speak like yourself, and say a sentence
Which, as a grise or step, may help these lovers   200
Into your favour.
When remedies are past, the griefs are ended
By seeing the worst, which late on hopes depended.
To mourn a mischief that is past and gone
Is the next way to draw new mischief on.
What cannot be preserved when Fortune takes,
Patience her injury a mockery makes.
The robbed that smiles steals something from the thief;
He robs himself that spends a bootless grief.

BRABANTIO So let the Turk of Cyprus us beguile,   210
We lose it not so long as we can smile.
He bears the sentence well that nothing bears
But the free comfort which from thence he hears;
But he bears both the sentence and the sorrow
That to pay grief must of poor patience borrow.
These sentences, to sugar or to gall,

Being strong on both sides, are equivocal.
But words are words: I never yet did hear
That the bruised heart was piercéd through the ear.
I humbly beseech you, proceed to th'affairs of state.   22

DUKE   The Turk with a most mighty preparation makes for
Cyprus. Othello, the fortitude of the place is best
known to you; and though we have there a substitute
of most allowed sufficiency, yet opinion, a sovereign
mistress of effects, throws a more safer voice on you:
you must therefore be content to slubber the gloss of
your new fortunes with this more stubborn and bois-
terous expedition.

OTHELLO   The tyrant Custom, most grave senators,
Hath made the flinty and steel couch of war   2:
My thrice-driven bed of down. I do agnize
A natural and prompt alacrity
I find in hardness; and do undertake
These present wars against the Ottomites.
Most humbly therefore bending to your state,
I crave fit disposition for my wife,
Due reference of place and exhibition,
With such accommodation and besort
As levels with her breeding.

DUKE   Why, if you please,
Be't at her father's.

BRABANTIO   I'll not have it so.   2.

OTHELLO   Nor I.

DESDEM.   Nor I; I would not there reside,
To put my father in impatient thoughts
By being in his eye. Most gracious duke,
To my unfolding lend your prosperous ear,
And let me find a charter in your voice
T'assist my simpleness.

DUKE   What would you, Desdemona?

DESDEM.   That I did love the Moor to live with him,
My downright violence and scorn of fortunes
May trumpet to the world. My heart's subdued   2
Even to the very quality of my lord.
I saw Othello's visage in his mind,

And to his honours and his valiant parts
Did I my soul and fortunes consecrate.
So that, dear lords, if I be left behind,
A moth of peace, and he go to the war,
The rights for why I love him are bereft me,
And I a heavy interim shall support
By his dear absence. Let me go with him.

OTHELLO Let her have your voice.   260
Vouch with me, heaven, I therefore beg it not
To please the palate of my appetite;
Nor to comply with heat and young affects
In my distinct and proper satisfaction;
But to be free and bounteous to her mind.
And heaven defend your good souls that you think
I will your serious and great business scant
For she is with me. No, when light-winged toys
Of feathered Cupid seel with wanton dullness
My speculative and officed instruments,   270
That my disports corrupt and taint my business,
Let housewives make a skillet of my helm,
And all indign and base adversities
Make head against my estimation!

DUKE Be it as you shall privately determine,
Either for her stay or going; th'affair cries haste,
And speed must answer it.

I SENATOR You must away tonight.

OTHELLO   With all my heart.

DUKE At nine i'th'morning here we'll meet again.
Othello, leave some officer behind,   280
And he shall our commission bring to you;
With such things else of quality and respect
As doth import you.

OTHELLO   So please your grace, my ancient:
A man he is of honesty and trust;
To his conveyance I assign my wife,
With what else needful your good grace shall think
To be sent after me.

DUKE   Let it be so.
Good night to everyone. And, noble signior,

     If virtue no delighted beauty lack,

     Your son-in-law is far more fair than black.   290

1 SENATOR Adieu, brave Moor; use Desdemona well.

BRABANTIO Look to her, Moor, if thou hast eyes to see:

     She has deceived her father, and may thee.

OTHELLO My life upon her faith! [*Duke, Senators, Officers, etc. go*

          Honest Iago,

     My Desdemona must I leave to thee;

     I prithee, let thy wife attend on her,

     And bring them after in the best advantage.

     Come, Desdemona, I have but an hour

     Of love, of worldly matter and direction,

     To spend with thee: we must obey the time.   300

         [*Othello and Desdemona go out*

RODERIGO Iago!

IAGO What say'st thou, noble heart?

RODERIGO What will I do, think'st thou?

IAGO Why, go to bed and sleep.

RODERIGO I will incontinently drown myself.

IAGO If thou dost, I shall never love thee after. Why, thou silly gentleman!

RODERIGO It is silliness to live when to live is torment; and then have we a prescription to die when death is our physician.   310

IAGO O villainous! I have looked upon the world for four times seven years; and since I could distinguish betwixt a benefit and an injury, I never found a man that knew how to love himself. Ere I would say I would drown myself for the love of a guinea-hen, I would change my humanity with a baboon.

RODERIGO What should I do? I confess it is my shame to be so fond, but it is not in my virtue to amend it.

IAGO Virtue! A fig! 'tis in ourselves that we are thus or thus. Our bodies are gardens, to the which our wills are 320 gardeners; so that if we will plant nettles or sow lettuce, set hyssop and weed up tine, supply it with one gender of herbs or distract it with many, either to have it sterile with idleness or manured with industry — why, the power and corrigible authority of this lies in our wills. If

the beam of our lives had not one scale of reason to
poise another of sensuality, the blood and baseness of
our natures would conduct us to most preposterous
conclusions. But we have reason to cool our raging
motions, our carnal stings, our unbitted lusts; whereof I   330
take this, that you call love, to be a set or scion.

RODERIGO It cannot be.

IAGO It is merely a lust of the blood and a permission of the
will. Come, be a man. Drown thyself! Drown cats and
blind puppies. I have professed me thy friend, and I
confess me knit to thy deserving with cables of
perdurable toughness. I could never better stead thee
than now. Put money in thy purse; follow thou these
wars; defeat thy favour with an usurped beard. I say,
put money in thy purse. It cannot be that Desdemona   340
should long continue her love to the Moor – put
money in thy purse – nor he his to her: it was a violent
commencement, and thou shalt see an answerable se-
questration – put but money in thy purse. These Moors
are changeable in their wills – fill thy purse with
money. The food that to him now is as luscious as
locusts, shall be to him shortly as bitter as coloquintida.
She must change for youth: when she is sated with his
body, she will find the error of her choice. Therefore
put money in thy purse. If thou wilt needs damn thy-   350
self, do it a more delicate way than drowning. Make all
the money thou canst. If sanctimony and a frail vow
betwixt an erring barbarian and a supersubtle Venetian
be not too hard for my wits and all the tribe of hell,
thou shalt enjoy her; therefore make money. A pox of
drowning thyself! 'Tis clean out of the way. Seek thou
rather to be hanged in compassing thy joy than to be
drowned and go without her.

RODERIGO Wilt thou be fast to my hopes, if I depend on the
issue?   360

IAGO Thou art sure of me. Go, make money. I have told thee
often, and I retell thee again and again, I hate the Moor.
My cause is hearted; thine hath no less reason. Let us be
conjunctive in our revenge against him. If thou canst

cuckold him, thou dost thyself a pleasure, me a sport.
There are many events in the womb of time, which will
be delivered. Traverse! Go; provide thy money. We
will have more of this tomorrow. Adieu.

RODERIGO Where shall we meet i'th'morning?

IAGO At my lodging. 370

RODERIGO I'll be with thee betimes.

IAGO Go to; farewell. Do you hear, Roderigo?

RODERIGO What say you?

IAGO No more of drowning, do you hear?

RODERIGO I am changed.

IAGO Go to; farewell. Put money enough in your purse.

RODERIGO I'll sell all my land. [goes

IAGO Thus do I ever make my fool my purse;
For I mine own gained knowledge should profane
If I would time expend with such a snipe 380
But for my sport and profit. I hate the Moor;
And it is thought abroad that 'twixt my sheets
He's done my office. I know not if't be true;
Yet I, for mere suspicion in that kind,
Will do as if for surety. He holds me well;
The better shall my purpose work on him.
Cassio's a proper man: let me see now;
To get his place, and to plume up my will
In double knavery. How? How? Let's see:
After some time to abuse Othello's ear 390
That he is too familiar with his wife;
He hath a person and a smooth dispose
To be suspected – framed to make women false.
The Moor is of a free and open nature
That thinks men honest that but seem to be so,
And will as tenderly be led by th'nose
As asses are.
I have't. It is engendered. Hell and night
Must bring this monstrous birth to the world's light.

[goes

ACT 2 SCENE I

A sea-port in Cyprus. An open place near the quay

Enter MONTANO *and two Gentlemen*

MONTANO What from the cape can you discern at sea?
I GENT'MAN Nothing at all: it is a high-wrought flood;
      I cannot 'twixt the heaven and the main
      Descry a sail.
MONTANO Methinks the wind hath spoke aloud at land;
      A fuller blast ne'er shook our battlements.
      If it hath ruffianed so upon the sea,
      What ribs of oak, when mountains melt on them,
      Can hold the mortise? What shall we hear of this?
2 GENT'MAN A segregation of the Turkish fleet: 10
      For do but stand upon the foaming shore,
      The chidden billow seems to pelt the clouds;
      The wind-shaked surge, with high and monstrous mane,
      Seems to cast water on the burning Bear,
      And quench the guards of th'ever-fixéd pole.
      I never did like molestation view
      On the enchaféd flood.
MONTANO   If that the Turkish fleet
      Be not ensheltered and embayed, they are drowned;
      It is impossible they bear it out.

Enter a third Gentleman

3 GENT'MAN News, lads! Our wars are done: 20
      The desperate tempest hath so banged the Turks
      That their designment halts. A noble ship of Venice
      Hath seen a grievous wreck and sufferance
      On most part of their fleet.
MONTANO How! Is this true?
3 GENT'MAN   The ship is here put in,
      A Veronesa; Michael Cassio,
      Lieutenant to the warlike Moor Othello,
      Is come on shore; the Moor himself at sea,
      And is in full commission here for Cyprus.

MONTANO	I am glad on't; 'tis a worthy governor. 30
3 GENT'MAN	But this same Cassio, though he speak of comfort
	Touching the Turkish loss, yet he looks sadly,
	And prays the Moor be safe; for they were parted
	With foul and violent tempest.
MONTANO	Pray heaven he be;
	For I have served him, and the man commands
	Like a full soldier. Let's to the sea-side, ho!
	As well to see the vessel that's come in
	As to throw out our eyes for brave Othello,
	Even till we make the main and th'aerial blue
	An indistinct regard.
3 GENT'MAN	Come, let's do so; 40
	For every minute is expectancy
	Of more arrivance.

Enter CASSIO

CASSIO	Thanks you, the valiant of this warlike isle,
	That so approve the Moor! O, let the heavens
	Give him defence against the elements,
	For I have lost him on a dangerous sea.
MONTANO	Is he well shipped?
CASSIO	His bark is stoutly timbered, and his pilot
	Of very expert and approved allowance;
	Therefore my hopes, not forfeited to death,
	Stand in bold cure. 50

[*a cry heard:* 'A sail, a sail, a sail!'

Enter a fourth Gentleman

CASSIO	What noise?
4 GENT'MAN	The town is empty; on the brow o'th'sea
	Stand ranks of people, and they cry 'A sail!'
CASSIO	My hopes do shape him for the Governor. [*guns heard*
2 GENT'MAN	They do discharge their shot of courtesy:
	Our friends at least.
CASSIO	I pray you, sir, go forth,
	And give us truth who 'tis that is arrived.
2 GENT'MAN	I shall. [*goes*
MONTANO	But, good lieutenant, is your general wived? 60
CASSIO	Most fortunately: he hath achieved a maid

That paragons description and wild fame;
One that excels the quirks of blazoning pens,
And in th'essential vesture of creation
Does tire the ingener.

Re-enter second Gentleman

                      How now! Who has put in?

2 GENT'MAN 'Tis one Iago, ancient to the general.

CASSIO   He's had most favourable and happy speed:
Tempests themselves, high seas, and howling winds,
The guttered rocks, and congregated sands,
Traitors insteeped to clog the guiltless keel,   70
As having sense of beauty, do omit
Their mortal natures, letting go safely by
The divine Desdemona.

MONTANO   What is she?

CASSIO   She that I spake of, our great captain's captain,
Left in the conduct of the bold Iago;
Whose footing here anticipates our thoughts
A se'nnight's speed. Great Jove, Othello guard,
And swell his sail with thine own powerful breath
That he may bless this bay with his tall ship,
Make love's quick pants in Desdemona's arms,   80
Give renewed fire to our extincted spirits,
And bring all Cyprus comfort.

Enter DESDEMONA, EMILIA, IAGO, RODERIGO, *and Attendants*

                      O, behold,
The riches of the ship is come on shore!
You men of Cyprus, let her have your knees.
Hail to thee, lady! And the grace of heaven,
Before, behind thee, and on every hand,
Enwheel thee round!

DESDEM.   I thank you, valiant Cassio.
What tidings can you tell me of my lord?

CASSIO   He is not yet arrived; nor know I aught
But that he's well and will be shortly here.   90

DESDEM.   O, but I fear – How lost you company?

CASSIO   The great contention of the sea and skies
Parted our fellowship. But, hark! A sail!

               [a cry heard, 'A sail, a sail!', *and then guns*

2 GENT.   They give their greeting to the citadel:
           This likewise is a friend.

CASSIO   See for the news.
                               [Gentleman goes
           Good ancient, you are welcome.
           [to Emilia]   Welcome, mistress.
           Let it not gall your patience, good Iago,
           That I extend my manners; 'tis my breeding
           That gives me this bold show of courtesy.   *[kisses her*

IAGO   Sir, would she give you so much of her lips   100
           As of her tongue she oft bestows on me,
           You'ld have enough.

DESDEM.   Alas, she has no speech.

IAGO   In faith, too much;
           I find it still when I have list to sleep.
           Marry, before your ladyship, I grant,
           She puts her tongue a little in her heart
           And chides with thinking.

EMILIA   You have little cause to say so.

IAGO   Come on, come on; you are pictures out of doors,
           bells in your parlours, wild-cats in your kitchens; saints   110
           in your injuries, devils being offended; players in your
           housewifery, and hussies in your beds.

DESDEM.   O, fie upon thee, slanderer!

IAGO   Nay, it is true, or else I am a Turk:
           You rise to play, and go to bed to work.

EMILIA   You shall not write my praise.

IAGO   No, let me not.

DESDEM.   What wouldst thou write of me, if thou shouldst
                                  praise me?

IAGO   O gentle lady, do not put me to't;
           For I am nothing if not critical.

DESDEM.   Come on, assay – There's one gone to the harbour?   120

IAGO   Ay, madam.

DESDEM.   I am not merry; but I do beguile
           The thing I am by seeming otherwise.
           Come, how wouldst thou praise me?

IAGO   I am about it; but indeed my invention comes from my

pate as birdlime does from frieze – it plucks out brains
and all. But my muse labours, and thus she is delivered.
If she be fair and wise, fairness and wit,
The one's for use, the other useth it.

DESDEM. Well praised! How if she be black and witty?   130

IAGO If she be black, and thereto have a wit,
She'll find a white that shall her blackness hit.

DESDEM. Worse and worse.

EMILIA How if fair and foolish?

IAGO She never yet was foolish that was fair;
For even her folly helped her to an heir.

DESDEM. These are old fond paradoxes to make fools laugh
i'th'alehouse. What miserable praise hast thou for her
that's foul and foolish?

IAGO There's none so foul, and foolish thereunto,   140
But does foul pranks which fair and wise ones do.

DESDEM. O heavy ignorance! Thou praisest the worst best. But
what praise couldst thou bestow on a deserving
woman indeed – one that in the authority of her merit
did justly put on the vouch of very malice?

IAGO She that was ever fair, and never proud,
Had tongue at will, and yet was never loud,
Never lacked gold, and yet went never gay,
Fled from her wish, and yet said 'Now I may';
She that, being angered, her revenge being nigh,   150
Bade her wrong stay, and her displeasure fly;
She that in wisdom never was so frail
To change the cod's head for the salmon's tail;
She that could think, and ne'er disclose her mind,
See suitors following, and not look behind;
She was a wight, if ever such wight were –

DESDEM. To do what?

IAGO To suckle fools and chronicle small beer.

DESDEM. O most lame and impotent conclusion! Do not learn of
him, Emilia, though he be thy husband. How say you,   160
Cassio? Is he not a most profane and liberal counsellor?

CASSIO He speaks home, madam. You may relish him more in
the soldier than in the scholar.

IAGO [aside] He takes her by the palm. Ay, well said, whisper.

With as little a web as this will I ensnare as great a fly
as Cassio. Ay, smile upon her, do; I will gyve thee in
thine own courtship. You say true: 'tis so, indeed. If
such tricks as these strip you out of your lieutenantry, it
had been better you had not kissed your three fingers
so oft, which now again you are most apt to play the sir 170
in. Very good; well kissed! An excellent courtesy! 'Tis
so, indeed. Yet again your fingers to your lips? Would
they were clyster-pipes for your sake!

[*trumpets within*

[*aloud*] The Moor! I know his trumpet.

CASSIO   'Tis truly so.
DESDEM.   Let's meet him and receive him.
CASSIO   Lo where he comes!

Enter OTHELLO *and Attendants*

OTHELLO   O my fair warrior!
DESDEM.   My dear Othello!
OTHELLO   It gives me wonder great as my content
To see you here before me. O my soul's joy!
If after every tempest come such calms,
May the winds blow till they have wakened death! 180
And let the labouring bark climb hills of seas
Olympus-high and duck again as low
As hell's from heaven! If it were now to die,
'Twere now to be most happy; for I fear,
My soul hath her content so absolute
That not another comfort like to this
Succeeds in unknown fate.
DESDEM.   The heavens forbid
But that our loves and comforts should increase
Even as our days do grow!
OTHELLO   Amen to that, sweet powers!
I cannot speak enough of this content: 190
It stops me here; it is too much of joy.
And this, and this, the greatest discords be   [*they kiss*
That e'er our hearts shall make!
IAGO   O, you are well tuned now! But I'll set down the pegs
that make this music, as honest as I am.
OTHELLO   Come, let's to the castle.

News, friends: our wars are done; the Turks are
                                                    drowned.
How does my old acquaintance of this isle?
Honey, you shall be well desired in Cyprus;
I have found great love amongst them. O my sweet,   200
I prattle out of fashion, and I dote
In mine own comfort. I prithee, good Iago,
Go to the bay, and disembark my coffers;
Bring thou the master to the citadel–
He is a good one, and his worthiness
Does challenge much respect. Come, Desdemona,
Once more well met at Cyprus.
                         [*all but Iago and Roderigo depart*

IAGO   Do thou meet me presently at the harbour. Come
          hither. If thou be'st valiant – as they say base men
          being in love have then a nobility in their natures   210
          more than is native to them – list me. The lieutenant
          tonight watches on the court of guard. First, I must tell
          thee this: Desdemona is directly in love with him.

RODERIGO With him! Why, 'tis not possible.

IAGO   Lay thy finger thus, and let thy soul be instructed.
          Mark me with what violence she first loved the Moor
          but for bragging and telling her fantastical lies. And will
          she love him still for prating? – Let not thy discreet
          heart think it. Her eye must be fed; and what delight
          shall she have to look on the devil? When the blood is   220
          made dull with the act of sport, there should be – again
          to inflame it and to give satiety a fresh appetite –
          loveliness in favour, sympathy in years, manners, and
          beauties; all which the Moor is defective in. Now, for
          want of these required conveniencies, her delicate ten-
          derness will find itself abused, begin to heave the gorge,
          disrelish and abhor the Moor. Very nature will instruct
          her in it and compel her to some second choice. Now,
          sir, this granted – as it is a most pregnant and unforced
          position – who stands so eminent in the degree of this   230
          fortune as Cassio does? – A knave very voluble; no
          further conscionable than in putting on the mere form
          of civil and humane seeming, for the better compassing

of his salt and most hidden loose affection. Why, none;
why, none – a slipper and subtle knave; a finder-out of
occasions; that has an eye can stamp and counterfeit
advantages, though true advantage never present itself;
a devilish knave! Besides, the knave is handsome,
young, and hath all those requisites in him that folly
and green minds look after; a pestilent complete knave; 24
and the woman hath found him already.

RODERIGO I cannot believe that in her; she's full of most blest
condition.

IAGO Blest fig's-end! The wine she drinks is made of grapes.
If she had been blest, she would never have loved the
Moor. Blest pudding! Didst thou not see her paddle
with the palm of his hand? Didst not mark that?

RODERIGO Yes, that I did; but that was but courtesy.

IAGO Lechery, by this hand; an index and obscure prologue
to the history of lust and foul thoughts. They met so 25
near with their lips that their breaths embraced together – villanous thoughts, Roderigo! When these
mutualities so marshal the way, hard at hand comes the
master and main exercise, th'incorporate conclusion.
Pish! But, sir, be you ruled by me. I have brought you
from Venice. Watch you tonight; for the command,
I'll lay't upon you. Cassio knows you not; I'll not be
far from you. Do you find some occasion to anger
Cassio, either by speaking too loud or tainting his
discipline, or from what other course you please which 26
the time shall more favourably minister.

RODERIGO Well.

IAGO Sir, he's rash and very sudden in choler, and haply may
strike at you – provoke him that he may; for even out
of that will I cause these of Cyprus to mutiny, whose
qualification shall come into no true taste again but by
the displanting of Cassio. So shall you have a shorter
journey to your desires by the means I shall then have
to prefer them, and the impediment most profitably
removed, without the which there were no expectation 27
of our prosperity.

RODERIGO I will do this, if you can bring it to any opportunity.

IAGO	I warrant thee. Meet me by and by at the citadel. I must fetch his necessaries ashore. Farewell.
RODERIGO	Adieu. *[goes*
IAGO	That Cassio loves her, I do well believe't;

That she loves him, 'tis apt and of great credit.
The Moor, howbeit that I endure him not,
Is of a constant, loving, noble nature;
And I dare think he'll prove to Desdemona   280
A most dear husband. Now, I do love her too,
Not out of absolute lust – though peradventure
I stand accountant for as great a sin –
But partly led to diet my revenge
For that I do suspect the lusty Moor
Hath leaped into my seat, the thought whereof
Doth like a poisonous mineral gnaw my inwards;
And nothing can or shall content my soul
Till I am evened with him, wife for wife;
Or failing so, yet that I put the Moor   290
At least into a jealousy so strong
That judgment cannot cure. Which thing to do,
If this poor trash of Venice, whom I leash
For his quick hunting, stand the putting on,
I'll have our Michael Cassio on the hip,
Abuse him to the Moor in the rank garb –
For I fear Cassio with my night-cap too –
Make the Moor thank me, love me, and reward me,
For making him egregiously an ass,
And practising upon his peace and quiet   300
Even to madness. 'Tis here, but yet confused;
Knavery's plain face is never seen till used.   *[goes*

SCENE 2

A street

Enter a Herald with a proclamation; people following

HERALD   It is Othello's pleasure, our noble and valiant general,
that, upon certain tidings now arrived importing the
mere perdition of the Turkish fleet, every man put
himself into triumph; some to dance, some to make
bonfires, each man to what sport and revels his addic-
tion leads him: for, besides these beneficial news, it is
the celebration of his nuptial. So much was his pleasure
should be proclaimed. All offices are open, and there is
full liberty of feasting from this present hour of five till
the bell have told eleven. Heaven bless the isle of 10
Cyprus and our noble general Othello!   [*he moves on*

SCENE 3

A hall in the citadel

Enter OTHELLO, DESDEMONA, CASSIO, *and Attendants*

OTHELLO   Good Michael, look you to the guard tonight.
             Let's teach ourselves that honourable stop,
             Not to outsport discretion.

CASSIO   Iago hath direction what to do;
             But notwithstanding with my personal eye
             Will I look to't.

OTHELLO   Iago is most honest.
             Michael, good night; tomorrow with your earliest
             Let me have speech with you. Come, my dear love,
             The purchase made, the fruits are to ensue;
             That profit's yet to come 'tween me and you.   10
             Good night.

                [*Othello, Desdemona, and Attendants depart*

Enter IAGO

CASSIO   Welcome, Iago; we must to the watch.

IAGO	Not this hour, lieutenant; 'tis not yet ten o'clock. Our general cast us thus early for the love of his Desdemona; who let us not therefore blame: he hath not yet made wanton the night with her, and she is sport for Jove.
CASSIO	She's a most exquisite lady.
IAGO	And, I'll warrant her, full of game.
CASSIO	Indeed she's a most fresh and delicate creature.
IAGO	What an eye she has! Methinks it sounds a parley to 20 provocation.
CASSIO	An inviting eye; and yet methinks right modest.
IAGO	And when she speaks, is it not an alarum to love?
CASSIO	She is indeed perfection.
IAGO	Well, happiness to their sheets! Come, lieutenant, I have a stoup of wine; and here without are a brace of Cyprus gallants that would fain have a measure to the health of black Othello.
CASSIO	Not tonight, good Iago; I have very poor and unhappy brains for drinking. I could well wish courtesy would 30 invent some other custom of entertainment.
IAGO	O, they are our friends — but one cup; I'll drink for you.
CASSIO	I have drunk but one cup tonight, and that was craftily qualified too, and behold what innovation it makes here. I am unfortunate in the infirmity and dare not task my weakness with any more.
IAGO	What, man! 'Tis a night of revels; the gallants desire it.
CASSIO	Where are they?
IAGO	Here at the door; I pray you, call them in. 40
CASSIO	I'll do't; but it dislikes me. [goes
IAGO	If I can fasten but one cup upon him, With that which he hath drunk tonight already, He'll be as full of quarrel and offence As my young mistress' dog. Now my sick fool Roderigo, Whom love hath turned almost the wrong side out, To Desdemona hath tonight caroused Potations pottle-deep; and he's to watch. Three else of Cyprus, noble swelling spirits, That hold their honours in a wary distance, 50 The very elements of this warlike isle,

Have I tonight flustered with flowing cups;
And they watch too. Now, 'mongst this flock of
                                                    drunkards,
Am I to put our Cassio in some action
That may offend the isle. But here they come;
If consequence do but approve my dream,
My boat sails freely, both with wind and stream.

Re-enter CASSIO; *with him* MONTANO *and Gentlemen; Servants*
following with wine

CASSIO   'Fore God, they have given me a rouse already.
MONTANO   Good faith, a little one; not past a pint, as I am a soldier.
IAGO   Some wine, ho!   60
             [*sings*] And let me the canakin clink, clink;
                        And let me the canakin clink;
                           A soldier's a man;
                           O, man's life's but a span;
                        Why, then, let a soldier drink.
             Some wine, boys!
CASSIO   'Fore God, an excellent song.
IAGO   I learned it in England, where indeed they are most
             potent in potting; your Dane, your German, and your
             swag-bellied Hollander – drink, ho! – Are nothing to   70
             your English.
CASSIO   Is your Englishman so exquisite in his drinking?
IAGO   Why, he drinks you with facility your Dane dead drunk;
             he sweats not to overthrow your Almain; he gives your
             Hollander a vomit ere the next pottle can be filled.
CASSIO   To the health of our general!
MONTANO   I am for it, lieutenant, and I'll do you justice.
IAGO   O sweet England!
             [*sings*] King Stephen was and-a worthy peer,
                        His breeches cost him but a crown;   80
                        He held them sixpence all too dear,
                        With that he called the tailor lown.

                        He was a wight of high renown,
                        And thou art but of low degree;
                        'Tis pride that pulls the country down;
                        Then take thy auld cloak about thee.

	Some wine, ho!	
CASSIO	Why, this is a more exquisite song than the other.	
IAGO	Will you hear't again?	
CASSIO	No; for I hold him to be unworthy of his place that	90
	does those things. Well, God's above all; and there be	
	souls must be saved, and there be souls must not be	
	saved.	
IAGO	It's true, good lieutenant.	
CASSIO	For mine own part – no offence to the general, nor any	
	man of quality – I hope to be saved.	
IAGO	And so do I too, lieutenant.	
CASSIO	Ay, but, by your leave, not before me; the lieutenant is	
	to be saved before the ancient. Let's have no more of	
	this; let's to our affairs. God forgive us our sins! Gentle-	100
	men, let's look to our business. Do not think,	
	gentlemen, I am drunk; this is my ancient; this is my	
	right hand, and this is my left hand. I am not drunk	
	now: I can stand well enough, and I speak well enough.	
ALL	Excellent well.	
CASSIO	Why, very well then; you must not think then that I	
	am drunk. [*goes out*	
MONTANO	To th'platform, masters; come, let's set the watch.	
IAGO	You see this fellow that is gone before:	
	He is a soldier fit to stand by Caesar	110
	And give direction; and do but see his vice –	
	'Tis to his virtue a just equinox,	
	The one as long as th'other. 'Tis pity of him.	
	I fear the trust Othello puts him in,	
	On some odd time of his infirmity,	
	Will shake this island.	
MONTANO	But is he often thus?	
IAGO	'Tis evermore the prologue to his sleep:	
	He'll watch the horologe a double set,	
	If drink rock not his cradle.	
MONTANO	It were well	
	The general were put in mind of it.	120
	Perhaps he sees it not, or his good nature	
	Prizes the virtue that appears in Cassio,	
	And looks not on his evil: is not this true?	

Enter RODERIGO

IAGO   How, now, Roderigo!
          I pray you, after the lieutenant; go.   [*Roderigo goes*

MONTANO And 'tis great pity that the noble Moor
          Should hazard such a place as his own second
          With one of an ingraft infirmity:
          It were an honest action to say
          So to the Moor.

IAGO   Not I, for this fair island: 130
          I do love Cassio well, and would do much
          To cure him of this evil.   [*a cry within*, 'Help! Help!'
                       But hark! What noise?

Re-enter CASSIO, *pursuing* RODERIGO

CASSIO   'Zounds, you rogue, you rascal!

MONTANO What's the matter, lieutenant?

CASSIO   A knave teach me my duty! I'll beat the knave
          Into a twiggen bottle.

RODERIGO   Beat me!

CASSIO   Dost prate, rogue?
                         [*striking Roderigo*

MONTANO Nay, good lieutenant; pray sir, hold your hand.

CASSIO   Let go, sir, or I'll knock you o'er the mazard.

MONTANO Come, come, you're drunk.

CASSIO   Drunk!   [*they fight* 140

IAGO   Away, I say; go out and cry a mutiny.   [*Roderigo goes*
          [*aloud*] Nay, good lieutenant! God's will, gentlemen!
          Help, ho! – lieutenant – sir – Montano – sir –
          Help, masters! – Here's a goodly watch indeed!
                       [*a bell rings*
          Who's that that rings the bell? – Diablo, ho!
          The town will rise. God's will, lieutenant, hold;
          You will be shamed for ever.

Re-enter OTHELLO *and Attendants*

OTHELLO What is the matter here?

MONTANO   'Zounds, I bleed still.
          I am hurt to th'death. He dies.   [*assailing Cassio again*

OTHELLO   Hold, for your lives!

IAGO   Hold, ho! Lieutenant – sir – Montano – gentlemen –   150

	Have you forgot all sense of place and duty?
	The general speaks to you; hold, hold, for shame!
OTHELLO	Why, how now, ho! From whence ariseth this?

OTHELLO Why, how now, ho! From whence ariseth this?
Are we turned Turks, and to ourselves do that
Which heaven hath forbid the Ottomites?
For Christian shame, put by this barbarous brawl.
He that stirs next to carve for his own rage
Holds his soul light; he dies upon his motion.
Silence that dreadful bell; it frights the isle
From her propriety. What is the matter, masters?   160
Honest Iago, that look'st dead with grieving,
Speak who began this; on thy love, I charge thee.

IAGO I do not know. Friends all but now, even now,
In quarter and in terms like bride and groom
Divesting them for bed; and then, but now,
As if some planet had unwitted men,
Swords out, and tilting one at other's breast,
In opposition bloody. I cannot speak
Any beginning to this peevish odds;
And would in action glorious I had lost   170
Those legs that brought me to a part of it!

OTHELLO How comes it, Michael, you are thus forgot?

CASSIO I pray you, pardon me; I cannot speak.

OTHELLO Worthy Montano, you were wont be civil;
The gravity and stillness of your youth
The world hath noted, and your name is great
In mouths of wisest censure: what's the matter
That you unlace your reputation thus,
And spend your rich opinion for the name
Of a night-brawler? Give me answer to it.   180

MONTANO Worthy Othello, I am hurt to danger;
Your officer, Iago, can inform you –
While I spare speech, which something now
                        offends me –
Of all that I do know; nor know I aught
By me that's said or done amiss this night –
Unless self-charity be sometimes a vice,
And to defend ourselves it be a sin
When violence assails us.

OTHELLO   Now, by heaven,
My blood begins my safer guides to rule,
And passion, having my best judgment collied,   19
Assays to lead the way. If I once stir,
Or do but lift this arm, the best of you
Shall sink in my rebuke. Give me to know
How this foul rout began, who set it on,
And he that is approved in this offence,
Though he had twinned with me, both at a birth,
Shall lose me. What! In a town of war,
Yet wild, the people's hearts brimful of fear,
To manage private and domestic quarrel,
In night, and on the court and guard of safety!   20
'Tis monstrous. Iago, who began't?
MONTANO If partially affined, or leagued in office,
Thou dost deliver more or less than truth,
Thou art no soldier.
IAGO   Touch me not so near;
I had rather have this tongue cut from my mouth
Than it should do offence to Michael Cassio;
Yet, I persuade myself, to speak the truth
Shall nothing wrong him. This it is, general.
Montano and myself being in speech,
There comes a fellow crying out for help,   21
And Cassio following with determined sword
To execute upon him. Sir, this gentleman
Steps in to Cassio and entreats his pause;
Myself the crying fellow did pursue,
Lest by his clamour – as it so fell out –
The town might fall in fright; he, swift of foot,
Outran my purpose; and I returned the rather
For that I heard the clink and fall of swords,
And Cassio high in oath; which till tonight
I ne'er might say before. When I came back –   22
For this was brief – I found them close together
At blow and thrust; even as again they were
When you yourself did part them.
More of this matter can I not report;
But men are men; the best sometimes forget.

Though Cassio did some little wrong to him,
As men in rage strike those that wish them best,
Yet surely Cassio, I believe, received
From him that fled some strange indignity,
Which patience could not pass.

OTHELLO   I know, Iago,   230
Thy honesty and love doth mince this matter,
Making it light to Cassio. Cassio, I love thee;
But never more be officer of mine.

           Re-enter DESDEMONA, *attended*

Look if my gentle love be not raised up!
I'll make thee an example.

DESDEM.   What's the matter?

OTHELLO   All's well, dear sweeting; come away to bed.
Sir, for your hurts, myself will be your surgeon.
              [*they lead Montano away*
Iago, look with care about the town,
And silence those whom this vile brawl distracted.
Come, Desdemona: 'tis the soldiers' life   240
To have their balmy slumbers waked with strife.
         [*all but Iago and Cassio depart*

IAGO   What, are you hurt, lieutenant?

CASSIO   Ay, past all surgery.

IAGO   Marry, heaven forbid!

CASSIO   Reputation, reputation, reputation! O, I have lost my
reputation! I have lost the immortal part of myself,
and what remains is bestial. My reputation, Iago, my
reputation!

IAGO   As I am an honest man, I thought you had received
some bodily wound; there is more sense in that than in 250
reputation. Reputation is an idle and most false imposi-
tion; oft got without merit and lost without deserving.
You have lost no reputation at all, unless you repute
yourself such a loser. What, man! There are ways to
recover the general again. You are but now cast in his
mood, a punishment more in policy than in malice;
even so as one would beat his offenceless dog to affright
an imperious lion. Sue to him again, and he's yours.

CASSIO   I will rather sue to be despised than to deceive so good a

commander with so light, so drunken, and so indiscreet 2•
an officer. Drunk! And speak parrot! And squabble!
Swagger! Swear! And discourse fustian with one's own
shadow! O thou invisible spirit of wine, if thou hast no
name to be known by, let us call thee devil!

IAGO   What was he that you followed with your sword?
         What had he done to you?

CASSIO   I know not.

IAGO   Is't possible?

CASSIO   I remember a mass of things, but nothing distinctly; a
         quarrel, but nothing wherefore. O, that men should 2•
         put an enemy in their mouths to steal away their
         brains! That we should, with joy, pleasance, revel and
         applause, transform ourselves into beasts!

IAGO   Why, but you are now well enough. How came you
         thus recovered?

CASSIO   It hath pleased the devil drunkenness to give place to
         the devil wrath: one unperfectness shows me another,
         to make me frankly despise myself.

IAGO   Come, you are too severe a moraller. As the time, the
         place, and the condition of this country stands, I could 2•
         heartily wish this had not befallen; but since it is as it
         is, mend it for your own good.

CASSIO   I will ask him for my place again; he shall tell me I am a
         drunkard! Had I as many mouths as Hydra, such an
         answer would stop them all. To be now a sensible man,
         by and by a fool, and presently a beast! O strange! Every
         inordinate cup is unblest, and the ingredience is a devil.

IAGO   Come, come, wine is a good familiar creature, if it be
         well used; exclaim no more against it. And, good
         lieutenant, I think you think I love you.   2•

CASSIO   I have well approved it, sir. I drunk!

IAGO   You or any man living may be drunk at a time. I'll tell
         you what you shall do. Our general's wife is now the
         general: I may say so in this respect, for that he hath
         devoted and given up himself to the contemplation,
         mark and denotement of her parts and graces. Confess
         yourself freely to her; importune her help to put you in
         your place again. She is of so free, so kind, so apt, so

blessed a disposition, she holds it a vice in her goodness
not to do more than she is requested. This broken joint 300
between you and her husband entreat her to splinter;
and, my fortunes against any lay worth naming, this
crack of your love shall grow stronger than it was before.

CASSIO You advise me well.

IAGO I protest, in the sincerity of love and honest kindness.

CASSIO I think it freely; and betimes in the morning I will
beseech the virtuous Desdemona to undertake for me.
I am desperate of my fortunes if they check me here.

IAGO You are in the right. Good night, lieutenant; I must to
the watch. 310

CASSIO Good night, honest Iago. [goes

IAGO And what's he then that says I play the villain,
When this advice I give is free and honest,
Probal to thinking, and indeed the course
To win the Moor again? For 'tis most easy
Th'inclining Desdemona to subdue
In any honest suit. She's framed as fruitful
As the free elements. And then for her
To win the Moor, were't to renounce his baptism,
All seals and symbols of redeeméd sin, 320
His soul is so enfettered to her love
That she may make, unmake, do what she list,
Even as her appetite shall play the god
With his weak function. How am I then a villain
To counsel Cassio to this parallel course,
Directly to his good? Divinity of hell!
When devils will the blackest sins put on,
They do suggest at first with heavenly shows,
As I do now; for while this honest fool
Plies Desdemona to repair his fortunes, 330
And she for him pleads strongly to the Moor,
I'll pour this pestilence into his ear,
That she repeals him for her body's lust;
And by how much she strives to do him good,
She shall undo her credit with the Moor.
So will I turn her virtue into pitch,
And out of her own goodness make the net

That shall enmesh them all.

Enter RODERIGO

                          How now, Roderigo!

RODERIGO I do follow here in the chase, not like a hound that
hunts, but one that fills up the cry. My money is 3.
almost spent; I have been tonight exceedingly well
cudgelled; and I think the issue will be, I shall have so
much experience for my pains; and so, with no money
at all and a little more wit, return again to Venice.

IAGO   How poor are they that have not patience!
What wound did ever heal but by degrees?
Thou know'st we work by wit and not by witchcraft,
And wit depends on dilatory time.
Does't not go well? Cassio hath beaten thee,
And thou by that small hurt hast cashiered Cassio. 3.
Though other things grow fair against the sun,
Yet fruits that blossom first will first be ripe.
Content thyself awhile. By th'mass, 'tis morning;
Pleasure and action make the hours seem short.
Retire thee; go where thou art billeted.
Away, I say; thou shalt know more hereafter.
Nay, get thee gone.   *[Roderigo goes*
                 Two things are to be done:
My wife must move for Cassio to her mistress –
I'll set her on –
Myself the while to draw the Moor apart, 3
And bring him jump when he may Cassio find
Soliciting his wife. Ay, that's the way;
Dull not device by coldness and delay.   *[goes*

ACT 3 SCENE 1

The citadel. Outside Othello's lodging

Enter CASSIO *and some Musicians*

CASSIO   Masters, play here; I will content your pains; Something
              that's brief; and bid 'Good morrow, general'.   [*music*

Enter Clown

CLOWN   Why, masters, have your instruments been in Naples,
              that they speak i'th'nose thus?

1 MUSIC'N   How, sir, how?

CLOWN   Are these, I pray you, wind instruments?

1 MUSIC'N   Ay, marry, are they, sir.

CLOWN   O, thereby hangs a tail.

1 MUSIC'N   Whereby hangs a tale, sir?

CLOWN   Marry, sir, by many a wind instrument that I know.   10
              But, masters, here's money for you! And the general so
              likes your music, that he desires you, for love's sake, to
              make no more noise with it.

1 MUSIC'N   Well, sir, we will not.

CLOWN   If you have any music that may not be heard, to't
              again; but, as they say, to hear music the general does
              not greatly care.

1 MUSIC'N   We have none such, sir.

CLOWN   Then put up your pipes in your bag, for I'll away. Go;
              vanish into air; away!   [*Musicians go* 20

CASSIO   Dost thou hear, my honest friend?

CLOWN   No, I hear not your honest friend; I hear you.

CASSIO   Prithee, keep up thy quillets. There's a poor piece of gold
              for thee: if the gentlewoman that attends the general's
              wife be stirring, tell her there's one Cassio entreats her a
              little favour of speech. Wilt thou do this?

CLOWN   She is stirring, sir; if she will stir hither, I shall seem to
              notify unto her.

CASSIO   Do, good my friend.   [*Clown goes*

Enter IAGO

              In happy time, Iago.

IAGO   You have not been abed then?   30
CASSIO   Why, no; the day had broke before we parted.
            I have made bold, Iago,
            To send in to your wife: my suit to her
            Is that she will to virtuous Desdemona
            Procure me some access.
IAGO   I'll send her to you presently;
            And I'll devise a mean to draw the Moor
            Out of the way, that your converse and business
            May be more free.
CASSIO   I humbly thank you for't.   [*Iago goes*
                              I never knew
            A Florentine more kind and honest.   40

                        Enter EMILIA

EMILIA   Good morrow, good lieutenant: I am sorry
            For your displeasure; but all will sure be well.
            The general and his wife are talking of it,
            And she speaks for you stoutly. The Moor replies
            That he you hurt is of great fame in Cyprus
            And great affinity, and that in wholesome wisdom
            He might not but refuse you; but he protests he
                                            loves you,
            And needs no other suitor but his liking
            To take the safest occasion by the front
            To bring you in again.
CASSIO   Yet, I beseech you,   50
            If you think fit, or that it may be done,
            Give me advantage of some brief discourse
            With Desdemon alone.
EMILIA   Pray you, come in;
            I will bestow you where you shall have time
            To speak your bosom freely.
CASSIO   I am much bound to you.
                                                    [*they go*

SCENE 2

A room in the citadel

Enter OTHELLO, IAGO, *and Gentlemen*

OTHELLO These letters give, Iago, to the pilot,
And by him do my duties to the senate.
That done, I will be walking on the works;
Repair there to me.

IAGO   Well, my good lord, I'll do't. [*goes*

OTHELLO This fortification, gentlemen, shall we see't?

GENT'MEN We'll wait upon your lordship.   [*they go*

SCENE 3

Before the citadel

Enter DESDEMONA, CASSIO, *and* EMILIA

DESDEM. Be thou assured, good Cassio, I will do
All my abilities in thy behalf.

EMILIA Good madam, do; I warrant it grieves my husband
As if the case were his.

DESDEM. O, that's an honest fellow. Do not doubt, Cassio,
But I will have my lord and you again
As friendly as you were.

CASSIO   Bounteous madam,
Whatever shall become of Michael Cassio,
He's never anything but your true servant.

DESDEM. I know't; I thank you. You do love my lord;   10
You have known him long; and be you well assured
He shall in strangeness stand no farther off
Than in a politic distance.

CASSIO   Ay, but, lady,
That policy may either last so long,
Or feed upon such nice and waterish diet,
Or breed itself so out of circumstance,
That, I being absent, and my place supplied,

	My general will forget my love and service.	
DESDEM.	Do not doubt that: before Emilia here	
	I give thee warrant of thy place. Assure thee,	20
	If I do vow a friendship, I'll perform it	
	To the last article. My lord shall never rest:	
	I'll watch him tame, and talk him out of patience;	
	His bed shall seem a school, his board a shrift;	
	I'll intermingle everything he does	
	With Cassio's suit. Therefore be merry, Cassio;	
	For thy solicitor shall rather die	
	Than give thy cause away.	

Enter OTHELLO *and* IAGO, *at a distance*

EMILIA	Madam, here comes my lord.	
CASSIO	Madam, I'll take my leave.	30
DESDEM.	Why, stay, and hear me speak.	
CASSIO	Madam, not now: I am very ill at ease,	
	Unfit for mine own purposes.	
DESDEM.	Well, do your discretion. [*Cassio goes*	
IAGO	Ha! I like not that.	
OTHELLO	What dost thou say?	
IAGO	Nothing, my lord; or if – I know not what.	
OTHELLO	Was not that Cassio parted from my wife?	
IAGO	Cassio, my lord! No, sure, I cannot think it,	
	That he would steal away so guilty-like,	40
	Seeing you coming.	
OTHELLO	I do believe 'twas he.	
DESDEM.	How now, my lord!	
	I have been talking with a suitor here,	
	A man that languishes in your displeasure.	
OTHELLO	Who is't you mean?	
DESDEM.	Why, your lieutenant, Cassio. Good my lord,	
	If I have any grace or power to move you,	
	His present reconciliation take;	
	For if he be not one that truly loves you,	
	That errs in ignorance and not in cunning,	50
	I have no judgment in an honest face.	
	I prithee, call him back.	
OTHELLO	Went he hence now?	
DESDEM.	Ay, sooth; so humbled,	

	That he hath left part of his grief with me
	To suffer with him. Good love, call him back.
OTHELLO	Not now, sweet Desdemon; some other time.
DESDEM.	But shall't be shortly?
OTHELLO	The sooner, sweet, for you.
DESDEM.	Shall't be tonight at supper?
OTHELLO	No, not tonight.
DESDEM.	Tomorrow dinner then?
OTHELLO	I shall not dine at home:

OTHELLO: I meet the captains at the citadel.   60

DESDEM. Why then, tomorrow night; or Tuesday morn;
On Tuesday noon, or night; on Wednesday morn.
I prithee, name the time; but let it not
Exceed three days. In faith, he's penitent;
And yet his trespass, in our common reason –
Save that, they say, the wars must make example
Out of their best – is not almost a fault
T'incur a private check. When shall he come?
Tell me, Othello. I wonder in my soul
What you would ask me that I should deny,   70
Or stand so mammering on. What! Michael Cassio,
That came a-wooing with you, and so many a time,
When I have spoke of you dispraisingly,
Hath ta'en your part – to have so much to do
To bring him in! Trust me, I could do much –

OTHELLO Prithee, no more. Let him come when he will;
I will deny thee nothing.

DESDEM. Why, this is not a boon;
'Tis as I should entreat you wear your gloves,
Or feed on nourishing dishes, or keep you warm,
Or sue to you to do peculiar profit   80
To your own person. Nay, when I have a suit
Wherein I mean to touch your love indeed,
It shall be full of poise and difficult weight,
And fearful to be granted.

OTHELLO I will deny thee nothing.
Whereon, I do beseech thee, grant me this,
To leave me but a little to myself.

DESDEM. Shall I deny you? No; farewell, my lord.

OTHELLO	Farewell, my Desdemona, I'll come straight.
DESDEM.	Emilia, come. Be as your fancies teach you;
	Whate'er you be, I am obedient. 90

[Desdemona and Emilia go

OTHELLO	Excellent wretch! Perdition catch my soul
	But I do love thee; and when I love thee not
	Chaos is come again.
IAGO	My noble lord –
OTHELLO	What dost thou say, Iago?
IAGO	Did Michael Cassio,
	When you wooed my lady, know of your love?
OTHELLO	He did, from first to last. Why dost thou ask?
IAGO	But for a satisfaction of my thought;
	No further harm.
OTHELLO	Why of thy thought, Iago?
IAGO	I did not think he had been acquainted with her.
OTHELLO	O, yes, and went between us very oft. 100
IAGO	Indeed!
OTHELLO	Indeed? Ay, indeed. Discern'st thou aught in that?
	Is he not honest?
IAGO	Honest, my lord?
OTHELLO	Honest? Ay, honest.
IAGO	My lord, for aught I know.
OTHELLO	What dost thou think?
IAGO	Think, my lord?
OTHELLO	Think, my lord! Alas, thou echo'st me,
	As if there were some monster in thy thought 110
	Too hideous to be shown. Thou dost mean something:
	I heard thee say even now, thou likedst not that,
	When Cassio left my wife. What didst not like?
	And when I told thee he was of my counsel
	In my whole course of wooing, thou criedst 'Indeed!'
	And didst contract and purse thy brow together,
	As if thou then hadst shut up in thy brain
	Some horrible conceit. If thou dost love me,
	Show me thy thought..
IAGO	My lord, you know I love you.
OTHELLO	I think thou dost; 120
	And for I know thou'rt full of love, and honest,

              And weigh'st thy words before thou giv'st them breath,
              Therefore these stops of thine fright me the more:
              For such things in a false disloyal knave
              Are tricks of custom; but in a man that's just
              They're close dilations, working from the heart
              That passion cannot rule.

IAGO   For Michael Cassio,
              I dare be sworn I think that he is honest.

OTHELLO I think so too.

IAGO   Men should be what they seem;
              Or those that be not, would they might seem none!   130

OTHELLO Certain, men should be what they seem.

IAGO   Why then, I think Cassio's an honest man.

OTHELLO Nay, yet there's more in this.
              I prithee, speak to me as to thy thinkings,
              As thou dost ruminate, and give thy worst of thought
              The worst of words.

IAGO   Good my lord, pardon me:
              Though I am bound to every act of duty,
              I am not bound to that all slaves are free to.
              Utter my thoughts! Why, say they are vile and false –   140
              As where's that palace whereinto foul things
              Sometimes intrude not? Who has a breast so pure,
              But some uncleanly apprehensions
              Keep leets and law–days, and in session sit
              With meditations lawful?

OTHELLO Thou dost conspire against thy friend, Iago,
              If thou but think'st him wronged and mak'st his ear
              A stranger to thy thoughts.

IAGO   I do beseech you –
              Though I perchance am vicious in my guess,
               As, I confess, it is my nature's plague
              To spy into abuses, and oft my jealousy   150
              Shapes faults that are not – that your wisdom then,
              From one that so imperfectly conceits,
              Would take no notice, nor build yourself a trouble
              Out of his scattering and unsure observance.
              It were not for your quiet nor your good,
              Nor for my manhood, honesty, or wisdom,

To let you know my thoughts.

OTHELLO   What dost thou mean?

IAGO   Good name in man and woman, dear my lord,
            Is the immediate jewel of their souls:
            Who steals my purse steals trash – 'tis something,   160
                                            nothing;
            'Twas mine, 'tis his, and has been slave to thousands;
            But he that filches from me my good name
            Robs me of that which not enriches him
            And makes me poor indeed.

OTHELLO   I'll know thy thoughts!

IAGO   You cannot, if my heart were in your hand;
            Nor shall not, while 'tis in my custody.

OTHELLO   Ha!

IAGO   O, beware, my lord, of jealousy;
            It is the green-eyed monster, which doth mock
            The meat it feeds on: that cuckold lives in bliss
            Who, certain of his fate, loves not his wronger;   170
            But, O, what damnéd minutes tells he o'er
            Who dotes, yet doubts, suspects, yet fondly loves!

OTHELLO   O misery!

IAGO   Poor and content is rich, and rich enough;
            But riches fineless is as poor as winter
            To him that ever fears he shall be poor.
            Good heaven the souls of all my tribe defend
            From jealousy!

OTHELLO   Why, why is this?
            Think'st thou I'd make a life of jealousy,
            To follow still the changes of the moon   180
            With fresh suspicions? No; to be once in doubt
            Is once resolved. Exchange me for a goat,
            When I shall turn the business of my soul
            To such exsufflicate and blown surmise
            Matching thy inference. 'Tis not to make me jealous
            To say my wife is fair, loves company,
            Is free of speech, sings, plays and dances well;
            Where virtue is, these are more virtuous;
            Nor from mine own weak merits will I draw
            The smallest fear or doubt of her revolt;   190

           For she had eyes and chose me. No, Iago:
           I'll see before I doubt; when I doubt, prove;
           And on the proof, there is no more but this,
           Away at once with love or jealousy!

IAGO   I am glad of it; for now I shall have reason
           To show the love and duty that I bear you
           With franker spirit. Therefore, as I am bound,
           Receive it from me. I speak not yet of proof.
           Look to your wife; observe her well with Cassio;
           Wear your eye thus not jealous nor secure: 200
           I would not have your free and noble nature
           Out of self-bounty be abused. Look to't:
           I know our country disposition well;
           In Venice they do let heaven see the pranks
           They dare not show their husbands; their best conscience
           Is not to leave't undone, but keep't unknown.

OTHELLO   Dost thou say so?

IAGO   She did deceive her father, marrying you:
           And when she seemed to shake and fear your looks,
           She loved them most.

OTHELLO   And so she did.

IAGO   Why then,   210
           She that so young could give out such a seeming,
           To seel her father's eyes up close as oak,
           He thought 'twas witchcraft – but I am much to blame;
           I humbly do beseech you of your pardon
           For too much loving you.

OTHELLO   I am bound to thee for ever.

IAGO   I see this hath a little dashed your spirits.

OTHELLO   Not a jot, not a jot.

IAGO   In faith, I fear it has.
           I hope you will consider what is spoke
           Comes from my love. But I do see you're moved.
           I am to pray you not to strain my speech   220
           To grosser issues nor to larger reach
           Than to suspicion.

OTHELLO   I will not.

IAGO   Should you do so, my lord,
           My speech should fall into such vile success

As my thoughts aimed not at. Cassio's my worthy
friend —
My lord, I see you're moved.

OTHELLO   No, not much moved:
I do not think but Desdemona's honest.

IAGO   Long live she so! And long live you to think so!

OTHELLO   And yet, how nature erring from itself —

IAGO   Ay, there's the point: as — to be bold with you —   230
Not to affect many proposéd matches
Of her own clime, complexion, and degree,
Whereto we see in all things nature tends —
Foh! One may smell, in such, a will most rank,
Foul disproportion, thoughts unnatural.
But pardon me: I do not in position
Distinctly speak of her; though I may fear
Her will, recoiling to her better judgment,
May fall to match you with her country forms,
And happily repent.

OTHELLO   Farewell, farewell.   240
If more thou dost perceive, let me know more;
Set on thy wife to observe. Leave me, Iago.

IAGO   [going] My lord, I take my leave.

OTHELLO   Why did I marry? This honest creature doubtless
Sees and knows more, much more, than he unfolds.

IAGO   [returning]
My lord, I would I might entreat your honour
To scan this thing no further. Leave it to time:
Although 'tis fit that Cassio have his place —
For sure he fills it up with great ability —
Yet if you please to hold him off awhile,   250
You shall by that perceive him and his means;
Note if your lady strain his entertainment
With any strong or vehement importunity —
Much will be seen in that. In the mean time,
Let me be thought too busy in my fears —
As worthy cause I have to fear I am —
And hold her free, I do beseech your honour.

OTHELLO   Fear not my government.

IAGO   I once more take my leave.   [goes

OTHELLO   This fellow's of exceeding honesty,   260
     And knows all qualities, with a learnéd spirit,
     Of human dealings. If I do prove her haggard,
     Though that her jesses were my dear heart-strings,
     I'd whistle her off and let her down the wind
     To prey at fortune. Haply, for I am black
     And have not those soft parts of conversation
     That chamberers have, or for I am declined
     Into the vale of years – yet that's not much –
     She's gone; I am abused, and my relief
     Must be to loathe her. O curse of marriage,   270
     That we can call these delicate creatures ours,
     And not their appetites! I had rather be a toad,
     And live upon the vapour of a dungeon,
     Than keep a corner in the thing I love
     For others' uses. Yet, 'tis the plague of great ones;
     Prerogatived are they less than the base;
     'Tis destiny unshunnable, like death:
     Even then this forkéd plague is fated to us
     When we do quicken. Look where she comes:

         Re-enter DESDEMONA *and* EMILIA

     If she be false, O, then heaven mocks itself!   280
     I'll not believe't.

DESDEM.   How now, my dear Othello!
     Your dinner, and the generous islanders
     By you invited, do attend your presence.

OTHELLO   I am to blame.

DESDEM.   Why do you speak so faintly?
     Are you not well?

OTHELLO   I have a pain upon my forehead here.

DESDEM.   Faith, that's with watching; 'twill away again:
     Let me but bind it hard, within this hour
     It will be well.

OTHELLO   Your napkin is too little;
         [he puts the handkerchief from him; and she drops it
     Let it alone. Come, I'll go in with you.   290

DESDEM.   I am very sorry that you are not well.
                [Othello and Desdemona go

EMILIA   I am glad I've found this napkin:
          This was her first remembrance from the Moor;
          My wayward husband hath a hundred times
          Wooed me to steal it; but she so loves the token,
          For he conjured her she should ever keep it,
          That she reserves it evermore about her
          To kiss and talk to. I'll have the work ta'en out,
          And give't Iago. What he will do with it
          Heaven knows, not I: 300
          I nothing but to please his fantasy.

                         Re-enter IAGO

IAGO   How now! What do you here alone?
EMILIA   Do not you chide; I have a thing for you.
IAGO   A thing, for me? It is a common thing –
EMILIA   Ha!
IAGO   To have a foolish wife.
EMILIA   O, is that all? What will you give me now
          For that same handkerchief?
IAGO   What handkerchief?
EMILIA   What handkerchief!
          Why, that the Moor first gave to Desdemona;   310
          That which so often you did bid me steal.
IAGO   Hast stole it from her?
EMILIA   No, faith; she let it drop by negligence,
          And, to th'advantage, I being here took't up.
          Look, here it is.
IAGO   A good wench; give it me.
EMILIA   What will you do with't, that you've been so earnest
          To have me filch it?
IAGO   [*snatching it*]   Why, what's that to you?
EMILIA   If't be not for some purpose of import,
          Give't me again. Poor lady, she'll run mad
          When she shall lack it.   320
IAGO   Be not acknown on't; I have use for it.
          Go, leave me.   [*Emilia goes*
          I will in Cassio's lodging lose this napkin,
          And let him find it. Trifles light as air
          Are to the jealous confirmations strong
          As proofs of holy writ: this may do something.

The Moor already changes with my poison:
Dangerous conceits are in their natures poisons
Which at the first are scarce found to distaste
But, with a little act upon the blood,   330
Burn like the mines of sulphur.

Re-enter OTHELLO

                         I did say so:
Look where he comes! Not poppy, nor mandragora,
Nor all the drowsy syrups of the world,
Shall ever medicine thee to that sweet sleep
Which thou owedst yesterday.

OTHELLO   Ha! Ha! False to me?

IAGO   Why, how now, general! No more of that.

OTHELLO Avaunt! Be gone! Thou hast set me on the rack:
I swear 'tis better to be much abused
Than but to know't a little.

IAGO   How now, my lord!

OTHELLO What sense had I of her stolen hours of lust?   340
I saw't not, thought it not, it harmed not me:
I slept the next night well, fed well, was merry;
I found not Cassio's kisses on her lips.
He that is robbed, not wanting what is stolen,
Let him not know't, and he's not robbed at all.

IAGO   I am sorry to hear this.

OTHELLO I had been happy, if the general camp,
Pioneers and all, had tasted her sweet body,
So I had nothing known. O, now for ever
Farewell the tranquil mind! Farewell content!   350
Farewell the pluméd troops, and the big wars
That make ambition virtue – O, farewell!
Farewell the neighing steed and the shrill trump,
The spirit-stirring drum, th'ear-piercing fife,
The royal banner, and all quality,
Pride, pomp, and circumstance, of glorious war!
And, O you mortal engines, whose rude throats
Th'immortal Jove's dread clamours counterfeit,
Farewell! Othello's occupation's gone!

IAGO   Is't possible, my lord?   360

OTHELLO Villain, be sure thou prove my love a whore;

    Be sure of it; give me the ocular proof;
               [takes him by the throat
    Or, by the worth of mine eternal soul,
    Thou hadst been better have been born a dog
    Than answer my waked wrath!

IAGO   Is't come to this?

OTHELLO Make me to see't; or, at the least, so prove it,
    That the probation bear no hinge nor loop
    To hang a doubt on; or woe upon thy life!

IAGO My noble lord –

OTHELLO If thou dost slander her and torture me,   37
    Never pray more; abandon all remorse;
    On horror's head horrors accumulate;
    Do deeds to make heaven weep, all earth amazed;
    For nothing canst thou to damnation add
    Greater than that.

IAGO   O grace! O heaven forgive me!
    Are you a man? Have you a soul, or sense?
    God bu'y you; take mine office. O wretched fool,
    That liv'st to make thine honesty a vice!
    O monstrous world! Take note, take note, O world,
    To be direct and honest is not safe.   38
    I thank you for this profit, and from hence
    I'll love no friend sith love breeds such offence.

OTHELLO Nay, stay; thou shouldst be honest.

IAGO I should be wise; for honesty's a fool,
    And loses that it works for.

OTHELLO   By the world,
    I think my wife be honest, and think she is not;
    I think that thou art just, and think thou art not:
    I'll have some proof. Her name, that was as fresh
    As Dian's visage, is now begrimed and black
    As mine own face. If there be cords, or knives, 39
    Poison, or fire, or suffocating streams,
    I'll not endure it. Would I were satisfied!

IAGO I see, sir, you are eaten up with passion:
    I do repent me that I put it to you.
    You would be satisfied?

OTHELLO   Would! Nay, and will.

IAGO   And may; but how? How satisfied, my lord?
            Would you, the supervisor, grossly gape on –
            Behold her topped?
OTHELLO   Death and damnation! O!
IAGO   It were a tedious difficulty, I think,
            To bring them to that prospect: damn them then,   400
            If ever mortal eyes do see them bolster
            More than their own! What then? How then?
            What shall I say? Where's satisfaction?
            It is impossible you should see this,
            Were they as prime as goats, as hot as monkeys,
            As salt as wolves in pride, and fools as gross
            As ignorance made drunk. But yet, I say,
            If imputation and strong circumstance,
            Which lead directly to the door of truth,
            Will give you satisfaction, you might have't.   410
OTHELLO   Give me a living reason she's disloyal.
IAGO   I do not like the office;
            But sith I am entered in this cause so far,
            Pricked to't by foolish honesty and love,
            I will go on. I lay with Cassio lately,
            And being troubled with a raging tooth,
            I could not sleep.
            There are a kind of men so loose of soul,
            That in their sleeps will mutter their affairs:
            One of this kind is Cassio.   420
            In sleep I heard him say 'Sweet Desdemona,
            Let us be wary, let us hide our loves';
            And then, sir, would he gripe and wring my hand,
            Cry 'O sweet creature!' and then kiss me hard,
            As if he plucked up kisses by the roots,
            That grew upon my lips; then laid his leg
            Over my thigh, and sighed, and kissed, and then
            Cried 'Curséd fate that gave thee to the Moor!'
OTHELLO   O monstrous! Monstrous!
IAGO   Nay, this was but his dream.
OTHELLO   But this denoted a foregone conclusion: 430
            'Tis a shrewd doubt, though it be but a dream.
IAGO   And this may help to thicken other proofs

That do demonstrate thinly.

OTHELLO   I'll tear her all to pieces.

IAGO   Nay, but be wise: yet we see nothing done;
           She may be honest yet. Tell me but this:
           Have you not sometimes seen a handkerchief
           Spotted with strawberries in your wife's hand?

OTHELLO   I gave her such a one; 'twas my first gift.

IAGO   I know not that; but such a handkerchief –
           I am sure it was your wife's – did I today   440
           See Cassio wipe his beard with.

OTHELLO   If it be that –

IAGO   If it be that, or any that was hers,
           It speaks against her with the other proofs.

OTHELLO   O, that the slave had forty thousand lives!
           One is too poor, too weak for my revenge.
           Now do I see 'tis true. Look: here, Iago,
           All my fond love thus do I blow to heaven –
           'Tis gone.
           Arise, black vengeance, from thy hollow cell!
           Yield up, O love, thy crown and hearted throne   450
           To tyrannous hate! Swell, bosom, with thy fraught,
           For 'tis of aspics' tongues!

IAGO   Yet be content.

OTHELLO   O, blood, blood, blood!

IAGO   Patience, I say; your mind perhaps may change.

OTHELLO   Never, Iago: like to the Pontic sea,
           Whose icy current and compulsive course
           Ne'er feels retiring ebb, but keeps due on
           To the Propontic and the Hellespont;
           Even so my bloody thoughts, with violent pace,
           Shall ne'er look back, ne'er ebb to humble love,   460
           Till that a capable and wide revenge
           Swallow them up. Now, by yond marble heaven,
           In the due reverence of a sacred vow   [kneels
           I here engage my words.

IAGO   Do not rise yet.   [kneels
           Witness you ever-burning lights above,
           You elements that clip us round about,
           Witness that here Iago doth give up

The execution of his wit, hands, heart,
To wrongèd Othello's service! Let him command,
And to obey shall be without remorse,   470
What bloody business ever.   [*they rise*

OTHELLO   I greet thy love,
Not with vain thanks, but with acceptance bounteous,
And will upon the instant put thee to't:
Within these three days let me hear thee say
That Cassio's not alive.

IAGO   My friend is dead;
'Tis done at your request. But let her live.

OTHELLO   Damn her, lewd minx! O, damn her! damn her!
Come, go with me apart; I will withdraw,
To furnish me with some swift means of death
For the fair devil. Now art thou my lieutenant.   480

IAGO   I am your own for ever.   [*they go*

SCENE 4

The same

Enter DESDEMONA, EMILIA, *and Clown*

DESDEM.   Do you know, sirrah, where Lieutenant Cassio lies?

CLOWN   I dare not say he lies anywhere.

DESDEM.   Why, man?

CLOWN   He's a soldier; and for one to say a soldier lies, is
stabbing.

DESDEM.   Go to: where lodges he?

CLOWN   To tell you where he lodges, is to tell you where I lie.

DESDEM.   Can anything be made of this?

CLOWN   I know not where he lodges; and for me to devise a
lodging, and say he lies here or he lies there, were to   10
lie in mine own throat.

DESDEM.   Can you inquire him out, and be edified by report?

CLOWN   I will catechize the world for him: that is, make questions
and by them answer.

DESDEM.   Seek him; bid him come hither. Tell him I have moved
my lord on his behalf, and hope all will be well.

CLOWN   To do this is within the compass of man's wit, and

	therefore I will attempt the doing it. *[goes*
DESDEM.	Where should I lose that handkerchief, Emilia?
EMILIA	I know not, madam. 20
DESDEM.	Believe me, I had rather lose my purse
	Full of crusadoes; and but my noble Moor
	Is true of mind and made of no such baseness
	As jealous creatures are, it were enough
	To put him to ill thinking.
EMILIA	Is he not jealous?
DESDEM.	Who, he! I think the sun where he was born
	Drew all such humours from him.
EMILIA	Look where he comes!
DESDEM.	I will not leave him now till Cassio
	Be called to him.

Enter OTHELLO

                                        How is't with you, my lord?

OTHELLO	Well, my good lady. [*aside*] O, hardness to dissemble! 30
	How do you, Desdemona?
DESDEM.	Well, my good lord.
OTHELLO	Give me your hand: this hand is moist, my lady.
DESDEM.	It yet hath felt no age nor known no sorrow.
OTHELLO	This argues fruitfulness and liberal heart:
	Hot, hot, and moist. This hand of yours requires
	A sequester from liberty, fasting and prayer,
	Much castigation, exercise devout;
	For there's a young and sweating devil here
	That commonly rebels. 'Tis a good hand,
	A frank one.
DESDEM.	You may, indeed, say so; 40
	For 'twas that hand that gave away my heart.
OTHELLO	A liberal hand: the hearts of old gave hands;
	But our new heraldry is hands, not hearts.
DESDEM.	I cannot speak of this. Come now, your promise.
OTHELLO	What promise, chuck?
DESDEM.	I have sent to bid Cassio come speak with you.
OTHELLO	I have a salt and sorry rheum offends me;
	Lend me thy handkerchief.
DESDEM.	Here, my lord.
OTHELLO	That which I gave you. 50

DESDEM.   I have it not about me.
OTHELLO   Not?
DESDEM.   No, indeed, my lord.
OTHELLO   That's a fault. That handkerchief
Did an Egyptian to my mother give;
She was a charmer, and could almost read
The thoughts of people: she told her, while she kept it
'Twould make her amiable and subdue my father
Entirely to her love; but if she lost it
Or made a gift of it, my father's eye   60
Should hold her loathéd and his spirits should hunt
After new fancies. She dying gave it me,
And bid me, when my fate would have me wive,
To give it her. I did so; and take heed on't:
Make it a darling like your precious eye;
To lose't or give't away were such perdition
As nothing else could match.
DESDEM.   Is't possible?
OTHELLO   'Tis true. There's magic in the web of it:
A sibyl, that had numbered in the world
The sun to course two hundred compasses,   70
In her prophetic fury sewed the work;
The worms were hallowed that did breed the silk;
And it was dyed in mummy which the skilful
Conserved of maidens' hearts.
DESDEM.   Indeed! Is't true?
OTHELLO   Most veritable; therefore look to't well.
DESDEM.   Then would to God that I had never seen't!
OTHELLO   Ha! Wherefore?
DESDEM.   Why do you speak so startingly and rash?
OTHELLO   Is't lost? Is't gone? Speak, is it out o'th'way?
DESDEM.   Heaven bless us!   80
OTHELLO   Say you?
DESDEM.   It is not lost; but what an if it were?
OTHELLO   How!
DESDEM.   I say it is not lost.
OTHELLO   Fetch't; let me see't.
DESDEM.   Why, so I can, sir, but I will not now.
This is a trick to put me from my suit:

Pray you, let Cassio be received again.

OTHELLO   Fetch me the handkerchief: my mind misgives.

DESDEM.   Come, come;   90

You'll never meet a more sufficient man.

OTHELLO   The handkerchief!

DESDEM.   I pray, talk me of Cassio.

OTHELLO   The handkerchief!

DESDEM.   A man that all his time

Hath founded his good fortunes on your love,

Shared dangers with you –

OTHELLO   The handkerchief!

DESDEM.   In sooth, you are to blame.

OTHELLO   Away!   [he goes

EMILIA   Is not this man jealous?

DESDEM.   I ne'er saw this before.   100

Sure there's some wonder in this handkerchief:

I am most unhappy in the loss of it.

EMILIA   'Tis not a year or two shows us a man:

They are all but stomachs and we all but food;

They eat us hungerly, and when they are full

They belch us. Look you, Cassio and my husband

Enter CASSIO *and* IAGO

IAGO   There is no other way: 'tis she must do't;

And, lo, the happiness! Go and importune her.

DESDEM.   How now, good Cassio! What's the news with you?

CASSIO   Madam, my former suit: I do beseech you   110

That, by your virtuous means, I may again

Exist and be a member of his love

Whom I with all the office of my heart

Entirely honour. I would not be delayed:

If my offence be of such mortal kind

That nor my service past nor present sorrow,

Nor purposed merit in futurity,

Can ransom me into his love again,

But to know so must be my benefit;

So shall I clothe me in a forced content   120

And shut myself up in some other course

To fortune's alms.

DESDEM.   Alas, thrice-gentle Cassio!

My advocation is not now in tune;
My lord is not my lord, nor should I know him
Were he in favour as in humour altered.
So help me every spirit sanctified,
As I have spoken for you all my best
And stood within the blank of his displeasure
For my free speech! You must awhile be patient:
What I can do I will; and more I will　　　　　　130
Than for myself I dare – let that suffice you.

IAGO　　　Is my lord angry?

EMILIA　　　　　　　　　He went hence but now,
And certainly in strange unquietness.

IAGO　　　Can he be angry? I have seen the cannon
When it hath blown his ranks into the air
And, like the devil, from his very arm
Puffed his own brother; and is he angry?
Something of moment then: I will go meet him;
There's matter in't indeed if he be angry.

DESDEM.　I prithee, do so.　　　　　　　[Iago goes
　　　　　　　　　　Something sure of state,　　　140
Either from Venice, or some unhatched practice
Made demonstrable here in Cyprus to him,
Hath puddled his clear spirit; and in such cases
Men's natures wrangle with inferior things,
Though great ones are their object. 'Tis even so;
For let our finger ache, and it indues
Our other healthful members to a sense
Of pain. Nay, we must think men are not gods,
Nor of them look for such observancy
As fits the bridal. Beshrew me much, Emilia,　　150
I was, unhandsome warrior as I am,
Arraigning his unkindness with my soul;
But now I find I had suborned the witness,
And he's indicted falsely.

EMILIA　　Pray heaven it be state matters, as you think,
And no conception nor no jealous toy
Concerning you.

DESDEM.　Alas the day, I never gave him cause!

EMILIA　　But jealous souls will not be answered so;

| | They are not ever jealous for the cause, | 160 |

They are not ever jealous for the cause,   160
But jealous for they're jealous: 'tis a monster
Begot upon itself, born on itself.

DESDEM.   Heaven keep that monster from Othello's mind!

EMILIA   Lady, amen.

DESDEM.   I will go seek him. Cassio, walk hereabout:
If I do find him fit, I'll move your suit,
And seek to effect it to my uttermost.

CASSIO   I humbly thank your ladyship.

                    [*Desdemona and Emilia depart*

                    Enter BIANCA

BIANCA   Save you, friend Cassio!

CASSIO   What make you from home?
How is it with you, my most fair Bianca?   170
In faith, sweet love, I was coming to your house.

BIANCA   And I was going to your lodging, Cassio.
What, keep a week away? Seven days and nights?
Eight score eight hours? And lovers' absent hours,
More tedious than the dial eight score times?
O weary reckoning!

CASSIO   Pardon me, Bianca:
I have this while with leaden thoughts been pressed;
But I shall in a more continuate time
Strike off this score of absence. Sweet Bianca,
                    [*giving Desdemona's handkerchief*
Take me this work out.

BIANCA   O Cassio, whence came this?   180
This is some token from a newer friend:
To the felt absence now I feel a cause;
Is't come to this? Well, well.

CASSIO   Go to, woman!
Throw your vile guesses in the devil's teeth,
From whence you have them. You are jealous now
That this is from some mistress, some remembrance:
No, by my faith, Bianca.

BIANCA   Why, whose is it?

CASSIO   I know not neither. I found it in my chamber.
I like the work well. Ere it be demanded –
As like enough it will – I'd have it copied: 190

            Take it, and do't; and leave me for this time.

BIANCA   Leave you! Wherefore?

CASSIO   I do attend here on the general;
            And think it no addition, nor my wish,
            To have him see me womaned.

BIANCA   Why, I pray you?

CASSIO   Not that I love you not.

BIANCA   But that you do not love me.
            I pray you, bring me on the way a little;
            And say if I shall see you soon at night.

CASSIO   'Tis but a little way that I can bring you,
            For I attend here; but I'll see you soon.   200

BIANCA   'Tis very good; I must be circumstanced.   [*they go*

ACT 4 SCENE 1

The same

Enter OTHELLO *and* IAGO

IAGO   Will you think so?
OTHELLO   Think so, Iago!
IAGO   What,
            To kiss in private?
OTHELLO   An unauthorized kiss.
IAGO   Or to be naked with her friend in bed
            An hour or more, not meaning any harm?
OTHELLO   Naked in bed, Iago, and not mean harm!
            It is hypocrisy against the devil:
            They that mean virtuously and yet do so,
            The devil their virtue tempts and they tempt heaven.
IAGO   So they do nothing, 'tis a venial slip:
            But if I give my wife a handkerchief –   10
OTHELLO   What then?
IAGO   Why, then, 'tis hers, my lord; and being hers,
            She may, I think, bestow't on any man.
OTHELLO   She is protectress of her honour too:
            May she give that?
IAGO   Her honour is an essence that's not seen;
            They have it very oft that have it not:
            But for the handkerchief –
OTHELLO   By heaven, I would most gladly have forgot it.
            Thou said'st – O, it comes o'er my memory,   20
            As doth the raven o'er the infected house,
            Boding to all – he had my handkerchief.
IAGO   Ay, what of that?
OTHELLO   That's not so good now.
IAGO   What
            If I had said I had seen him do you wrong?
            Or heard him say – as knaves be such abroad,
            Who having, by their own importunate suit,
            Or voluntary dotage of some mistress,
            Convincéd or supplied them, cannot choose

	But they must blab –	
OTHELLO	Hath he said anything?	
IAGO	He hath, my lord; but, be you well assured,	30
	No more than he'll unswear.	
OTHELLO	What hath he said?	
IAGO	Faith, that he did – I know not what he did.	
OTHELLO	What? What?	
IAGO	Lie –	
OTHELLO	With her?	
IAGO	With her, on her; what you will,	
OTHELLO	Lie with her! Lie on her! – We say lie on her, when	

OTHELLO   Lie with her! Lie on her! – We say lie on her, when
they belie her. – Lie with her! 'Zounds, that's fulsome!
Handkerchief – confessions – handkerchief! To confess and be hanged for his labour; first, to be, hanged;
and then to confess. I tremble at it. Nature would not
invest herself in such shadowing passion without some 40
instruction. It is not words that shakes me thus. Pish!
Noses, ears, and lips. Is't possible? – Confess? – Handkerchief? – O devil!   [*falls in a trance*

IAGO   Work on,
My medicine, work! Thus credulous fools are caught;
And many worthy and chaste dames even thus,
All guiltless, meet reproach. What, ho! My lord!
My lord, I say! Othello!

Enter CASSIO

How now, Cassio!

CASSIO   What's the matter?
IAGO   My lord is fallen into an epilepsy.   50
This is his second fit; he had one yesterday.
CASSIO   Rub him about the temples.
IAGO   No, forbear;
The lethargy must have his quiet course;
If not, he foams at mouth, and by and by
Breaks out to savage madness. Look, he stirs.
Do you withdraw yourself a little while.
He will recover straight; when he is gone,
I would on great occasion speak with you. [*Cassio goes*
How is it, general? Have you not hurt your head?

OTHELLO   Dost thou mock me?

IAGO   I mock you! No, by heaven.   60
          Would you would bear your fortune like a man!

OTHELLO   A hornéd man's a monster and a beast.

IAGO   There's many a beast then in a populous city,
          And many a civil monster.

OTHELLO   Did he confess it?

IAGO   Good sir, be a man:
          Think every bearded fellow that's but yoked
          May draw with you. There's millions now alive
          That nightly lie in those unproper beds
          Which they dare swear peculiar; your case is better.
          O, 'tis the spite of hell, the fiend's arch-mock,   70
          To lip a wanton in a secure couch,
          And to suppose her chaste! No, let me know;
          And knowing what I am, know what shall be.

OTHELLO   O, thou art wise; 'tis certain.

IAGO   Stand you awhile apart;
          Confine yourself but in a patient list.
          Whilst you were here o'erwhelméd with your grief –
          A passion most unsuiting such a man –
          Cassio came hither; I shifted him away,
          And laid good scuse upon your ecstasy;
          Bade him anon return and speak with me;   80
          The which he promised. Do but encave yourself,
          And mark the fleers, the gibes, and notable scorns,
          That dwell in every region of his face;
          For I will make him tell the tale anew,
          Where, how, how oft, how long ago and when
          He hath and is again to cope your wife.
          I say, but mark his gestures. Marry, patience;
          Or I shall say you're all in all a spleen,
          And nothing of a man.

OTHELLO   Dost thou hear, Iago?
          I will be found most cunning in my patience;   90
          But – dost thou hear? – Most bloody.

IAGO   That's not amiss;
          But yet keep time in all. Will you withdraw?
                                        [*Othello retires*

Now will I question Cassio of Bianca,
A hussy that by selling her desires
Buys herself bread and clothes: it is a creature
That dotes on Cassio; as 'tis the strumpet's plague
To beguile many and be beguiled by one.
He, when he hears of her, cannot refrain
From the excess of laughter. Here he comes.

Re-enter CASSIO

	As he shall smile, Othello shall go mad;	100
	And his unbookish jealousy must construe	
	Poor Cassio's smiles, gestures, and light behaviours,	
	Quite in the wrong. How do you now, lieutenant?	
CASSIO	The worser that you give me the addition	
	Whose want even kills me.	
IAGO	Ply Desdemona well, and you are sure on't.	
	Now, if this suit lay in Bianca's power,	
	How quickly should you speed!	
CASSIO	Alas, poor caitiff!	
OTHELLO	Look how he laughs already!	
IAGO	I never knew a woman love man so.	110
CASSIO	Alas, poor rogue! I think, in faith, she loves me.	
OTHELLO	Now he denies it faintly, and laughs it out.	
IAGO	Do you hear, Cassio?	
OTHELLO	Now he importunes him to tell it o'er.	
	Go to; well said, well said.	
IAGO	She gives it out that you shall marry her.	
	Do you intend it?	
CASSIO	Ha, ha, ha!	
OTHELLO	Do you triumph, Roman? Do you triumph?	
CASSIO	I marry her! What, a customer! I prithee, bear some	120
	charity to my wit; do not think it so unwholesome.	
	Ha, ha, ha!	
OTHELLO	So, so, so, so; they laugh that win.	
IAGO	Faith, the cry goes that you marry her.	
CASSIO	Prithee, say true.	
IAGO	I am a very villain else.	
OTHELLO	Have you scored me? Well.	
CASSIO	This is the monkey's own giving out: she is persuaded	

	I will marry her, out of her own love and flattery, not out of my promise.

I will marry her, out of her own love and flattery, not
out of my promise.   130

OTHELLO   Iago beckons me; now he begins the story.

CASSIO   She was here even now; she haunts me in every place.
I was the other day talking on the sea-bank with
certain Venetians; and thither comes the bauble, and,
by this hand, falls me thus about my neck –

OTHELLO   Crying 'O dear Cassio!' As it were: his gesture imports it.

CASSIO   So hangs, and lolls, and weeps upon me; so shakes, and
pulls me: ha, ha, ha!

OTHELLO   Now he tells how she plucked him to my chamber. O, I
see that nose of yours, but not that dog I shall throw it to.   140

CASSIO   Well, I must leave her company.

IAGO   Before me! Look where she comes!

CASSIO   'Tis such another fitchew! Marry, a perfumed one!

Enter BIANCA

What do you mean by this haunting of me?

BIANCA   Let the devil and his dam haunt you! What did you
mean by that same handkerchief you gave me even
now? I was a fine fool to take it. I must take out the
work? A likely piece of work that you should find it in
your chamber and not know who left it there! This is
some minx's token, and I must take out the work?   150
There; give it your hobby-horse. Wheresoever you
had it, I'll take out no work on't.

CASSIO   How now, my sweet Bianca! How now! How now!

OTHELLO   By heaven, that should be my handkerchief!

BIANCA   An you'll come to supper tonight, you may; an you
will not, come when you are next prepared for.   [*goes*

IAGO   After her, after her.

CASSIO   Faith, I must; she'll rail in the street else.

IAGO   Will you sup there?

CASSIO   Faith, I intend so.   160

IAGO   Well, I may chance to see you; for I would very fain
speak with you.

CASSIO   Prithee, come; will you?

IAGO   Go to; say no more.   [*Cassio goes*

OTHELLO   [*comes forward*] How shall I murder him, Iago?

IAGO   Did you perceive how he laughed at his vice?

OTHELLO	O Iago!
IAGO	And did you see the handkerchief?
OTHELLO	Was that mine?
IAGO	Yours, by this hand – and to see how he prizes the foolish woman your wife! She gave it him, and he hath given it his whore.
OTHELLO	I would have him nine years a-killing. A fine woman! A fair woman! A sweet woman!
IAGO	Nay, you must forget that.
OTHELLO	Ay, let her rot, and perish, and be damned tonight; for she shall not live. No, my heart is turned to stone: I strike it, and it hurts my hand. O, the world hath not a sweeter creature: she might lie by an emperor's side and command him tasks.
IAGO	Nay, that's not your way.
OTHELLO	Hang her! I do but say what she is: so delicate with her needle, an admirable musician – O, she will sing the savageness out of a bear – of so high and plenteous wit and invention –
IAGO	She's the worse for all this.
OTHELLO	O, a thousand, thousand times – and then, of so gentle a condition!
IAGO	Ay, too gentle.
OTHELLO	Nay, that's certain; but yet the pity of it, Iago! O Iago, the pity of it, Iago!
IAGO	If you be so fond over her iniquity, give her patent to offend; for, if it touch not you, it comes near nobody.
OTHELLO	I will chop her into messes – cuckold me!
IAGO	O, 'tis foul in her.
OTHELLO	With mine officer!
IAGO	That's fouler.
OTHELLO	Get me some poison, Iago – this night. I'll not expostulate with her, lest her body and beauty unprovide my mind again – this night, Iago.
IAGO	Do it not with poison: strangle her in her bed, even the bed she hath contaminated.
OTHELLO	Good, good: the justice of it pleases; very good.
IAGO	And for Cassio, let me be his undertaker: you shall hear more by midnight.

170

180

190

200

OTHELLO   Excellent good.   [*a trumpet sounds*]
                    What trumpet is that same?
IAGO   I warrant, something from Venice.

          Enter LODOVICO, DESDEMONA, *and Attendants*

                              'Tis Lodovico!
          This comes from the duke; and see, your wife is
                              with him.
LODOVICO God save you, worthy general!
OTHELLO   With all my heart, sir.
LODOVICO The duke and senators of Venice greet you.   210
                              [*gives him a letter*
OTHELLO   I kiss the instrument of their pleasures.
                              [*opens and reads*
DESDEM.   And what's the news, good cousin Lodovico?
IAGO   I am very glad to see you, signior;
          Welcome to Cyprus.
LODOVICO I thank you. How does Lieutenant Cassio?
IAGO   Lives, sir.
DESDEM.   Cousin, there's fallen between him and my lord
          An unkind breach; but you shall make all well.
OTHELLO   Are you sure of that?
DESDEM.   My lord?   220
OTHELLO   [*reads*] 'This fail you not to do, as you will – '
LODOVICO He did not call; he's busy in the paper.
          Is there division 'twixt my lord and Cassio?
DESDEM.   A most unhappy one; I would do much
          T' atone them, for the love I bear to Cassio.
OTHELLO   Fire and brimstone!
DESDEM.   My lord?
OTHELLO   Are you wise?
DESDEM.   What, is he angry?
LODOVICO   May be the letter moved him;
          For, as I think, they do command him home,   230
          Deputing Cassio in his government.
DESDEM.   By my troth, I am glad on't.
OTHELLO   Indeed!
DESDEM.   My lord?
OTHELLO   I am glad to see you mad.
DESDEM.   Why, sweet Othello!

OTHELLO	Devil! *[striking her*
DESDEM.	I have not deserved this.
LODOVICO	My lord, this would not be believed in Venice,
	Though I should swear I saw't. 'Tis very much.
	Make her amends; she weeps.
OTHELLO	O devil, devil!
	If that the earth could teem with woman's tears,
	Each drop she falls would prove a crocodile.
	Out of my sight!
DESDEM.	I will not stay to offend you. *[going*
LODOVICO	Truly, an obedient lady.
	I do beseech your lordship, call her back.
OTHELLO	Mistress!
DESDEM.	My lord?
OTHELLO	What would you with her, sir?
LODOVICO	Who, I, my lord?
OTHELLO	Ay; you did wish that I would make her turn.
	Sir, she can turn and turn, and yet go on
	And turn again; and she can weep, sir, weep;
	And she's obedient, as you say, obedient,
	Very obedient. Proceed you in your tears. –
	Concerning this, sir, – O well-painted passion! –
	I am commanded home. – Get you away;
	I'll send for you anon. – Sir, I obey the mandate,
	And will return to Venice. – Hence, avaunt! –
	[Desdemona goes
	Cassio shall have my place. And, sir, tonight,
	I do entreat that we may sup together.
	You are welcome, sir, to Cyprus. – Goats and monkeys!
	[he goes
LODOVICO	Is this the noble Moor whom our full senate
	Call all in all sufficient? Is this the nature
	Whom passion could not shake? Whose solid virtue
	The shot of accident nor dart of chance
	Could neither graze nor pierce?
IAGO	He is much changed.
LODOVICO	Are his wits safe? Is he not light of brain?
IAGO	He's that he is. I may not breathe my censure
	What he might be; if what he might he is not,

Line numbers in right margin: 240 (at "Each drop she falls..."), 250 (at "And she's obedient..."), 260 (at "Call all in all sufficient...").

I would to heaven he were!

LODOVICO   What, strike his wife!

IAGO   Faith, that was not so well; yet would I knew
              That stroke would prove the worst!

LODOVICO   Is it his use?
              Or did the letters work upon his blood,   27
              And new-create this fault?

IAGO   Alas, alas!
              It is not honesty in me to speak
              What I have, seen and known. You shall observe him,
              And his own courses will denote him so
              That I may save my speech; do but go after,
              And mark how he continues.

LODOVICO I am sorry that I am deceived in him.   [they go

SCENE 2

A room in the citadel

Enter OTHELLO *and* EMILIA

OTHELLO   You have seen nothing, then?

EMILIA   Nor ever heard, nor ever did suspect.

OTHELLO   Yes, you have seen Cassio and she together.

EMILIA   But then I saw no harm, and then I heard
          Each syllable that breath made up between them.

OTHELLO   What, did they never whisper?

EMILIA   Never, my lord.

OTHELLO   Nor send you out o'th'way?

EMILIA   Never.

OTHELLO   To fetch her fan, her gloves, her mask, nor nothing?

EMILIA   Never, my lord.   10

OTHELLO   That's strange.

EMILIA   I durst, my lord, to wager she is honest,
          Lay down my soul at stake. If you think other,
          Remove your thought: it doth abuse your bosom.
          If any wretch have put this in your head,
          Let heaven requite it with the serpent's curse!
          For if she be not honest, chaste, and true,

There's no man happy: the purest of their wives
Is foul as slander.

OTHELLO   Bid her come hither; go. [*Emilia goes*
She says enough; yet she's a simple bawd   20
That cannot say as much. This is a subtle whore,
A closet lock and key of villainous secrets;
And yet she'll kneel and pray; I have seen her do't.

Enter DESDEMONA *with* EMILIA

DESDEM.   My lord, what is your will?
OTHELLO   Pray, chuck, come hither.
DESDEM.   What is your pleasure?
OTHELLO   Let me see your eyes;
Look in my face.
DESDEM.   What horrible fancy's this?
OTHELLO   [*to Emilia*] Some of your function, mistress:
Leave procreants alone and shut the door;
Cough, or cry hem, if anybody come –
Your mystery, your mystery; nay, dispatch.   30
                              [*Emilia goes out*
DESDEM.   Upon my knees, what doth your speech import?
I understand a fury in your words,
But not the words.
OTHELLO   Why, what art thou?
DESDEM.   Your wife, my lord; your true and loyal wife.
OTHELLO   Come, swear it, damn thyself;
Lest, being like one of heaven, the devils themselves
Should fear to seize thee. Therefore be double-damned:
Swear thou art honest.
DESDEM.   Heaven doth truly know it.
OTHELLO   Heaven truly knows that thou art false as hell.   40
DESDEM.   To whom, my lord? With whom? How am I false?
OTHELLO   Ah, Desdemon! Away! Away! Away!
DESDEM.   Alas the heavy day! Why do you weep?
Am I the motive of these tears, my lord?
If haply you my father do suspect
An instrument of this your calling back,
Lay not your blame on me; if you have lost him,
Why, I have lost him too.
OTHELLO   Had it pleased heaven

To try me with affliction; had they rained
All kind of sores and shames on my bare head,   50
Steeped me in poverty to the very lips,
Given to captivity me and my utmost hopes,
I should have found in some place of my soul
A drop of patience; but, alas, to make me
A fixéd figure for the time of scorn
To point his slow unmoving finger at!
Yet could I bear that too; well, very well;
But there, where I have garnered up my heart,
Where either I must live or bear no life,
The foundation from the which my current runs,   60
Or else dries up – to be discarded thence!
Or keep it as a cistern for foul toads
To knot and gender in! Turn thy complexion there,
Patience, thou young and rose-lipped cherubin,
Ay, there, look grim as hell!

DESDEM.   I hope my noble lord esteems me honest.

OTHELLO   O, ay; as summer flies are in the shambles,
That quicken even with blowing. O thou weed,
Who art so lovely fair and smell'st so sweet
That the sense aches at thee, would thou hadst ne'er
                                        been born!   70

DESDEM.   Alas, what ignorant sin have I committed?

OTHELLO   Was this fair paper, this most goodly book,
Made to write 'whore' upon? What committed!
Committed! O thou public commoner!
I should make very forges of my cheeks,
That would to cinders burn up modesty,
Did I but speak thy deeds. What committed!
Heaven stops the nose at it, and the moon winks;
The bawdy wind, that kisses all it meets,
Is hushed within the hollow mine of earth,   80
And will not hear it. What committed!
Impudent strumpet!

DESDEM.   By heaven, you do me wrong.

OTHELLO   Are not you a strumpet?

DESDEM.   No, as I am a Christian.
If to preserve this vessel for my lord

From any other foul unlawful touch
Be not to be a strumpet, I am none.

OTHELLO   What, not a whore?

DESDEM.   No, as I shall be saved.

OTHELLO   Is't possible?

DESDEM.   O, heaven forgive us!

OTHELLO   I cry you mercy then:
I took you for that cunning whore of Venice   90
That married with Othello.
[raising his voice]   You, mistress,
That have the office opposite to Saint Peter,
And keep the gate of hell!

Re-enter EMILIA

                    You, you, ay, you.
We've done our course; there's money for your pains:
I pray you, turn the key, and keep our counsel.   [goes

EMILIA   Alas, what does this gentleman conceive?
How do you, madam? How do you, my good lady?

DESDEM.   Faith, half asleep.

EMILIA   Good madam, what's the matter with my lord?

DESDEM.   With who?   100

EMILIA   Why, with my lord, madam.

DESDEM.   Who is thy lord?

EMILIA   He that is yours, sweet lady.

DESDEM.   I have none: do not talk to me, Emilia;
I cannot weep, nor answers have I none
But what should go by water. Prithee, tonight
Lay on my bed my wedding sheets – remember;
And call thy husband hither.

EMILIA   Here's a change indeed!   [goes

DESDEM.   'Tis meet I should be used so, very meet.
How have I been behaved, that he might stick
The small'st opinion on my least misuse?   110

Re-enter EMILIA *with* IAGO

IAGO   What is your pleasure, madam? How is't with you?

DESDEM.   I cannot tell. Those that do teach young babes
Do it with gentle means and easy tasks:
He might have chid me so; for, in good faith,

I am a child to chiding.

IAGO   What's the matter, lady?

EMILIA   Alas, Iago, my lord hath so bewhored her,
          Thrown such despite and heavy terms upon her,
          As true heart cannot bear.

DESDEM.   Am I that name, Iago?

IAGO   What name, fair lady?

DESDEM.   Such as she said my lord did say I was.   120

EMILIA   He called her whore: a beggar in his drink
          Could not have laid such terms upon his callet.

IAGO   Why did he so?

DESDEM.   I do not know; I am sure I am none such.

IAGO   Do not weep, do not weep. Alas the day!

EMILIA   Hath she forsook so many noble matches,
          Her father, and her country, and her friends,
          To be called whore? Would it not make one weep?

DESDEM.   It is my wretched fortune.

IAGO   Beshrew him for't!
          How comes this trick upon him?

DESDEM.   Nay, heaven doth know.   130

EMILIA   I will be hanged, if some eternal villain,
          Some busy and insinuating rogue,
          Some cogging, cozening slave, to get some office,
          Have not devised this slander; I'll be hanged else.

IAGO   Fie, there is no such man; it is impossible.

DESDEM.   If any such there be, heaven pardon him!

EMILIA   A halter pardon him! And hell gnaw his bones!
          Why should he call her whore? Who keeps her
                                                company?
          What place, what time, what form, what likelihood?
          The Moor's abused by some most villainous knave,   140
          Some base notorious knave, some scurvy fellow.
          O heaven, that such companions thou'ldst unfold,
          And put in every honest hand a whip
          To lash the rascals naked through the world
          Even from the east to th'west!

IAGO   Speak within door.

EMILIA   O, fie upon them! Some such squire he was
          That turned your wit the seamy side without,

And made you to suspect me with the Moor.

IAGO　You are a fool; go to.

DESDEM.　　　　　　　　　　Alas, Iago,
What shall I do to win my lord again?　　　　　　　150
Good friend, go to him; for, by·this light of heaven,
I know not how I lost him. Here I kneel:
If e'er my will did trespass 'gainst his love
Either in discourse of thought or actual deed,
Or that mine eyes, mine ears, or any sense,
Delighted them in any other form,
Or that I do not yet, and ever did,
And ever will, though he do shake me off
To beggarly divorcement, love him dearly,
Comfort forswear me! Unkindness may do much;　　160
And his unkindness may defeat my life,
But never taint my love. I cannot say 'whore':
It does abhor me now I speak the word;
To do the act that might the addition earn
Not the world's mass of vanity could make me.

IAGO　I pray you, be content; 'tis but his humour:
The business of the state does him offence,
And he does chide with you.

DESDEM.　　　　　　　　　　If 'twere no other!

IAGO　'Tis but so, I warrant.　　　　　　[*trumpets sound*
Hark how these instruments summon to supper!　　170
The messengers of Venice stay the meat:
Go in, and weep not; all things shall be well.

　　　　　　　　　　　　　[*Desdemona and Emilia go*

　　　　　　　　Enter RODERIGO

How now, Roderigo!

RODERIGO　I do not find that thou deal'st justly with me.

IAGO　What in the contrary?

RODERIGO　Every day thou daff'st me with some device, Iago; and
rather, as it seems to me now, keep'st from me all
conveniency than suppliest me with the least advantage
of hope. I will indeed no longer endure it; nor am I yet
persuaded to put up in peace what already I have　180
foolishly suffered.

IAGO　Will you hear me, Roderigo?

RODERIGO Faith, I have heard too much; for your words and performances are no kin together.

IAGO You charge me most unjustly.

RODERIGO With nought but truth. I have wasted myself out of my means. The jewels you have had from me to deliver to Desdemona would half have corrupted a votarist. You have told me she hath received them and returned me expectations and comforts of sudden 19 respect and acquaintance; but I find none.

IAGO Well; go to; very well.

RODERIGO Very well! Go to! I cannot go to, man; nor 'tis not very well. By this hand, I think 'tis very scurvy, and begin to find myself fopped in it.

IAGO Very well.

RODERIGO I tell you 'tis not very well. I will make myself known to Desdemona. If she will return me my jewels, I will give over my suit and repent my unlawful solicitation; if not, assure yourself I will seek satisfaction of you. 2c

IAGO You have said now.

RODERIGO Ay, and said nothing but what I protest intendment of doing.

IAGO Why, now I see there's mettle in thee; and even from this instant do build on thee a better opinion than ever before. Give me thy hand, Roderigo: thou hast taken against me a most just exception ; but yet, I protest, I have dealt most directly in thy affair.

RODERIGO It hath not appeared.

IAGO I grant indeed it hath not appeared, and your suspicion 2\ is not without wit and judgment. But, Roderigo, if thou hast that in thee indeed, which I have greater reason to believe now than ever − I mean purpose, courage, and valour − this night show it: if thou the next night following enjoy not Desdemona, take me from this world with treachery and devise engines for my life.

RODERIGO Well, what is it? Is it within reason and compass?

IAGO Sir, there is especial commission come from Venice to depute Cassio in Othello's place.

RODERIGO Is that true? Why then, Othello and Desdemona return 2. again to Venice.

IAGO   O, no; he goes into Mauritania, and takes away with him the fair Desdemona, unless his abode be lingered here by some accident: wherein none can be so determinate as the removing of Cassio.

RODERIGO How do you mean removing of him?

IAGO   Why, by making him uncapable of Othello's place; knocking out his brains.

RODERIGO And that you would have me do?

IAGO   Ay, if you dare do yourself a profit and a right. He sups 230
tonight with a harlotry, and thither will I go to him: he knows not yet of his honourable fortune. If you will watch his going thence, which I will fashion to fall out between twelve and one, you may take him at your pleasure. I will be near to second your attempt, and he shall fall between us. Come, stand not amazed at it, but go along with me; I will show you such a necessity in his death that you shall think yourself bound to put it on him. It is now high supper-time, and the night grows to waste. About it. 240

RODERIGO I will hear further reason for this.

IAGO   And you shall be satisfied.   [*they go*

SCENE 3

Another room in the citadel

Enter OTHELLO, LODOVICO, DESDEMONA, EMILIA, *and Attendants*

LODOVICO I do beseech you, sir, trouble yourself no further.

OTHELLO   O, pardon me; 'twill do me good to walk.

LODOVICO Madam, good night; I humbly thank your ladyship.

DESDEM.   Your honour is most welcome.

OTHELLO   Will you walk, sir?
O, Desdemona!

DESDEM.   My lord?

OTHELLO   Get you to bed on th'instant; I will be returned forthwith. Dismiss your attendant there: look't be done.

DESDEM.   I will, my lord.   [*Othello, Lodovico, and Attendants go*

EMILIA   How goes it now? He looks gentler than he did. 10

DESDEM.   He says he will return incontinent:

| | He hath commanded me to go to bed, |
| | And bade me to dismiss you. |

EMILIA   Dismiss me!

DESDEM.   It was his bidding; therefore, good Emilia,
          Give me my nightly wearing, and adieu:
          We must not now displease him.

EMILIA   I would you had never seen him!

DESDEM.   So would not I: my love doth so approve him,
          That even his stubbornness, his checks, his frowns –
          Prithee, unpin me – have grace and favour in them.   20

EMILIA   I have laid those sheets you bade me on the bed.

DESDEM.   All's one. Good faith, how foolish are our minds!
          If I do die before thee, prithee, shroud me
          In one of those same sheets.

EMILIA   Come, come, you talk.

DESDEM.   My mother had a maid called Barbara.
          She was in love; and he she loved proved mad
          And did forsake her. She had a song of 'willow' –
          An old thing 'twas, but it expressed her fortune,
          And she died singing it. That song tonight
          Will not go from my mind. I have much to do   30
          But to go hang my head all at one side
          And sing it like poor Barbara. Prithee, dispatch.

EMILIA   Shall I go fetch your night-gown?

DESDEM.   No, unpin me here.
          This Lodovico is a proper man.

EMILIA   A very handsome man.

DESDEM.   He speaks well.

EMILIA   I know a lady in Venice would have walked barefoot
          to Palestine for a touch of his nether lip.

DESDEM.   [sings] The poor soul sat sighing by a sycamore tree,
                      Sing all a green willow;   40
                  Her hand on her bosom, her head on her knee,
                      Sing willow, willow, willow:
                  The fresh streams ran by her, and murmured
                                              her moans;
                      Sing willow, willow, willow;
                  Her salt tears fell from her, and softened the
                                              stones –

       Lay by these –
            Sing willow, willow, willow;
       Prithee, hie thee; he'll come anon –
            Sing all a green willow must be my garland.
            Let nobody blame him; his scorn I approve –   50
       Nay, that's not next. Hark! Who is't that knocks?

EMILIA   It's the wind.

DESDEM.   [*sings*] I called my love false love; but what said he
                                         then?
            Sing willow, willow, willow;
          If I court moe women, you'll couch with moe
                                      men.
       So, get thee gone; good night. Mine eyes do itch;
       Does that bode weeping?

EMILIA   'Tis neither here nor there.

DESDEM.   I have heard it said so. O, these men, these men!
       Dost thou in conscience think – tell me, Emilia –
       That there be women do abuse their husbands   60
       In such gross kind?

EMILIA   There be some such, no question.

DESDEM.   Wouldst thou do such a deed for all the world?

EMILIA   Why, would not you?

DESDEM.   No, by this heavenly light!

EMILIA   Nor I neither by this heavenly light: I might do't as
       well i'th'dark.

DESDEM.   Wouldst thou do such a deed for all the world?

EMILIA   The world's a huge thing: it is a great prize for a small
       vice.

DESDEM.   In troth, I think thou wouldst not.

EMILIA   In troth, I think I should; and undo't when I had 70
       done't. Marry, I would not do such a thing for a joint-
       ring, nor for measures of lawn, nor for gowns,
       petticoats, nor caps, nor any petty exhibition. But for all
       the whole world – ud's pity, who would not make her
       husband a cuckold to make him a monarch? I should
       venture purgatory for't.

DESDEM.   Beshrew me, if I would do such a wrong for the whole
       world.

EMILIA   Why, the wrong is but a wrong i'th'world; and having

the world for your labour, 'tis a wrong in your own 80
world, and you might quickly make it right.

DESDEM. I do not think there is any such woman.

EMILIA Yes, a dozen; and as many to th'vantage as would store
the world they played for.
But I do think it is their husbands' faults
If wives do fall. Say that they slack their duties
And pour our treasures into foreign laps,
Or else break out in peevish jealousies,
Throwing restraint upon us; or say they strike us,
Or scant our former having in despite – 90
Why, we have galls, and though we have some grace,
Yet have we some revenge. Let husbands know
Their wives have sense like them: they see, and smell,
And have their palates both for sweet and sour,
As husbands have. What is it that they do
When they change us for others? Is it sport?
I think it is. And doth affection breed it?
I think it doth. Is't frailty that thus errs?
It is so too. And have not we affections,
Desires for sport, and frailty, as men have? 100
Then let them use us well: else let them know,
The ills we do, their ills instruct us so.

DESDEM. Good night, good night.   [*Emilia goes*
                   Heaven me such uses send,
Not to pick bad from bad, but by bad mend!   [*goes*

ACT 5 SCENE I

A street

Enter IAGO *and* RODERIGO

IAGO	Here, stand behind this bulk; straight will he come.
	Wear thy good rapier bare, and put it home;
	Quick, quick; fear nothing; I'll be at thy elbow.
	It makes us, or it mars us; think on that,
	And fix most firm thy resolution.
RODERIGO	Be near at hand; I may miscarry in't.
IAGO	Here, at thy hand. Be bold, and take thy stand. *[retires*
RODERIGO	I have no great devotion to the deed;
	And yet he hath given me satisfying reasons.
	'Tis but a man gone. Forth, my sword: he dies. 10
IAGO	I have rubbed this young quat almost to the sense,
	And he grows angry. Now, whether he kill Cassio,
	Or Cassio him, or each do kill the other,
	Every way makes my gain: live Roderigo,
	He calls me to a restitution large
	Of gold and jewels that I bobbed from him,
	As gifts to Desdemona –
	It must not be; if Cassio do remain,
	He hath a daily beauty in his life
	That makes me ugly; and besides, the Moor 20
	May unfold me to him – there stand I in much peril.
	No, he must die. Be't so. I hear him coming.

Enter CASSIO

RODERIGO	I know his gait; 'tis he. Villain, thou diest!
	[makes a pass at Cassio
CASSIO	That thrust had been mine enemy indeed,
	But that my coat is better than thou think'st.
	I will make proof of thine. *[draws, and wounds Roderigo*
RODERIGO	O, I am slain!
	[Iago from behind strikes at Cassio's legs, and hurries off
CASSIO	I am maimed for ever. Help, ho! Murder! Murder!
	[falls

Enter OTHELLO

OTHELLO	The voice of Cassio: Iago keeps his word.
RODERIGO	O, villain that I am!
OTHELLO	It is even so.
CASSIO	O, help, ho! Light! A surgeon!

30

OTHELLO	'Tis he. O brave Iago, honest and just,
	That hast such noble sense of thy friend's wrong!
	Thou teachest me: minion, your dear lies dead,
	And your unblest fate hies. Strumpet, I come!
	Forth of my heart, those charms, thine eyes, are blotted;
	Thy bed lust-stained shall with lust's blood be spotted.

[*he goes*

Enter LODOVICO *and* GRATIANO

CASSIO	What, ho! No watch? No passage? Murder! Murder!
GRATIANO	'Tis some mischance; the voice is very direful.
CASSIO	O, help!
LODOVICO	Hark!

40

RODERIGO	O wretched villain!
LODOVICO	Two or three groan. It is a heavy night;
	These may be counterfeits: let's think't unsafe
	To come in to the cry without more help.

[*they stand aside*

RODERIGO	Nobody come? Then shall I bleed to death.
LODOVICO	Hark!

Re-enter IAGO, *with a light*

GRATIANO	Here's one comes in his shirt, with light and weapons.
IAGO	Who's there? Whose noise is this that cries on murder?
LODOVICO	We do not know.
IAGO	Did not you hear a cry?
CASSIO	Here, here! For heaven's sake, help me!
IAGO	What's the matter?

50

GRATIANO	This is Othello's ancient, as I take it.
LODOVICO	The same indeed; a very valiant fellow.
IAGO	What are you here that cry so grievously?
CASSIO	Iago? O, I am spoiled, undone by villains!
	Give me some help.
IAGO	O me, lieutenant! What villains have done this?
CASSIO	I think that one of them is hereabout,

	And cannot make away.	
IAGO	O treacherous villains!	
	What are you there? [*spies Lodovico and Gratiano*	
	Come in and give some help.	
RODERIGO	O, help me here!	60
CASSIO	That's one of them.	
IAGO	O murderous slave! O villain!	
	[*stabs Roderigo*	
RODERIGO	O damned Iago! O inhuman dog!	
IAGO	Kill men i'th'dark! Where be these bloody thieves?	
	How silent is this town! Ho! Murder! Murder!	
	[*Lodovico and Gratiano come forward*	
	What may you be? Are you of good or evil?	
LODOVICO	As you shall prove us, praise us.	
IAGO	Signior Lodovico?	
LODOVICO	He, sir.	
IAGO	I cry you mercy. Here's Cassio hurt by villains.	
GRATIANO	Cassio!	70
IAGO	How is't, brother?	
CASSIO	My leg is cut in two.	
IAGO	Marry, heaven forbid!	
	Light, gentlemen: I'll bind it with my shirt.	

Enter BIANCA

BIANCA	What is the matter, ho? Who is't that cried?	
IAGO	Who is't that cried!	
BIANCA	O my dear Cassio!	
	My sweet Cassio! O Cassio, Cassio, Cassio!	
IAGO	O notable strumpet! Cassio, may you suspect	
	Who they should be that have thus mangled you?	
CASSIO	No.	80
GRATIANO	I am sorry to find you thus: I have been to seek you.	
IAGO	Lend me a garter. So. O, for a chair,	
	To bear him easily hence!	
BIANCA	Alas, he faints! O Cassio, Cassio, Cassio!	
IAGO	Gentlemen all, I do suspect this trash	
	To be a party in this injury.	
	Patience awhile, good Cassio. Come, come;	
	Lend me a light. Know we this face or no?	

Alas, my friend and my dear countryman
Roderigo? No – yes, sure; 'tis Roderigo.   90
GRATIANO What, of Venice?
IAGO Even he, sir. Did you know him?
GRATIANO   Know him! Ay.
IAGO Signior Gratiano? I cry your gentle pardon:
These bloody accidents must excuse my manners,
That so neglected you.
GRATIANO   I am glad to see you.
IAGO How do you, Cassio? O, a chair, a chair!
GRATIANO Roderigo!
IAGO He, he, 'tis he. [*a chair brought*] O, that's well said;
                                              the chair.
Some good man bear him carefully from hence;
I'll fetch the general's surgeon. [*to Bianca*] For you,
                                              mistress,   100
Save you your labour. He that lies slain here, Cassio,
Was my dear friend: what malice was between you?
CASSIO None in the world; nor do I know the man.
IAGO [*to Bianca*]
What, look you pale? O, bear him out o'th'air.
              [*Cassio is borne in, and the body of Roderigo removed*
Stay you, good gentlemen. Look you pale, mistress?
Do you perceive the gastness of her eye?
Nay, if you stare, we shall hear more anon.
Behold her well; I pray you, look upon her:
Do you see, gentlemen? Nay, guiltiness will speak,
Though tongues were out of use.   110

Enter EMILIA

EMILIA 'Las, what's the matter? What's the matter, husband?
IAGO Cassio hath here been set on in the dark
By Roderigo, and fellows that are scaped:
He's almost slain, and Roderigo dead.
EMILIA Alas, good gentleman! Alas, good Cassio!
IAGO This is the fruits of whoring. Prithee, Emilia,
Go know of Cassio where he supped tonight.
What, do you shake at that?
BIANCA He supped at my house; but I therefore shake not.

IAGO	O, did he so? I charge you, go with me.	120
EMILIA	O, fie upon thee, strumpet!	
BIANCA	I am no strumpet; but of life as honest	
	As you that thus abuse me.	
EMILIA	As I! Foh! Fie upon thee!	
IAGO	Kind gentlemen, let's see poor Cassio dressed.	
	Come, mistress, you must tell's another tale.	
	Emilia, run you to the citadel,	
	And tell my lord and lady what hath happed.	
	Will you go on afore? [aside] This is the night	
	That either makes me or fordoes me quite. [they go	

SCENE 2

A chamber in the citadel; Desdemona asleep in her bed

Enter OTHELLO *with a light; he locks the door*

OTHELLO It is the cause, it is the cause, my soul.
Let me not name it to you, you chaste stars!
It is the cause. Yet I'll not shed her blood,
Nor scar that whiter skin of hers than snow
And smooth as monumental alabaster –
Yet she must die, else she'll betray more men.
Put out the light, and then put out the light:
If I quench thee, thou flaming minister,
I can again thy former light restore
Should I repent me; but once put out thy light,   10
Thou cunning'st pattern of excelling nature,
I know not where is that Promethean heat
That can thy light relume.   [*sets down the taper*
                   When I have plucked the rose,
I cannot give it vital growth again,
It needs must wither: I'll smell it on the tree. [*kisses her*
O balmy breath, that dost almost persuade
Justice to break her sword! One more, one more.
Be thus when thou art dead, and I will kill thee,
And love thee after. One more, and that's the last.
So sweet was ne'er so fatal. I must weep,   20

But they are cruel tears; this sorrow's heavenly:
It strikes where it doth love. She wakes.

DESDEM. Who's there? Othello?

OTHELLO Ay, Desdemona.

DESDEM. Will you come to bed, my lord?

OTHELLO Have you prayed tonight, Desdemona?

DESDEM.   Ay, my lord.

OTHELLO If you bethink yourself of any crime
Unreconciled as yet to heaven and grace,
Solicit for it straight.

DESDEM. Alack, my lord, what may you mean by that?   30

OTHELLO Well, do it, and be brief; I will walk by:
I would not kill thy unpreparéd spirit;
No – heaven forfend! – I would not kill thy soul.

DESDEM. Talk you of killing?

OTHELLO Ay, I do.

DESDEM. Then heaven have mercy on me!

OTHELLO Amen, with all my heart!

DESDEM. If you say so, I hope you will not kill me.

OTHELLO Hum!

DESDEM. And yet I fear you; for you're fatal then   40
When your eyes roll so. Why I should fear I know not,
Since guiltiness I know not; but yet I feel I fear.

OTHELLO Think on thy sins.

DESDEM.   They are loves I bear to you.

OTHELLO Ay, and for that thou diest.

DESDEM. That death's unnatural that kills for loving.
Alas, why gnaw you so your nether lip?
Some bloody passion shakes your very frame:
These are portents; but yet I hope, I hope,
They do not point on me.

OTHELLO   Peace, and be still!

DESDEM. I will so. What's the matter?   50

OTHELLO That handkerchief which I so loved and gave thee,
Thou gav'st to Cassio.

DESDEM.   No, by my life and soul!
Send for the man, and ask him.

OTHELLO   Sweet soul, take heed,
Take heed of perjury: thou art on thy death-bed,

DESDEM. Ay, but not yet to die.
OTHELLO   Yes, presently;
Therefore confess thee freely of thy sin;
For to deny each article with oath
Cannot remove nor choke the strong conception
That I do groan withal. Thou art to die.
DESDEM. O Lord have mercy on me!
OTHELLO   I say, amen.   60
DESDEM. And have you mercy too! I never did
Offend you in my life; never loved Cassio
But with such general warranty of heaven
As I might love. I never gave him token.
OTHELLO By heaven, I saw my handkerchief in's hand.
O perjured woman! Thou dost stone my heart,
And mak'st me call what I intend to do
A murder, which I thought a sacrifice.
I saw the handkerchief.
DESDEM.   He found it then;
I never gave it him. Send for him hither: 70
Let him confess a truth.
OTHELLO   He hath confessed.
DESDEM. What, my lord?
OTHELLO That he hath used thee.
DESDEM.   How? Unlawfully?
OTHELLO Ay.
DESDEM. He will not say so.
OTHELLO   No, his mouth is stopped;
Honest Iago hath ta'en order for't.
DESDEM. O, my fear interprets! What, is he dead?
OTHELLO Had all his hairs been lives, my great revenge
Had stomach for them all.
DESDEM. Alas, he is betrayed, and I undone!   80
OTHELLO Out, strumpet! Weep'st thou for him to my face?
DESDEM. O, banish me, my lord, but kill me not!
OTHELLO Down, strumpet!
DESDEM. Kill me tomorrow; let me live tonight!
OTHELLO Nay, if you strive —
DESDEM. But half an hour!
OTHELLO   Being done, there is no pause.

DESDEM.	But while I say one prayer!
OTHELLO	It is too late. [*he smothers her*
EMILIA	[*at the door without*]
	My lord, my lord! What, ho! My lord, my lord!
OTHELLO	What noise is this? – Not dead? Not yet quite dead?
	I that am cruel am yet merciful;
	I would not have thee linger in thy pain.
	So, so.
EMILIA	[*without*] What, ho! My lord, my lord!
OTHELLO	Who's there?
EMILIA	[*without*]
	O, good my lord, I'd speak a word with you!
OTHELLO	Yes: 'tis Emilia. – By and by. – She's dead.
	'Tis like she comes to speak of Cassio's death;
	The noise was high. Ha! No more moving?
	Still as the grave. Shall she come in? Were't good?
	I think she stirs again. No. What's best to do?
	If she come in, she'll sure speak to my wife –
	My wife! My wife! What wife? I have no wife.
	O, insupportable! O heavy hour!
	Methinks it should be now a huge eclipse
	Of sun and moon, and that th'affrighted globe
	Should yawn at alteration.
EMILIA	[*without*] I do beseech
	That I may speak with you. O, good my lord!
OTHELLO	I had forgot thee: O, come in, Emilia.
	Soft; by and by. Let me the curtains draw.
	Where art thou? [*unlocks the door*

Enter EMILIA

	What's the matter with thee now?
EMILIA	O, my good lord, yonder's foul murder done!
OTHELLO	What, now?
EMILIA	But now, my lord.
OTHELLO	It is the very error of the moon;
	She comes more nearer earth than she was wont
	And makes men mad.
EMILIA	Cassio, my lord, hath killed a young Venetian
	Called Roderigo.
OTHELLO	Roderigo killed!

90

10

11

	And Cassio killed!
EMILIA	No, Cassio is not killed.
OTHELLO	Not Cassio killed! Then murder's out of tune,
	And sweet revenge grows harsh.
DESDEM.	O, falsely, falsely murdered!
EMILIA	Alas, what cry is that? 120
OTHELLO	That! What?
EMILIA	Out, and alas! That was my lady's voice.

                                        [she draws back the curtain

	Help! Help, ho! Help! O lady, speak again!
	Sweet Desdemona! O sweet mistress, speak!
DESDEM.	A guiltless death I die.
EMILIA	O, who hath done this deed?
DESDEM.	Nobody: I myself. Farewell;
	Commend me to my kind lord: O, farewell! *[dies*
OTHELLO	Why, how should she be murdered?
EMILIA	Alas, who knows?
OTHELLO	You heard her say herself, it was not I. 130
EMILIA	She said so: I must needs report the truth.
OTHELLO	She's like a liar gone to burning hell:
	'Twas I that killed her.
EMILIA	O, the more angel she,
	And you the blacker devil!
OTHELLO	She turned to folly, and she was a whore.
EMILIA	Thou dost belie her, and thou art a devil.
OTHELLO	She was false as water.
EMILIA	Thou art rash as fire to say
	That she was false: O, she was heavenly true!
OTHELLO	Cassio did top her: ask thy husband else;
	O, I were damned beneath all depth in hell 140
	But that I did proceed upon just grounds
	To this extremity. Thy husband knew it all.
EMILIA	My husband!
OTHELLO	Thy husband.
EMILIA	That she was false to wedlock?
OTHELLO	Ay, with Cassio. Nay, had she been true,
	If heaven would make me such another world
	Of one entire and perfect chrysolite,
	I'd not have sold her for it.

EMILIA   My husband!

OTHELLO   Ay, 'twas he that told he on her first;   15
An honest man he is, and hates the slime
That sticks on filthy deeds.

EMILIA   My husband!

OTHELLO   What needs this iterance, woman? I say thy husband.

EMILIA   O mis'tress, villainy hath made mocks with love!
My husband say that she was false!

OTHELLO   He, woman:
I say thy husband; dost understand the word?
My friend, thy husband, honest, honest Iago.

EMILIA   If he say so, may his pernicious soul
Rot half a grain a day! He lies to th'heart.
She was too fond of her most filthy bargain.   16

OTHELLO   Ha!

EMILIA   Do thy worst:
This deed of thine is no more worthy heaven
Than thou wast worthy her.

OTHELLO   Peace, you were best.

EMILIA   Thou hast not half that power to do me harm
As I have to be hurt. O gull! O dolt!
As ignorant as dirt! Thou hast done a deed –
I care not for thy sword; I'll make thee known,
Though I lost twenty lives. Help! Help, ho! Help!
The Moor hath killed my mistress! Murder! Murder!   17

Enter MONTANO, GRATIANO, IAGO, *and others*

MONTANO   What is the matter? How now, general!

EMILIA   O, are you come, Iago? You have done well,
That men must lay their murders on your neck.

GRATIANO   What is the matter?

EMILIA   Disprove this villain, if thou be'st a man.
He says thou told'st him that his wife was false.
I know thou didst not, thou'rt not such a villain.
Speak, for my heart is full.

IAGO   I told him what I thought, and told no more
Than what he found himself was apt and true.   18

EMILIA   But did you ever tell him she was false?

IAGO   I did.

EMILIA   You told a lie, an odious, damnéd lie;

	Upon my soul, a lie, a wicked lie!
	She false with Cassio! Did you say with Cassio?
IAGO	With Cassio, mistress. Go to, charm your tongue.
EMILIA	I will not charm my tongue; I am bound to speak:
	My mistress here lies murdered in her bed –
ALL	O heavens forfend!
EMILIA	And your reports have set the murder on. 190
OTHELLO	Nay, stare not, masters: it is true indeed.
GRATIANO	'Tis a strange truth.
MONTANO	O monstrous act!
EMILIA	Villainy, villainy, villainy!
	I think upon't; I think – I smell't: O villainy!
	I thought so then; I'll kill myself for grief:
	O villainy, villainy!
IAGO	What, are you mad? I charge you, get you home.
EMILIA	Good gentlemen, let me have leave to speak:
	'Tis proper I obey him, but not now.
	Perchance, Iago, I will ne'er go home. 200
OTHELLO	O! O! O! [falls on the bed
EMILIA	Nay, lay thee down and roar;
	For thou hast killed the sweetest innocent
	That e'er did lift up eye.
OTHELLO	[rising] O, she was foul!
	I scarce did know you, uncle. There lies your niece,
	Whose breath indeed these hands have newly stopped.
	I know this act shows horrible and grim.
GRATIANO	Poor Desdemon! I am glad thy father's dead.
	Thy match was mortal to him, and pure grief
	Shore his old thread in twain. Did he live now,
	This sight would make him do a desperate turn, 210
	Yea, curse his better angel from his side,
	And fall to reprobance.
OTHELLO	'Tis pitiful; but yet Iago knows
	That she with Cassio hath the act of shame
	A thousand times committed. Cassio confessed it;
	And she did gratify his amorous works
	With that recognizance and pledge of love
	Which I first gave her – I saw it in his hand:
	It was a handkerchief, an antique token

My father gave my mother.   22

EMILIA   O God! O heavenly God!

IAGO   'Zounds! Hold your peace.

EMILIA   'Twill out, 'twill out. I peace!
          No, I will speak as liberal as the north;
          Let heaven and men and devils, let them all,
          All, all, cry shame against me, yet I'll speak.

IAGO   Be wise, and get you home.

EMILIA   I will not.
                          [Iago offers to stab her

GRATIANO   Fie!
          Your sword upon a woman!

EMILIA   O thou dull Moor! That handkerchief thou speak'st of
          I found by fortune, and did give my husband;
          For often with a solemn earnestness,   23
          More than indeed belonged to such a trifle,
          He begged of me to steal it.

IAGO   Villainous whore!

EMILIA   She give it Cassio! No, alas, I found it,
          And I did give't my husband.

IAGO   Filth, thou liest!

EMILIA   By heaven, I do not, I do not, gentlemen.
          O murderous coxcomb! What should such a fool
          Do with so good a wife?

OTHELLO   Are there no stones in heaven
          But what serve for the thunder? Precious villain!
                  *[he runs at Iago, but Montano disarms him; in the
                  confusion, Iago stabs Emilia from behind and escapes*

GRATIANO The woman falls; sure, he hath killed his wife.

EMILIA   Ay, ay. O, lay me by my mistress' side.   24

GRATIANO He's gone, but his wife's killed.

MONTANO   'Tis a notorious villain. Take you this weapon,
          Which I have here recovered from the Moor.
          Come, guard the door without; let him not pass,
          But kill him rather. I'll after that same villain,
          For 'tis a damnéd slave. *[all but Othello and Emilia depart*

OTHELLO   I am not valiant neither,
          But every puny whipster gets my sword.
          But why should honour outlive honesty?

Let it go all.

EMILIA   What did thy song bode, lady?

Hark, canst thou hear me? I will play the swan,   250
And die in music. [*singing*] Willow, willow, willow.
Moor, she was chaste; she loved thee, cruel Moor;
So come my soul to bliss, as I speak true;
So speaking as I think, alas, I die.   [*dies*

OTHELLO   I have another weapon in this chamber:
It was a sword of Spain, the ice brook's temper –
O, here it is. Uncle, I must come forth.

GRATIANO [*at the door*] If thou attempt it, it will cost thee dear:
Thou hast no weapon, and perforce must suffer.

OTHELLO   Look in upon me then, and speak with me,   260
Or, naked as I am, I will assault thee.

Re-enter GRATIANO

GRATIANO What is the matter?

OTHELLO   Behold, I have a weapon:
A better never did itself sustain
Upon a soldier's thigh. I have seen the day
That with this little arm and this good sword
I have made my way through more impediments
Than twenty times your stop – but, O vain boast!
Who can control his fate? – 'Tis not so now.
Be not afraid, though you do see me weaponed:
Here is my journey's end, here is my butt   270
And very sea-mark of my utmost sail.
Do you go back dismayed? 'Tis a lost fear:
Man but a rush against Othello's breast,
And he retires. Where should Othello go?
Now, [*he turns to the bed*] how dost thou look now?
                          O ill-starred wench!
Pale as thy smock! When we shall meet at compt,
This look of thine will hurl my soul from heaven,
And fiends will snatch at it. Cold, cold, my girl!
Even like thy chastity.
O curséd, curséd slave! Whip me, ye devils,   280
From the possession of this heavenly sight!
Blow me about in winds! Roast me in sulphur!

Wash me in steep-down gulfs of liquid fire!
O Desdemon! Dead Desdemon! Dead! O! O!

Enter LODOVICO, MONTANO, CASSIO *carried in a chair, and Officers*
with IAGO, *prisoner*

LODOVICO Where is this rash and most unfortunate man?
OTHELLO   That's he that was Othello: here I am.
LODOVICO Where is that viper? Bring the villain forth.
OTHELLO   I look down towards his feet: but that's a fable;
          If that thou be'st a devil, I cannot kill thee.

                                              [*wounds Iago*

LODOVICO Wrench his sword from him.
IAGO   I bleed, sir, but not killed. 290
OTHELLO   I am not sorry neither: I'd have thee live;
          For, in my sense, 'tis happiness to die.
LODOVICO O thou Othello, that wert once so good,
          Fallen in the practice of a damnéd slave,
          What shall be said to thee?
OTHELLO   Why, anything:
          An honourable murderer, if you will;
          For nought did I in hate, but all in honour.
LODOVICO This wretch hath part confessed his villainy.
          Did you and he consent in Cassio's death?
OTHELLO   Ay.   300
CASSIO   Dear general, I never gave you cause.
OTHELLO   I do believe it, and I ask your pardon.
          Will you, I pray, demand that demi-devil
          Why he hath thus ensnared my soul and body?
IAGO   Demand me nothing: what you know, you know;
          From this time forth I never will speak word.
LODOVICO What, not to pray?
GRATIANO   Torments will ope your lips.
OTHELLO   Well, thou dost best.
LODOVICO Sir, you shall understand what hath befallen,
          Which, as I think, you know not. Here is a letter, 310
          Found in the pocket of the slain Roderigo,
          And here another: the one of them imports
          The death of Cassio to be undertook
          By Roderigo.

OTHELLO O villain!

CASSIO   Most heathenish and most gross!

LODOVICO Now here's another discontented paper,
          Found in his pocket too: and this, it seems,
          Roderigo meant t'have sent this damnéd villain;
          But that, belike, Iago in the nick
          Came in and satisfied him.

OTHELLO   O the pernicious caitiff!   320
          How came you, Cassio, by that handkerchief
          That was my wife's?

CASSIO   I found it in my chamber:
          And he himself confessed but even now
          That there he dropped it for a special purpose
          Which wrought to his desire.

OTHELLO   O fool! Fool! Fool!

CASSIO   There is besides, in Roderigo's letter,
          How he upbraids Iago that he made him
          Brave me upon the watch; whereon it came
          That I was cast; and even but now he spake –
          After long seeming dead – Iago hurt him,   330
          Iago set him on.

LODOVICO You must forsake this room, and go with us;
          Your power and your command is taken off,
          And Cassio rules in Cyprus. For this slave,
          If there be any cunning cruelty
          That can torment him much and hold him long,
          It shall be his. You shall close prisoner rest,
          Till that the nature of your fault be known
          To the Venetian state. Come, bring away.

OTHELLO Soft you; a word or two before you go.   340
          I have done the state some service, and they know't,
          No more of that. I pray you, in your letters,
          When you shall these unlucky deeds relate,
          Speak of me as I am; nothing extenuate,
          Nor set down aught in malice. Then must you speak
          Of one that loved not wisely but too well;
          Of one not easily jealous but, being wrought,
          Perplexed in the extreme; of one whose hand,
          Like the base Indian, threw a pearl away

        Richer than all his tribe; of one whose subdued eyes,   350
        Albeit unuséd to the melting mood,
        Drop tears as fast as the Arabian trees
        Their medicinable gum – Set you down this;
        And say besides, that in Aleppo once,
        Where a malignant and a turbaned Turk
        Beat a Venetian and traduced the state,
        I took by th'throat the circumciséd dog,
        And smote him – thus.   *[he stabs himself*

LODOVICO O bloody period!

GRATIANO   All that's spoke is marred.

OTHELLO I kissed thee ere I killed thee: no way but this,   360
        Killing myself, to die upon a kiss.
                        [falls on the bed, and dies

CASSIO   This did I fear, but thought he had no weapon;
        For he was great of heart.

LODOVICO *[to Iago]*   O Spartan dog,
        More fell than anguish, hunger, or the sea!
        Look on the tragic loading of this bed –
        This is thy work. The object poisons sight;
        Let it be hid. *[they draw the curtains]* Gratiano, keep
                                 the house,
        And seize upon the fortunes of the Moor,
        For they succeed on you. To you, lord governor,
        Remains the censure of this hellish villain,   370
        The time, the place, the torture: O, enforce it!
        Myself will straight aboard, and to the state
        This heavy act with heavy heart relate.   *[they go*

KING LEAR

INTRODUCTION

King Lear was first printed in 1608, and appeared in a substantially different version in 1623, probably representing the author's revisions of the original text. It uses a story known to Shakespeare from historical sources, especially from the *Chronicles* of Elizabethan historian Raphael Holinshed, the major source for the history plays and for *Macbeth*. It also reworks an existing anonymous play, *The True Chronicle History of King Leir*, but Shakespeare's manipulation of this familiar material produces his own highly original creation. The play's plot concerns Lear, old king of ancient Britain, who asks his three daughters how much they love him in order to divide up his kingdom between them. The two elder daughters, Goneril and Regan, satisfy their father's test through overstated and insincere protestations of affection. Only Cordelia, Lear's favourite, is unable to take part in this charade, and her angry father divides the land between his other daughters. Disgraced and disinherited, Cordelia is claimed as wife by the King of France, and leaves with her husband. Lear's faith in Goneril and Regan proves entirely misplaced, as they contrive to turn their father out of doors with only his Fool for company. In the madness and mental collapse which follows, Lear comes intermittently to realise his folly. Hearing of her father's situation, Cordelia arrives at Dover with a French army. In a subplot, the nobleman Gloucester's bastard son, Edmund, turns his father against his legitimate son, Edgar. Edgar dresses as a madman in order to stay close to his father, who has been tortured on the orders of Goneril and Regan and blinded. Both sisters are in love with Edmund, and in her passion, Goneril kills Regan and herself. Cordelia is hanged and Lear dies.

From this brief synopsis, it is clear that *King Lear* is a bleak story. Unlike versions of the Lear tale which allow a happy ending, Shakespeare's play is unremitting in its pessimism. Samuel Johnson was famously so upset by the death of Cordelia that he could not bear to reread the last scenes of the play, and many critics and readers since the eighteenth century have felt similarly devastated by *King Lear*'s desperate and desolate conclusion, in which the apocalypse of personal and political tragedy finishes with the banalities of Edgar's final words and the solemn tableau of the 'dead march'. The recognition scene between Cordelia and Lear which ought to set the play on the way to a resolution only ushers forth an ending – death – and in this cruel manipulation of expectations, Shakespeare is working against all the analogues from which the play is drawn. Lear's death, with the body of Cordelia in his arms, is agonisingly slow: like his remaining subjects, we want it to be over.

Perhaps it is this refusal to submit to fictitious comforts which makes the play so modern: it represents an existential view of a world in which no benevolent God or other agent will ensure that the good are rewarded and the bad punished, and there seems to be no mechanism to limit human cruelty and suffering. 'Humanity must perforce prey on itself,' says Albany, 'Like monsters of the deep' (4.2.49–50). While this may seem modern – parallels have been drawn with the plays of Samuel Beckett – *King Lear* is also the Shakespearean tragedy which comes closest to the art of the ancient Greek tragedians in its unflinching dissection of human torment. Alluding to this tragic model, Gloucester's attribution of a terrible arbitrary power to the gods, 'As flies to wanton boys are we to th' gods; They kill us for their sport' (4.1.36–37), seems to reduce human capacity for self-determination, but in the end humanity cannot duck responsibility. Gloucester's own belief in the gods is undermined by his speech renouncing the world (4.6.34–40): there are no gods, only mortals, the play seems to say, as Gloucester throws himself off an imaginary cliff produced through the theatrical trickery of the disguised Edgar. By contrast Edmund recalls Iago's belief in his own self-sufficiency and repudiates superstition, mocking the human tendency to 'admirable evasion' in 'mak[ing] guilty of our disasters the sun, the moon and stars' (1.2.114–23). Readings of the play which have attempted to salvage it as a Christian allegory seem wilfully inappropriate – the type of rationalisation that a character within the play might try to make of his predicament in the face of the crushing misery which is fundamentally inexplicable. While it does make use of biblical allusion and parallel – the story of Job, for example, or Cordelia as a Christ-like redemptive sacrifice – the play seems to pick up different ideologies, expressed at different moments and through different characters, in an attempt to explain human life, without fixing on any transcendent ideology, except perhaps a bitter stoicism. 'Nothing will come of nothing' (1.1.89), Lear tells Cordelia in the opening scene, and the play goes on to explore the implications of that nothingness in a senseless world without consolation.

King Lear approaches and constructs nothingness through its repeated motif of the loss of personal and social identity. Disguise is a physical symbol of these transformations, but whereas in Shakespeare's comedies, disguises are the means by which social and personal integration and identification are achieved, in King Lear these features work towards fragmentation and destruction. From the first scene in which Lear divests himself of kingship to Edgar's disguise as a madman, from the disinheriting of Cordelia to the blinding of Gloucester, the play systematically dismantles all the comforts of stable and continuous identity. Lear's bitter joking at his treatment in Goneril's court asks the question the play goes on to anatomise: 'Who is it that can tell me who I am?' (1.4.218). The play offers several answers but does not seem to endorse a single response. 'Royal Lear' and 'old man' (1.1.138, 145) Kent announces in the first scene; 'infirm and choleric' and one who 'hath ever but slenderly known himself' (1.1.289–95) is the judgment of Goneril and Regan; 'a poor, infirm, weak, and despised old man' (3.2.20), as Lear identifies himself. 'Lear's shadow', responds the Fool, representing the disintegration of Lear's substantive person as he is reduced to a pale imitation of his former self. 'Now thou art an O without a figure, [. . .] thou art nothing' (1.4.181–83) All the main characters undergo change, but none more so than Lear himself. In instigating the self-indulgent test in the first scene of the play, Lear begins a series of changes. While his first act in the play is willed and purposive, his subsequent behaviour is not so controlled, and he undergoes a shocking and irreversible personal collapse. Unaware that his whole identity is bound up with his position, after abdicating his authority and banishing his daughter he loses not only his kingdom but his reason and his very self. One way of making sense of this progression is to see in it an accompanying spiritual or mental transformation: by this logic, Lear loses material and social riches, but comes to a closer knowledge of a more fundamental truth. This, too, seems illusory. Lear's lessons are harsh ones, but they do him little good, and his self-knowledge at the end of the play is as partial and myopic as before, and as unable to stave off the inevitable destruction. He is by turns testy, misogynistic, clear-sighted and self-justificatory, and it is hard to make him an admirable or likeable character, although he has moments of extreme, even unbearable, pathos.

The play's dissection of reason and insanity is one of its most striking themes. Lear's madness, Edgar's disguise as a Bedlam beggar, and the gnomic wisdom of the Fool, coincide to offer an oblique commentary on the play world and propose alternative methods of understanding it. 'Folly' and its cognates 'fool' and 'foolishness' reverberate through the play, and this theme is often articulated and encapsulated by the character named for it. Court fools had a particular liberty in medieval and Renaissance society, and were privileged to speak wittily and critically of their masters: Goneril refers to 'your all-licensed fool' (1.4.189). Lear's Fool goads him unrelentingly for his folly in giving away the kingdom, but is also curiously tender in following his master through his deprivations. His is more a function than a character: it is significant that he has no name beyond that of his role. As the Fool disappears, Lear comes to recognise his own foolishness: 'I am a very foolish fond old man' (4.7.60); but this comes too late and ineffectually. All is foolish – in the sense of being meaningless – the play avers: 'When we are born, we cry that we are come To this great stage of fools' (4.6.182–83), a theatrical metaphor which amply expresses the emptiness of human existence. Associated with this grim insight is the play's thematisation of language. Cordelia's simple, catastrophic and proud refusal to engage in the linguistic inflation of her sisters' responses to Lear's test inaugurates a motif about true and false speech throughout the play. The truest speech turns out to be the most riddling or evasive, in the words of the Fool, or in Cordelia's aside telling the audience that her 'love's More ponderous than my tongue' (1.1.76–77). At the play's conclusion, Edgar urges the depleted cast to 'Speak what we feel, not what we ought to say' (5.3.324), as if genuine and unaffected speech can heal the play's pain. It was, however, exactly such speech, in the mouth of Cordelia at the beginning of the play, which set the tragic events in motion. In this recollection of its opening scene, the play's conclusion underlines *King Lear*'s refusal of the possibility of final reconciliation.

The scene: Britain

CHARACTERS IN THE PLAY

LEAR, *king of Britain*
KING OF FRANCE
DUKE OF BURGUNDY
DUKE OF CORNWALL, *husband to Regan*
DUKE OF ALBANY, *husband to Goneril*
EARL OF KENT
EARL OF GLOUCESTER
EDGAR, *son to Gloucester*
EDMUND, *bastard son to Gloucester*
CURAN, *a courtier*
OSWALD, *steward to Goneril*
OLD MAN, *tenant to Gloucester*
DOCTOR
FOOL

GONERIL
REGAN } *daughters of Lear*
CORDELIA

Gentleman, Herald, Captains, Knights of Lear's train, Messengers, Soldiers, Attendants, Servants

KING LEAR

ACT I SCENE I

The throne-room in King Lear's palace

'*Enter* KENT, GLOUCESTER, *and* EDMUND'

KENT   I thought the king had more affected the Duke of
          Albany than Cornwall.

GLO'STER It did always seem so to us; but now, in the division of
          the kingdom, it appears not which of the dukes he
          values most, for equalities are so weighed that curiosity
          in neither can make choice of either's moiety.

KENT   Is not this your son, my lord?

GLO'STER His breeding, sir, hath been at my charge. I have so
          often blushed to acknowledge him that now I am
          brazed to 't.   10

KENT   I cannot conceive you.

GLO'STER Sir, this young fellow's mother could; whereupon she
          grew round-wombed, and had indeed, sir, a son for
          her cradle ere she had a husband for her bed. Do you
          smell a fault?

KENT   I cannot wish the fault undone, the issue of it being so
          proper.

GLO'STER But I have a son, sir, by order of law, some year elder
          than this, who yet is no dearer in my account. Though
          this knave came something saucily to the world before 20
          he was sent for, yet was his mother fair; there was
          good sport at his making, and the whoreson must be
          acknowledged. Do you know this noble gentleman,
          Edmund?

EDMUND   No, my lord.

GLO'STER My lord of Kent. Remember him hereafter as my
          honourable friend.

EDMUND   My services to your lordship.

KENT   I must love you, and sue to know you better.

EDMUND   Sir, I shall study deserving.   30

GLO'STER He hath been out nine years, and away he shall again.
          [*A sennet sounded*] The king is coming.

'Enter one bearing a coronet.' *'Enter* KING LEAR, CORNWALL,
ALBANY, GONERIL, REGAN, CORDELIA, *and attendants'*

LEAR	Attend the lords of France and Burgundy, Gloucester.
GLO'STER	I shall, my liege. [*he goes out, attended by Edmund*
LEAR	Meantime we shall express our darker purpose.

Give me the map there. Know that we have divided
In three our kingdom; and 'tis our fast intent
To shake all cares and business from our age,
Conferring them on younger strengths while we
Unburdened crawl toward death. Our son of
                                        Cornwall,   40
And you, our no less loving son of Albany,
We have this hour a constant will to publish
Our daughters' several dowers, that future strife
May be prevented now. The princes, France and
                                        Burgundy,
Great rivals in our youngest daughter's love,
Long in our court have made their amorous sojourn,
And here are to be answered. Tell me, my daughters
(Since now we will divest us both of rule,
Interest of territory, cares of state),
Which of you shall we say doth love us most,   50
That we our largest bounty may extend
Where nature doth with merit challenge, Goneril,
Our eldest-born, speak first.

GONERIL   Sir, I love you more than word can wield the matter;
Dearer than eyesight, space and liberty;
Beyond what can be valued rich or rare;
No less than life with grace, health, beauty, honour;
As much as child e'er loved, or father found:
A love that makes breath poor, and speech unable.
Beyond all manner of 'so much' I love you.   60

CORDELIA   What shall Cordelia speak? Love, and be silent.
LEAR   [*showing the map*]
Of all these bounds, even from this line to this,
With shadowy forests and with champaigns riched,
With plenteous rivers and wide-skirted meads,
We make thee lady. To thine and Albany's issues
Be this perpetual. What says our second daughter,

Our dearest Regan, wife of Cornwall?

REGAN   I am made of that self metal as my sister,
And prize me at her worth. In my true heart
I find she names my very deed of love   70
Only she comes too short, that I profess
Myself an enemy to all other joys
Which the most precious spirit of sense possesses,
And find I am alone felicitate
In your dear Highness' love.

CORDELIA   Then poor Cordelia!
And yet not so, since I am sure my love's
More ponderous than my tongue.

LEAR   To thee and thine, hereditary ever,
Remain this ample third of our fair kingdom,
No less in space, validity, and pleasure   80
Than that conferred on Goneril. Now, our joy,
Although our last and least, to whose young love
The vines of France and milk of Burgundy
Strive to be interessed, what can you say to draw
A third more opulent than your sisters? Speak.

CORDELIA   Nothing, my lord.

LEAR   Nothing?

CORDELIA   Nothing.

LEAR   Nothing will come of nothing; speak again.

CORDELIA   Unhappy that I am, I cannot heave   90
My heart into my mouth. I love your Majesty
According to my bond, no more nor less.

LEAR   How, how, Cordelia? Mend your speech a little,
Lest you may mar your fortunes.

CORDELIA   Good my lord,
You have begot me, bred me, loved me. I
Return those duties back as are right fit,
Obey you, love you, and most honour you.
Why have my sisters husbands, if they say
They love you all? Haply, when I shall wed,
That lord whose hand must take my plight shall carry   100
Half my love with him, half my care and duty.
Sure I shall never marry like my sisters,
To love my father all.

LEAR	But goes thy heart with this?
CORDELIA	Ay, my good lord.
LEAR	So young, and so untender?
CORDELIA	So young, my lord, and true.
LEAR	Let it be so; thy truth then be thy dower!

For, by the saxred radiance of the sun,
The mysteries of Hecate and the night,
By all the operation of the orbs   110
From whom we do esist and cease to be,
Here I disclaim all my paternal care,
Propinquity and property of blood,
And as a stranger to my heart and me
Hold thee from this for ever. The barbarous Scythian,
Or he that makes his generation messes
To gorge his appetite, shall to my bosom
Be as well neighboured, pitied, and relieved,
As thou my sometime daughter.

KENT   Good my liege –

LEAR   Peace, Kent!   120
Come not between the dragon and his wrath.
I loved her most, and thought to set my rest
On her kind nursery. [*to Cordelia*] Hence, and avoid
                                                    my sight! –
So be my grave my peace as here I give
Her father's heart from her. Call France! Who stirs?
Call Burgundy! [*A courtier hurries forth*]
                    Cornwall and Albany,
With my two daughters' dowers digest the third;
Let pride, which she calls plainness, marry her.
I do invest you jointly with my power,
Pre-eminence, and all the large effects   130
That troop with majesty. Ourself, by monthly course,
With reservation of an hundred knights
By you to be sustained, shall our abode
Make with you by due turn. Only we shall retain
The name and all th' addition to a king: the sway,
Revenue, execution of the rest,
Belovéd sons, be yours; which to confirm,
This coronet part between you.

KENT   Royal Lear,
        Whom I have ever honoured as my king,
        Loved as my father, as my master followed,   140
        As my great patron thought on in my prayers –

LEAR   The bow is bent and drawn; make from the shaft.

KENT   Let it fall rather, though the fork invade
        The region of my heart! Be Kent unmannerly
        When Lear is mad. What wouldst thou do, old man?
        Think'st thou that duty shall have dread to speak
        When power to flattery bows? To plainness honour's
                                      bound
        When majesty stoops to folly. Reserve thy state,
        And in thy best consideration check
        This hideous rashness. Answer my life my judgment,   150
        Thy youngest daughter does not love thee least,
        Nor are those empty-hearted whose low sounds
        Reverb no hollowness.

LEAR   Kent, on thy life, no more!

KENT   My life I never held but as a pawn
        To wage against thine enemies; ne'er feared to lose it,
        Thy safety being motive.

LEAR   Out of my sight!

KENT   See better, Lear, and let me still remain
        The true blank of thine eye.

LEAR   Now by Apollo –

KENT   Now by Apollo, king,
        Thou swear'st thy gods in vain.

LEAR   O vassal! miscreant!   160
                      [*laying his hand on his sword*

ALBANY, C'WALL   Dear sir, forbear!

KENT   Kill thy physician, and the fee bestow
        Upon the foul disease. Revoke thy gift,
        Or, whilst I can vent clamour from my throat,
        I'll tell thee thou dost evil.

LEAR   Hear me, recreant,
        On thine allegiance, hear me!
        That thou hast sought to make us break our vow –
        Which we durst never yet – and with strained pride
        To come betwixt our sentence and our power –

Which nor our nature nor our place can bear, –   170
Our potency made good, take thy reward.
Five days we do allot thee for provision
To shield thee from disasters of the world,
And on the sixth to turn thy hated back
Upon our kingdom. If, on the tenth day following,
Thy banished trunk be found in our dominions,
The moment is thy death. Away! By Jupiter,
This shall not be revoked.

KENT   Fare thee well, king; sith thus thou wilt appear,
Freedom lives hence and banishment is here.   180
[to Cordelia]
The gods to their dear shelter take thee, maid,
That justly think'st and hast most rightly said.
[to Goneril and Regan]
And your large speeches may your deeds approve,
That good effects may spring from words of love.
Thus Kent, O princes, bids you all adieu;
He'll shape his old course in a country new.   [he goes

'Flourish'. Re-enter GLOUCESTER, with FRANCE,
BURGUNDY, and attendants

GLO'STER Here's France and Burgundy, my noble lord.
LEAR   My lord of Burgundy,
We first address toward you, who with this king
Hath rivalled for our daughter. What in the least   190
Will you require in present dower with her,
Or cease your quest of love?
BURG'DY   Most royal majesty,
I crave no more than hath your highness offered –
Nor will you tender less?
LEAR   Right noble Burgundy,
When she was dear to us, we did hold her so;
But now her price is fall'n. Sir, there she stands.
If aught within that little seeming-substance,
Or all of it, with our displeasure pieced,
And nothing more, may fitly like your grace,
She's there, and she is yours.
BURG'DY   I know no answer.   200
LEAR   Will you, with those infirmities she owes,

           Unfriended, new adopted to our hate,
           Dowered with our curse and strangered with our oath,
           Take her or leave her?

BURG'DY   Pardon me, royal sir.
           Election makes not up on such conditions.

LEAR   Then leave her, sir; for, by the power that made me,
           I tell you all her wealth. [*to France*] For you, great king,
           I would not from your love make such a stray
           To match you where I hate; therefore beseech you
           T' avert your liking a more worthier way   210
           Than on a wretch whom Nature is ashamed
           Almost t' acknowledge hers.

FRANCE   This is most strange,
           That she whom even but now was your best object,
           The argument of your praise, balm of your age,
           The best, the dearest, should in this trice of time
           Commit a thing so monstrous to dismantle
           So many folds of favour. Sure her offence
           Must be of such unnatural degree
           That monsters it, or your fore-vouched affection
           Fall into taint; which to believe of her   220
           Must be a faith that reason without miracle
           Should never plant in me.

CORDELIA   I yet beseech your majesty –
           If for I want that glib and oily art
           To speak and purpose not, since what I well intend,
           I'll do 't before I speak – that you make known
           It is no vicious blot, murder or foulness,
           No unchaste action or dishonoured step,
           That hath deprived me of your grace and favour;
           But even for want of that for which I am richer –
           A still-soliciting eye, and such a tongue   230
           That I am glad I have not, though not to have it
           Hath lost me in your liking.

LEAR   Better thou
           Hadst not been born than not t' have pleased me better.

FRANCE   Is it but this – a tardiness in nature
           Which often leaves the history unspoke
           That it intends? My lord of Burgundy,

What say you to the lady? Love's not love
When it is mingled with regards that stands
Aloof from th' entire point. Will you have her?
She is herself a dowry.

BURG'DY   Royal king,   240
Give but that portion which yourself proposed,
And here I take Cordelia by the hand,
Duchess of Burgundy.

LEAR   Nothing. I have sworn; I am firm.

BURG'DY   I am sorry then you have so lost a father
That you must lose a husband.

CORDELIA   Peace be with Burgundy!
Since that respect and fortunes are his love,
I shall not be his wife.

FRANCE   Fairest Cordelia, that art most rich, being poor;
Most choice, forsaken; and most loved, despised;   250
Thee and thy virtues here I seize upon.
Be it lawful I take up what's cast away.
Gods, gods! 'Tis strange that from their cold'st neglect
My love should kindle to inflamed respect.
Thy dowerless daughter, king, thrown to my chance,
Is queen of us, of ours, and our fair France.
Not all the dukes of wat'rish Burgundy
Can buy this unprized precious maid of me.
Bid them farewell, Cordelia, though unkind;
Thou losest here, a better where to find.   260

LEAR   Thou hast her, France; let her be thine, for we
Have no such daughter, nor shall ever see
That face of hers again. Therefore be gone
Without our grace, our love, our benison.
Come, noble Burgundy.

'Flourish'. LEAR, BURGUNDY, CORNWALL, ALBANY,
GLOUCESTER, and attendants depart

FRANCE   Bid farewell to your sisters.

CORDELIA   The jewels of our father, with washed eyes
Cordelia leaves you. I know you what you are,
And like a sister am most loath to call
Your faults as they are named. Love well our father;
To your professéd bosoms I commit him   270

But yet, alas, stood I within his grace,
I would prefer him to a better place.
So farewell to you both.

REGAN   Prescribe not us our duty.

GONERIL   Let your study
Be to content your lord, who hath received you
At Fortune's alms. You have obedience scanted,
And well are worth the want that you have wanted.

CORDELIA Time shall unfold what plighted cunning hides,
Who covert faults at last with shame derides.
Well may you prosper.

FRANCE   Come, my fair Cordelia.   280
                              [*he leads her away*

GONERIL   Sister, it is not little I have to say of what most nearly
appertains to us both. I think our father will hence
tonight.

REGAN   That's most certain, and with you; next month with us.

GONERIL   You see how full of changes his age is. The observation we have made of it hath not been little. He always
loved our sister most, and with what poor judgment
he hath now cast her off appears too grossly.

REGAN   'Tis the infirmity of his age; yet he hath ever but
slenderly known himself.   290

GONERIL   The best and soundest of his time hath been but rash;
then must we look from his age to receive, not alone
the imperfections of long-engraffed condition, but
therewithal the unruly waywardness that infirm and
choleric years bring with them.

REGAN   Such unconstant starts are we like to have from him as
this of Kent's banishment.

GONERIL   There is further compliment of leave-taking between
France and him. Pray you let us hit together. If our
father carry authority with such disposition as he bears, 300
this last surrender of his will but offend us.

REGAN   We shall further think of it.

GONERIL   We must do something, and i' th' heat.

                                        [*they go*

SCENE 2

A room in the Earl of Gloucester's castle

Enter EDMUND, *with a letter*

EDMUND   Thou, Nature, art my goddess; to thy law
          My services are bound. Wherefore should I
          Stand in the plague of custom, and permit
          The curiosity of nations to deprive me,
          For that I am some twelve or fourteen moonshines
          Lag of a brother? Why bastard? wherefore base?
          When my dimensions are as well compact,
          My mind as generous, and my shape as true,
          As honest madam's issue? Why brand they us
          With base? With baseness? Bastardy? Base, base?   10
          Who, in the lusty stealth of Nature, take
          More composition and fierce quality
          Than doth, within a dull, stale, tiréd bed,
          Go to th' creating a whole tribe of fops
          Got 'tween a sleep and wake? Well then,
          Legitimate Edgar, I must have your land.
          Our father's love is to the bastard Edmund
          As to th' legitimate. Fine word, 'legitimate'!
          Well, my legitimate, if this letter speed,
          And my invention thrive, Edmund the base   20
          Shall top th' legitimate. I grow, I prosper.
          Now, gods, stand up for bastards!

'Enter GLOUCESTER*'*

GLO'STER   Kent banished thus? And France in choler parted?
          And the king gone tonight? Prescribed his power?
          Confined to exhibition? All this done
          Upon the gad? – Edmund, how now? What news?
EDMUND   So please your lordship, none.
                                      [*putting the letter in his pocket*
GLO'STER   Why so earnestly seek you to put up that letter?
EDMUND   I know no news, my lord.
GLO'STER   What paper were you reading?   30
EDMUND   Nothing, my lord.

GLO'STER   No? What needed then that terrible dispatch of it into
           your pocket? The quality of nothing hath not such
           need to hide itself. Let's see. Come, if it be nothing, I
           shall not need spectacles.

EDMUND   I beseech you, sir, pardon me. It is a letter from my
           brother that I have not all o'er-read; and for so much as
           I have perused, I find it not fit for your o'erlooking.

GLO'STER   Give me the letter, sir.

EDMUND   I shall offend either to detain or give it. The contents,   40
           as in part I understand them, are to blame.

GLO'STER   Let's see, let's see.

EDMUND   I hope, for my brother's justification, he wrote this but
           as an essay or taste of my virtue.

GLO'STER   ['reads'] 'This policy and reverence of age makes the
           world bitter to the best of our times, keeps our fortunes
           from us till our oldness cannot relish them. I begin to
           find an idle and fond bondage in the oppression of aged
           tyranny, who sways, not as it hath power, but as it is
           suffered. Come to me, that of this I may speak more. If   50
           our father would sleep till I waked him, you should
           enjoy half his revenue for ever, and live the beloved of
           your brother. Edgar.'
               Hum! Conspiracy? 'Sleep till I waked him, you
           should enjoy half his revenue.' My son Edgar! Had he
           a hand to write this? A heart and brain to breed it in?
           When came you to this? Who brought it?

EDMUND   It was not brought me, my lord: there's the cunning of
           it. I found it thrown in at the casement of my closet.

GLO'STER   You know the character to be your brother's?   60

EDMUND   If the matter were good, my lord, I durst swear it were
           his; but, in respect of that, I would fain think it were not.

GLO'STER   It is his.

EDMUND   It is his hand, my lord; but I hope his heart is not in
           the contents.

GLO'STER   Has he never before sounded you in this business?

EDMUND   Never, my lord. But I have heard him oft maintain it
           to be fit that, sons at perfect age, and fathers declined,
           the father should be as ward to the son, and the son
           manage his revenue.   70

GLO'STER O villain, villain! His very opinion in the letter! Abhorred villain! Unnatural, detested, brutish villain!
Worse than brutish! Go, sirrah, seek him. I'll apprehend him. Abominable villain! Where is he?

EDMUND I do not well know, my lord. If it shall please you to
suspend your indignation against my brother till you
can derive from him better testimony of his intent, you
should run a certain course; where, if you violently
proceed against hum, mistaking his purpose, it would
make a great gap in your own honour, and shake in   80
pieces the heart of his obedience. I dare pawn down
my life for him that he hath writ this to feel my
affection to your honour, and to no other pretence of
danger.

GLO'STER Think you so?

EDMUND If your honour judge it meet, I will place you where
you shall hear us confer of this and by an auricular
assurance have your satisfaction, and that without any
further delay than this very evening.

GLO'STER He cannot be such a monster!   90

EDMUND Nor is not, sure.

GLO'STER To his father, that so tenderly and entirely loves him!
Heaven and earth! Edmund, seek him out; wind me
into him, I pray you; frame the business after your
own wisdom. I would unstate myself to be in a due
resolution.

EDMUND I will seek him, sir, presently; convey the business as I
shall find means, and acquaint you withal.

GLO'STER These late eclipses in the sun and moon portend no
good to us. Though the wisdom of nature can reason   100
it thus and thus, yet nature finds itself scourged by the
sequent effects. Love cools, friendship falls off, brothers
divide. In cities, mutinies; in countries, discord; in
palaces, treason; and the bond cracked 'twixt son and
father. This villain of mine comes under the prediction; there's son against father: the king falls from bias
of nature; there's father against child. We have seen
the best of our time. Machinations, hollowness,
treachery, and all ruinous disorders follow us disquietly

to our graves. Find out this villain, Edmund; it shall 110
lose thee nothing; do it carefully. And the noble and
true-hearted Kent banished; his offence, honesty! 'Tis
strange.   [*he goes*

EDMUND This is the excellent foppery of the world that when
we are sick in fortune, often the surfeits of our own
behaviour, we make guilty of our disasters the sun, the
moon and stars; as if we were villains on necessity, fools
by heavenly compulsion, knaves, thieves, and treachers
by spherical predominance, drunkards, liars, and
adulterers by an enforced obedience of planetary 120
influence, and all that we are evil in by a divine
thrusting on. An admirable evasion of whoremaster
man, to lay his goatish disposition to the charge of a
star! My father compounded with my mother under
the Dragon's tail, and my nativity was under Ursa
Major, so that it follows I am rough and lecherous. Fut,
I should have been that I am, had the maidenliest star
in the firmament twinkled on my bastardizing. Edgar —

'Enter EDGAR*'*

Pat! he comes, like the catastrophe of the old comedy.
My cue is villainous melancholy, with a sigh like Tom 130
o' Bedlam — O these eclipses do portend these divisions.
[*humming sadly*] Fa, sol, la, me.

EDGAR How now, brother Edmund? What serious contem-
plation are you in?

EDMUND I am thinking, brother, of a prediction I read this other
day, what should follow these eclipses.

EDGAR Do you busy yourself with that?

EDMUND I promise you, the effects he writes of succeed unhappily, as of unnaturalness between the child and the
parent, death, dearth, dissolutions of ancient amities, 140
divisions in state, menaces and maledictions against
king and nobles, needless diffidences, banishment of
friends, dissipation of cohorts, nuptial breaches, and I
know not what.

EDGAR How long have you been a sectary astronomical?

EDMUND When saw you my father last?

EDGAR   The night gone by.

EDMUND   Spake you with him?

EDGAR   Ay, two hours together.

EDMUND   Parted you in good terms? Found you no displeasure 150
            in him, by word nor countenance?

EDGAR   None at all.

EDMUND   Bethink yourself wherein you may have offended him;
            and at my entreaty forbear his presence until some
            little time hath qualified the heat of his displeasure,
            which at this instant so rageth in him that with the
            mischief of your person it would scarcely allay.

EDGAR   Some villain hath done me wrong.

EDMUND   That's my fear. I pray you have a continent forbear-
            ance till the speed of his rage goes slower; and, as I say, 160
            retire with me to my lodging, from whence I will fitly
            bring you to hear my lord speak. Pray ye, go; there's
            my key. If you do stir abroad, go armed.

EDGAR   Armed, brother?

EDMUND   Brother, I advise you to the best. I am no honest man
            if there be any good meaning toward you. I have told
            you what I have seen and heard – but faintly, nothing
            like the image and horror of it. Pray you, away!

EDGAR   Shall I hear from you anon?

EDMUND   I do serve you in this business.   [*Edgar goes* 170
            A credulous father! And a brother noble,
            Whose nature is so far from doing harms
            That he suspects none; on whose foolish honesty
            My practices ride easy! I see the business.
            Let me, if not by birth, have lands by wit;
            All with me's meet that I can fashion fit.   [*he goes*

SCENE 3

A room in the Duke of Albany's palace

Enter GONERIL *and* OSWALD, *her steward*

GONERIL Did my father strike my gentleman for
      chiding of his fool?

OSWALD Ay, madam.

GONERIL By day and night he wrongs me. Every hour
      He flashes into one gross crime or other
      That sets us all at odds. I'll not endure it.
      His knights grow riotous, and himself upbraids us
      On every trifle. When he returns from hunting
      I will not speak with him: say I am sick.
      If you come slack of former services,   10
      You shall do well; the fault of it I'll answer.

                                        [horns heard

OSWALD He's coming, madam; I hear him.

GONERIL Put on what weary negligence you please,
      You and your fellows; I'd have it come to question.
      If he distaste it, let him to my sister,
      Whose mind and mine I know in that are one,
      Not to be overruled. Idle old man,
      That still would manage those authorities
      That he hath given away! Now, by my life,
      Old fools are babes again, and must be used   20
      With checks as flatteries, when they are seen abused.
      Remember what I have said.

OSWALD   Well, madam.

GONERIL And let his knights have colder looks among you;
      What grows of it, no matter. Advise your fellows so.
      I would breed from hence occasions, and I shall,
      That I may speak. I'll write straight to my sister
      To hold my very course. Prepare for dinner.

                                        [they go

SCENE 4

A hall in the same

'Enter KENT*' disguised*

KENT   If but as well I other accents borrow,
That can my speech diffuse, my good intent
May carry through itself to that full issue
For which I razed my likeness. Now, banished Kent,
If thou canst serve where thou dost stand condemned,
So may it come thy master whom thou lov'st
Shall find thee full of labours.

Horns heard. LEAR *enters from hunting, with knights and attendants*

LEAR   Let me not stay a jot for dinner; go get it ready.
[*attendant goes out*] How now! What art thou?

KENT   A man, sir.   10

LEAR   What dost thou profess? What would'st thou with us?

KENT   I do profess to be no less than I seem, to serve him
truly that will put me in trust, to love him that is
honest, to converse with him that is wise and says
little, to fear judgment, to fight when I cannot choose,
and to eat no fish.

LEAR   What art thou?

KENT   A very honest-hearted fellow, and as poor as the king.

LEAR   If thou be'st as poor for a subject as he's for a king,
thou art poor enough. What would'st thou?   20

KENT   Service.

LEAR   Who would'st thou serve?

KENT   You.

LEAR   Dost thou know me, fellow?

KENT   No, sir; but you have that in your countenance which
I would fain call master.

LEAR   What's that?

KENT   Authority.

LEAR   What services canst thou do?

KENT   I can keep honest counsel, ride, run, mar a curious tale   30
in telling it, and deliver a plain message bluntly; that

which ordinary men are fit for I am qualified in, and
the best of me is diligence.

LEAR   How old art thou?

KENT   Not so young, sir, to love a woman for singing, nor so
old to dote on her for anything. I have years on my
back forty-eight.

LEAR   Follow me; thou shalt serve me. If I like thee no worse
after dinner I will not part from thee yet. Dinner, ho!
Dinner! Where's my knave? My fool? Go you and call 40
my fool hither.   [*attendant goes out*

Enter OSWALD

You! You, sirrah! Where's my daughter?

OSWALD   [*crossing the hall without pausing*] So please you —
                                          [*goes out*

LEAR   What says the fellow there? Call the clotpoll back!
[*knight goes out*] Where's my fool? Ho! I think the
world's asleep. [*knight returns*] How now? Where's that
mongrel?

KNIGHT   He says, my lord, your daughter is not well.

LEAR   Why came not the slave back to me when I called him?

KNIGHT   Sir, he answered me in the roundest manner he would 50
not.

LEAR   He would not?

KNIGHT   My lord, I know not what the matter is, but to my
judgment your highness is not entertained with that
ceremonious affection as you were wont. There's a
great abatement of kindness appears as well in the
general dependants as in the duke himself also and
your daughter.

LEAR   Ha! Say'st thou so?

KNIGHT   I beseech you pardon me, my lord, if I be mistaken, 60
for my duty cannot be silent when I think your highness wronged.

LEAR   Thou but rememb'rest me of mine own conception. I
have perceived a most faint neglect of late, which I
have rather blamed as mine own jealous curiosity than
as a very pretence and purpose of unkindness; I will
look further into't. But where's my fool? I have not
seen him this two days.

KNIGHT   Since my young lady's going into France, sir, the fool
            hath much pined away.   70
LEAR   No more of that; I have noted it well. Go you and tell
            my daughter I would speak with her. [*Attendant goes out*]
            Go you, call hither my fool. [*Second attendant goes out*]

                              OSWALD *returns*

            O you sir, you, come you hither, sir. Who am I, sir?
OSWALD   My lady's father.
LEAR   'My lady's father', my lord's knave? You whoreson
            dog, you slave, you cur!
OSWALD   I am none of these, my lord; I beseech your pardon.
LEAR   Do you bandy looks with me, you rascal?   [*strikes him*
OSWALD   I'll not be strucken, my lord.   80
KENT   Nor tripped neither, you base football player.
                                        [*tripping up his heels*
LEAR   I thank thee, fellow. Thou serv'st me, and I'll love thee.
KENT   Come, sir, arise, away! I'll teach you differences.
            Away, away! If you will measure your lubber's length
            again, tarry; but away! Go to; have you wisdom?
            [*Oswald goes*] So.
LEAR   Now, my friendly knave, I thank thee. There's earnest
            of thy service. [*giving money*]

                              Enter FOOL

FOOL   Let me hire him too. Here's my coxcomb.
                                        [*offers Kent his cap*
LEAR   How now, my pretty knave? How dost thou?   90
FOOL   Sirrah, you were best take my coxcomb.
KENT   Why, fool?
FOOL   Why? For taking one's part that's out of favour. Nay,
            an thou canst not smile as the wind sits, thou'lt catch
            cold shortly. There, take my coxcomb! Why, this fel-
            low has banished two on's daughters, and did the third
            a blessing against his will. If thou follow him thou
            must needs wear my coxcomb. How now, nuncle?
            Would I had two coxcombs and two daughters!
LEAR   Why, my boy?   100
FOOL   If I gave them all my living, I'd keep my coxcombs
            myself. There's mine; beg another of thy daughters.

LEAR   Take heed, sirrah – the whip.

FOOL   Truth's a dog must to kennel; he must be whipped out,
          when the Lady's brach may stand by th' fire and stink.

LEAR   A pestilent gall to me!

FOOL   Sirrah, I'll teach thee a speech.

LEAR   Do.

FOOL   Mark it, nuncle!
               Have more than thou showest,   110
               Speak less than thou knowest,
               Lend less than thou owest,
               Ride more than thou goest,
               Learn more than thou trowest,
               Set less than thou throwest;
               Leave thy drink and thy whore,
               And keep in-a-door,
               And thou shalt have more
               Than two tens to a score.

KENT   This is nothing, fool.   120

FOOL   Then 'tis like the breath of an unfee'd lawyer – you
          gave me nothing for't. Can you make no use of noth-
          ing, nuncle?

LEAR   Why, no, boy; nothing can be made out of nothing.

FOOL   [to Kent] Prithee tell him, so much the rent of his land
          comes to. He will not believe a fool.

LEAR   A bitter fool!

FOOL   Dost thou know the difference, my boy, between a
          bitter fool and a sweet one?

LEAR   No, lad; teach me.   130

FOOL   That lord that counselled thee
               To give away thy land,
               Come place him here by me –
               Do thou for him stand.
               The sweet and bitter fool
               Will presently appear:
               The one in motley here,   [pointing to himself
               The other found out there!   [pointing to Lear

LEAR   Dost thou call me fool, boy?

FOOL   All thy other titles thou hast given away; that thou   140
          wast born with.

KENT   This is not altogether fool, my lord.

FOOL   No, faith, lords and great men will not let me; if I had
         a monopoly out, they would have part on't: and ladies
         too, they will not let me have all the fool to myself;
         they'll be snatching. Nuncle, give me an egg, and I'll
         give thee two crowns.

LEAR   What two crowns shall they be?

FOOL   Why, after I have cut the egg i'th'middle and eat up the
         meat, the two crowns of the egg. When thou clovest   15
         thy crown i'th'middle and gav'st away both parts, thou
         bor'st thine ass on thy back o'er the dirt. Thou hadst
         little wit in thy bald crown when thou gav'st thy golden
         one away. If I speak like myself in this, let him be
         whipped that first finds it so.
         [*singing*]
                 Fools had ne'er less grace in a year;
                     For wise men are grown foppish,
                 And know not how their wits to wear,
                     Their manners are so apish.

LEAR   When were you wont to be so full of songs, sirrah?   16

FOOL   I have used it, nuncle, e'er since thou mad'st thy
         daughters thy mothers – for when thou gav'st them
         the rod and putt'st down thine own breeches,
         [*singing*]
                 Then they for sudden joy did weep,
                     And I for sorrow sung,
                 That such a king should play bo-peep,
                     And go the fools among.
         Prithee, nuncle, keep a schoolmaster that can teach thy
         fool to lie: I would fain learn to lie.

LEAR   An you lie, sirrah, we'll have you whipped.   17

FOOL   I marvel what kin thou and thy daughters are: they'll
         have me whipped for speaking true, thou'lt have me
         whipped for lying; and sometimes I am whipped for
         holding my peace. I had rather be any kind o' thing
         than a fool: and yet I would not be thee, nuncle; thou
         hast pared thy wit o' both sides and left nothing i'th'
         middle. Here comes one o' the parings.

                         '*Enter* GONERIL'

LEAR   How now, daughter? What makes that frontlet on?
             You are too much of late i'th'frown.

FOOL   Thou wast a pretty fellow when thou hadst no need to   180
             care for her frowning; now thou art an O without a
             figure. I am better than thou art now; I am a fool thou
             art nothing. [to Goneril] Yes, forsooth, I will hold my
             tongue; so your face bids me, though you say nothing.
                Mum, mum:
                  He that keeps nor crust nor crumb,
                  Weary of all, shall want some.
             [pointing to Lear] That's a shelled peascod.

GONERIL   Not only, sir, this your all-licensed fool
             But other of your insolent retinue   190
             Do hourly carp and quarrel, breaking forth
             In rank and not-to-be-enduréd riots.
             I had thought, by making this well known unto you,
             To have found a safe redress; but now grow fearful,
             By what yourself too late have spoke and done,
             That you protect this course, and put it on
             By your allowance; which if you should, the fault
             Would not scape censure, nor the redresses sleep
             Which, in the tender of a wholesome weal,
             Might in their working do you that offence,   200
             Which else were shame, that then necessity
             Will call discreet proceeding.

FOOL   For you know, nuncle,
                The hedge-sparrow fed the cuckoo so long
                That it had it head bit off by it young.
             So out went the candle, and we were left darkling.

LEAR   Are you our daughter?

GONERIL   I would you would make use of your good wisdom
             (Whereof I know you are fraught) and put away
             These dispositions which of late transport you   210
             From what you rightly are.

FOOL   May not an ass know when the cart draws the horse?
                Whoop, Jug! I love thee.

LEAR   Does any here know me? This is not Lear.
             Does Lear walk thus, speak thus? Where are his eyes?
             Either his notion weakens, his discernings

	Are lethargied – Ha! Waking? 'Tis not so?
	Who is it that can tell me who I am?
FOOL	Lear's shadow!
LEAR	I would learn that; for by the marks 220
	Of sovereignty, knowledge, and reason,
	I should be false persuaded I had daughters.
FOOL	Which they will make an obedient father.
LEAR	Your name, fair gentlewoman?
GONERIL	This admiration, sir, is much o' th' savour
	Of other your new pranks. I do beseech you
	To understand my purposes aright.
	As you are old and reverend, should be wise.
	Here do you keep a hundred knights and squires –
	Men so disordered, so debauched and bold, 230
	That this our court, infected with their manners,
	Shows like a riotous inn. Epicurism and lust
	Makes it more like a tavern or a brothel
	Than a graced palace. The shame itself doth speak
	For instant remedy. Be then desired,
	By her that else will take the thing she begs,
	A little to disquantity your train;
	And the remainders, that shall still depend,
	To be such men as may besort your age
	Which know themselves and you.
LEAR	Darkness and devils! 240
	Saddle my horses; call my train together!
	Degenerate bastard, I'll not trouble thee;
	Yet have I left a daughter.
GONERIL	You strike my people, and your disordered rabble
	Make servants of their betters.

'Enter ALBANY'

LEAR	Woe that too late repents! – O, are you come?
	Is it your will? Speak, sir! – Prepare my horses.
	Ingratitude, thou marble-hearted fiend,
	More hideous when thou show'st thee in a child
	Than the sea-monster!
ALBANY	Pray, sir, be patient. 25
LEAR	[to Goneril] Detested kite, thou liest!

My train are men of choice and rarest parts,
That all particulars of duty know,
And in the most exact regard support
The worships of their name. O most small fault,
How ugly didst thou in Cordelia show,
Which, like an engine, wrenched my frame of nature
From the fixed place, drew from my heart all love,
And added to the gall. O Lear, Lear, Lear!
Beat at this gate that let thy folly in   [*striking his head* 260
And thy dear judgment out! Go, go, my people.
                                  [*knights and Kent go*

ALBANY   My lord, I am guiltless, as I am ignorant
Of what hath moved you.

LEAR   It may be so, my lord.
Hear, Nature; hear, dear goddess; hear!
Suspend thy purpose, if thou didst intend
To make this creature fruitful.
Into her womb convey sterility;
Dry up in her the organs of increase;
And from her derogate body never spring
A babe to honour her! If she must teem,   270
Create her child of spleen, that it may live
And be a thwart disnatured torment to her.
Let it stamp wrinkles in her brow of youth,
With cadent tears fret channels in her cheeks,
Turn all her mother's pains and benefits
To laughter and contempt, that she may feel
How sharper than a serpent's tooth it is
To have a thankless child! Away, away!   [*he rushes forth*

ALBANY   Now, gods that we adore, whereof comes this?

GONERIL   Never afflict yourself to know more of it,   280
But let his disposition have that scope
As dotage gives it.

                   LEAR *returns distraught*

LEAR   What, fifty of my followers at a clap?
Within a fortnight?

ALBANY   What's the matter, sir?

LEAR   I'll tell thee. [*to Goneril*] Life and death! I am ashamed
That thou hast power to shake my manhood thus;

That these hot tears, which break from me perforce,
Should make thee worth them. Blasts and fogs upon
                thee!
Th'untented woundings of a father's curse
Pierce every sense about thee! Old fond eyes,   290
Beweep this cause again, I'll pluck ye out,
And cast you, with the waters that you loose,
To temper clay. Yea, is't come to this?
Ha! Let it be so. I have another daughter,
Who I am sure is kind and comfortable.
When she shall hear this of thee, with her nails
She'll flay thy wolvish visage. Thou shalt find
That I'll resume the shape which thou dost think
I have cast off for ever.   *[he goes*

GONERIL   Do you mark that?   300
ALBANY   I cannot be so partial, Goneril,
To the great love I bear you –
GONERIL   Pray you, content. What, Oswald, ho!
[*to the Fool*]
You sir, more knave than fool, after your master!
FOOL   Nuncle Lear, nuncle Lear! Tarry; take the fool with
thee.
    A fox, when one has caught her,
    And such a daughter,
    Should sure to the slaughter,
    If my cap would buy a halter.
    So the fool follows after.   *[he runs off* 310
GONERIL   This man hath had good counsel! A hundred knights?
'Tis politic and safe to let him keep
At point a hundred knights; yes, that on every dream,
Each buzz, each fancy, each complaint, dislike,
He may enguard his dotage with their powers,
And hold our lives in mercy. Oswald, I say!
ALBANY   Well, you may fear too far.
GONERIL   Safer than trust too far.
Let me still take away the harms I fear,
Not fear still to be taken. I know his heart.
What he hath uttered I have writ my sister.   320
If she sustain him and his hundred knights,

When I have showed th'unfitness –

Enter OSWALD

                        How now, Oswald?
What, have you writ that letter to my sister?

OSWALD   Ay, madam.

GONERIL   Take you some company, and away to horse!
Inform her full of my particular fear,
And thereto add such reasons of your own
As may compact it more. Get you gone,
And hasten your return.   [*Oswald goes*]
                 No, no, my lord,
This milky gentleness and course of yours   330
Though I condemn not, yet, under pardon,
You are much more attaxed for want of wisdom
Than praised for harmful mildness.

ALBANY   How far your eyes may pierce I cannot tell:
Striving to better, oft we mar what's well.

GONERIL   Nay, then –

ALBANY   Well, well; th'event.   [*they go*

SCENE 5

Court before the same

Enter LEAR, KENT, *and* FOOL

LEAR   Go you before to Cornwall with these letters. Acquaint
my daughter no further with anything you know than
comes from her demand out of the letter. If your
diligence be not speedy, I shall be there afore you.

KENT   I will not sleep, my lord, till I have delivered your
letter.   [*he goes*

FOOL   If a man's brains were in's heels, were't not in danger
of kibes?

LEAR   Ay, boy.

FOOL   Then I prithee be merry; thy wit shall not go slip-shod.   10

LEAR   Ha, ha, ha!

FOOL   Shalt see thy other daughter will use thee kindly; for,
though she's as like this as a crab's like an apple, yet I

	can tell what I can tell.
LEAR	What canst tell, boy?
FOOL	She will taste as like this as a crab does to a crab. Thou canst tell why one's nose stands i'th'middle on's face?
LEAR	No.
FOOL	Why, to keep one's eyes of either side's nose, that what a man cannot smell out, he may spy into.

20

LEAR	I did her wrong.
FOOL	Canst tell how an oyster makes his shell?
LEAR	No.
FOOL	Nor I neither; but I can tell why a snail has a house.
LEAR	Why?
FOOL	Why, to put's head in; not to give it away to his daughters, and leave his horns without a case.
LEAR	I will forget my nature. So kind a father! Be my horses ready?
FOOL	Thy asses are gone about 'em. The reason why the seven stars are no moe than seven is a pretty reason.

30

LEAR	Because they are not eight.
FOOL	Yes, indeed; thou would'st make a good fool.
LEAR	To take 't again perforce! Monster Ingratitude!
FOOL	If thou wert my fool, nuncle, I'd have thee beaten for being old before thy time.
LEAR	How's that?
FOOL	Thou should'st not have been old till thou hadst been wise.
LEAR	O let me not be mad, not mad, sweet heaven! Keep me in temper; I would not be mad!

40

Enter Gentleman

	How now! Are the horses ready?
GENT'MAN	Ready, my lord.
LEAR	Come, boy.
FOOL	She that's a maid now, and laughs at my departure, Shall not be a maid long, unless things be cut shorter.

[they go

ACT 2 SCENE I

A court within the castle of the Earl of Gloucester

    'Enter EDMUND *and* CURAN*', meeting*

EDMUND	Save thee, Curan.
CURAN	And you, sir. I have been with your father, and given him notice that the Duke of Cornwall and Regan his Duchess will be here with him this night.
EDMUND	How comes that?
CURAN	Nay, I know not. You have heard of the news abroad, I mean the whispered ones, for they are yet but ear-bussing arguments?
EDMUND	Not I. Pray you, what are they?
CURAN	Have you heard of no likely wars toward 'twixt the 10 Dukes of Cornwall and Albany?
EDMUND	Not a word.
CURAN	You may do, then, in time. Fare you well, sir. *[he goes*
EDMUND	The Duke be here tonight? The better! Best! This weaves itself perforce into my business. My father hath set guard to take my brother; And I have one thing, of a queasy question, Which I must act. Briefness and fortune, work! Brother, a word! Descend! Brother, I say!

        'Enter EDGAR*'*

	My father watches: O sir, fly this place!	20
	Intelligence is given where you are hid.	
	You have now the good advantage of the night.	
	Have you not spoken 'gainst the Duke of Cornwall?	
	He's coming hither, now i'th'night, i'th' haste,	
	And Regan with him. Have you nothing said	
	Upon his party 'gainst the Duke of Albany?	
	Advise yourself.	
EDGAR	I am sure on't, not a word.	
EDMUND	I hear my father coming. Pardon me,	
	In cunning I must draw my sword upon you.	30
	Draw, seem to defend yourself; now quit you well. –	

Yield! Come before my father. Light, ho! Here! –
Fly, brother. – Torches, torches!   [*Edgar hastens away*
                    So; farewell.
Some blood drawn on me would beget opinion
Of my more fierce endeavour.   [*wounds his arm*
                  I have seen drunkards
Do more than this in sport – Father, father!
Stop, stop! No help?

    '*Enter* GLOUCESTER, *and servants with torches*'

GLO'STER   Now, Edmund, where's the villain?
EDMUND   Here stood he in the dark, his sharp sword out,
Mumbling of wicked charms, conjuring the moon
To stand auspicious mistress.
GLO'STER   But where is he?
EDMUND   Look, sir, I bleed.
GLO'STER   Where is the villain, Edmund?   40
EDMUND   Fled this way, sir, when by no means he could –
GLO'STER   Pursue him, ho! Go after.   [*Some servants go*
              By no means what?
EDMUND   Persuade me to the murder of your lordship.
But that I told him the revenging gods
'Gainst parricides did all the thunder bend,
Spoke with how manifold and strong a bond
The child was bound to th'father – sir, in fine,
Seeing how loathly opposite I stood
To his unnatural purpose, in fell motion
With his preparéd sword he charges home   50
My unprovided body, latched mine arm;
And when he saw my best alarumed spirits,
Bold in the quarrel's right, roused to th'encounter,
Or whether gasted by the noise I made,
Full suddenly he fled.
GLO'STER   Let him fly far:
Not in this land shall he remain uncaught;
And found – dispatch. The noble Duke my master,
My worthy arch and patron, comes tonight.
By his authority I will proclaim it,
That he which finds him shall deserve our thanks,   60

        Bringing the murderous coward to the stake;
        He that conceals him, death.
EDMUND   When I dissuaded him from his intent,
        And found him pight to do it, with curst speech
        I threatened to discover him. He replied,
        'Thou unpossessing bastard, dost thou think,
        If I would stand against thee, would the reposal
        Of any trust, virtue, or worth in thee
        Make thy words faithed? No. What I should deny,
        (As this I would – ay, though thou didst produce   70
        My very character) I'd turn it all
        To thy suggestion, plot, and damnéd practice;
        And thou must make a dullard of the world,
        If they not thought the profits of my death
        Were very pregnant and potential spurs
        To make thee seek it.'
GLO'STER   O strange and fastened villain!
        Would he deny his letter, said he? I never got him.
                                [*a tucket heard*
        Hark, the Duke's trumpet! I know not why he comes.
        All ports I'll bar; the villain shall not scape;
        The Duke must grant me that. Besides, his picture   80
        I will send far and near, that all the kingdom
        May have due note of him; and of my land,
        Loyal and natural boy, I'll work the means
        To make thee capable.

        Enter CORNWALL, REGAN, *and attendants*

CORNWALL How now, my noble friend? Since I came hither,
        Which I can call but now, I have heard strange news.
REGAN   If it be true, all vengeance comes too short
        Which can pursue th'offender. How dost, my lord?
GLO'STER O madam, my old heart is cracked, it's cracked.
REGAN   What! Did my father's godson seek your life?   90
        He whom my father named, your Edgar?
GLO'STER O lady, lady, shame would have it hid!
REGAN   Was he not companion with the riotous knights
        That tended upon my father?
GLO'STER I know not, madam. 'Tis too bad, too bad!

EDMUND   Yes, madam; he was of that consort.

REGAN   No marvel, then, though he were ill affected.
'Tis they have put him on the old man's death,
To have th'expense and waste of his revenues.
I have this present evening from my sister   100
Been well informed of them, and with such cautions
That, if they come to sojourn at my house,
I'll not be there.

CORNWALL   Nor I, assure thee, Regan.
Edmund, I hear that you have shown your father
A childlike office.

EDMUND   It was my duty, sir.

GLO'STER   He did bewray his practice; and received
This hurt you see, striving to apprehend him.

CORNWALL Is he pursued?

GLO'STER   Ay, my good lord.

CORNWALL If he be taken, he shall never more
Be feared of doing harm. Make your own purpose,   110
How in my strength you please. For you, Edmund,
Whose virtue and obedience doth this instant
So much commend itself, you shall be ours.
Natures of such deep trust we shall much need;
You we first seize on.

EDMUND   I shall serve you, sir,
Truly, however else.

GLO'STER   For him I thank your Grace.

CORNWALL You know not why we came to visit you?

REGAN   Thus out of season, threading dark-eyed night:
Occasions, noble Gloucester, of some prize,
Wherein we must have use of your advice.   120
Our father he hath writ, so hath our sister,
Of differences, which I best thought it fit
To answer from our home. The several messengers
From hence attend dispatch. Our good old friend,
Lay comforts to your bosom, and bestow
Your needful counsel to our businesses,
Which craves the instant use.

GLO'STER   I serve you, madam.
Your Graces are right welcome.   ['Flourish'. They go

SCENE 2

Before Gloucester's castle

Enter KENT *and* OSWALD, *meeting*

OSWALD   Good dawning to thee, friend. Art of this house?

KENT   Ay.

OSWALD   Where may we set our horses?

KENT   I'th'mire.

OSWALD   Prithee, if thou lov'st me, tell me.

KENT   I love thee not.

OSWALD   Why then, I care not for thee.

KENT   If I had thee in Lipsbury Pinfold, I would make thee care for me.

OSWALD   Why dost thou use me thus? I know thee not.   10

KENT   Fellow, I know thee.

OSWALD   What dost thou know me for?

KENT   A knave, a rascal, an eater of broken meats; a base, proud, shallow, beggarly, three-suited, hundred-pound, filthy worsted-stocking knave; a lily-livered, action-taking, whoreson, glass-gazing, super-serviceable, finical rogue; one-trunk-inheriting slave; one that wouldst be a bawd in way of good service, and art nothing but the composition of a knave, beggar, coward, pandar, and the son and heir of a mongrel bitch: one whom I will   20 beat into clamorous whining if thou deniest the least syllable of thy addition.

OSWALD   Why, what a monstrous fellow art thou, thus to rail on one that is neither known of thee nor knows thee!

KENT   What a brazen-heed varlet art thou, to deny thou knowest me! Is it two days since I tripped up thy heels and beat thee before the king? Draw, you rogue; for, though it be night, yet the moon shines. I'll make a sop o' th' moonshine of you, you whoreson cullionly barber-monger. Draw!   [*drawing his sword*   30

OSWALD   Away! I have nothing to do with thee.

KENT   Draw, you rascal! You come with letters against the

king, and take Vanity the puppet's part against the royalty of her father. Draw, you rogue, or I'll so carbonado
your shanks! Draw, you rascal! Come your ways!

OSWALD   Help, ho! Murder! Help!

KENT   Strike, you slave! Stand, rogue! Stand, you neat slave!
         Strike!   [*beating him*

OSWALD   Help, ho! Murder, murder!

Enter EDMUND *with his rapier drawn*

EDMUND   How now? What's the matter? Part!   40

KENT   With you, goodman boy, if you please! Come, I'll
         flesh ye; come on, young master!

Enter CORNWALL, REGAN, GLOUCESTER *and servants*

GLO'STER Weapons? Arms? What is the matter here?

CORNWALL Keep peace, upon your lives!
         He dies that strikes again. What is the matter?

REGAN   The messengers from our sister and the king!

CORNWALL What is your difference? Speak.

OSWALD   I am scarce in breath, my lord.

KENT   No marvel, you have so bestirred your valour. You
         cowardly rascal, Nature disclaims in thee; a tailor made 50
         thee.

CORNWALL Thou art a strange fellow; a tailor make a man?

KENT   A tailor, sir. A stone-cutter or a painter could not have
         made him so ill, though they had been but two years
         o'th'trade.

CORNWALL Speak yet, how grew your quarrel?

OSWALD   This ancient ruffian, sir, whose life I have spared
         At suit of his grey beard –

KENT   Thou whoreson zed, thou unnecessary letter! My lord,
         if you will give me leave, I will tread this unbolted 60
         villain into mortar and daub the wall of a jakes with
         him. Spare my grey beard, you wagtail?

CORNWALL Peace, sirrah!
         You beastly knave, know you no reverence?

KENT   Yes, sir; but anger hath a privilege.

CORNWALL Why art thou angry?

KENT   That such a slave as this should wear a sword,
         Who wears no honesty. Such smiling rogues as these,

Like rats, oft bite the holy cords atwain
Which are too intrince t'unloose: smooth every passion 70
That in the natures of their lords rebel,
Bring oil to fire, snow to the colder moods;
Renege, affirm, and turn their halcyon beaks
With every gale and vary of their masters,
Knowing nought (like dogs) but following.
A plague upon your epileptic visage!
Smile you my speeches, as I were a fool?
Goose, if I had you upon Sarum plain,
I'd drive ye cackling home to Camelot.

CORNWALL What, art thou mad, old fellow?   80

GLO'STER How fell you out? Say that.

KENT   No contraries hold more antipathy
Than I and such a knave.

CORNWALL Why dost thou call him knave? What is his fault?

KENT   His countenance likes me not.

CORNWALL No more perchance does mine, nor his, nor hers.

KENT   Sirs, 'tis my occupation to be plain:
I have seen better faces in my time
Than stands on any shoulder that I see
Before me at this instant.

CORNWALL   This is some fellow,   90
Who, having been praised for bluntness, doth affect
A saucy roughness, and constrains the garb
Quite from his nature. He cannot flatter, he!
An honest mind and plain, he must speak truth!
An they will take it, so; if not, he's plain.
These kind of knaves I know which in this plainness
Harbour more craft and more corrupter ends
Than twenty silly-ducking observants
That stretch their duties nicely.

KENT   Sir, in good faith, in sincere verity,   100
Under th'allowance of your great aspect,
Whose influence, like the wreath of radiant fire
On flick'ring Phoebus' front –

CORNWALL   What mean'st by this?

KENT   To go out of my dialect, which you discommend so
much. I know, sir, I am no flatterer. He that beguiled

you in a plain accent was a plain knave, which for my
part I will not be, though I should win your displeasure
to entreat me to 't.

CORNWALL What was th'offence you gave him?

OSWALD   I never gave him any.
It pleased the king his master very late
To strike at me upon his misconstruction
When he, compact, and flattering his displeasure,
Tripped me behind: being down, insulted, railed
And put upon him such a deal of man
That worthied him, got praises of the king
For him attempting who was self-subdued,
And, in the fleshment of this dread exploit,
Drew on me here again.

KENT   None of these rogues and cowards
But Ajax is their fool.

CORNWALL   Fetch forth the stocks!
You stubborn ancient knave, you reverend braggart,
We'll teach you!

KENT   Sir, I am too old to learn.
Call not your stocks for me; I serve the king,
On whose employment I was sent to you.
You shall do small respect, show too bold malice
Against the grace and person of my master,
Stocking his messenger.

CORNWALL   Fetch forth the stocks!
As I have life and honour, there shall he sit till noon.

REGAN   Till noon? Till night, my lord, and all night too.

KENT   Why, madam, if I were your father's dog,
You should not use me so.

REGAN   Sir, being his knave, I will.

CORNWALL This is a fellow of the self-same colour
Our sister speaks of. Come, bring away the stocks.
                                        [*stocks brought out*

GLO'STER Let me beseech your Grace not to do so.
His fault is much, and the good king his master
Will check him for't. Your purposed low correction
Is such as basest and contemnéd'st wretches
For pilf'rings and most common trespasses

110

120

130

          Are punished with. The king must take it ill
          That he, so slightly valued in his messenger,   140
          Should have him thus restrained.

CORNWALL   I'll answer that.

REGAN   My sister may receive it much more worse
          To have her gentleman abused, assaulted,
          For following her affairs. Put in his legs.

                              [Kent is put in the stocks
          Come, my lord, away.

                     [all go in except Gloucester and Kent

GLO'STER   I am sorry for thee, friend; 'tis the duke's pleasure,
          Whose disposition, all the world well knows,
          Will not be rubbed nor stopped. I'll entreat for thee.

KENT   Pray do not, sir. I have watched, and travelled hard.
          Some time I shall sleep out, the rest I'll whistle.   150
          A good man's fortune may grow out at heels.
          Give you good morrow!

GLO'STER   The duke's to blame in this; 'twill be ill taken. *[he goes*

KENT   Good king, that must approve the common saw,
          Thou out of heaven's benediction com'st
          To the warm sun!
          Approach, thou beacon to this under globe,
          That by thy comfortable beams I may
          Peruse this letter. Nothing almost sees miracles
          But misery. I know 'tis from Cordelia,   160
          Who hath most fortunately been informed
          Of my obscuréd course, and shall find time
          From this enormous state, seeking to give
          Losses their remedies. All weary and o'erwatched,
          Take vantage, heavy eyes, not to behold
          This shameful lodging.
          Fortune, good night; smile once more; turn thy wheel.

                                    [sleeps

SCENE 3

The open country

'Enter EDGAR*'*

EDGAR   I heard myself proclaimed,
And by the happy hollow of a tree
Escaped the hunt. No port is free, no place
That guard and most unusual vigilance
Does not attend my taking. Whiles I may scape
I will preserve myself; and am bethought
To take the basest and most poorest shape
That ever penury in contempt of man
Brought near to beast. My face I'll grime with filth,
Blanket my loins, elf all my hairs in knots,   10
And with presented nakedness outface
The winds and persecutions of the sky.
The country gives me proof and precedent
Of Bedlam beggars who, with roaring voices,
Strike in their numbed and mortified bare arms
Pins, wooden pricks, nails, sprigs of rosemary;
And with this horrible object, from low farms,
Poor pelting villages, sheep-cotes, and mills,
Sometimes with lunatic bans, sometime with prayers,
Enforce their charity. 'Poor Turlygod, poor Tom!'   20
That's something yet! Edgar I nothing am.   *[he goes*

SCENE 4

Before Gloucester's castle. Kent in the stocks

Enter LEAR, FOOL *and Gentleman*

LEAR   'Tis strange that they should so depart from home,
And not send back my messenger.

GENT'MAN   As I learned,
The night before there was no purpose in them
Of this remove.

KENT	Hail to thee, noble master!
LEAR	Ha!
	Mak'st thou this shame thy pastime?
KENT	No, my lord.
FOOL	Ha, ha! He wears cruel garters. Horses are tied by the
	heads, dogs and bears by th' neck, monkeys by th'
	loins, and men by th' legs. When a man's over-lusty at
	legs, then he wears wooden nether-stocks.
LEAR	What's he that hath so much thy place mistook
	To set thee here?
KENT	It is both he and she,
	Your son and daughter.
LEAR	No.
KENT	Yes.
LEAR	No, I say.
KENT	I say yea.
LEAR	No, no, they would not.
KENT	Yes, yes, they have.
LEAR	By Jupiter, I swear no!
KENT	By Juno, I swear ay!
LEAR	They durst not do 't,
	They could not, would not do 't; 'tis worse than murder
	To do upon respect such violent outrage.
	Resolve me with all modest haste which way
	Thou mightst deserve or they impose this usage,
	Coming from us.
KENT	My lord, when at their home
	I did commend your Highness' letters to them,
	Ere I was risen from the place that showed
	My duty kneeling, came there a reeking post,
	Stewed in his haste, half breathless, panting forth
	From Goneril his mistress salutations;
	Delivered letters, spite of intermission,
	Which presently they read: on whose contents
	They summoned up their meiny, straight took horse,
	Commanded me to follow and attend
	The leisure of their answer, gave me cold looks:
	And meeting here the other messenger,
	Whose welcome I perceived had poisoned mine –

10

20

30

Being the very fellow which of late
Displayed so saucily against your Highness –   40
Having more man than wit about me, drew.
He raised the house with loud and coward cries.
Your son and daughter found this trespass worth
The shame which here it suffers.

FOOL   Winter's not gone yet if the wild geese fly that way.
      Fathers that wear rags
        Do make their children blind,
      But fathers that bear bags
        Shall see their children kind.
      Fortune, that arrant whore,   50
        Ne'er turns the key to th' poor.
But for all this thou shalt have as many dolours for thy
daughters as thou canst tell in a year.

LEAR   O how this mother swells up toward my heart!
Hysterica passio! Down, thou climbing sorrow;
Thy element's below. Where is this daughter?

KENT   With the earl, sir, here within.

LEAR   Follow me not; stay here.   [*he goes in*

GENT   Made you no more offence but what you speak of?

KENT   None.   60
How chance the king comes with so small a number?

FOOL   An thou hadst been set i'th'stocks for that question,
thou'dst well deserved it.

KENT   Why, fool?

FOOL   We'll set thee to school to an ant, to teach thee there's
no labouring i'th'winter. All that follow their noses are
led by their eyes but blind men, and there's not a nose
among twenty but can smell him that's stinking. Let go
thy hold when a great wheel runs down a hill, lest it
break thy neck with following; but the great one that   70
goes upward, let him draw thee after. When a wise
man gives thee better counsel, give me mine again. I
would ha' none but knaves use it, since a fool gives it.
      That sir which serves and seeks for gain
        And follows but for form,
     Will pack when it begins to rain
        And leave thee in the storm.

    But I will tarry; the Fool will stay
    And let the wise man fly.
The knave turns fool that runs away;   80
    The Fool no knave, perdy.

KENT   Where learned you this, fool?

FOOL   Not i'th'stocks, fool!

    Re-enter LEAR *with* GLOUCESTER

LEAR   Deny to speak with me? They are sick, they are weary,
They have travelled all the night? Mere fetches; ay,
The images of revolt and flying off.
Fetch me a better answer.

GLO'STER   My dear lord,
You know the fiery quality of the duke,
How unremovable and fixed he is
In his own course.

LEAR   Vengeance! plague! death! confusion! 90
Fiery? What quality? Why, Gloucester, Gloucester,
I'd speak with the Duke of Cornwall and his wife.

GLO'STER   Well, my good lord, I have informed them so.

LEAR   Informed them? Dost thou understand me, man?

GLO'STER   Ay, my good lord.

LEAR   The king would speak with Cornwall; the dear father
Would with his daughter speak, commands her service.
Are they informed of this? My breath and blood!
Fiery? The fiery duke? Tell the hot duke that –
No, but not yet; may be he is not well: 100
Infirmity doth still neglect all office
Whereto our health is bound. We are not ourselves
When nature, being oppressed, commands the mind
To suffer with the body. I'll forbear,
And am fall'n out with my more headier will
To take the indisposed and sickly fit
For the sound man. [*looking on Kent*]
                    Death on my state! Wherefore
Should he sit here? This act persuades me
That this remotion of the duke and her
Is practice only. Give me my servant forth.   110
Go tell the duke and 's wife I'd speak with them
Now, presently; bid them come forth and hear me,

Or at their chamber door I'll beat the drum
Till it cry sleep to death.

GLO'STER   I would have all well betwixt you.   [goes

LEAR   O me, my heart! My rising heart! But down!

FOOL   Cry to it, nuncle, as the cockney did to the eels when
she put 'em i' th' paste alive. She knapped 'em o'th'
coxcombs with a stick and cried 'Down, wantons,
down!' 'Twas her brother that, in pure kindness to his
horse, buttered his hay.   120

Re-enter GLOUCESTER, *with* CORNWALL, REGAN *and servants*

LEAR   Good morrow to you both.

CORNWALL   Hail to your Grace!
                              [*'Kent here set at liberty'*

REGAN   I am glad to see your Highness.

LEAR   Regan, I think you are. I know what reason
I have to think so; if thou shouldst not be glad,
I would divorce me from thy mother's tomb,
Sepulchring an adultress. [*to Kent*] O, are you free?
Some other time for that. – Beloved Regan,
Thy sister's naught. O Regan, she hath tied
Sharp-toothed unkindness, like a vulture, here.   130
                              [*points to his heart*
I can scarce speak to thee; thou'lt not believe
With how depraved a quality – O Regan!

REGAN   I pray you, sir, take patience. I have hope
You less know how to value her desert
Than she to scant her duty.

LEAR   Say? How is that?

REGAN   I cannot think my sister in the least
Would fail her obligation. If, sir, perchance
She have restrained the riots of your followers,
'Tis on such ground, and to such wholesome end,
As clears her from all blame.   140

LEAR   My curses on her!

REGAN   O sir, you are old;
Nature in you stands on the very verge
Of his confine. You should be ruled and led
By some discretion that discerns your state
Better than you yourself. Therefore I pray you

        That to our sister you do make return;
        Say you have wronged her.

LEAR   Ask her forgiveness?
        Do you but mark how this becomes the house!
        'Dear daughter, I confess that I am old: [*kneeling*
        Age is unnecessary; on my knees I beg   150
        That you'll vouchsafe me raiment, bed, and food!'

REGAN   Good sir, no more; these are unsightly tricks.
        Return you to my sister.

LEAR   [*rising*]   Never, Regan!
        She hath abated me of half my train,
        Looked black upon me, struck me with her tongue
        Most serpent-like upon the very heart.
        All the stored vengeances of heaven fall
        On her ingrateful top. Strike her young bones,
        You taking airs, with lameness!

CORNWALL   Fie, sir, fie!

LEAR   You nimble lightnings, dart your blinding flames   160
        Into her scornful eyes! Infect her beauty,
        You fen-sucked fogs, drawn by the pow'rful sun
        To fall and blister her!

REGAN   O the blest gods!
        So will you wish on me when the rash mood –

LEAR   No, Regan, thou shalt never have my curse.
        Thy tender-hefted nature shall not give
        Thee o'er to harshness. Her eyes are fierce; but thine
        Do comfort and not burn. 'Tis not in thee
        To grudge my pleasures, to cut off my train,
        To bandy hasty words, to scant my sizes,   170
        And in conclusion to oppose the bolt
        Against my coming in. Thou better know'st
        The offices of nature, bond of childhood,
        Effects of courtesy, dues of gratitude:
        Thy half o' th' kingdom hast thou not forgot,
        Wherein I thee endowed.

REGAN   Good sir, to th' purpose.

LEAR   Who put my man i' th' stocks?

                                [*tucket heard*

CORNWALL   What trumpet's that?

REGAN   I know't – my sister's. This approves her letter,
             That she would soon be here.

                                    Enter OSWALD

                                             Is your lady come?
LEAR   This is a slave, whose easy-borrowed pride   180
             Dwells in the sickly grace of her he follows.
             Out, varlet, from my sight!
CORNWALL   What means your Grace?
LEAR   Who stocked my servant? Regan, I have good hope
             Thou didst not know on't.

                                    Enter GONERIL

                                             Who comes here? O heavens,
             If you do love old men, if your sweet sway
             Allow obedience, if you yourselves are old,
             Make it your cause; send down and take my part!
             [*to Goneril*] Art not ashamed to look upon this beard?
             O Regan! will you take her by the hand?
GONERIL   Why not by th' hand, sir? How have I offended?   190
             All's not offence that indiscretion finds
             And dotage terms so.
LEAR   O sides, you are too tough!
             Will you yet hold? How came my man i' th' stocks?
CORNWALL I set him there, sir; but his own disorders
             Deserved much less advancement.
LEAR   You? Did you?
REGAN   I pray you, father, being weak, seem so.
             If, till the expiration of your month,
             You will return and sojourn with my sister,
             Dismissing half your train, come then to me.
             I am now from home, and out of that provision   200
             Which shall be needful for your entertainment.
LEAR   Return to her? And fifty men dismissed?
             No, rather I abjure all roofs, and choose
             To wage against the enmity o'th'air,
             To be a comrade with the wolf and owl –
             Necessity's sharp pinch! Return with her?
             Why, the hot-blooded France, that dowerless took
             Our youngest born, I could as well be brought

To knee his throne and, squire-like, pension beg
To keep base life afoot. Return with her?   210
Persuade me rather to be slave and sumpter
To this detested groom.   [*looking at Oswald*
GONERIL   At your choice, sir.
LEAR · I prithee, daughter, do not make me mad.
I will not trouble thee, my child; farewell:
We'll no more meet, no more see one another.
But yet thou art my flesh, my blood, my daughter –
Or rather a disease that's in my flesh,
Which I must needs call mine. Thou art a boil,
A plague-sore, or embosséd carbuncle
In my corrupted blood. But I'll not chide thee: 220
Let shame come when it will, I do not call it;
I do not bid the thunder-bearer shoot,
Nor tell tales of thee to high-judging Jove.
Mend when thou canst; be better at thy leisure:
I can be patient; I can stay with Regan,
I and my hundred knights.
REGAN   Not altogether so.
I looked not for you yet, nor am provided
For your fit welcome. Give ear, sir, to my sister;
For those that mingle reason with your passion
Must be content to think you old, and so –   230
But she knows what she does.
LEAR   Is this well spoken?
REGAN I dare avouch it, sir. What! Fifty followers?
Is it not well? What should you need of more?
Yea, or so many, sith that both charge and danger
Speak 'gainst so great a number? How in one house
Should many people, under two commands,
Hold amity? 'Tis hard, almost impossible.
GONERIL Why might not you, my lord, receive attendance
From those that she calls servants, or from mine?
REGAN Why not, my lord? If then they chanced to slack ye,   240
We could control them. If you will come to me
(For now I spy a danger), I entreat you
To bring but five and twenty: to no more
Will I give place or notice.

LEAR   I gave you all —
REGAN   And in good time you gave it.
LEAR   Made you my guardians, my depositaries,
            But kept a reservation to be followed
            With such a number. What! Must I come to you
            With five and twenty? Regan, said you so?
REGAN   And speak 't again, my lord; no more with me.   25
LEAR   Those wicked creatures yet do look well-favoured
            When others are more wicked; not being the worst
            Stands in some rank of praise.
            [to Goneril]   I'll go with thee.
            Thy fifty yet doth double five and twenty,
            And thou art twice her love.
GONERIL   Hear me, my lord.
            What need you five and twenty, ten, or five,
            To follow in a house where twice so many
            Have a command to tend you?
REGAN   What need one?
LEAR   O reason not the need! Our basest beggars
            Are in the poorest things superfluous.   26
            Allow not nature more than nature needs,
            Man's life is cheap as beast's. Thou art a lady;
            If only to go warm were gorgeous,
            Why, nature needs not what thou gorgeous wear'st,
            Which scarcely keeps thee warm. But for true need —
            You heavens, give me patience — patience I need!
            You see me here, you gods, a poor old man,
            As full of grief as age, wretched in both.
            If it be you that stirs these daughters' hearts
            Against their father, fool me not so much   27
            To bear it tamely; touch me with noble anger,
            And let not women's weapons, water drops,
            Stain my man's cheeks. No, you unnatural hags,
            I will have such revenges on you both
            That all the world shall — I will do such things —
            What they are yet I know not, but they shall be
            The terrors of the earth! You think I'll weep;
            No, I'll not weep: [storm heard approaching
            I have full cause of weeping, but this heart

Shall break into a hundred thousand flaws 280
Or ere I'll weep. O Fool, I shall go mad!
[he goes forth, the FOOL, GLOUCESTER, *and* KENT *following*

CORNWALL Let us withdraw; 'twill be a storm.
REGAN   This house is little: the old man and's people
Cannot be well bestowed.
GONERIL 'Tis his own blame; hath put himself from rest,
And must needs taste his folly.
REGAN   For his particular, I'll receive him gladly,
But not one follower.
GONERIL   So am I purposed.
Where is my lord of Gloucester?
CORNWALL Followed the old man forth.
        [Gloucester re-enters]   He is returned. 290
GLO'STER The king is in high rage.
CORNWALL   Whither is he going?
GLO'STER He calls to horse, but will I know not whither.
CORNWALL Tis best to give him way; he leads himself.
GONERIL My lord, entreat him by no means to stay.
GLO'STER Alack, the night comes on, and the bleak winds
Do sorely ruffle. For many miles about
There's scarce a bush.
REGAN   O sir, to wilful men
The injuries that they themselves procure
Must be their schoolmasters. Shut up your doors;
He is attended with a desperate train, 300
And what they may incense him to, being apt
To have his ear abused, wisdom bids fear.
CORNWALL Shut up your doors, my lord; 'tis a wild night:
My Regan counsels well. Come out o' th' storm.
                                        [they go in

ACT 3 SCENE 1

A heath

A storm with thunder and lightning.
Enter KENT *and a Gentleman meeting*

KENT   Who's there besides foul weather?
GENT'MAN One minded like the weather, most unquietly.
KENT   I know you. Where's the King?
GENT'MAN Contending with the fretful elements;
            Bids the wind blow the earth into the sea,
            Or swell the curléd waters 'bove the main,
            That things might change or cease; tears his white hair,
            Which the impetuous blasts with eyeless rage
            Catch in their fury and make nothing of;
            Strives in his little world of man to out-storm   10
            The to-and-fro-conflicting wind and rain.
            This night, wherein the cub-drawn bear would couch,
            The lion and the belly-pinchéd wolf
            Keep their fur dry, unbonneted he runs,
            And bids what will take all.
KENT   But who is with him?
GENT'MAN None but the Fool, who labours to outjest
            His heart-struck injuries.
KENT   Sir, I do know you,
            And dare upon the warrant of my note
            Commend a dear thing to you. There is division,
            Although as yet the face of it is covered   20
            With mutual cunning, 'twixt Albany and Cornwall,
            Who have – as who have not that their great stars
            Throned and set high? – servants, who seem no less,
            Which are to France the spies and speculations
            Intelligent of our state. What hath been seen,
            Either in snuffs and packings of the Dukes,
            Or the hard rein which both of them hath borne
            Against the old kind King; or something deeper
            Whereof perchance these are but furnishings –
            But true it is from France there comes a power   30

Into this scattered kingdom, who already,
Wise in our negligence, have secret feet
In some of our best ports and are at point
To show their open banner. Now to you:
If on my credit you dare build so far
To make your speed to Dover, you shall find
Some that will thank you, making just report
Of how unnatural and bemadding sorrow
The King hath cause to plain.
I am a gentleman of blood and breeding,   40
And from some knowledge and assurance offer
This office to you.

GENT'MAN I will talk further with you.

KENT   No, do not.
For confirmation that I am much more
Than my out-wall, open this purse and take
What it contains. If you shall see Cordelia
(As fear not but you shall), show her this ring,
And she will tell you who your fellow is
That yet you do not know. Fie on this storm!
I will go seek the King.   50

GENT'MAN Give me your hand. Have you no more to say?

KENT   Few words, but, to effect, more than all yet –
That when we have found the King (in which your pain
That way, I'll this) he that first lights on him
Holla the other.   [*they go their separate ways*

SCENE 2

Another part of the heath

'Storm still.' Enter LEAR *and* FOOL

LEAR   Blow, winds, and crack your cheeks! Rage! Blow!
You cataracts and hurricanoes, spout
Till you have drenched our steeples, drowned the cocks!
You sulph'rous and thought-executing fires,
Vaunt-couriers of oak-cleaving thunderbolts,
Singe my white head! And thou, all-shaking thunder,
Strike flat the thick rotundity o'th'world,

           Crack Nature's moulds, all germens spill at once
           That make ingrateful man!

FOOL   O nuncle, court holy water in a dry house is better than 10
           this rain-water out o' door. Good nuncle, in; ask thy
           daughters blessing! Here's a night pities neither wise
           men nor fools.

LEAR   Rumble thy bellyful! Spit, fire! spout, rain!
           Nor rain, wind, thunder, fire are my daughters.
           I tax not you, you elements, with unkindness:
           I never gave you kingdom, called you children;
           You owe me no subscription. Then let fall
           Your horrible pleasure. Here I stand your slave,
           A poor, infirm, weak, and despised old man   20
           But yet I call you servile ministers,
           That will with two pernicious daughters join
           Your high-engendered battles 'gainst a head
           So old and white as this. O, ho! 'Tis foul!

FOOL   He that has a house to put's head in has a good head-
           piece.
             The codpiece that will house
               Before the head has any,
             The head and he shall louse:
               So beggars marry many.   30
             The man that makes his toe
               What he his heart should make
             Shall of a corn cry woe,
               And turn his sleep to wake.
           For there was never yet fair woman but she made
           mouths in a glass.

Enter KENT

LEAR   No, I will be the pattern of all patience;
           I will say nothing.

KENT   Who's there?

FOOL   Marry, here's grace and a codpiece; that's a wise man 40
           and [*pointing at Lear*] a fool.

KENT   Alas, sir, are you here? Things that love night
           Love not such nights as these. The wrathful skies
           Gallow the very wanderers of the dark

And make them keep their caves. Since I was man,
Such sheets of fire, such bursts of horrid thunder,
Such groans of roaring wind and rain, I never
Remember to have heard. Man's nature cannot carry
Th'affliction nor the fear.

LEAR   Let the great gods,
That keep this dreadful pudder o'er our heads,   50
Find out their enemies now. Tremble, thou wretch
That hast within thee undivulgéd crimes
Unwhipped of justice. Hide thee, thou bloody hand,
Thou perjured, and thou simular of virtue
That art incestuous. Caitiff, to pieces shake,
That under covert and convenient seeming
Hast practised on man's life. Close pent-up guilts,
Rive your concealing continents, and cry
These dreadful summoners grace. I am a man
More sinned against than sinning.

KENT   Alack, bare-headed?   60
Gracious my lord, hard by here is a hovel;
Some friendship will it lend you 'gainst the tempest:
Repose you there, while I to this hard house
(More harder than the stones whereof 'tis raised,
Which even but now, demanding after you,
Denied me to come in) return, and force
Their scanted courtesy.

LEAR   My wits begin to turn.
Come on, my boy. How dost, my boy? Art cold?
I am cold myself. Where is this straw, my fellow?
The art of our necessities is strange,   70
And can make vile things precious. Come, your hovel.
Poor fool and knave, I have one part in my heart
That's sorry yet for thee.

FOOL   [sings]
            He that has and a little tiny wit –
                With heigh-ho, the wind and the rain –
            Must make content with his fortunes fit,
                Though the rain it raineth every day.

LEAR   True, boy. Come, bring us to this hovel.

                                          [Lear and Kent go

FOOL   · This is a brave night to cool a courtesan! I'll speak a
       prophecy ere I go: 80

> When priests are more in word than matter;
> When brewers mar their malt with water;
> When nobles are their tailors' tutors;
> No heretics burned, but wenches' suitors;
> Then shall the realm of Albion
> Come to great confusion.

> When every case in law is right;
> No squire in debt nor no poor knight;
> When slanders do not live in tongues,
> Nor cutpurses come not to throngs;   90
> When usurers tell their gold i'th'field,
> And bawds and whores do churches build;
> Then comes the time, who lives to see 't,
> That going shall be used with feet.

This prophecy Merlin shall make, for I live before
his time.   [goes

SCENE 3

A room in Gloucester's castle

'Enter GLOUCESTER *and* EDMUND, *with lights*'

GLO'STER Alack, alack, Edmund, I like not this unnatural dealing.
          When I desired their leave that I might pity him, they
          took from me the use of mine own house, charged me
          on pain of perpetual displeasure neither to speak of
          him, entreat for him, or any way sustain him.

EDMUND   Most savage and unnatural!

GLO'STER Go to; say you nothing. There is division between the
          Dukes, and a worse matter than that. I have received a
          letter this night – 'tis dangerous to be spoken – I have
          locked the letter in my closet. These injuries the King   10
          now bears will be revenged home. There is part of a
          power already footed; we must incline to the King. I
          will look him and privily relieve him; go you and

maintain talk with the Duke, that my charity be not of him perceived; if he ask for me, I am ill and gone to bed. If I die for it (as no less is threat'ned me), the King, my old master, must be relieved. There is strange things toward, Edmund; pray you be careful.   *[he goes*

EDMUND   This courtesy, forbid thee, shall the Duke
     Instantly know, and of that letter too.   20
     This seems a fair deserving, and must draw me
     That which my father loses – no less than all.
     The younger rises when the old doth fall.

                                  [he goes

SCENE 4

The heath. Before a hovel. 'Storm still'

'Enter LEAR, KENT, *and* FOOL*'*

KENT   Here is the place, my lord; good my lord, enter:
     The tyranny of the open night's too rough
     For nature to endure.

LEAR   Let me alone.

KENT   Good my lord, enter here.

LEAR   Wilt break my heart?

KENT   I had rather break mine own. Good my lord, enter.

LEAR   Thou think'st 'tis much that this contentious storm
     Invades us to the skin: so 'tis to thee;
     But where the greater malady is fixed,
     The lesser is scarce felt. Thou'dst shun a bear;
     But if thy flight lay toward the roaring sea,   10
     Thou'dst meet the bear i'th'mouth. When the
                                 mind's free,
     The body's delicate; this tempest in my mind
     Doth from my senses take all feeling else
     Save what beats there – filial ingratitude!
     Is it not as this mouth should tear this hand
     For lifting food to 't? But I will punish home.
     No, I will weep no more. In such a night
     To shut me out? Pour on; I will endure.
     In such a night as this? O Regan, Goneril!

Your old kind father whose frank heart gave all!   20
O, that way madness lies; let me shun that!
No more of that.

KENT   Good my lord, enter here.

LEAR   Prithee go in thyself, seek thine own ease;
This tempest will not give me leave to ponder
On things would hurt me more. But I'll go in.
[*to the Fool*] In, boy, go first. You houseless poverty –
Nay, get thee in; I'll pray, and then I'll sleep.

                                        [*Fool goes in*

Poor naked wretches, whereso'er you are,
That bide the pelting of this pitiless storm,
How shall your houseless heads and unfed sides,   30
Your looped and windowed raggedness, defend you
From seasons such as these? O, I have ta'en
Too little care of this! Take physic, pomp;
Expose thyself to feel what wretches feel,
That thou mayst shake the superflux to them
And show the heavens more just.

EDGAR   [*within*] Fathom and half, fathom and half! Poor Tom!

                         [*the Fool runs out from the hovel*

FOOL   Come not in here, nuncle, here's a spirit. Help me,
help me!

KENT   Give me thy hand. Who's there?   40

FOOL   A spirit, a spirit! He says his name's poor Tom.

KENT   What art thou that dost grumble there i'th'straw?
Come forth!

Enter EDGAR, *disguised as a madman, from the hovel*

EDGAR   Away! The foul fiend follows me!
Through the sharp hawthorn blow the cold winds.
Humh! Go to thy bed and warm thee.

LEAR   Didst thou give all to thy daughters? And art thou
come to this?

EDGAR   Who gives anything to poor Tom? Whom the foul
fiend hath led through fire and through flame, through   50
ford and whirlpool, o'er bog and quagmire; that hath
laid knives under his pillow, and halters in his pew; set
ratsbane by his porridge; made him proud of heart, to
ride on a bay trotting horse over four-inched bridges,

	to course his own shadow for a traitor. Bless thy five wits! Tom's a-cold. O, do de, do de, do de. Bless thee from whirlwinds, star-blasting, and taking! Do poor Tom some charity, whom the foul fiend vexes. There could I have him now – and there – and there again – and there! ['*storm still*' 60
LEAR	What, has his daughters brought him to this pass? Couldst thou save nothing? Wouldst thou give 'em all?
FOOL	Nay, he reserved a blanket; else we had been all shamed.
LEAR	Now all the plagues that in the pendulous air Hang fated o'er men's faults light on thy daughters!
KENT	He hath no daughters, sir.
LEAR	Death, traitor! Nothing could have subdued nature To such a lowness but his unkind daughters. Is it the fashion that discarded fathers Should have thus little mercy on their flesh? 70 Judicious punishment! 'Twas this flesh begot Those pelican daughters.
EDGAR	Pillicock sat on Pillicock Hill. Alow! alow, loo, loo!
FOOL	This cold night will turn us all to fools and madmen
EDGAR	Take heed o'th'foul fiend. Obey thy parents, keep thy word justly, swear not, commit not with man's sworn spouse, set not thy sweet heart on proud array. Tom's a-cold.
LEAR	What hast thou been? 80
EDGAR	A servingman, proud in heart and mind; that curled my hair, wore gloves in my cap; served the lust of my mistress' heart, and did the act of darkness with her; swore as many oaths as I spake words and broke them in the sweet face of heaven- one that slept in the contriving of lust, and waked to do it. Wine loved I deeply, dice dearly; and in woman out-paramoured the Turk. False of heart, light of ear, bloody of hand; hog in sloth, fox in stealth, wolf in greediness, dog in madness, lion in prey. Let not the creaking of shoes nor the 90 rustling of silks betray thy poor heart to woman. Keep thy foot out of brothels, thy hand out of plackets, thy pen from lenders' books, and defy the foul fiend.

Still through the hawthorn blows the cold wind,
Says suum, mun, hey nonny nonny.
Dolphin my boy, boy! – sessa! let him trot by.

[*'storm still'*

LEAR   Thou wert better in a grave than to answer with thy
uncovered body this extremity of the skies. Is man no
more than this? Consider him well. Thou ow'st the
worm no silk, the beast no hide, the sheep no wool,   100
the cat no perfume. Ha! Here's three on's are sophisti-
cated: thou art the thing itself. Unaccommodated man
is no more but such a poor, bare, forked animal as
thou art. Off, off, you lendings! Come, unbutton here!

[*strives to tear off his clothes*

FOOL   Prithee, nuncle, be contented; 'tis a naughty night to
swim in!

Sees GLOUCESTER *approaching 'with a torch'*

Now a little fire in a wild field were like an old
lecher's heart – small spark, all the rest on's body cold.
Look, here comes a walking fire.

EDGAR   This is the foul Flibbertigibbet. He begins at curfew,   110
and walks till first cock. He gives the web and the pin,
squinies the eye, and makes the harelip; mildews the
white wheat, and hurts the poor creature of earth.

S'Withold footed thrice the 'old::
He met the nightmare and her ninefold
Bid her alight
And her troth plight –
And aroint thee, witch, aroint thee!

KENT   How fares your grace?
LEAR   What's he?   120
KENT   Who's there? What is't you seek?
GLO'STER   What are you there? Your names?
EDGAR   Poor Tom, that eats the swimming frog, the toad, the
tadpole, the wall-newt and the water; that in the fury
of his heart, when the foul fiend rages, eats cow-dung
for sallets, swallows the old rat and the ditch-dog,
drinks the green mantle of the standing pool; who is
whipped from tithing to tithing, and stock-punished

and imprisoned; who hath had three suits to his back,
six shirts to his body,   130

    Horse to ride, and weapon to wear;
    But mice and rats and such small deer
    Have been Tom's food for seven long year.

Beware my follower. Peace, Smulkin; peace, thou fiend!

GLO'STER   What, hath your Grace no better company?

EDGAR   The Prince of Darkness is a gentleman! Modo he's
called, and Mahu.

GLO'STER   Our flesh and blood, my lord, is grown so vile,
That it doth hate what gets it.

EDGAR   Poor Tom's a-cold.   140

GLO'STER   Go in with me; my duty cannot suffer
T' obey in all your daughters' hard commands.
Though their injunction be to bar my doors
And let this tyrannous night take hold upon you,
Yet have I ventured to come seek you out
And bring you where both fire and food is ready.

LEAR   First let me talk with this philosopher.
What is the cause of thunder?

KENT   Good my lord, take his offer; go into th' house.

LEAR   I'll talk a word with this same learned Theban.   150
What is your study?

EDGAR   How to prevent the fiend and to kill vermin.

LEAR   Let me ask you one word in private.

KENT   Importune him once more to go, my lord;
His wits begin t' unsettle.   [*'storm still'*

GLO'STER   Canst thou blame him?
His daughters seek his death. Ah, that good Kent!
He said it would be thus, poor banished man!
Thou sayest the King grows mad; I'll tell thee, friend,
I am almost mad myself. I had a son,
Now outlawed from my blood: he sought my life   160
But lately, very late: I loved him, friend,
No father his son dearer: true to tell thee,
The grief hath crazed my wits. What a night's this!
I do beseech your Grace –

LEAR   O cry you mercy, sir.
Noble philosopher, your company.

EDGAR   Tom's a-cold.

GLO'STER In, fellow, there, into th' hovel; keep thee warm.

LEAR   Come, let's in all.

KENT   This way, my lord.

LEAR   With him;
          I will keep still with my philosopher.

KENT   Good my lord, soothe him; let him take the fellow.   170

GLO'STER Take him you on.

KENT   Sirrah, come on; go along with us.

LEAR   Come, good Athenian.

GLO'STER No words, no words; hush!

EDGAR   Child Roland to the dark tower came.
              His word was still 'Fie, foh, and fum.
              I smell the blood of a British man.'   [*they go*

SCENE 5

A room in Gloucester's castle

'Enter CORNWALL *and* EDMUND*'*

CORNWALL I will have my revenge ere I depart his house.

EDMUND   How, my lord, I may be censured, that nature thus
          gives way to loyalty, something fears me to think of.

CORNWALL I now perceive it was not altogether your brother's evil
          disposition made him seek his death; but a provoking
          merit, set awork by a reproveable badness in himself.

EDMUND   How malicious is my fortune, that I must repent to be
          just! This is the letter he spoke of, which approves him
          an intelligent party to the advantages of France. O
          heavens! That this treason were not – or not I the   10
          detector!

CORNWALL Go with me to the Duchess.

EDMUND   If the matter of this paper be certain, you have mighty
          business in hand.

CORNWALL True or false, it hath made thee Earl of Gloucester.
          Seek out where thy father is, that he may be ready for
          our apprehension.

EDMUND   [*aside*] If I find him comforting the King, it will stuff his

suspicion more fully. [*to Cornwall*] I will persever in my
course of loyalty, though the conflict be sore between 20
that and my blood.

CORNWALL I will lay trust upon thee; and thou shalt find a dearer
father in my love.   [*they leave*

SCENE 6

A room in a farmhouse adjoining Gloucester's castle

Enter GLOUCESTER *and* KENT

GLO'STER Here is better than the open air; take it thankfully. I
will piece out the comfort with what addition I can: I
will not be long from you.

KENT All the power of his wits have given way to his impa-
tience. The gods reward your kindness!

                                         [*Gloucester goes out*

Enter LEAR, EDGAR, *and* FOOL

EDGAR Frateretto calls me, and tells me Nero is an angler in
the lake of darkness. Pray, innocent, and beware the
foul fiend.

FOOL Prithee, nuncle, tell me whether a madman be a gentleman or a yeoman.   10

LEAR A king, a king!

FOOL No, he's a yeoman that has a gentleman to his son; for
he's a mad yeoman that sees his son a gentleman before
him.

LEAR To have a thousand with red burning spits
Come hizzing in upon 'em!

EDGAR The foul fiend bites my back.

FOOL He's mad that trusts in the tameness of a wolf, a horse's
health, a boy's love, or a whore's oath.

LEAR It shall be done; I will arraign them straight.   20
[*to Edgar*] Come sit thou here, most learned justicer;
[*to the Fool*]
Thou sapient sir, sit here. Now, you she-foxes –

EDGAR Look where he stands and glares! Want'st thou eyes at
trial, madam?

          [*sings*]　Come o'er the burn, Bessy, to me.

FOOL   [*sings*]   Her boat hath a leak,
                  And she must not speak
            Why she dares not come over to thee.

EDGAR   The foul fiend haunts poor Tom in the voice of a
nightingale. Hoppedance cries in Tom's belly for two 30
white herring. Croak not, black angel; I have no food
for thee.

KENT   How do you, sir? Stand you not so amazed.
Will you lie down and rest upon the cushions?

LEAR   I'll see their trial first. Bring in their evidence.
[*to Edgar*] Thou robéd man of justice, take thy place;
[*to the Fool*] And thou, his yokefellow of equity,
Bench by his side.
[*to Kent*]   You are o'th'commission;
Sit you too.

EDGAR   Let us deal justly.   40
             Sleepest or wakest thou, jolly shepherd?
                Thy sheep be in the corn;
             And for one blast of thy minikin mouth
                Thy sheep shall take no harm.
     Purr the cat is gray.

LEAR   Arraign her first; 'tis Goneril. I here take my oath
before this honourable assembly, she kicked the poor
king, her father.

FOOL   Come hither, mistress; is your name Goneril?

LEAR   She cannot deny it.   50

FOOL   Cry you mercy, I took you for a joined-stool.

LEAR   Ant here's another, whose warped looks proclaim
What stone her heart is made on. Stop her there!
Arms, arms, sword, fire! Corruption in the place!
False justicer, why hast thou let her scape?

EDGAR   Bless thy five wits!

KENT   O pity! Sir, where is the patience now
That you so oft have boasted to retain?

EDGAR   My tears begin to take his part so much
They mar my counterfeiting.   60

LEAR   The little dogs and all,
Tray, Blanche, and Sweetheart; see, they bark at me.

EDGAR   Tom will throw his head at them. Avaunt, you curs!
                  Be thy mouth or black or white,
                  Tooth that poisons if it bite;
                  Mastiff, greyhound, mongrel grim,
                  Hound or spaniel, brach or lym,
                  Or bobtail tyke or trundle-tail,
                  Tom will make him weep and wail;
                  For, with throwing thus my head,   70
                  Dogs leaped the hatch, and all are fled.
          Do, de, de, de. Sessa! Come, march to wakes and fairs
          and market towns. Poor Tom, thy horn is dry.

LEAR   Then let them anatomize Regan; see what breeds
          about her heart. Is there any cause in nature that make
          these hard hearts? [*to Edgar*] You, sir, I entertain for
          one of my hundred; only I do not like the fashion of
          your garments. You will say they are Persian; but let
          them be changed.

KENT   Now good my lord, lie here and rest awhile.   80

LEAR   Make no noise, make no noise; draw the curtains. So,
          so; we'll go to supper i'th'morning.

FOOL   And I'll go to bed at noon.

Enter GLOUCESTER

GLO'STER   Come hither, friend. Where is the King my master?

KENT   Here, sir: but trouble him not; his wits are gone.

GLO'STER   Good friend, I prithee take him in thy arms.
          I have o'erheard a plot of death upon him.
          There is a litter ready; lay him in't,
          And drive toward Dover, friend, where thou shalt meet
          Both welcome and protection. Take up thy master;   90
          If thou should'st dally half an hour, his life,
          With thine, and all that offer to defend him,
          Stand in assuréd loss. Take up, take up
          And follow me, that will to some provision
          Give thee quick conduct.

KENT   Oppresséd nature sleeps
          This rest might yet have balmed thy broken sinews,
          Which, if convenience will not allow,
          Stand in hard cure.
          [*to the Fool*]   Come, help to bear thy master;

Thou must not stay behind.

GLO'STER   Come, come, away!
       [Gloucester, Kent and the Fool leave, carrying Lear

EDGAR   When we our betters see bearing our woes,   100
    We scarcely think our miseries our foes.
    Who alone suffers, suffers most i'th'mind,
    Leaving free things and happy shows behind.
    But then the mind much sufferance doth o'erskip
    When grief hath mates, and bearing fellowship.
    Haw light and portable my pain seems now,
    When that which makes me bend makes the King bow.
    He childed as I fathered! Tom, away!
    Mark the high noises, and thyself bewray
    When false opinion, whose wrong thoughts defile thee,   110
    In thy just proof repeals and reconciles thee.
    What will hap more tonight, safe scape the King!
    Lurk, lurk.   *[he goes*

SCENE 7

A room in Gloucester's castle

Enter CORNWALL, REGAN, GONERIL, EDMUND, *and Servants*

CORNWALL *[to Goneril]* Post speedily to my lord your husband;
    show him this letter: the army of France is landed.
    Seek out the traitor Gloucester.

REGAN   Hang him instantly.

GONERIL   Pluck out his eyes.

CORNWALL Leave him to my displeasure. Edmund, keep you our
    sister company. The revenges we are bound to take
    upon your traitorous father are not fit for your behold-
    ing. Advise the Duke, where you are going, to a most
    festinate preparation: we are bound to the like. Our   10
    posts shall be swift and intelligent betwixt us. Farewell,
    dear sister; farewell, my Lord of Gloucester.

Enter OSWALD

How now? Where's the King?

OSWALD   My Lord of Gloucester hath conveyed him hence.

Some five or six and thirty of his knights,
Hot questrists after him, met him at gate,
Who, with some other of the lord's dependants,
Are gone with him toward Dover, where they boast
To have well-arméd friends.

CORNWALL   Get horses for your mistress.
GONERIL Farewell, sweet lord, and sister.   20
CORNWALL Edmund, farewell.   [*Goneril, Edmund and Oswald go*
                    Go seek the traitor Gloucester;
Pinion him like a thief, bring him before us.
                              [*Servants go*
Though well we may not pass upon his life
Without the form of justice, yet our power
Shall do a court'sy to our wrath, which men
May blame, but not control.

        Re-enter Servants, with GLOUCESTER *prisoner*

                    Who's there? The traitor?
REGAN   Ingrateful fox! 'tis he.
CORNWALL Bind fast his corky arms.
GLO'STER What means your Graces? Good my friends, consider
         You are my guests. Do me no foul play, friends.   30
CORNWALL Bind him, I say.   [*Servants bind him*
REGAN   Hard, hard. O filthy traitor!
GLO'STER Unmerciful lady as you are, I'm none.
CORNWALL To this chair bind him. Villain, thou shalt find –
                          [*Regan plucks his beard*
GLO'STER By the kind gods, 'tis most ignobly done
         To pluck me by the beard.
REGAN   So white, and such a traitor?
GLO'STER   Naughty lady,
         These hairs which thou dost ravish from my chin
         Will quicken and accuse thee. I am your host:
         With robbers' hands my hospitable favours
         You should not ruffle thus. What will you do?   40
CORNWALL Come, sir. What letters had you late from France?
REGAN   Be simple-answered, for we know the truth.
CORNWALL And what confederacy have you with the traitors
         Late footed in the kingdom?
REGAN   To whose hands

You have sent the lunatic king. Speak.

GLO'STER I have a letter, guessingly set down,
          Which came from one that's of a neutral heart,
          And not from one opposed.

CORNWALL   Cunning.

REGAN   And false.

CORNWALL Where hast thou sent the King?

GLO'STER   To Dover.

REGAN   Wherefore to Dover? Wast thou not charged at peril — 50

CORNWALL Wherefore to Dover? Let him answer that.

GLO'STER I am tied to th' stake, and I must stand the course.

REGAN   Wherefore to Dover?

GLO'STER Because I would not see thy cruel nails
          Pluck out his poor old eyes, nor thy fierce sister
          In his anointed flesh rash boarish fangs.
          The sea, with such a storm as his loved head
          In hell-black night endured, would have buoyed up,
          And quenched the stelléd fires;
          Yet, poor old heart, he holp the heavens to rain.   60
          If wolves had at thy gate howled that dearn time,
          Thou should'st have said 'Good porter, turn the key'.
          All cruels else subscribe: but I shall see
          The wingéd Vengeance overtake such children.

CORNWALL See 't shalt thou never. Fellows, hold the chair.
          Upon these eyes of thine I'll set my foot.

GLO'STER He that will think to live till he be old,
          Give me some help. O cruel! O you gods!

REGAN   One site will mock another. Th'other too!

CORNWALL If you see vengeance —

I SERVANT   Hold your hand, my lord!   70
          I have served you ever since I was a child,
          But better service have I never done you
          Than now to bid you hold.

REGAN   How, now, you dog?

I SERVANT If you did wear a beard upon your chin,
          I'd shake it on this quarrel.

REGAN   What do you mean?

CORNWALL My villain?   [he unsheathes his sword

I SERVANT Nay, then, come on, and take the chance of anger.

REGAN   [*to another Servant*] Give me thy sword. A peasant
                             stand up thus?
             [*'she takes a sword and runs at him behind'*
1 SERVANT O, I am slain! My lord, you have one eye left
          To see some mischief on him. O!   [*he dies* 80
CORNWALL Lest it see more, prevent it. Out, vile jelly!
          Where is thy lustre now?
GLO'STER All dark and comfortless! Where's my son Edmund?
          Edmund, enkindle all the sparks of nature
          To quit this horrid act.
REGAN   Out, treacherous villain!
          Thou call'st on him that hates thee. It was he
          That made the overture of thy treasons to us,
          Who is too good to pity thee.
GLO'STER O, my follies! Then Edgar was abused.
          Kind gods, forgive me that, and prosper him!   90
REGAN   Go thrust him out at gates, and let him smell
          His way to Dover.   [*they lead him out
             How is 't, my lord? How look you?
CORNWALL I have received a hurt. Follow me, lady.
          Turn out that eyeless villain. Throw this slave
          Upon the dunghill. Regan, I bleed apace.
          Untimely comes this hurt. Give me your arm.
                [*he goes in, supported by Regan
2 SERVANT I'll never care what wickedness I do,
          If this man come to good.
3 SERVANT   If she live long,
          And in the end meet the old course of death,
          Women will all turn monsters.   100
2 SERVANT Let's follow the old earl, and get the bedlam
          To lead him where he would; his roguish madness
          Allows itself to anything.
3 SERVANT Go thou; I'll fetch some flax and whites of eggs
          To apply to his bleeding face. Now heaven help him!
                             [*they go

ACT 4 SCENE 1

The heath

'Enter EDGAR*'*

EDGAR   Yet better thus, and known to be contemned,
Than still contemned and flattered. To be worst,
The lowest and most dejected thing of Fortune,
Stands still in esperance, lives not in fear.
The lamentable change is from the best;
The worst returns to laughter. Welcome, then,
Thou unsubstantial air that I embrace:
The wretch that thou hast blown unto the worst
Owes nothing to thy blasts.

    'Enter GLOUCESTER, *led by an* OLD MAN*'*

                       But who comes here?
My father, poorly eyed! World, world, O world!   10
But that thy strange mutations make us hate thee,
Life would not yield to age.

OLD MAN   O my good lord,
I have been your tenant, and your father's tenant,
These fourscore years.

GLO'STER   Away, get thee away! Good friend, be gone:
Thy comforts can do me no good at all;
Thee they may hurt.

OLD MAN   You cannot see your way.

GLO'STER   I have no way, and therefore want no eyes;
I stumbled when I saw. Full oft 'tis seen
Our means secure us, and our mere defects   20
Prove our commodities. O dear son Edgar,
The food of thy abuséd father's wrath!
Might I but live to see thee in my touch,
I'd say I had eyes again

OLD MAN   How now? Who's there?

EDGAR   O gods! Who is't can say 'I am at the worst'?
I am worse than e'er I was.

OLD MAN   'Tis poor mad Tom.

EDGAR   And worse I may be yet: the worst is not
So long as we can say 'This is the worst'.

OLD MAN   Fellow, where goest?

GLO'STER   Is it a beggar-man?

OLD MAN   Madman, and beggar too.   30

GLO'STER   He has some reason, else he could not beg.
I' th' last night's storm I such a fellow saw,
Which made me think a man a worm. My son
Came then into my mind, and yet my mind
Was then scarce friends with him: I have heard more
                                 since.
As flies to wanton boys are we to th' gods;
They kill us for their sport.

EDGAR   How should this be?
Bad is the trade that must play fool to sorrow,
Ang'ring itself and others. – Bless thee, master!

GLO'STER   Is that the naked fellow?

OLD MAN   Ay, my lord.   40

GLO'STER   Then prithee get thee away. If, for my sake,
Thou wilt o'ertake us hence a mile or twain
I' th' way toward Dover, do it for ancient love;
And bring some covering for this naked soul
Which I'll entreat to lead me.

OLD MAN   Alack, sir, he is mad!

GLO'STER   'Tis the time's plague when madmen lead the blind.
Do as I bid thee; or rather do thy pleasure:
Above the rest, be gone.

OLD MAN   I'll bring him the best 'parel that I have,
Come on't what will.   [*he goes*

GLO'STER   Sirrah, naked fellow!   50

EDGAR   Poor Tom's a-cold. [*aside*] I cannot daub it further.

GLO'STER   Come hither, fellow.

EDGAR   And yet I must. Bless thy sweet eyes, they bleed!

GLO'STER   Know'st thou the way to Dover?

EDGAR   Both stile and gate, horseway and footpath. Poor Tom
hath been scared out of his good wits. Bless thee, good
man's son, from the foul fiend! Five fiends have been in
poor Tom at once: as Obidicut, of lust; Hobbididence,
prince of darkness; Mahu, of stealing; Modo, of murder;

Flibbertigibbet, of mocking and mowing, who since 60
possesses chambermaids and waiting-women. So, bless
thee, master!

GLO'STER   Here, take this purse, thou whom the heavens' plagues
Have humbled to all strokes: that I am wretched
Makes thee the happier; Heavens, deal so still!
Let the superfluous and lust-dieted man,
That slaves your ordinance, that will not see
Because he does not feel, feel your power quickly;
So distribution should undo excess,
And each man have enough. Dost thou know Dover?   70

EDGAR   Ay, master.

GLO'STER   There is a cliff, whose high and bending head
Looks fearfully in the confinéd deep.
Bring me but to the very brim of it,
And I'll repair the misery thou dost bear
With something rich about me. From that place
I shall no leading need.

EDGAR   Give me thy arm;
Poor Tom shall lead thee.   [they go

SCENE 2

Before the Duke of Albany's palace

Enter GONERIL *and* EDMUND

GONERIL   Welcome, my lord. I marvel our mild husband
Not met us on the way.

Enter OSWALD

                          Now, where's your master?

OSWALD   Madam, within; but never man so changed.
I told him of the army that was landed;
He smiled at it: I told him you were coming;
His answer was, 'The worse'. Of Gloucester's treachery
And of the loyal service of his son
When I informed him, then he called me sot
And told me I had turned the wrong side out.
What most he should dislike seems pleasant to him;   10

What like, offensive.

GONERIL [*to Edmund*]   Then shall you go no further.
It is the cowish terror of his spirit,
That dares not undertake; he'll not feel wrongs
Which tie him to an answer. Our wishes on the way
May prove effects. Back, Edmund, to my brother;
Hasten his musters and conduct his powers:
I must change arms at home and give the distaff
Into my husband's hands. This trusty servant
Shall pass between us: ere long you are like to hear
(If you dare venture in your own behalf)   20
A mistress's command. Wear this. [*giving a favour*]
                              Spare speech;
Decline your head: this kiss, if it durst speak,
Would stretch thy spirits up into the air.
Conceive, and fare thee well.

EDMUND Yours in the ranks of death!

GONERIL   My most dear Gloucester!
                                        [*Edmund goes*

O, the difference of man and man!
To thee a woman's services are due;
A fool usurps my bed.

OSWALD   Madam, here comes my lord.
                                        [*he goes*

'Enter ALBANY*'*

GONERIL I have been worth the whistling.

ALBANY   O Goneril,
You are not worth the dust which the rude wind   30
Blows in your face! I fear your disposition.
That nature which contemns it origin
Cannot be bordered certain in itself.
She that herself will sliver and disbranch
From her material sap, perforce must wither
And come to deadly use.

GONERIL No more! The text is foolish.

ALBANY Wisdom and goodness to the vile seem vile;
Filths savour but themselves. What have you done?
Tigers, not daughters, what have you performed?   40

A father, and a gracious agéd man,
Whose reverence even the head-lugged bear would lick,
Most barbarous, most degenerate, have you madded.
Could my good brother suffer you to do it?
A man, a prince, by him so benefited!
If that the heavens do not their visible spirits
Send quickly down to tame these vile offences,
It will come
Humanity must perforce prey on itself
Like monsters of the deep.

GONERIL   Milk-livered man!   50
That bear'st a cheek for blows, a head for wrongs:
Who hast not in thy brows an eye discerning
Thine honour from thy suffering; that not know'st
Fools do those villains pity who are punished
Ere they have done their mischief. Where's thy drum?
France spreads his banners in our noiseless land,
With pluméd helm thy state begins to threat,
Whilst thou, a moral fool, sits still and cries
'Alack, why does he so?'

ALBANY   See thyself, devil!
Proper deformity shows not in the fiend   60
So horrid as in woman.

GONERIL   O vain fool!

ALBANY   Thou changéd and self-covered thing, for shame
Bemonster not thy feature! Were't my fitness
To let these hands obey my blood,
They are apt enough to dislocate and tear
Thy flesh and bones: howe'er thou art a fiend,
A woman's shape doth shield thee.

GONERIL   Marry, your manhood! Mew!

'Enter a Messenger'

ALBANY   What news?

MESSENGER O, my good lord, the Duke of Cornwall's dead,   70
Slain by his servant, going to put out
The other eye of Gloucester.

ALBANY   Gloucester's eyes!

MESSENGER A servant that he bred, thrilled with remorse,

  Opposed against the act, bending his sword
  To his great master; who, thereat enraged,
  Flew on him, and amongst them felled him dead;
  But not without that harmful stroke which since
  Hath plucked him after.

ALBANY   This shows you are above,
  You justicers, that these our nether crimes
  So speedily can venge! But, O poor Gloucester!   80
  Lost he his other eye?

MESSENGER   Both, both, my lord.
  This letter, madam, craves a speedy answer;
  'Tis from your sister.   [*presents a letter*

GONERIL   One way I like this well;
  But being widow, and my Gloucester with her,
  May all the building in my fancy pluck
  Upon my hateful life. Another way
  The news is not so tart. – I'll read, and answer.
                [*she goes out*

ALBANY   Where was his son when they did take his eyes?
MESSENGER Come with my lady hither.
ALBANY   He is not here.
MESSENGER No, my good lord; I met him back again.   90
ALBANY   Knows he the wickedness?
MESSENGER Ay, my good lord; 'twas he informed against him,
  And quit the house on purpose, that their punishment
  Might have the freer course.

ALBANY   Gloucester, I live
  To thank thee for the love thou show'dst the King,
  And to revenge thine eyes. Come hither, friend;
  Tell me what more thou know'st.   [*they go*

SCENE 3

The French camp near Dover

'Enter KENT *and a Gentleman'*

KENT   Why the King of France is so suddenly gone back
          know you no reason?

GENT'MAN Something he left imperfect in the state, which since
          his coming forth is thought of, which imports to the
          kingdom so much fear and danger that his personal
          return was most required and necessary.

KENT   Who hath he left behind him general?

GENT'MAN The Marshal of France, Monsieur La Far.

KENT   Did your letters pierce the queen to any demonstration
          of grief?   10

GENT'MAN Ay, sir; she took them, read them in my presence,
          And now and then an ample tear trilled down
          Her delicate cheek. It seemed she was a queen
          Over her passion, who, most rebel-like,
          Sought to be king o'er her.

KENT   O, then it moved her.

GENT'MAN Not to a rage; patience and sorrow strove
          Who should express her goodliest. You have seen
          Sunshine and rain at once; her smiles and tears
          Were like, a better way: those happy smilets
          That played on her ripe lip seemed not to know   20
          What guests were in her eyes, which parted thence
          As pearls from diamonds dropped. In brief,
          Sorrow would be a rarity most beloved
          If all could so become it.

KENT   Made she no verbal question?

GENT'MAN Faith, once or twice she heaved the name of 'father'
          Pantingly forth, as if it pressed her heart;
          Cried 'Sisters, sisters! Shame of ladies! Sisters!
          Kent! Father! Sisters! What, i'th'storm? i'th'night?
          Let pity not believe it!' There she shook
          The holy water from her heavenly eyes   30
          That clamour moistened; then away she started

To deal with grief alone.

KENT It is the stars,
The stars above us, govern our conditions;
Else one self mate and make could not beget
Such different issues. You spoke not with her since?

GENT'MAN No.

KENT Was this before the King returned?

GENT'MAN No, since.

KENT Well, sir, the poor distresséd Lear's i'th'town,
Who sometime, in his better tune, remembers
What we are come about, and by no means   40
Will yield to see his daughter.

GENT'MAN Why, good sir?

KENT A sovereign shame so elbows him: his own unkindness,
That stripped her from his benediction, turned her
To foreign casualties, gave her dear rights
To his dog-hearted daughters — these things sting
His mind so venomously that burning shame
Detains him from Cordelia.

GENT'MAN Alack, poor gentleman!

KENT Of Albany's and Cornwall's powers you heard not?

GENT'MAN 'Tis so, they are afoot.

KENT Well, sir, I'll bring you to our master Lear   50
And leave you to attend him. Some dear cause
Will in concealment wrap me up awhile;
When I am known aright, you shall not grieve
Lending me this acquaintance. I pray you go
Along with me.   [they go

SCENE 4

The same

Enter, with drum and colours, CORDELIA, *Doctor, and Soldiers*

CORDELIA Alack, 'tis he! Why, he was met even now
        As mad as the vexed sea, singing aloud,
        Crowned with rank fumiter and furrow-weeds,
        With hardocks, hemlock, nettles, cuckoo-flowers,
        Darnel, and all the idle weeds that grow
        In our sustaining corn. A century send forth;
        Search every acre in the high-grown field,
        And bring him to our eye.   *[an Officer goes*
                        What can man's wisdom
        In the restoring his bereavéd sense?
        He that helps him take all my outward worth.   10
DOCTOR There is means, madam.
        Our foster-nurse of nature is repose,
        The which he lacks. That to provoke in him
        Are many simples operative, whose power
        Will close the eye of anguish.
CORDELIA   All blest secrets,
        All you unpublished virtues of the earth,
        Spring with my tears! Be aidant and remediate
        In the good man's distress! – Seek, seek for him,
        Lest his ungoverned rage dissolve the life
        That wants the means to lead it.

Enter Messenger

MESSENGER   News, madam!   20
        The British powers are marching hitherward.
CORDELIA 'Tis known before; our preparation stands
        In expectation of them. O dear father,
        It is thy business that I go about!
        Therefore great France
        My mourning and importuned tears hath pitied.
        No blown ambition doth our arms incite,
        But love, dear love, and our aged father's right.
        Soon may I hear and see him!   *[they go*

SCENE 5

Gloucester's castle

Enter REGAN *and* OSWALD

REGAN   But are my brother's powers set forth?
OSWALD   Ay, madam.
REGAN   Himself in person there?
OSWALD   Madam, with much ado.
         Your sister is the better soldier.
REGAN   Lord Edmund spake not with your lord at home?
OSWALD   No, madam.
REGAN   What might import my sister's letter to him?
OSWALD   I know not, lady.
REGAN   Faith, he is posted hence on serious matter.
         It was great ignorance, Gloucester's eyes being out,
         To let him live: where he arrives he moves   10
         All hearts against us. Edmund, I think, is gone,
         In pity of his misery, to dispatch
         His nighted life; moreover, to descry
         The strength o'th'enemy.
OSWALD   I must needs after him, madam, with my letter.
REGAN   Our troops set forth tomorrow. Stay with us;
         The ways are dangerous.
OSWALD   I may not, madam;
         My lady charged my duty in this business.
REGAN   Why should she write to Edmund? Might not you
         Transport her purposes by word? Belike,   20
         Some things, I know not what. I'll love thee much –
         Let me unseal the letter.
OSWALD   Madam, I had rather –
REGAN   I know your lady does not love her husband;
         I am sure of that: and at her late being here
         She gave strange oeillades and most speaking looks
         To noble Edmund. I know you are of her bosom.
OSWALD   I, madam!
REGAN   I speak in understanding: you are: I know't;
         Therefore I do advise you take this note.

My lord is dead; Edmund and I have talked,   30
And more convenient is he for my hand
Than for your lady's. You may gather more.
If you do find him, pray you give him this;
And when your mistress hears thus much from you,
I pray desire her call her wisdom to her.
So fare you well.
If you do chance to hear of that blind traitor,
Preferment falls on him that cuts him off.

OSWALD   Would I could meet him, madam! I should show
What party I do follow.

REGAN   Fare thee well.   [*they go* 40

SCENE 6

The country near Dover

'*Enter* GLOUCESTER, *and* EDGAR' *dressed like a peasant*

GLO'STER   When shall I come to th' top of that same hill?
EDGAR   You do climb up it now; look how we labour.
GLO'STER   Methinks the ground is even.
EDGAR   Horrible steep.
            Hark, do you hear the sea?
GLO'STER   No, truly.
EDGAR   Why, then your other senses grow imperfect
            By your eyes' anguish.
GLO'STER   So may it be indeed.
            Methinks thy voice is altered, and thou speak'st
            In better phrase and matter than thou didst.
EDGAR   You're much deceived: in nothing am I changed
            But in my garments.
GLO'STER   Methinks you're better spoken.   10
EDGAR   Come on, sir, here's the place: stand still; how fearful
            And dizzy 'tis to cast one's eyes so low!
            The crows and choughs that wing the midway air
            Show scarce so gross as beetles. Half way down
            Hangs one that gathers samphire – dreadful trade!
            Methinks he seems no bigger than his head.
            The fishermen that walk upon the beach

Appear like mice: and yond tall anchoring bark
Diminished to her cock; her cock a buoy
Almost too small for sight. The murmuring surge,   20
That on th'unnumbered idle pebble chafes,
Cannot be heard so high. I'll look no more,
Lest my brain turn and the deficient sight
Topple down headlong.

GLO'STER   Set me where you stand.

EDGAR   Give me your hand. You are now within a foot
Of th'extreme verge. For all beneath the moon
Would I not leap upright.

GLO'STER   Let go my hand.
Here, friend, 's another purse, in it a jewel
Well worth a poor man's taking. Fairies and gods
Prosper it with thee! Go thou further off: 30
Bid me farewell, and let me hear thee going.

EDGAR   Now fare ye well, good sir.

GLO'STER   With all my heart!

EDGAR   Why I do trifle thus with his despair
Is done to cure it.

GLO'STER   O you mighty gods!   ['*he kneels*'
This world I do renounce, and in your sights
Shake patiently my great affliction off.
If I could bear it longer, and not fall
To quarrel with your great opposeless wills,
My snuff and loathéd part of nature should
Burn itself out. If Edgar live, O bless him!   40
Now, fellow, fare thee well.

EDGAR   Gone, sir; farewell!
[*Gloucester falls forward, and swoons*
And yet I know not how conceit may rob
The treasury of life when life itself
Yields to the theft. Had he been where he thought,
By this had thought been past. [*aloud*] Alive, or dead?
Ho, you sir! Friend! Hear you, sir! Speak!
[*aside*] Thus might he pass indeed: yet he revives.
[*aloud*] What are you, sir?

GLO'STER   . Away, and let me die.

EDGAR   Hadst thou been aught but gossamer, feathers, air,

(So many fathom down precipitating),   50
Thou'dst shivered like an egg: but thou dost breathe,
Hast heavy substance, bleed'st not, speak'st, art sound.
Ten masts at each make not the altitude
Which thou hast perpendicularly fell:
Thy life's a miracle. Speak yet again.

GLO'STER   But have I fall'n, or no?

EDGAR   From the dread summit of this chalky bourn.
Look up a-height; the shrill-gorged lark so far
Cannot be seen, or heard. Do but look up.

GLO'STER   Alack, I have no eyes.   60
Is wretchedness deprived that benefit
To end itself by death? 'Twas yet some comfort
When misery could beguile the tyrant's rage
And frustrate his proud will.

EDGAR   Give me your arm.
Up; so. How is't? Feel you your legs? You stand.

GLO'STER   Too well, too well.

EDGAR   This is above all strangeness.
Upon the crown o'th'cliff what thing was that
Which parted from you?

GLO'STER   A poor unfortunate beggar.

EDGAR   As I stood here below methought his eyes
Were two full moons; he had a thousand noses,   70
Horns whelked and waved like the enridgéd sea.
It was some fiend. Therefore, thou happy father,
Think that the clearest gods, who make them honours
Of men's impossibilities, have preserved thee.

GLO'STER   I do remember now. Henceforth I'll bear
Affliction till it do cry out itself
'Enough, enough', and die. That thing you speak of,
I took it for a man. Often 'twould say
'The fiend, the fiend', – he led me to that place.

EDGAR   Bear free and patient thoughts.

Enter LEAR, *crowned with wild flowers and nettles*

                                    But who comes here?   80
The safer sense will ne'er accommodate
His master thus.

LEAR	No, they cannot touch me for coining; I am the king himself.
EDGAR	O thou side-piercing sight!
LEAR	Nature's above art in that respect. There's your press-money. That fellow handles his bow like a crow-keeper: draw me a clothier's yard. Look, look, a mouse! Peace, peace; this piece of toasted cheese will do't. There' my gauntlet; I'll prove it on a giant. Bring up the brown 90 bills. O, well flown, bird; i'th' clout, i'th'clout: hewgh! Give the word.
EDGAR	Sweet marjoram.
LEAR	Pass.
GLO'STER	I know that voice.
LEAR	Ha! Goneril with a white beard? They flattered me like a dog, and told me I had the white hairs in my beard ere the black ones were there. To say 'ay' and 'no' to everything that I said! 'Ay', and 'no' too, was no good divinity. When the rain came to wet me once and the 100 wind to make me chatter, when the thunder would not peace at my bidding, there I found 'em, there I smelt 'em out! Go to, they are not men o' their words: they told me I was everything; 'tis a lie − I am not ague-proof.
GLO'STER	The trick of that voice I do well remember: Is't not the King?
LEAR	[*touching his crown*] Ay, every inch a king! When I do stare, see how the subject quakes. I pardon that man's life. What was thy cause? 110 Adultery? Thou shalt not die. Die for adultery? No! The wren goes to 't, and the small gilded fly Does lecher in my sight. Let copulation thrive: for Gloucester's bastard son Was kinder to his father than my daughters Got 'tween the lawful sheets. To 't, luxury, pell-mell! For I lack soldiers. Behold yond simp'ring dame Whose face between her forks presages snow, 120 That minces virtue and does shake the head

To hear of pleasure's name;
The fitchew nor the soiléd horse goes to 't
With a more riotous appetite.
Down from the waist they are centaurs,
Though women all above.
But to the girdle do the gods inherit,
Beneath is all the fiend's.
There's hell, there's darkness, there is the sulphurous pit;
Burning, scalding, stench, consumption: fie, fie, fie,
                                                pah, pah!   130
Give me an ounce of civet; good apothecary, sweeten
my imagination: there's money for thee.

GLO'STER   O, let me kiss that hand!

LEAR   Let me wipe it first; it smells of mortality.

GLO'STER   O ruined piece of Nature! This great world
Shall so wear out to naught. Dost thou know me?

LEAR   I remember thine eyes well enough. Dost thou squiny
at me?
No, do thy worst, blind Cupid; I'll not love.
Read thou this challenge; mark but the penning of it.   140

GLO'STER   Were all thy letters suns, I could not see.

EDGAR   I would not take this from report. It is,
And my heart breaks at it.

LEAR   Read.

GLO'STER   What! With the case of eyes?

LEAR   O ho, are you there with me? No eyes in your head, nor
no money in your purse? Your eyes are in a heavy case,
your purse in a light; yet you see how this world goes.

GLO'STER   I see it feelingly.

LEAR   What! Art mad? A man may see how this world goes   150
with no eyes. Look with thine ears: see how yond
justice rails upon yond simple thief. Hark in thine ear:
change places and, handy-dandy, which is the justice,
which is the thief? Thou hast seen a farmer's dog bark
at a beggar?

GLO'STER   Ay, sir.

LEAR   And the creature run from the cur? There thou
mightst behold the great image of authority – a dog's
obeyed in office.

Thou rascal beadle, hold thy bloody hand!   160
Why dost thou lash that whore? Strip thy own back;
Thou hotly lusts to use her in that kind
For which thou whipp'st her. The usurer hangs the
                                                    cozener.
Through tattered clothes great vices do appear;
Robes and furred gowns hide all. Plate sin with gold,
And the strong lance of justice hurtless breaks:
Arm it in rags, a pigmy's straw does pierce it.
None does offend, none, I say none. I'll able 'em;
Take that of me, my friend, who have the power
To seal th'accuser's lips. Get thee glass eyes   170
And, like a scurvy politician, seem
To see the things thou dost not. Now, now, now, now!
Pull off my boots: harder, harder! So.

EDGAR   O, matter and impertinency mixed!
          Reason in madness!

LEAR   If thou wilt weep my fortunes, take my eyes.
          I know thee well enough; thy name is Gloucester.
          Thou must be patient. We came crying hither;
          Thou know'st the first time that we smell the air
          We wawl and cry. I will preach to thee: mark!   180

GLO'STER Alack, alack the day!

LEAR   When we are born, we cry that we are come
          To this great stage of fools. This' a good block!
                                        [*taking off the crown*
          It were a delicate stratagem to shoe
          A troop of horse with felt: I'll put't in proof,
          And when I have stol'n upon these son-in-laws,
          Then kill, kill, kill, kill, kill, kill!

          'Enter a Gentleman' with attendants

GENT'MAN O, here he is: lay hand upon him. Sir,
          Your most dear daughter –

LEAR   No rescue? What, a prisoner? I am even   190
          The natural fool of Fortune. Use me well;
          You shall have ransom. Let me have surgeons;
          I am cut to th'brains.

GENT'MAN   You shall have anything.

LEAR   No seconds? All myself?
            Why, this would make a man a man of salt,
            To use his eyes for garden water-pots,
            Ay, and laying autumn's dust. I will die bravely,
            Like a smug bridegroom. What! I will be jovial.
            Come, come, I am a king, masters, know you that?
GENT'MAN   You are a royal one, and we obey you.   200
LEAR   Then there's life in't. Come, an you get it you shall get
            it by running. Sa, sa, sa, sa.
                                    [he runs away; attendants follow
GENT'MAN   A sight most pitiful in the meanest wretch,
            Past speaking of in a king! Thou hast one daughter
            Who redeems nature from the general curse
            Which twain have brought her to.
EDGAR   Hail, gentle sir!
GENT'MAN   Sir, speed you. What's your will?
EDGAR   Do you hear aught, sir, of a battle toward?
GENT'MAN   Most sure, and vulgar: everyone hears that,
            Which can distinguish sound.
EDGAR   But, by your favour,   210
            How near's the other army?
GENT'MAN   Near, and on speedy foot: the main descry
            Stands on the hourly thought.
EDGAR   I thank you, sir: that's all.
GENT'MAN   Though that the queen on special cause is here,
            Her army is moved on.
EDGAR   I thank you, sir.
                                    [Gentleman goes
GLO'STER   You ever-gentle gods, take my breath from me;
            Let not my worser spirit tempt me again
            To die before you please!
EDGAR   Well pray you, father.
GLO'STER   Now, good sir, what are you?
EDGAR   A most poor man, made tame to Fortune's blows,   220
            Who, by the art of known and feeling sorrows,
            Am pregnant to good pity. Give me your hand;
            I'll lead you to some biding.
GLO'STER   Hearty thanks:
            The bounty and the benison of Heaven

To boot, and boot!

Enter OSWALD

OSWALD   A proclaimed prize! Most happy!
That eyeless head of thine was first framed flesh
To raise my fortunes. Thou old unhappy traitor,
Briefly thyself remember; the sword is out
That must destroy thee.

GLO'STER   Now let thy friendly hand
Put strength enough to't.   [*Edgar interposes*

OSWALD   Wherefore, bold peasant,   230
Dar'st thou support a published traitor? Hence,
Lest that th'infection of his fortune take
Like hold on thee. Let go his arm.

EDGAR   Chill not let go, zir, without vurther cagion.

OSWALD   Let go, slave, or thou diest.

EDGAR   Good gentleman, go your gate, and let poor voke pass.
An 'chud ha' bin zwaggered out of my life, 'twould
not ha' bin zo long as 'tis by a vortnight. Nay, come
not near th'old man; keep out, che vor' ye, or Ice try
whither your costard or my ballow be the harder. 240
Chill be plain with you.

OSWALD   Out, dunghill!   [*'they fight'*

EDGAR   Chill pick your teeth, zir. Come; no matter vor your
foins.   [*Oswald falls*

OSWALD   Slave, thou hast slain me. Villain, take my purse:
If ever thou wilt thrive, bury my body,
And give the letters which thou find'st about me
To Edmund, Earl of Gloucester; seek him out
Upon the British party. O, untimely death! Death!
                             [*'he dies'*

EDGAR   I know thee well — a serviceable villain,   250
As duteous to the vices of thy mistress
As badness would desire.

GLO'STER   What, is he dead?

EDGAR   Sit you down, father; rest you.
Let's see these pockets; the letters that he speaks of
May be my friends. He's dead; I am only sorry
He had no other deathsman. Let us see.
Leave, gentle wax; and, manners, blame us not:

To know our enemies' minds we rip their hearts;
Their papers is more lawful.   [*'reads the letter'*

Let our reciprocal vows be rememb'red. You have 260
many opportunities to cut him off: if your will
want not, time and place will be fruitfully offered.
There is nothing done if he return the conqueror:
then am I the prisoner, and his bed my gaol; from
the loathed warmth wherof deliver me, and supply
the place for your labour.

    Your (wife, so I would say) affectionate servant,
                                Goneril.

O indistinguished space of woman's will!
A plot upon her virtuous husband's life,   270
And the exchange my brother! Here in the sands
Thee I'll rake up, thou post unsanctified
Of murderous lechers; and in the mature time
With this ungracious paper strike the sight
Of the death-practised Duke. For him 'tis well
That of thy death and business I can tell.

GLO'STER The King is mad; how stiff is my vile sense
That I stand up and have ingenious feeling
Of my huge sorrows! Better I were distract:
So should my thoughts be severed from my griefs, 280
And woes by wrong imaginations lose
The knowledge of themselves.   [*'drum afar off'*

EDGAR   Give me your hand:
Far off methinks I hear the beaten drum.
Come, father, I'll bestow you with a friend.   [*they go*

SCENE 7

A tent in the French camp

Enter CORDELIA, KENT, DOCTOR *and Gentleman*

CORDELIA O thou good Kent, how shall I live and work
To match thy goodness? My life will be too short,
And every measure fail me.

KENT To be acknowledged, madam, is oe'r-paid.
All my reports go with the modest truth;
Nor more, nor clipped, but so.

CORDELIA   Be better suited:
These weeds are memories of those worser hours;
I prithee put them off.

KENT   Pardon, dear madam;
Yet to be known shortens my made intent.
My boon I make it that you know me not   10
Till time, and I, think meet.

CORDELIA Then be't so, my good lord.
[*to the Doctor*]   How does the King?

DOCTOR Madam, sleeps still.

CORDELIA O you kind gods,
Cure this great breach in his abuséd nature!
Th'untuned and jarring senses. O, wind up
Of this child-changéd father!

DOCTOR   So please your Majesty
That we may wake the king? He hath slept long.

CORDELIA Be governed by your knowledge, and proceed
I'th'sway of your own will. Is he arrayed?   20

GENT'MAN Ay, madam: in the heaviness of sleep
We put fresh garments on him.

DOCTOR Be by, good madam, when we do awake him;
I doubt not of his temperance.

CORDELIA   Very well.

'Enter LEAR *asleep in a chair carried by servants',*
clad in his royal robes. Soft music

DOCTOR Please you draw near. Louder the music there!

CORDELIA O my dear father, restoration hang

Thy medicine on my lips, and let this kiss
Repair those violent harms that my two sisters
Have in thy reverence made!
KENT   Kind and dear princess!
CORDELIA Had you not been their father, these white flakes   30
Did challenge pity of them. Was this a face
To be opposed against the warring winds?
To stand against the deep dread-bolted thunder
In the most terrible and nimble stroke
Of quick cross lightning? To watch – poor perdu! –
With this thin helm? Mine enemy's dog,
Though he had bit me, should have stood that night
Against my fire; and wast thou fain, poor father,
To hovel thee with swine and rogues forlorn,
In short and musty straw? Alack, alack!   40
'Tis wonder that thy life and wits at once
Had not concluded all. He wakes; speak to him.
DOCTOR   Madam, do you; 'tis fittest.
CORDELIA How does my royal lord? How fares your Majesty?
LEAR   You do me wrong to take me out o'th'grave:
Thou art a soul in bliss; but I am bound
Upon a wheel of fire, that mine own tears
Do scald like molten lead.
CORDELIA   Sir, do you know me?
LEAR   You are a spirit, I know; when did you die?
CORDELIA Still, still, far wide!   50
DOCTOR   He's scarce awake; let him alone awhile.
LEAR   Where have I been? Where am I? Fair daylight?
I am mightily abused; I should e'en die with pity
To see another thus. I know not what to say.
I will not swear these are my hands: let's see;
I feel this pin prick. Would I were assured
Of my condition!
CORDELIA [kneels]   O, look upon me, sir,
And hold your hand in benediction o'er me;
No, sir, you must not kneel.   [seeing him about to rise
LEAR   Pray do not mock me;
I am a very foolish fond old man,   60
Fourscore and upward, not an hour more nor less;

And, to deal plainly,
I fear I am not in my perfect mind.
Methinks I should know you, and know this man,
Yet I am doubtful: for I am mainly ignorant
What place this is; and all the skill I have
Remembers not these garments, nor I know not
Where I did lodge last night. Do not laugh at me,
For (as I am a man) I think this lady
To be my child Cordelia.

CORDELIA   And so I am: I am!   70

LEAR   Be your tears wet? Yes, faith: I pray weep not.
If you have poison for me, I will drink it:
I know you do not love me, for your sisters
Have (as I do remember) done me wrong;
You have some cause; they have not.

CORDELIA   No cause, no cause.

LEAR   Am I in France?

KENT   In your own kingdom, sir.

LEAR   Do not abuse me.

DOCTOR   Be comforted, good madam: the great rage,
You see, is killed in him; and yet it is danger
To make him even o'er the time he has lost.   80
Desire him to go in; trouble him no more
Till further settling.

CORDELIA Will't please your Highness walk?

LEAR   You must bear with me. Pray you now, forget and forgive; I am old and foolish.   [all go but Kent and Gentleman

GENT'MAN Holds it true, sir, that the Duke of Cornwall was so slain?

KENT   Most certain, sir.

GENT'MAN Who is conductor of his people?

KENT   As 'tis said, the bastard son of Gloucester.

GENT'MAN They say Edgar, his banished son, is with the Earl of 90
Kent in Germany.

KENT   Report is changeable. 'Tis time to look about; the
powers of the kingdom approach apace.

GENT'MAN The arbitrement is like to be bloody. Fare you well, sir.
[goes

KENT   My point and period will be throughly wrought,
Or well or ill, as this day's battle's fought.   [goes

ACT 5 SCENE 1

The British camp near Dover

'*Enter, with drum and colours,* EDMUND, REGAN, *officers, and soldiers*'

EDMUND   Know of the Duke if his last purpose hold,
         Or whether since he is advised by aught
         To change the course; he's full of alteration
         And self-reproving; bring his constant pleasure.
                              [*to an officer, who goes out*

REGAN   Our sister's man is certainly miscarried.

EDMUND   'Tis to be doubted, madam.

REGAN   Now, sweet lord,
         You know the goodness I intend upon you.
         Tell me – but truly – but then speak the truth –
         Do you not love my sister?

EDMUND   In honoured love.

REGAN   But have you never found my brother's way   10
         To the forfended place?

EDMUND   That thought abuses you.

REGAN   I am doubtful that you have been conjunct
         And bosomed with her, as far as we call hers.

EDMUND   No, by mine honour, madam.

REGAN   I never shall endure her: dear my lord,
         Be not familiar with her.

EDMUND   Fear me not.
         She and the Duke her husband!

     '*Enter, with drum and colours,* ALBANY, GONERIL, *soldiers*'

GONERIL I had rather lose the battle than that sister
         Should loosen him and me.

ALBANY   Our very loving sister, well be-met.   20
         Sir, this I hear: the King is come to his daughter,
         With others whom the rigour of our state
         Forced to cry out. Where I could not be honest,
         I never yet was valiant: for this business,
         It touches us as France invades our land,
         Not bolds the King, with others whom, I fear,

Most just and heavy causes make oppose.

EDMUND   Sir, you speak nobly.

REGAN   Why is this reasoned?

GONERIL   Combine together 'gainst the enemy;
          For these domestic and particular broils   30
          Are not the question here.

ALBANY   Let's then determine
          With th'ancient of war on our proceeding.

EDMUND   I shall attend you presently at your tent.

REGAN   Sister, you'll go with us?

GONERIL   No.

REGAN   Tis most convenient; pray go with us.

GONERIL   O ho, I know the riddle. – I will go.

          As they are going out, enter EDGAR *disguised*

EDGAR   If e'er your Grace had speech with man so poor,
          Hear me one word.

ALBANY   I'll overtake you.
                              [*all but Albany and Edgar depart*
                                    Speak.

EDGAR   Before you fight the battle, ope this letter.   40
          If you have victory, let the trumpet sound
          For him that brought it: wretched though I seem,
          I can produce a champion that will prove
          What is avouchéd there. If you miscarry,
          Your business of the world hath so an end,
          And machination ceases. Fortune love you!

ALBANY   Stay till I have read the letter.

EDGAR   I was forbid it.
          When time shall serve, let but the herald cry,
          And I'll appear again.

ALBANY   Why, fare thee well;
          I will o'erlook thy paper.   [*Edgar goes* 50

                      EDMUND *returns*

EDMUND   The enemy's in view; draw up your powers.
          Here is the guess of their true strength and forces,
          By diligent discovery; but your haste
          Is now urged on you.

ALBANY   We will greet the time.   [*he goes*

EDMUND   To both these sisters have I sworn my love;
         Each jealous of the other, as the stung
         Are of the adder. Which of them shall I take?
         Both? One? Or neither? Neither can be enjoyed
         If both remain alive: to take the widow
         Exasperates, makes mad her sister Goneril;   60
         And hardly shall I carry out my side,
         Her husband being alive. Now then, we'll use
         His countenance for the battle, which being done,
         Let her who would be rid of him devise
         His speedy taking off. As for the mercy
         Which he intends to Lear and to Cordelia,
         The battle done, and they within our power,
         Shall never see his pardon: for my state
         Stands on me to defend, not to debate.   [he goes

SCENE 2

A field between the two camps

'Alarum'. Enter the French army, CORDELIA *leading* LEAR
by the hand, and pass by

'Enter EDGAR *and* GLOUCESTER*'*

EDGAR   Here, father, take the shadow of this tree
         For your good host. Pray that the right may thrive.
         If ever I return to you again,
         I'll bring you comfort.
GLO'STER   Grace go with you, sir! [*Edgar goes*

'Alarum' heard from the battlefield hard by, and later a 'retreat'

Enter EDGAR

EDGAR   Away, old man; give me thy hand, away!
         King Lear hath lost, he and his daughter ta'en.
         Give me thy hand; come on!
GLO'STER No further, sir; a man may rot even here.
EDGAR   What, in ill thoughts again? Men must endure   10
         Their going hence, even as their coming hither;
         Ripeness is all. Come on.
GLO'STER   And that's true too.   [*they go*

SCENE 3

The British camp near Dover

'Enter in conquest with drum and colours, EDMUND; LEAR *and*
CORDELIA *as prisoners; soldiers, Captain*

EDMUND   Some officers take them away: good guard,
Until their greater pleasures first be known
That are to censure them.

CORDELIA   We are not the first
Who with best meaning have incurred the worst.
For thee, oppressèd King, I am cast down;
Myself could else out-frown false Fortune's frown.
Shall we not see these daughters and these sisters?

LEAR   No, no, no, no! Come, let's away to prison:
We two alone will sing like birds i'th'cage;
When thou dost ask me blessing, I'll kneel down   10
And ask of thee forgiveness. So we'll live,
And pray, and sing, and tell old tales, and laugh
At gilded butterflies, and hear poor rogues
Talk of court news; and we'll talk with them too –
Who loses and who wins, who's in, who's out –
And take upon 's the mystery of things,
As if we were God's spies; and we'll wear out,
In a walled prison, packs and sects of great ones
That ebb and flow by th'moon.

EDMUND   Take them away.

LEAR   Upon such sacrifices, my Cordelia,   20
The gods themselves throw incense. Have I caught thee?
He that parts us shall bring a brand from heaven
And fire us hence like foxes. Wipe thine eyes;
The good-years shall devour them, flesh and fell,
Ere they shall make us weep! We'll see 'em starved first.
Come.   [*Lear and Cordelia are led away under guard*

EDMUND   Come hither, captain; hark.
Take thou this note;
[*giving a paper*]   go follow them to prison.
One step I have advanced thee; if thou dost

As this instructs thee, thou dost make thy way   30
To noble fortunes. Know thou this, that men
Are as the time is: to be tender-minded
Does not become a sword: thy great employment
Will not bear question; either say thou'lt do't,
Or thrive by other means.

CAPTAIN   I'll do't, my lord.

EDMUND   About it; and write happy when thou'st done.
Mark – I say instantly; and carry it so
As I have set it down.

CAPTAIN   I cannot draw a cart, nor eat dried oats;
If it be man's work I'll do't.   [he goes   40

'Flourish. Enter ALBANY, GONERIL, REGAN, Soldiers'

ALBANY   Sir, you have showed today your valiant strain,
And Fortune led you well. You have the captives
Who were the opposites of this day's strife:
I do require them of you, so to use them
As we shall find their merits and our safety
May equally determine.

EDMUND   Sir, I thought it fit
To send the old and miserable King
To some retention and appointed guard;
Whose age had charms in it, whole title more,
To pluck the common bosom on his side   50
And turn our impressed lances in our eyes
Which do command them. With him I sent the Queen,
My reason all the same; and they are ready
Tomorrow, or at further space, t'appear
Where you shall hold your session. At this time
We sweat and bleed: the friend hath lost his friend;
And the best quarrels, in the heat, are cursed
By those that feel their sharpness.
The question of Cordelia and her father
Requires a fitter place.

ALBANY   Sir, by your patience,   60
I hold you but a subject of this war,
Not as a brother.

REGAN   That's as we list to grace him.

Methinks our pleasure might have been demanded
Ere you had spoke so far. He led our powers,
Bore the commission of my place and person
The which immediacy may well stand up
And call itself your brother.

GONERIL   Not so hot!
In his own grace he doth exalt himself
More than in your addition.

REGAN   In my rights
By me invested, he compeers the best.   70

ALBANY   That were the most if he should husband you.

REGAN   Jesters do oft prove prophets.

GONERIL   Holla, holla!
That eye that told you so looked but asquint.

REGAN   Lady, I am not well, else I should answer
From a full-flowing stomach. General,
Take thou my soldiers, prisoners, patrimony:
Dispose of them, of me; the walls are thine.
Witness the world that I create thee here
My lord and master.

GONERIL   Mean you to enjoy him?

ALBANY   The let-alone lies not in your good will.   80

EDMUND   Nor in thine, lord.

ALBANY   Half-blooded fellow, yes.

REGAN   [*to Edmund*]
Let the drum strike; and prove my title thine.

ALBANY   Stay yet; hear reason. Edmund, I arrest thee
On capital treason, and, in thy attaint,
                              [*pointing to Goneril*
This gilded serpent. For your claim, fair sister,
I bar it in the interest of my wife;
'Tis she is sub-contracted to this lord,
And I, her husband, contradict your banns.
If you will marry, make your loves to me;
My lady is bespoke.

GONERIL   An interlude!   90

ALBANY   Thou art armed, Gloucester: let the trumpet sound;
If none appear to prove upon thy person
Thy heinous, manifest, and many treasons,

                There is my pledge!   [*throwing down a glove*
                                    I'll make it on thy heart,
                Ere I taste bread, thou art in nothing less
                Than I have here proclaimed thee.
REGAN   Sick, O sick!
(GONERIL   If not, I'll ne'er trust medicine.
EDMUND   There's my exchange!   [*throwing down a glove*
                                What in the world he is
                That names me traitor, villain-like he lies.
                Call by the trumpet; he that dares approach,   10
                On him, on you – who not? – I will maintain
                My truth and honour firmly.
ALBANY   A herald, ho!
EDMUND   A herald, ho, a herald!
ALBANY   Trust to thy single virtue; for the soldiers,
                All levied in my name, have in my name
                Took their discharge.
REGAN   My sickness grows upon me.
ALBANY   She is not well; convey her to my tent.
                                        [*Regan is led away*

                    Enter a HERALD

                Come hither, herald – Let the trumpet sound –
                And read out this.   [*a trumpet sounds*
HERALD   [*reads*] If any man of quality or degree within the lists   1
                of the army will maintain upon Edmund, supposed
                Earl of Gloucester, that he is a manifold traitor, let him
                appear by the third sound of the trumpet. He is bold in
                his defence.   ['*first trumpet*'
                Again!   ['*second trumpet*'
                Again!   ['*third trumpet*'

        An answering trumpet is heard. Enter EDGAR, *in armour*

ALBANY   Ask him his purposes – why he appears
                Upon this call o'th'trumpet.
HERALD   What are you?
                Your name, your quality, and why you answer
                This present summons?
EDGAR   Know my name is lost;   12
                By treason's tooth bare-gnawn and canker-bit:

           Yet am I noble as the adversary
           I come to cope.
ALBANY   Which is that adversary?
EDGAR   What's he that speaks for Edmund, Earl of Gloucester?
EDMUND   Himself: what say'st thou to him?
EDGAR   Draw thy sword,
           That, if my speech offend a noble heart,
           Thy arm may do thee justice; here is mine:
           Behold, it is the privilege of mine honours,
           My oath, and my profession. I protest,
           Maugre thy strength, place, youth, and eminence,   130
           Despite thy victor-sword and fire-new fortune,
           Thy valour and thy heart, thou art a traitor,
           False to thy gods, thy brother, and thy father,
           Conspirant 'gainst this high illustrious prince,
           And, from th'extremest upward of thy head
           To the descent and dust below thy foot,
           A most toad-spotted traitor. Say thou no,
           This sword, this arm, and my best spirits are bent
           To prove upon thy heart, whereto I speak,
           Thou liest.
EDMUND   In wisdom I should ask thy name;   140
           But since thy outside looks so fair and warlike,
           And that thy tongue some say of breeding breathes,
           What safe and nicely I might well delay
           By rule of knighthood, I disdain and spurn.
           Back do I toss these treasons to thy head,
           With the hell-hated lie o'erwhelm thy heart,
           Which, for they yet glance by and scarcely bruise,
           This sword of mine shall give them instant way
           Where they shall rest for ever. Trumpets, speak!
           'Alarums'. They fight. Edmund falls
ALBANY   Save him, save him!
GONERIL   This is practice, Gloucester: 150
           By th' law of war thou wast not bound to answer
           An unknown opposite: thou art not vanquished,
           But cozened and beguiled.
ALBANY   Shut your mouth, dame,

Or with this paper shall I stop it. –
[*to Edgar*]   Hold, sir –
                         [*showing Goneril her name on the letter*
Thou worse than any name, read thine own evil.
No tearing, lady! I perceive you know it.

GONERIL   Say if I do – the laws are mine, not thine;
Who can arraign me for't?

ALBANY   Most monstrous! O!
Know'st thou this paper?

GONERIL   Ask me not what I know. [*goes*

ALBANY   Go after her: she's desperate; govern her.   [*officer goes*   160

EDMUND   What you have charged me with, that have I done,
And more, much more; the time will bring it out:
'Tis past, and so am I. But what are thou
That hast this fortune on me? If thou'rt noble,
I do forgive thee.

EDGAR   Let's exchange charity.
I am no less in blood than thou art, Edmund;
If more, the more thou'st wronged me.
My name is Edgar, and thy father's son.
The gods are just, and of our pleasant vices
Make instruments to plague us: 170
The dark and vicious place where thee he got
Cost him his eyes.

EDMUND   Thou'st spoken right, 'tis true.
The wheel is come full circle; I am here.

ALBANY   [*to Edgar*] Methought thy very gait did prophesy
A royal nobleness: I must embrace thee;
Let sorrow split my heart if ever I
Did hate thee or thy father.

EDGAR   Worthy prince, I know't.

ALBANY   Where have you hid yourself?
How have you known the miseries of your father?

EDGAR   By nursing them, my lord. List a brief tale;   180
And when 'tis told, O that my heart would burst!
The bloody proclamation to escape
That followed me so near (O, our life's sweetness!
That we the pain of death would hourly die,
Rather than die at once!) taught me to shift

Into a madman's rags, t'assume a semblance
That very dogs disdained: and in this habit
Met I my father with his bleeding rings,
Their precious stones new lost; became his guide,
Led him, begged for him, saved him from despair;   190
Never (O fault!) revealed myself unto him
Until some half hour past, when I was armed.
Not sure, though hoping, of this good success,
I asked his blessing, and from first to last
Told him our pilgrimage. But his flawed heart
(Alack, too weak the conflict to support)
'Twixt two extremes of passion, joy and grief,
Burst smilingly.

EDMUND   This speech of yours hath moved me,
And shall perchance do good: but speak you on;
You look as you had something more to say.   200

ALBANY   If there be more, more woeful, hold it in,
For I am almost ready to dissolve,
Hearing of this.

EDGAR   This would have seemed a period
To such as love not sorrow; but another,
To amplify too much, would make much more,
And top extremity. Whilst I
Was big in clamour, came there in a man,
Who, having seen me in my worst estate,
Shunned my abhorred society; but then, finding
Who 'twas that so endured, with his strong arms   210
He fastened on my neck and bellowed out
As he'd burst heaven: threw him on my father;
Told the most piteous tale of Lear and him
That ever ear received, which in recounting
His grief grew puissant and the strings of life
Began to crack: twice then the trumpets sounded,
And there I left him tranced.

ALBANY   But who was this?

EDGAR   Kent, sir, the banished Kent, who in disguise
Followed his enemy king and did him service
Improper for a slave.   220

    'Enter a Gentleman', 'with a bloody knife'

GENT'MAN Help, help! O help!

EDGAR   What kind of help?

ALBANY   Speak, man!

EDGAR   What means this bloody knife?

GENT'MAN   'Tis hot, it smokes;
          It came even from the heart of – O, she's dead!

ALBANY   Who dead? Speak, man!

GENT'MAN Your lady, sir, your lady: and her sister
          By her is poisoned; she confesses it.

EDMUND   I was contracted to them both; all three
          Now marry in an instant.

EDGAR   Here comes Kent.

                    Enter KENT

ALBANY   Produce the bodies, be they alive or dead.
                                          [*Gentleman goes*
          This judgment of the heavens, that makes us tremble,   230
          Touches us not with pity. [*notices Kent*] O, is this he?
          The time will not allow the compliment
          Which very manners urges.

KENT   I am come
          To bid my king and master aye good night.
          Is he not here?

ALBANY   Great thing of us forgot!
          Speak, Edmund; where's the king? And where's
                                                  Cordelia?
              [*'The bodies of Goneril and Regan are brought in'*
          See'st thou this object, Kent?

KENT   Alack, why thus?

EDMUND   Yet Edmund was beloved:
          The one the other poisoned for my sake,
          And after slew herself.   240

ALBANY   Even so. Cover their faces.

EDMUND   I pant for life. Some good I mean to do,
          Despite of mine own nature. Quickly send
          (Be brief in it) to th' castle, for my writ
          Is on the life of Lear and on Cordelia.
          Nay, send in time!

ALBANY   Run, run, O run!

EDGAR   To who, my lord? – Who has the office? Send
         Thy token of reprieve.

EDMUND   Well thought on. Take my sword,
         Give it to the captain.

ALBANY   Haste thee, for thy life!   250
                              [*Edgar hurries forth*

EDMUND   He hath commission from thy wife and me
         To hang Cordelia in the prison and
         To lay the blame upon her own despair,
         That she fordid herself.

ALBANY   The gods defend her!
         Bear him hence awhile.   [*Edmund is borne off*

         '*Enter* LEAR *with* CORDELIA *in his arms*', EDGAR,
                  Captain, and others following

LEAR   Howl, howl, howl! O, you are men of stones!
         Had I your tongues and eyes, I'd use them so
         That heaven's vault should crack! She's gone for ever.
         I know when one is dead, and when one lives;   260
         She's dead as earth. Lend me a looking-glass;
         If that her breath will mist or stain the stone,
         Why, then she lives.

KENT   Is this the promised end?

EDGAR   Or image of that horror.

ALBANY   Fall and cease!

LEAR   This feather stirs – she lives! If it be so,
         It is a chance which does redeem all sorrows
         That ever I have felt.

KENT   [*kneeling*]   O my good master!

LEAR   Prithee away!

EDGAR   'Tis noble Kent, your friend.

LEAR   A plague upon you, murderers, traitors all!
         I might have saved her; now she's gone for ever!   270
         Cordelia, Cordelia, stay a little – Ha?
         What is't thou say'st? – Her voice was ever soft,
         Gentle and low, an excellent thing in woman –
         I killed the slave that was a-hanging thee.

OFFICER 'Tis true, my lords, he did.

LEAR   Did I not, fellow?

I have seen the day, with my good biting falchion
I would have made them skip: I am old now,
And these same crosses spoil me. Who are you?
Mine eyes are not o' th' best; I'll tell you straight.

KENT   If Fortune brag of two she loved and hated,   280
            One of them we behold.

LEAR   This is a dull sight. Are you not Kent?

KENT   The same
            Your servant Kent. Where is your servant Caius?

LEAR   He's a good fellow, I can tell you that;
            He'll strike, and quickly too. He's dead and rotten.

KENT   No, my good lord; I am the very man –

LEAR   I'll see that straight.

KENT   That from your first of difference and decay
            Have followed your sad steps –

LEAR   You are welcome hither.

KENT   Nor no man else. All's cheerless, dark, and deadly.   290
            Your eldest daughters have fordone themselves,
            And desperately are dead.

LEAR   Ay, so I think.

ALBANY   He knows not what he says, and vain is it
            That we present us to him.

EDGAR   Very bootless.

            'Enter Captain'

CAPTAIN   Edmund is dead, my lord.

ALBANY   That's but a trifle here.
            You lords and noble friends, know our intent:
            What comfort to this great decay may come
            Shall be applied. For us, we will resign,
            During the life of this old majesty,
            To him our absolute power;
            [to Edgar and Kent]   to you your rights,   300
            With boot and such addition as your honours
            Have more than merited. All friends shall taste
            The wages of their virtue, and all foes
            The cup of their deservings. O see, see!

LEAR   And my poor fool is hanged! No, no, no life!
            Why should a dog, a horse, a rat have life,

And thou no breath at all? Thou'lt come no more,
Never, never, never, never, never!
Pray you, undo this button. Thank you, sir.
Do you see this? Look on her! Look – her lips!   310
Look there, look there!

EDGAR   He faints! My lord, my lord!

KENT   Break, heart! I prithee break.

EDGAR   Look up, my lord.

KENT   Vex not his ghost: O, let him pass; he hates him,
That would upon the rack of this tough world
Stretch him out longer.   [*Lear dies*

EDGAR   He is gone indeed.

KENT   The wonder is he hath endured so long;
He but usurped his life.

ALBANY   Bear them from hence. Our present business
Is general woe.
[*to Kent and Edgar*] Friends of my soul, you twain
Rule in this realm, and the gored state sustain.   320

KENT   I have a journey, sir, shortly to go:
My master calls me; I must not say no.

EDGAR   The weight of this sad time we must obey;
Speak what we feel, not what we ought to say.
The oldest hath borne most: we that are young
Shall never see so much, nor live so long.
        [*The bodies are borne out, all follow with 'a death march'*

MACBETH

INTRODUCTION

Macbeth is a dark thriller of a play, considerably shorter than the other four tragedies in this volume. Its highly compressed and bloody story is derived from historical sources, particularly Holinshed's *Chronicles of Scotland*, and it was written in 1606. In its treatment of Scottish history, the play is often seen to address the interests of James I, who gave his patronage to Shakespeare's company in 1603. James traced his ancestry from Banquo, and was well known to be interested in witchcraft, and *Macbeth* is a document of the relationship between the king and his players. In the play, Macbeth is a Scottish lord highly regarded for his valour in his country's wars. With his friend Banquo, he meets three witches who prophesy that he will become king, and that Banquo's children shall be kings. Macbeth and his wife kill the king, Duncan, and Macbeth becomes king. To safeguard his position of power, he arranges for Banquo to be killed, although Fleance, Banquo's son, escapes. Other murders are also ordered by the desperate yet haunted Macbeth. In England, forces loyal to Duncan's sons gather. Meeting the witches again, Macbeth feels reassured by their forecast, but their riddling prophecies have misled him. Lady Macbeth commits suicide, and in the battle Macbeth is killed by Macduff, whose wife and children the king has murdered. Duncan's heir Malcolm is crowned king of Scotland.

Macbeth is a tragedy preoccupied with the nature of what is manly. Lady Macbeth taunts her husband with 'When you durst do it, then you were a man' in response to his 'I dare do all that may become a man; Who dares do more is none.' (1.7.46–49) Physical prowess and moral scruple are in conflict as alternative indices of masculinity. The two murderers summoned by Macbeth to dispatch Banquo call themselves men, but Macbeth describes them as men only in so much as 'hounds and grey-hounds, mongrels, spaniels, curs, Shoughs, water-rugs, and demi-wolves' (3.1.92–93) are all dogs. Lady Macbeth asks 'Are you a man?' (3.4.58) when it seems her husband has lost his wits in the banquet, and Macbeth uses the same formulation when the ghost of Banquo disappears from his sight: 'I am a man again' (3.4.108). Malcolm urges Macduff to 'Dispute it like a man', when he hears of the slaughter of his family, but Macduff's response is to propose manliness as the fusing of the physical and emotional: 'I shall do so; But I must also feel it as a man' (4.3.220–21). Manliness is sometimes synonymous with humanity, sometimes with extreme brutality, in a conflict of meanings which represent, in miniature, the complex value-systems of the warlike society of Macbeth's Scotland.

The play is also concerned with women's role in men's lives. From the destructive prophecies of the witches and their bubbling cauldron which parodies natural reproduction in its catalogue of ingredients (Orson Welles' 1946 film of the play develops this suggestion in opening with the witches and the cauldron, from which they shape an effigy of Macbeth in a grotesque birth-ritual), to Lady Macbeth's denial of her femininity, the female is presented as monstrous and dangerous. Lady Macbeth calls on spirits to 'unsex' her (1.5.40) and to take away her maternal qualities: 'Come to my woman's breasts And take my milk for gall' (1.5.46–47). Berating Macbeth for his cowardice, she declares: 'I have given suck, and know How tender 'tis to love the babe that milks me' (1.7.54–55), but this child and the brightly chattering son of Macduff are evoked only in order to be murdered, either symbolically by Lady Macbeth who promises herself willing to 'dash[. . .] the brains out', or actually in the case of young Macduff. The play does not mention any children of the Macbeth line – the child to whom Lady Macbeth says she gave suck is never mentioned again – and this absence reinforces the unnatural sterility of his quest for power. It is Banquo who will found a dynasty, the witches prophesy, whereas Macbeth's is a 'fruitless crown' and 'barren sceptre' (3.1.60–61). Children play an important symbolic role in the play: the witches produce the apparitions of a 'bloody child' and a child-king; Macbeth describes his infirmity as 'the baby of a girl' (3.4.106); Hecate describes him as the witches' 'wayward son' (3.5.11), and even Lady Macbeth describes her husband as unweaned from goodness: 'too full o' th' milk of human kindness' (1.5.16). The play's concern with succession and royal dynasties is partly a feature of the circumstances of its original presentation. As the eighth generation of Banquo's line, James I was implied as the latest in the 'show of eight kings' (stage direction following 4.1.111) shown to Macbeth by the witches. (Part of the play's anxieties about motherhood may also refer to James' own mother, Mary Queen of Scots, who was executed by Elizabeth I and was thus an unsuitable connection for the new king and one whose influence was to be mistrusted and minimised). Given the play's apprehensive representation of women, therefore, it is entirely appropriate that Macbeth's nemesis should take the form of Macduff. Macduff's invincibility is signalled by the circumstances of his birth: the witches' prophecy that 'none of woman born Shall harm Macbeth' (4.1.80–81) is revealed, via the expedient of Macduff's birth by caesarian section 'from his mother's womb Untimely ripped', to be misleading. Macduff alone seems to have bypassed the inevitable vulnerability of men to women and to have rendered himself immune to women's influence.

Unlike the other tragic characters, Macbeth's crimes are all too obvious. He murders Duncan and causes many others to be murdered. *Macbeth* is not particularly concerned with the events which lead up to the crime, not over-interested in motive or explanation as, say *Othello* or *Hamlet* might be seen to be, but rather with observing and diagnosing the psychological effects of crime on the criminal. It might be assumed, then, that his characterisation offers a kind of moral clarity absent from the other plays. This is not so, however. In his soliloquies, Macbeth represents himself as a divided and increasingly tortured personality. He recognises his own flaw – his 'vaulting ambition, which o'erleaps itself' (1.7.27) – and when the witches' reassurances are revealed to be worthless, he resolves to fight on, in a reversion to the kind of valour which marked the admiring reports about him in the second scene of the play. Indeed, like the Thane of Cawdor whose title he gathers up as the first step towards greatness, it could be said of Macbeth that 'nothing in his life Became him like the leaving it' (1.4.7–8). The extent to which Macbeth is entirely culpable for his crimes is also arguable. The role of the witches in fanning his ambitious desires may be interpreted either as decisive or reflective. Do they control him as their puppet, encouraging him to kill Duncan and seize the crown? Or do they represent his hidden desires for power? If the former, their supernatural intervention may discharge Macbeth of some of the responsibility for the play's carnage; if the latter, they can be seen to make the play into a darker and more unsettling exploration of the psyche. If the witches are external agents, the fact that they do not reappear may be problematic – they are still roaming the blasted heath with apparently malevolent intent. If they are manifestations of Macbeth's own wishes, it is interesting that Banquo also sees them. In Holinshed's *Chronicles*, Shakespeare's major source for the play, Macbeth and Banquo are partners in crime. Macbeth's individual crimes also need to be seen in the context of a bloody and violent society, which valorises and rewards bloodthirsty brutality. Macbeth's first honour is given him by the king in recognition of his exploits, when his sword 'Smoked with bloody execution' and, without any ceremony, he 'unseamed [Macdonwald] from the nave to the chops' (1.2.18, 22). It is arguable that Macbeth's subsequent promotions are achieved through that same murderous instinct.

The language of the play is preoccupied with images of darkness. Actual darkness cloaks the murder of Duncan, metaphorical darkness spurs the deed. Lady Macbeth invokes 'thick night' and the 'dunnest smoke of hell' to shield her actions from view of heaven. Ironically, it is night-time when the true inescapability of what she has done is revealed; in her sleep-walking, the embodiment of Macbeth's murder of sleep (2.2.36), night becomes the theatre of the conscience, in which she can gain no forgetful peace. Macbeth reiterates this invocation, calling on 'seeling night' whose 'black agents' will undertake his work (3.2.46–53). It is night when Macbeth and Banquo meet in 2.1, and again when Banquo is murdered. Macbeth ponders on this hour when 'o'er the one half-world Nature seems dead and wicked dreams abuse The curtained sleep' (2.1.49–51). After the Macbeths' regicide, Ross describes an unnaturally dark day when 'dark night strangles the travelling lamp' and 'darkness does the face of earth entomb'

(2.4.7–9). Darkness represents the moral turmoil of the play-world and the predominance of evil; and thus when Siward tells Malcolm in the battle that 'the day almost itself professes yours' (5.7.27), the phrase is more than military convention. Malcolm's forces have been fighting for the day as well as during it, and their triumph represents a new dawn after a nightmarish darkness.

The Scene: Scotland and (in 4.3) England

CHARACTERS IN THE PLAY

DUNCAN, *King of Scotland*
MALCOLM   } *his sons*
DONALBAIN }
MACBETH, *at first a general, later King of Scotland*
BANQUO, *a general*
MACDUFF
LENNOX
ROSS
MENTEITH } *noblemen of Scotland*
ANGUS
CAITHNESS
FLEANCE, *son to Banquo*
SIWARD, *Earl of Northumberland, general of the
    English forces*
YOUNG SIWARD, *his son*
SETON, *armour-bearer to Macbeth*
A Boy, son to Macduff
A Captain
A Porter
An Old Man
An English Doctor
A Scotch Doctor
Three Murderers

LADY MACBETH
LADY MACDUFF
A Gentlewoman attending on Lady Macbeth
The Weird Sisters
HECATE
Apparitions

*Lords, Gentlemen, Officers, Soldiers, Attendants, and
Messengers*

MACBETH

ACT I SCENE I

'Thunder and lightning. Enter three Witches'

1 WITCH	When shall we three meet again
	In thunder, lightning, or in rain?
2 WITCH	When the hurlyburly's done,
	When the battle's lost and won.
3 WITCH	That will be ere the set of sun.
1 WITCH	Where the place?
2 WITCH	Upon the heath.
3 WITCH	There to meet with Macbeth.
1 WITCH	I come, Graymalkin!
2 WITCH	Paddock calls.
3 WITCH	Anon!
ALL	Fair is foul, and foul is fair:
	Hover through the fog and filthy air.

10

[they vanish in mist

SCENE 2

A camp

'Alarum'. 'Enter King' DUNCAN, 'MALCOLM, DONALBAIN,
LENNOX, *with attendants, meeting a bleeding Captain'*

DUNCAN   What bloody man is that? He can report,
As seemeth by his plight, of the revolt
The newest state.

MALCOLM   This is the sergeant,
Who like a good and hardy soldier fought
'Gainst my captivity. Hail, brave friend!
Say to the king the knowledge of the broil
As thou didst leave it.

CAPTAIN   Doubtful it stood,
As two spent swimmers that do cling together
And choke their art. The merciless Macdonwald
(Worthy to be a rebel, for to that

10

The multiplying villainies of nature
Do swarm upon him) from the Western Isles
Of kerns and gallowglasses is supplied,
And Fortune, on his damnéd quarrel smiling,
Showed like a rebel's whore: but all's too weak:
For brave Macbeth (well he deserves that name)
Disdaining fortune, with his brandished steel,
Which smoked with bloody execution,
Like Valour's minion carvéd out his passage,
Till he faced the slave;   20
Which ne'er shook hands, nor bade farewell to him,
Till he unseamed him from the nave to th' chops,
And fixed his head upon our battlements.

DUNCAN   O, valiant cousin! Worthy gentleman!

CAPTAIN   As whence the sun 'gins his reflection
Shipwracking storms and direful thunders break;
So from that spring whence comfort seemed to come
Discomfort swells: mark, king of Scotland, mark!
No sooner justice had, with valour armed,
Compelled these skipping kerns to trust their heels,   30
But the Norweyan lord, surveying vantage,
With furbished arms and new supplies of men,
Began a fresh assault.

DUNCAN: Dismayed not this
Our captains, Macbeth and Banquo?

CAPTAIN   Yes;
As sparrows, eagles; or the hare, the lion.
If I say sooth, I must report they were
As cannons overcharged with double cracks;
So they
Doubly redoubled strokes upon the foe:
Except they meant to bathe in reeking wounds,   40
Or memorize another Golgotha,
I cannot tell:
But I am faint, my gashes cry for help.

DUNCAN   So well thy words become thee as thy wounds,
They smack of honour both. Go get him surgeons.
                              [*attendants help him thence*
Who comes here?

'Enter Ross and Angus'

MALCOLM   The worthy thane of Ross.

LENNOX   What a haste looks through his eyes! So should he look
That seems to speak things strange.

ROSS   God save the king!

DUNCAN   Whence cam'st thou, worthy thane?

ROSS   From Fife, great king,   50
Where the Norweyan banners flout the sky,
And fan our people cold.
Norway himself, with terrible numbers,
Assisted by that most disloyal traitor
The thane of Cawdor, began a dismal conflict,
Till that Bellona's bridegroom, lapped in proof,
Confronted him with self-comparisons,
Point against point, rebellious arm 'gainst arm,
Curbing his lavish spirit: and, to conclude,
The victory fell on us.

DUNCAN   Great happiness!

ROSS   That now   60
Sweno, the Norways' king, craves composition;
Nor would we deign him burial of his men
Till he disburséd, at Saint Colme's Inch,
Ten thousand dollars to our general use.

DUNCAN   No more that thane of Cawdor shall deceive
Our bosom interest: go pronounce his present death,
And with his former title greet Macbeth.

ROSS   I'll see it done.

DUNCAN   What he hath lost, noble Macbeth hath won.

                                               [they go

SCENE 3

A barren heath

'Thunder. Enter the three Witches'

1 WITCH	Where hast thou been, sister?
2 WITCH	Killing swine.
3 WITCH	Sister, where thou?
1 WITCH	A sailor's wife had chestnuts in her lap,

And munched, and munched, and munched: 'Give
me', quoth I.
'Aroint thee, witch!' the rump-fed ronyon cries.
Her husband's to Aleppo gone, master o'th' Tiger:
But in a sieve I'll thither sail,
And, like a rat without a tail,
I'll do, I'll do, and I'll do.   10

2 WITCH I'll give thee a wind.
1 WITCH Th'art kind.
3 WITCH And I another.
1 WITCH I myself have all the other,
And the very ports they blow,
All the quarters that they know
I'th' shipman's card.
I will drain him dry as hay:
Sleep shall, neither night nor day
Hang upon his pent-house lid;   20
He shall live a man forbid:
Weary sev'nights nine times nine
Shall he dwindle, peak, and pine:
Though his bark cannot be lost,
Yet it shall be tempest-tost.
Look what I have.
2 WITCH Show me, show me.
1 WITCH Here I have a pilot's thumb,
Wrecked as homeward he did come.   [*'drum within'*
3 WITCH A drum, a drum!   30
Macbeth doth come.

They dance in a ring, whirling faster and faster

ALL   The Weïrd Sisters, hand in hand,
     Posters of the sea and land,
     Thus do go, about, about,
     Thrice to thine, and thrice to mine,
     And thrice again, to make up nine.
     Peace! the charm's wound up.
          [they stop suddenly, and a mist hides them

     'Enter MACBETH and BANQUO'

MACBETH So foul and fair a day I have not seen.
BANQUO How far is't called to Forres?   *[the mist thins*
             What are these,
     So withered, and so wild in their attire,   40
     That look not like th'inhabitants o'th'earth,
     And yet are on't? Live you? Or are you aught
     That man may question? You seem to understand me,
     By each at once her choppy finger laying
     Upon her skinny lips: you should be women,
     And yet your beards forbid me to interpret
     That you are so.
MACBETH   Speak, if you can: what are you?
1 WITCH All hail, Macbeth! Hail to thee, thane of Glamis!
2 WITCH All hail, Macbeth! Hail to thee, thane of Cawdor!
3 WITCH All hail, Macbeth! That shalt be king hereafter. 50
BANQUO Good sir, why do you start, and seem to fear
     Things that do sound so fair? I'th' name of truth,
     Are ye fantastical, or that indeed
     Which outwardly ye show? My noble partner
     You greet with present grace and great prediction
     Of noble having and of royal hope,
     That he seems rapt withal: to me you speak not.
     If you can look into the seeds of time,
     And say which grain will grow and which will not,
     Speak then to me, who neither beg nor fear 60
     Your favours nor your hate.
1 WITCH Hail!
2 WITCH Hail!
3 WITCH Hail!

I WITCH	Lesser than Macbeth, and greater.
2 WITCH	Not so happy, yet much happier.
3 WITCH	Thou shalt get kings, though thou be none:
	So all hail, Macbeth and Banquo!
I WITCH	Banquo and Macbeth, all hail! *[the mist thickens*
MACBETH	Stay, you imperfect speakers, tell me more 70
	By Sinel's death I know I am thane of Glamis,
	But how of Cawdor? The thane of Cawdor lives
	A prosperous gentleman; and to be king
	Stands not within the prospect of belief,
	No more than to be Cawdor. Say from whence
	You owe this strange intelligence, or why
	Upon this blasted heath you stop our way
	With such prophetic greeting. Speak, I charge you.
	[they disappear
BANQUO	The earth hath bubbles, as the water has,
	And these are of them: whither are they vanished? 80
MACBETH	Into the air; and what seemed corporal, melted,
	As breath into the wind. Would they had stayed!
BANQUO	Were such things here as we do speak about?
	Or have we eaten on the insane root
	That takes the reason prisoner?
MACBETH	Your children shall be kings.
BANQUO	You shall be king.
MACBETH	And thane of Cawdor too: Went it not so?
BANQUO	To th' selfsame tune and words. Who's here?

'Enter ROSS *and* ANGUS'

ROSS	The king hath happily received, Macbeth,
	The news of thy success: and when he reads 90
	Thy personal venture in the rebels' fight,
	His wonders and his praises do contend
	Which should be thine or his: silenced with that,
	In viewing o'er the rest o'th' self-same day,
	He finds thee in the stout Norweyan ranks,
	Nothing afeard of what thyself didst make
	Strange images of death. As thick as hail
	Came post with post, and every one did bear
	Thy praises in his kingdom's great defence,

      And poured them down before him.

ANGUS   We are sent   100
      To give thee from our royal master thanks,
      Only to herald thee into his sight,
      Not pay thee.

ROSS   And for an earnest of a greater honour,
      He bade me, from him, call thee thane of Cawdor:
      In which addition, hail, most worthy thane,
      For it is thine.

BANQUO   What, can the devil speak true?

MACBETH   The thane of Cawdor lives: why do you dress me
      In borrowed robes?

ANGUS   Who was the thane lives yet,
      But under heavy judgment bears that life   110
      Which he deserves to lose. Whether he was combined
      With those of Norway, or did line the rebel
      With hidden help and vantage, or that with both
      He laboured in his country's wreck, I know not;
      But treasons capital, confessed, and proved,
      Have overthrown him.

MACBETH   Glamis, and thane of Cawdor:
      The greatest is behind. [*aloud*] Thanks for your pains –
      [*aside to Banquo*]
      Do you not hope your children shall be kings,
      When those that gave the thane of Cawdor to me
      Promised no less to them?

BANQUO   That, trusted home,   120
      Might yet enkindle you unto the crown,
      Besides the thane of Cawdor. But 'tis strange:
      And oftentimes, to win us to our harm,
      The instruments of darkness tell us truths,
      Win us with honest trifles, to betray's
      In deepest consequence.
      Cousins, a word, I pray you.
                [*to Ross and Angus, who move towards him*

MACBETH   Two truths are told,
      As happy prologues to the swelling act
      Of the imperial theme. [*aloud*] I thank you, gentlemen.
      [*aside*] This supernatural soliciting   130

Cannot be ill; cannot be good. If ill,
Why hath it given me earnest of success,
Commencing in a truth? I am thane of Cawdor.
If good, why do I yield to that suggestion
Whose horrid image doth unfix my hair,
And make my seated heart knock at my ribs,
Against the use of nature? Present fears
Are less than horrible imaginings:
My thought, whose murder yet is but fantastical,
Shakes so my single state of man that function   14
Is smothered in surmise, and nothing is
But what is not.

BANQUO   Look how our partner's rapt.

MACBETH   If chance will have me king, why, chance may
                                     crown me,
Without my stir.

BANQUO   New honours come upon him,
Like our strange garments, cleave not to their mould
But with the aid of use.

MACBETH   Come what come may,
Time and the hour runs through the roughest day.

BANQUO   Worthy Macbeth, we stay upon your leisure.

MACBETH   Give me your favour: my dull brain was wrought
With things forgotten. Kind gentlemen, your pains   15
Are registered where every day I turn
The leaf to read them. Let us toward the king.
                                [*aside to Banquo*
Think upon what hath chanced; and at more time,
The interim having weighed it, let us speak
Our free hearts each to other.

BANQUO   Very gladly,

MACBETH   Till then, enough – Come, friends.
                                    [*they go forward*

SCENE 4

Forres. A room in the Palace

'Flourish. Enter King' DUNCAN, *'*MALCOLM,
DONALBAIN, LENNOX, *and Attendants'*

DUNCAN   Is execution done on Cawdor? Are not
Those in commission yet returned?

MALCOLM   My liege,
They are not yet come back. But I have spoke
With one that saw him die: who did report
That very frankly he confessed his treasons,
Implored your highness' pardon, and set forth
A deep repentance: nothing in his life
Became him like the leaving it; he died
As one that had been studied in his death,
To throw away the dearest thing he owed   10
As 'twere a careless trifle.

DUNCAN   There's no art
To find the mind's construction in the face:
He was a gentleman on whom I built
An absolute trust.

'Enter MALCOLM, BANQUO, ROSS, *and* ANGUS*'*

                  O worthiest cousin!
The sin of my ingratitude even now
Was heavy on me. Thou art so far before,
That swiftest wing of recompense is slow
To overtake thee. Would thou hadst less deserved,
That the proportion both of thanks and payment
Might have been mine! Only I have left to say,   20
More is thy due than more than all can pay.

MACBETH   The service and the loyalty I owe,
In doing it, pays itself. Your highness' part
Is to receive our duties: and our duties
Are to your throne and state children and servants,
Which do but what they should, by doing everything
Safe toward your love and honour.

DUNCAN   Welcome hither:
              I have begun to plant thee, and will labour
              To make thee full of growing. Noble Banquo,
              That hast no less deserved, nor must be known   30
              No less to have done so: let me infold thee,
              And hold thee to my heart.

BANQUO   There if I grow,
              The harvest is your own.

DUNCAN   My plenteous joys,
              Wanton in fulness, seek to hide themselves
              In drops of sorrow. Sons, kinsmen, thanes,
              And you whose places are the nearest, know,
              We will establish our estate upon
              Our eldest, Malcolm, whom we name hereafter
              The Prince of Cumberland: which honour must
              Not unaccompanied invest him only,   40
              But signs of nobleness, like stars, shall shine
              On all deservers. From hence to Inverness,
              And bind us further to you.

MACBETH   The rest is labour, which is not used for you:
              I'll be myself the harbinger, and make joyful
              The hearing of my wife with your approach;
              So humbly take my leave.

DUNCAN   My worthy Cawdor!

MACBETH   The Prince of Cumberland! That is a step
              On which I must fall down, or else o'er-leap,
              For in my way it lies. Stars, hide your fires!   50
              Let not light see my black and deep desires:
              The eye wink at the hand; yet let that be
              Which the eye fears, when it is done, to see.   [he goes

DUNCAN   True, worthy Banquo; he is full so valiant,
              And in his commendations I am fed;
              It is a banquet to me. Let's after him,
              Whose care is gone before to bid us welcome:
              It is a peerless kinsman.   ['Flourish'. They go

SCENE 5

Inverness. Before Macbeth's castle

'Enter MACBETH'S *wife alone, with a letter'*

LADY M.   [*reads*] 'They met me in the day of success; and I have
learned by the perfect'st report, they have more in them
than mortal knowledge. When I burned in desire to
question them further, they made themselves air, into
which they vanished. Whiles I stood rapt in the wonder
of it, came missives from the king, who all- hailed me,
'Thane of Cawdor', by which title, before, these Weird
Sisters saluted me, and referred me to the coming on of
time, with 'Hail, king that shalt be!' This have I thought
good to deliver thee (my dearest partner of greatness) 10
that thou mightst not lose the dues of rejoicing, by
being ignorant of what greatness is promised thee. Lay
it to thy heart, and farewell.'
Glamis thou art, and Cawdor, and shalt be
What thou art promised: yet do I fear thy nature,
It is too full o'th' milk of human kindness
To catch the nearest way: thou wouldst be great,
Art not without ambition, but without
The illness should attend it: what thou wouldst highly,
That wouldst thou holily; wouldst not play false, 20
And yet wouldst wrongly win: thou'ldst have,

                             great Glamis,
That which cries 'Thus thou must do', if thou have it,
And that which rather thou dost fear to do
Than wishest should be undone. Hie thee hither,
That I may pour my spirits in thine ear,
And chastise with the valour of my tongue
All that impedes thee from the golden round,
Which fate and metaphysical aid doth seem
To have thee crowned withal.

An attendant enters

ATTEN'T
What is your tidings?

ATTEN'T The king comes here tonight.

LADY M.   Thou'rt mad to say it!   30
Is not thy master with him? Who, were't so,
Would have informed for preparation.

ATTEN'T So please you, it is true: our thane is coming:
One of my fellows had the speed of him;
Who, almost dead for breath, had scarcely more
Than would make up his message.

LADY M.   Give him tending,
He brings great news. [*attendant goes*] The raven
himself is hoarse
That croaks the fatal entrance of Duncan
Under my battlements. Come, you spirits
That tend on mortal thoughts, unsex me here,   40
And fill me, from the crown to the toe, top-full
Of direst cruelty! Make thick my blood,
Stop up th'access and passage to remorse,
That no compunctious visitings of nature
Shake my fell purpose, nor keep peace between
Th'effect and it! Come to my woman's breasts,
 And take my milk for gall, you murd'ring ministers,
Wherever in your sightless substances
You wait on nature's mischief! Come, thick night,
And pall thee in the dunnest smoke of hell,   50
That my keen knife see not the wound it makes,
Nor heaven peep through the blanket of the dark,
To cry 'Hold, hold!'

'Enter MACBETH*'*

Great Glamis! Worthy Cawdor!
Greater than both, by the all-hail hereafter!
Thy letters have transported me beyond
This ignorant present, and I feel now
The future in the instant.

MACBETH   My dearest love,
Duncan comes here tonight.

LADY M.   And when goes hence?

MACBETH Tomorrow, as he purposes.

LADY M.   O, never

Shall sun that morrow see!   60
Your face, my thane, is as a book, where men
May read strange matters. To beguile the time,
Look like the time, bear welcome in your eye,
Your hand, your tongue: look like th'innocent flower,
But be the serpent under't. He that's coming
Must be provided for: and you shall put
This night's great business into my dispatch,
Which shall to all our nights and days to come
Give solely sovereign sway and masterdom.

MACBETH   We will speak further.

LADY M.   Only look up clear.   70
To alter favour ever is to fear:
Leave all the rest to me.   [*they go within*

SCENE 6

'*Hautboys*'. '*Enter King*' DUNCAN, '*MALCOLM, DONALBAIN,*
BANQUO, LENNOX, MACDUFF, ROSS, ANGUS, *and attendants*'

DUNCAN   This castle hath a pleasant seat; the air
Nimbly and sweetly recommends itself
Unto our gentle senses.

BANQUO   This guest of summer,
The temple-haunting martlet, does approve,
By his loved mansionry, that the heaven's breath
Smells wooingly here: no jutty, frieze,
Buttress, nor coign of vantage, but this bird
Hath made his pendent bed and procreant cradle:
Where they most breed and haunt, I have observed
The air is delicate.

'*Enter* LADY' MACBETH

DUNCAN   See, see! our honoured hostess!   10
The love that follows us sometime is our trouble,
Which still we thank as love. Herein I teach you
How you shall bid God 'ield us for your pains,
And thank us for your trouble.

LADY M.   All our service
In every point twice done, and then done double,

Were poor and single business to contend
Against those honours deep and broad, wherewith
Your majesty loads our house: for those of old,
And the late dignities heaped up to them,
We rest your hermits.

DUNCAN   Where's the thane of Cawdor?   20
We coursed him at the heels, and had a purpose
To be his purveyor: but he rides well,
And his great love (sharp as his spur) hath holp him
To his home before us. Fair and noble hostess,
We are your guest tonight.

LADY M.   Your servants ever
Have theirs, themselves, and what is theirs, in compt,
To make their audit at your highness' pleasure,
Still to return your own.

DUNCAN   Give me your hand:
Conduct me to mine host; we love him highly,
And shall continue our graces towards him.   30
By your leave, hostess.   [*he conducts her into the castle*

ACT I SCENE 7

*A court in Macbeth's castle, open to the sky, with doors to the rear, one
on the left the main gate or south entry, one on the right leading to rooms
within, and between them a covered recess running back, beneath a gallery,
to a third door, through which when ajar may be seen a flight of stairs to
an upper chamber. A bench with a table before it against a side wall.*

*'Hautboys. Torches. Enter a sewer' directing 'divers servants' who
pass 'with dishes and service' across the court. As they come through
the door on the right a sound of feasting is heard within. 'Then enter*
MACBETH' *from the same door*

MACBETH   If it were done, when 'tis done, then 'twere well
It were done quickly: if th'assassination
Could trammel up the consequence, and catch,
With his surcease, success; that but this blow
Might be the be-all and the end-all – here,
But here, upon this bank and shoal of time,
We'ld jump the life to come. But in these cases

We still have judgment here – that we but teach
Bloody instructions, which being taught return
To plague th'inventor: this even-handed justice   10
Commends th'ingredience of our poisoned chalice
To our own lips. He's here in double trust:
First, as I am his kinsman and his subject,
Strong both against the deed; then, as his host,
Who should against his murderer shut the door,
Not bear the knife myself. Besides, this Duncan
Hath borne his faculties so meek, hath been
So clear in his great office, that his virtues
Will plead like angels, trumpet-tongued, against
The deep damnation of his taking-off   20
And pity, like a naked new-born babe,
Striding the blast, or Heaven's cherubin, horsed
Upon the sightless couriers of the air,
Shall blow the horrid deed in every eye,
That tears shall drown the wind. I have no spur
To prick the sides of my intent, but only
Vaulting ambition, which o'erleaps itself,
And falls on th'other –

        '*Enter* LADY' MACBETH

             How now, what news?

LADY M.   He has almost supped: why have you left the chamber?
MACBETH   Hath he asked for me?
LADY M.   Know you not he has?   30
MACBETH   We will proceed no further in this business:
He hath honoured me of late, and I have bought
Golden opinions from all sorts of people,
Which would be worn now in their newest gloss,
Not cast aside so soon.
LADY M.   Was the hope drunk
Wherein you dressed yourself? Hath it slept since?
And wakes it now, to look so green and pale
At what it did so freely? From this time
Such I account thy love. Art thou afeard
To be the same in thine own act and valour   40
As thou art in desire? Wouldst thou have that
Which thou esteem'st the ornament of life,

And live a coward in thine own esteem,
Letting 'I dare not' wait upon 'I would',
Like the poor cat i'th'adage?

MACBETH   Prithee, peace:
I dare do all that may become a man;
Who dares do more, is none.

LADY M.   What beast was't then
That made you break this enterprise to me?
When you durst do it, then you were a man;
And, to be more than what you were, you would   50
Be so much more the man. Nor time nor place
Did then adhere, and yet you would make both:
They have made themselves, and that their fitness now
Does unmake you. I have given suck, and know
How tender 'tis to love the babe that milks me –
I would, while it was smiling in my face,
Have plucked my nipple from his boneless gums,
And dashed the brains out, had I so sworn as you
Have done to this.

MACBETH   If we should fail?

LADY M.   We fail?
But screw your courage to the sticking place,   60
And we'll not fail. When Duncan is asleep
(Whereto the rather shall his day's hard journey
Soundly invite him) his two chamberlains
Will I with wine and wassail so convince,
That memory, the warder of the brain,
Shall be a fume, and the receipt of reason
A limbec only: when in swinish sleep
Their drenchéd natures lie as in a death,
What cannot you and I perform upon
Th'unguarded Duncan? What not put upon   70
His spongy officers, who shall bear the guilt
Of our great quell?

MACBETH   Bring forth men-children only!
For thy undaunted mettle should compose
Nothing but males. Will it not be received,
When we have marked with blood those sleepy two
Of his own chamber, and used their very daggers,

That they have done't?

LADY M.   Who dares receive it other,
As we shall make our griefs and clamour roar
Upon his death?

MACBETH   I am settled, and bend up
Each corporal agent to this terrible feat.   80
Away, and mock the time with fairest show:
False face must hide what the false heart doth know.

                         [they return to the chamber

ACT 2 SCENE 1

The same, one or two hours later. 'Enter' from the back
'BANQUO, and FLEANCE with a torch before him'. They
come forward, leaving the door open behind them

BANQUO   How goes the night, boy?
FLEANCE   [*gazing at the sky*] The moon is down; I have not
                                                    heard the clock.
BANQUO   And she goes down at twelve.
FLEANCE   I take't, 'tis later, sir.
BANQUO   Hold, take my sword. There's husbandry in heaven,
          Their candles are all out. [*unclasps his belt with its dagger*
                                      Take thee that too.
          A heavy summons lies like lead upon me,
          And yet I would not sleep. Merciful powers,
          Restrain in me the curséd thoughts that nature
          Gives way to in repose! [*he starts*] Give me my sword,

'Enter' (from the right) 'MACBETH, and a servant, with a torch'

          Who's there?   10
MACBETH   A friend.
BANQUO   What, sir, not yet at rest? The king's a-bed.
          He hath been in unusual pleasure, and
          Sent forth great largess to your offices.
          This diamond he greets your wife withal,
          By the name of most kind hostess; and shut up
          In measureless content.
MACBETH   Being unprepared,
          Our will became the servant to defect,
          Which else should free have wrought.
BANQUO   All's well.
          I dreamt last night of the three Weird Sisters   20
          To you they have showed some truth.
MACBETH   I think not of them:
          Yet, when we can entreat an hour to serve,
          We would spend it in some words upon that business,
          If you would grant the time.
BANQUO   At your kind'st leisure.

MACBETH   If you shall cleave to my consent, when 'tis,
          It shall make honour for you.

BANQUO   So I lose none
          In seeking to augment it, but still keep
          My bosom franchised and allegiance clear,
          I shall be counselled.

MACBETH   Good repose the while!

BANQUO   Thanks, sir: the like to you!   30

                    [*Banquo and Fleance go to their chamber*

MACBETH   Go bid thy mistress, when my drink is ready,
          She strike upon the bell. Get thee to bed.

                    [*the servant goes; he sits at the table*

          Is this a dagger which I see before me,
          The handle toward my hand? Come, let me
                                            clutch thee:
          I have thee not, and yet I see thee still.
          Art thou not, fatal vision, sensible
          To feeling as to sight? Or art thou but
          A dagger of the mind, a false creation,
          Proceeding from the heat-oppressèd brain?
          I see thee yet, in form as palpable   40
          As this which now I draw.
          Thou marshall'st me the way that I was going,
          And such an instrument I was to use!   [*he rises*
          Mine eyes are made the fools o'th'other senses,
          Or else worth all the rest: I see thee still;
          And on thy blade and dudgeon gouts of blood,
          Which was not so before. There's no such thing:
          It is the bloody business which informs
          Thus to mine eyes. Now o'er the one half-world
          Nature seems dead, and wicked dreams abuse   50
          The curtained sleep; Witchcraft celebrates
          Pale Hecate's off'rings; and withered Murder,
          Alarumed by his sentinel, the wolf,
          Whose howl's his watch, thus with his stealthy pace,
          With Tarquin's ravishing strides, towards his design
          Moves like a ghost. Thou sure and firm-set earth,
          Hear not my steps, which way they walk, for fear
          Thy very stones prate of my whereabout,

And take the present horror from the time,
Which now suits with it. Whiles I threat, he lives: 60
Words to the heat of deeds too cold breath gives.

            [*'a bell rings'*

I go, and it is done: the bell invites me.
 Hear it not, Duncan, for it is a knell
That summons thee to heaven, or to hell.

       [*he steals out by the open door at back, and
         step by step climbs the stair. A pause*

SCENE 2

  LADY MACBETH *enters from the right, with a cup in her hand*

LADY M. That which hath made them drunk hath made me bold:
    What hath quenched them hath given me fire.
    [*she pauses*]   Hark! Peace:
    It was the owl that shrieked, the fatal bellman,
    Which gives the stern'st good-night. He is about it:
    The doors are open; and the surfeited grooms
    Do mock their charge with snores: I have drugged
                their possets,
    That death and nature do contend about them,
    Whether they live or die.
MACBETH [*within*]   Who's there? What, ho!
LADY M. Alack! I am afraid they have awaked,
    And 'tis not done: th'attempt and not the deed 10
    Confounds us. Hark! I laid their daggers ready,
    He could not miss 'em. Had he not resembled
    My father as he slept, I had done't.

  She turns as if making towards the stair, to find MACBETH
   *standing in the door, his arms bathed in blood and with
   two daggers clasped in his left hand. He totters forward*

             My husband !
MACBETH [*whispers*] I have done the deed. Didst thou not
                hear a noise?
LADY M. I heard the owl scream, and the crickets cry.
    Did not you speak?
MACBETH   When?

LADY M.   Now.

MACBETH   As I descended?

LADY M.   Ay.

MACBETH Hark!   [*they listen*
          Who lies i'th' second chamber?

LADY M.   Donalbain.

MACBETH This is a sorry sight.   20
                 [*stretching forth his right hand*

LADY M.   A foolish thought, to say a sorry sight.

MACBETH There's one did laugh in's sleep, and one cried 'Murder!'
          That they did wake each other: I stood and heard them:
          But they did say their prayers, and addressed them
          Again to sleep.

LADY M.   There are two lodged together.

MACBETH One cried 'God bless us!' and 'Amen' the other,
          As they had seen me with these hangman's hands:
          List'ning their fear, I could not say 'Amen',
          When they did say 'God bless us'.

LADY M.   Consider it not so deeply.   30

MACBETH But wherefore could not I pronounce 'Amen'?
          I had most need of blessing, and 'Amen'
          Stuck in my throat.

LADY M.   These deeds must not be thought
          After these ways; so, it will make us mad.

MACBETH Methought I heard a voice cry 'Sleep no more!
          Macbeth does murder sleep' – the innocent sleep,
          Sleep that knits up the ravelled sleave of care,
          The death of each day's life, sore labour's bath,
          Balm of hurt minds, great Nature's second course,
          Chief nourisher in life's feast, –

LADY M.   What do you mean?   40

MACBETH Still it cried 'Sleep no more!' to all the house:
          'Glamis hath murdered sleep, and therefore Cawdor
          Shall sleep no more: Macbeth shall sleep no more!'

LADY M.   Who was it that thus cried? Why, worthy thane,
          You do unbend your noble strength, to think
          So brainsickly of things. Go get some water,
          And wash this filthy witness from your hand.
          Why did you bring these daggers from the place?

They must lie there: go carry them, and smear
The sleepy grooms with blood.

MACBETH   I'll go no more: 50
am afraid to think what I have done;
Look on't again I dare not.

LADY M.   Infirm of purpose!
Give me the daggers: the sleeping and the dead
Are but as pictures: 'tis the eye of childhood
That fears a painted devil. If he do bleed,
I'll gild the faces of the grooms withal,
For it must seem their guilt.

                      [she goes up. A knocking heard

MACBETH   Whence is that knocking?
How is't with me, when every noise appals me?
What hands are here? Ha! They pluck out mine eyes!
Will all great Neptune's ocean wash this blood   60
Clean from my hand? No; this my hand will rather
The multitudinous seas incarnadine,
Making the green one red.

      LADY MACBETH *returns, closing the inner door*

LADY M.   My hands are of your colour; but I shame
To wear a heart so white. [*knocking*] I hear a knocking
At the south entry: retire we to our chamber:
A little water clears us of this deed:
How easy is it then! Your constancy
Hath left you unattended. [*knocking*]
                 Hark! More knocking.
Get on your nightgown, lest occasion call us   70
And show us to be watchers: be not lost
So poorly in your thoughts.

MACBETH   To know my deed, 'twere best not know myself.

                          [knocking

Wake Duncan with thy knocking! I would thou couldst!

                          [they go in

SCENE 3

The knocking grows yet louder; a drunken Porter enters the court

PORTER   Here's a knocking indeed! If a man were porter of hell-
gate, he should have old turning the key. [*knocking*]
Knock, knock, knock! Who's there, i'th' name of
Beelzebub? Here's a farmer, that hanged himself on
th'expectation of plenty: come in, time-server; have
napkins enow about you, here you'll sweat for't.
[*knocking*] Knock, knock! Who's there, in th'other devil's name? Faith, here's an equivocator, that could
swear in both the scales against either scale, who committed treason enough for God's sake, yet could not   10
equivocate to heaven: O, come in, equivocator. [*knocking*] Knock, knock, knock! Who's there? Faith, here's
an English tailor come hither, for stealing out of a
French hose: come in, tailor, here you may roast your
goose. [*knocking*] Knock, knock! Never at quiet! What
are you? But this place is too cold for hell. I'll devil-
porter it no further: I had thought to have let in some
of all professions, that go the primrose way to
th'everlasting bonfire. [*knocking*] Anon, anon! I pray
you, remember the porter.   [*opens the gate*   20

'*Enter* MACDUFF *and* LENNOX'

MACDUFF   Was it so late, friend, ere you went to bed, that you do
lie so late?

PORTER   Faith, sir, we were carousing till the second cock: and
drink, sir, is a great provoker of three things.

MACDUFF   What three things does drink especially provoke?

PORTER   Marry, sir, nose-painting, sleep, and urine. Lechery, sir,
it provokes and unprovokes: it provokes the desire, but
it takes away the performance. Therefore, much drink
may be said to be an equivocator with lechery: it makes
him, and it mars him; it sets him on, and it takes him   30
off; it persuades him, and disheartens him; makes him
stand to, and not stand to: in conclusion, equivocates
him in a sleep, and giving him the lie, leaves him.

MACDUFF   I believe drink gave thee the lie last night.

PORTER   That it did, sir, i'the very throat on me: but I requited
          him for his lie, and, I think, being too strong for him,
          though he took up my legs sometime, yet I made a
          shift to cast him.

MACDUFF   Is thy master stirring?

                   MACBETH *returns, in a dressing gown*

          Our knocking has awaked him; here he comes.   40

LENNOX   Good-morrow, noble sir.

MACBETH   Good-morrow, both.

MACDUFF   Is the king stirring, worthy thane?

MACBETH   Not yet.

MACDUFF   He did command me to call timely on him;
          I have almost slipped the hour.

MACBETH   I'll bring you to him.
                       [*they move towards the inner door*

MACDUFF   I know this is a joyful trouble to you;
          But yet 'tis one.

MACBETH   The labour we delight in physics pain.
          This is the door.   [*he points*

MACDUFF   I'll make so bold to call,
          For 'tis my limited service.   [*he goes in*

LENNOX   Goes the king hence today?   50

MACBETH   He does: he did appoint so.

LENNOX   The night has been unruly: where we lay,
          Our chimneys were blown down, and, as they say,
          Lamentings heard i'th'air, strange screams of death,
          And prophesying with accents terrible
          Of dire combustion and confused events
          New hatched to th' woeful time. The obscure bird
          Clamoured the livelong night: some say, the earth
          Was feverous and did shake.

MACBETH   'Twas a rough night.

LENNOX   My young remembrance cannot parallel   60
          A fellow to it.

                      MACDUFF *returns*

MACDUFF   O horror! horror! horror! Tongue, nor heart,
          Cannot conceive nor name thee!

MACBETH, LENNOX   What's the matter?
MACDUFF Confusion now hath made his masterpiece!
         Most sacrilegious murder hath broke ope
         The Lord's anointed temple, and stole thence
         The life o'th' building.
MACBETH What is't you say? The life?
LENNOX   Mean you his majesty?
MACDUFF Approach the chamber, and destroy your sight   70
         With a new Gorgon: do not bid me speak;
         See, and then speak yourselves. [*Macbeth and Lennox go*
                                        Awake! awake!
         Ring the alarum bell! Murder and treason!
         Banquo and Donalbain! Malcolm, awake!
         Shake off this downy sleep, death's counterfeit,
         And look on death itself! Up, up, and see
         The great doom's image! Malcolm! Banquo!
         As from your graves rise up, and walk like sprites,
         To countenance this horror!   [*'bell rings'*

              '*Enter* LADY' MACBETH *in a dressing gown*

LADY M.   What's the business,
         That such a hideous trumpet calls to parley   80
         The sleepers of the house? Speak, speak!
MACDUFF   O, gentle lady,
         'Tis not for you to hear what I can speak:
         The repetition, in a woman's ear,
         Would murder as it fell.

                   '*Enter* BANQUO' *half-clad*

                                 O Banquo! Banquo!
         Our royal master's murdered!
LADY M.   Woe, alas!
         What, in our house!
BANQUO   Too cruel, anywhere.
         Dear Duff, I prithee, contradict thyself,
         And say it is not so.

                   MACBETH *and* LENNOX *return*

MACBETH Had I but died an hour before this chance,
         I had lived a blessèd time; for from this instant   90
         There's nothing serious in mortality:

All is but toys: renown and grace is dead,
The wine of life is drawn, and the mere lees
Is left this vault to brag of.

>   MALCOLM *and* DONALBAIN *come in haste*
>   *through the door on the right*

DONALB'N: What is amiss?

MACBETH   You are, and do not know't:
The spring, the head, the fountain of your blood
Is stopped — the very source of it is stopped.

MACDUFF   Your royal father's murdered.

MALCOLM   O, by whom?

LENNOX   Those of his chamber, as it seemed, had done't:
Their hands and faces were all badged with blood,   100
So were their daggers, which unwiped we found
Upon their pillows:
They stared and were distracted, no man's life
Was to be trusted with them.

MACBETH   O, yet I do repent me of my fury,
That I did kill them.

MACDUFF   Wherefore did you so?

MACBETH   Who can be wise, amazed, temp'rate and furious,
Loyal and neutral, in a moment? No man:
Th'expedition of my violent love
Outrun the pauser, reason. Here lay Duncan,   110
His silver skin laced with his golden blood,
And his gashed stabs looked like a breach in nature
For ruin's wasteful entrance: there, the murderers,
Steeped in the colours of their trade, their daggers
Unmannerly breeched with gore: who could refrain,
That had a heart to love, and in that heart
Courage to make's love known?

LADY M.   [*seeming to faint*]   Help me hence, ho!

>   MACBETH *goes to her*

MACDUFF   Look to the lady.

MALCOLM   Why do we hold our tongues,
That most may claim this argument for ours?

DONALB'N   What should be spoken here, where our fate,   120
Hid in an auger-hole, may rush and seize us?

Let's away.
Our tears are not yet brewed.

MALCOLM   Nor our strong sorrow
Upon the foot of motion.   [*enter waiting-women*

BANQUO   [*directs them*]   Look to the lady. [*they lead her forth*
And when we have our naked frailties hid,
That suffer in exposure, let us meet,
And question this most bloody piece of work,
To know it further. Fears and scruples shake us:
In the great hand of God I stand, and thence
Against the undivulged pretence I fight   130
Of treasonous malice.

MACDUFF   And so do I.

ALL   So all.

MACBETH   Let's briefly put on manly readiness.
And meet i'th'hall together.

ALL   Well contented.
             [*all go in but Malcolm and Donalbain*

MALCOLM   What will you do? Let's not consort with them:
To show an unfelt sorrow is an office
Which the false man does easy. I'll to England.

DONALB'N   To Ireland, I: our separated fortune
Shall keep us both the safer: where we are
There's daggers in men's smiles: the near in blood,
The nearer bloody.

MALCOLM   This murderous shaft that's shot   140
Hath not yet lighted, and our safest way
Is to avoid the aim. Therefore to horse,
And let us not be dainty of leave-taking,
But shift away: there's warrant in that theft
Which steals itself when there's no mercy left.
                       [*they go*

SCENE 4

Before Macbeth's castle. A day strangely dark

'Enter ROSS *with an Old Man'*

OLD MAN   Threescore and ten I can remember well,
              Within the volume of which time I have seen
              Hours dreadful and things strange; but this sore night
              Hath trifled former knowings.

ROSS   [*looks up*]   Ha, good father,
              Thou seest the heavens, as troubled with man's act,
              Threatens his bloody stage: by th' clock 'tis day,
              And yet dark night strangles the travelling lamp:
              Is't night's predominance, or the day's shame,
              That darkness does the face of earth entomb,
              When living light should kiss it?

OLD MAN   'Tis unnatural,   10
              Even like the deed that's done. On Tuesday last
              A falcon towering in her pride of place
              Was by a mousing owl hawked at and killed.

ROSS   And Duncan's horses – a thing most strange and
                                                  certain –
              Beauteous and swift, the minions of their race,
              Turned wild in nature, broke their stalls, flung out,
              Contending 'gainst obedience, as they would make
              War with mankind.

OLD MAN   'Tis said they eat each other.

ROSS   They did so, to th'amazement of mine eyes,
              That looked upon't.

              MACDUFF *comes from the Castle*

                                  Here comes the good Macduff.   20
              How goes the world, sir, now?

MACDUFF   [*points at the sky*]   Why, see you not?

ROSS   Is't known who did this more than bloody deed?

MACDUFF   Those that Macbeth hath slain.

ROSS   Alas, the day!
              What good could they pretend?

MACDUFF   They were suborned.
         Malcolm and Donalbain, the king's two sons,
         Are stol'n away and fled, which puts upon them
         Suspicion of the deed.

ROSS   'Gainst nature still!
         Thriftless ambition, that wilt ravin up
         Thine own life's means! Then 'tis most like
         The sovereignty will fall upon Macbeth.   30

MACDUFF He is already named, and gone to Scone
         To be invested.

ROSS   Where is Duncan's body?

MACDUFF Carried to Colme kill,
         The sacred storehouse of his predecessors,
         And guardian of their bones.

ROSS   Will you to Scone?

MACDUFF No cousin, I'll to Fife.

ROSS   Well, I will thither.

MACDUFF Well, may you see things well done there: adieu!
         Lest our old robes sit easier than our new!

ROSS   Farewell, father.

OLD MAN God's benison go with you, and with those   40
         That would make good of bad and friends of foes!
                                [*they go*

[*Some weeks pass*]

ACT 3 SCENE 1

An audience chamber in the palace at Forres

BANQUO *enters*

BANQUO   Thou hast it now, King, Cawdor, Glamis, all,
          As the weird women promised, and I fear
          Thou play'dst most foully for't: yet it was said
          It should not stand in thy posterity,
          But that myself should be the root and father
          Of many kings. If there come truth from them –
          As upon thee, Macbeth, their speeches shine –
          Why, by the verities on thee made good,
          May they not be my oracles as well,
          And set me up in hope? But hush, no more.   10

'*Sennet sounded. Enter* MACBETH, *as King,* LADY' MACBETH,
as Queen, 'LENNOX, ROSS, *Lords and attendants*'

MACBETH   Here's our chief guest.
LADY M.   If he had been forgotten,
          It had been as a gap in our great feast,
          And all-thing unbecoming.
MACBETH   Tonight we hold a solemn supper, sir,
          And I'll request your presence.
BANQUO   Let your highness
          Command upon me, to the which my duties
          Are with a most indissoluble tie
          For ever knit.
MACBETH   Ride you this afternoon?
BANQUO   Ay, my good lord.
MACBETH   We should have else desired your good advice   20
          (Which still hath been both grave and prosperous)
          In this day's council; but we'll take tomorrow.
          Is't far you ride?
BANQUO   As far, my lord, as will fill up the time
          'Twixt this and supper. Go not my horse the better,

I must become a borrower of the night
For a dark hour or twain.

MACBETH   Fail not our feast.

BANQUO   My lord, I will not.

MACBETH We hear our bloody cousins are bestowed
In England and in Ireland, not confessing   30
Their cruel parricide, filling their hearers
With strange invention: but of that tomorrow,
When therewithal we shall have cause of state
Craving us jointly. Hie you to horse: adieu,
Till you return at night. Goes Fleance with you?

BANQUO   Ay, my good lord: our time does call upon's.

MACBETH I wish your horses swift and sure of foot;
And so I do commend you to their backs.
Farewell.   [Banquo goes
Let every man be master of his time   40
Till seven at night; to make society
The sweeter welcome, we will keep ourself
Till supper-time alone: while then, God be with you!
              [all depart but Macbeth and a servant
Sirrah, a word with you: attend those men
Our pleasure?

ATTEND'T They are, my lord, without the palace gate.

MACBETH Bring them before us.   [the servant goes
                        To be thus is nothing,
But to be safely thus: our fears in Banquo
Stick deep, and in his royalty of nature
Reigns that which would be feared. 'Tis much
                              he dares,   50
And, to that dauntless temper of his mind,
He hath a wisdom that doth guide his valour
To act in safety. There is none but he
Whose being I do fear: and under him
My Genius is rebuked, as it is said
Mark Antony's was by Caesar. He chid the Sisters,
When first they put the name of king upon me,
And bade them speak to him; then prophet-like
They hailed him father to a line of kings:
Upon my head they placed a fruitless crown,   60

And put a barren sceptre in my gripe,
Thence to be wrenched with an unlineal hand,
No son of mine succeeding. If't be so,
For Banquo's issue have I filed my mind,
For them the gracious Duncan have I murdered,
Put rancours in the vessel of my peace
Only for them, and mine eternal jewel
Given to the common enemy of man,
To make them kings, the seed of Banquo kings!
Rather than so, come Fate into the list,   70
And champion me to th'utterance. Who's there?

    The servant returns 'with two murderers'

Now go to the door, and stay there till we call.

                                          [*servant goes out*

Was it not yesterday we spoke together?

I MURD'R It was, so please your highness.

MACBETH   Well then, now
Have you considered of my speeches? Know
That it was he in the times past which held you
So under fortune, which you thought had been
Our innocent self: this I made good to you
In our last conference; passed in probation with you,
How you were borne in hand, how crossed,
                              the instruments,   80
Who wrought with them, and all things else that might
To half a soul and to a notion crazed
Say 'Thus did Banquo'.

I MURD'R   You made it known to us.

MACBETH I did so; and went further, which is now
Our point of second meeting. Do you find
Your patience so predominant in your nature,
That you can let this go? Are you so gospelled,
To pray for this good man, and for his issue,
Whose heavy hand hath bowed you to the grave
And beggared yours for ever?

I MURD'R   We are men, my liege.   90

MACBETH Ay, in the catalogue ye go for men,
As hounds and greyhounds, mongrels, spaniels, curs,

  Shoughs, water-rugs, and demi-wolves, are clept
  All by the name of dogs: the valued file
  Distinguishes the swift, the slow, the subtle,
  The housekeeper, the hunter, every one
  According to the gift which bounteous nature
  Hath in him closed, whereby he does receive
  Particular addition, from the bill
  That writes them all alike: and so of men.   100
  Now, if you have a station in the file,
  Not i'th' worst rank of manhood, say't,
  And I will put that business in your bosoms,
  Whose execution takes your enemy off,
  Grapples you to the heart and love of us,
  Who wear our health but sickly in his life
  Which in his death were perfect.

2 MURD'R   I am one, my liege,
  Whom the vile blows and buffets of the world
  Hath so incensed that I am reckless what
  I do to spite the world.

1 MURD'R   And I another   110
  So weary with disasters, tugged with fortune,
  That I would set my life on any chance,
  To mend it, or be rid on't.

MACBETH   Both of you
  Know Banquo was your enemy.

BOTH MURD'RS: True, my lord.

MACBETH So is he mine: and in such bloody distance
  That every minute of his being thrusts
  Against my near'st of life: and though I could
  With barefaced power sweep him from my sight
  And bid my will avouch it, yet I must not,
  For certain friends that are both his and mine, 120
  Whose loves I may not drop, but wail his fall
  Who I myself struck down: and thence it is
  That I to your assistance do make love,
  Masking the business from the common eye,
  For sundry weighty reasons.

2 MURD'R   We shall, my lord,
  Perform what you command us.

I MURD'R   Though our lives —
MACBETH   Your spirits shine through you. Within this hour at most
          I will advise you where to plant yourselves,
          Acquaint you with the perfect spy o'th' time,
          The moment on't, for't must be done tonight,   130
          And something from the palace; always thought
          That I require a clearness: and with him —
          To leave no rubs nor botches in the work —
          Fleance his son, that keeps him company,
          Whose absence is no less material to me
          Than is his father's, must embrace the fate
          Of that dark hour. Resolve yourselves apart;
          I'll come to you anon.
BOTH MURD'RS: We are resolved, my lord.
MACBETH   I'll call upon you straight; abide within.   [they go
          It is concluded: Banquo, thy soul's flight,   140
          If it find heaven, must find it out tonight.
                                      [he leaves by another door

                              SCENE 2

                  LADY MACBETH enters with a servant

LADY M.   Is Banquo gone from court?
SERVANT   Ay, madam, but returns again tonight.
LADY M.   Say to the king, I would attend his leisure
          For a few words.
SERVANT   Madam, I will.   [he goes
LADY M.   Nought's had, all's spent,
          Where our desire is got without content;
          'Tis safer to be that which we destroy
          Than by destruction dwell in doubtful joy.

                  MACBETH enters lost in thought

          How now, my lord! why do you keep alone,
          Of sorriest fancies your companions making,
          Using those thoughts which should indeed have died   10
          With them they think on? Things without all remedy
          Should be without regard: what's done, is done.

MACBETH   We have scorched the snake, not killed it:
She'll close and be herself, whilst our poor malice
Remains in danger of her former tooth.
But let the frame of things disjoint, both the
                                 worlds suffer,
Ere we will eat our meal in fear, and sleep
In the affliction of these terrible dreams
That shake us nightly: better be with the dead,
Whom we, to gain our peace, have sent to peace,   20
Than on the torture of the mind to lie
In restless ecstasy. Duncan is in his grave;
After life's fitful fever he sleeps well;
Treason has done his worst: nor steel, nor poison,
Malice domestic, foreign levy, nothing,
Can touch him further.

LADY M.   Come on;
Gentle my lord, sleek o'er your rugged looks,
Be bright and jovial among your guests tonight.

MACBETH   So shall I, love, and so I pray be you:
Let your remembrance apply to Banquo;   30
Present him eminence, both with eye and tongue:
Unsafe the while, that we
Must lave our honours in these flattering streams,
And make our faces vizards to our hearts,
Disguising what they are.

LADY M.   You must leave this.

MACBETH   O, full of scorpions is my mind, dear wife!
Thou know'st that Banquo and his Fleance lives.

LADY M.   But in them nature's copy's not eterne.

MACBETH   There's comfort yet, they are assailable,
Then be thou jocund: ere the bat hath flown   40
His cloistered flight, ere to black Hecate's summons
The shard-borne beetle with his drowsy hums
Hath rung night's yawning peal, there shall be done
A deed of dreadful note.

LADY M.   What's to be done?

MACBETH   Be innocent of the knowledge, dearest chuck,
Till thou applaud the deed. Come, seeling night,
Scarf up the tender eye of pitiful day,

And with thy bloody and invisible hand
Cancel and tear to pieces that great bond
Which keeps me paled! Light thickens, and the crow   50
Makes wing to th' rooky wood:
Good things of day begin to droop and drowse,
Whiles night's black agents to their preys do rouse.
Thou marvell'st at my words: but hold thee still;
Things bad begun make strong themselves by ill:
So, prithee, go with me.   [*they go*

SCENE 3

*A steep lane leading through a wood to gates of the royal park, some
way from the palace. The two murderers come up, with a third*

1 MURD'R But who did bid thee join with us?
3 MURD'R   Macbeth.
2 MURD'R He needs not our mistrust, since he delivers
         Our offices and what we have to do,
         To the direction just.
1 MURD'R   Then stand with us.
         The west yet glimmers with some streaks of day:
         Now spurs the lated traveller apace
         To gain the timely inn, and near approaches
         The subject of our watch.
3 MURD'R   Hark! I hear horses.
BANQUO   [*at a distance*]
         Give us a light there, ho!
2 MURD'R   Then 'tis he; the rest
         That are within the note of expectation   10
         Already are i'th' court.
1 MURD'R   His horses go about.
3 MURD'R Almost a mile: but he does usually –
         So all men do – from hence to th' palace gate
         Make it their walk.

   'BANQUO *and* FLEANCE *with a torch' are seen coming up the lane*

2 MURD'R   A light, a light!
3 MURD'R   'Tis he.

1 MURD'R Stand to't.
BANQUO   It will be rain tonight.
1 MURD'R   Let it come down.

[*1 Murderer strikes out the torch; the others set upon Banquo*

BANQUO   O, treachery! Fly, good Fleance, fly, fly, fly!
         Thou mayst revenge. O slave!

[*he dies; Fleance escapes*

3 MURD'R Who did strike out the light?
1 MURD'R   Was't not the way?
3 MURD'R There's but one down; the son is fled.
2 MURD'R   We have lost   20
          Best half of our affair.
1 MURD'R Well, let's away, and say how much is done.

[*they go*

SCENE 4

*The hall of the palace. At the upper end a dais with doors to left
and right, between which are two thrones and a table before them,
while a longer table, at right angles, extends down the room*

A 'banquet prepared. Enter MACBETH, LADY' MACBETH,
'ROSS, LENNOX, *Lords, and attendants'*

MACBETH You know your own degrees, sit down: at first
         And last, the hearty welcome.
LORDS   Thanks to your majesty.

*Macbeth leads Lady Macbeth to the dais; the Lords sit on
either side of the long table, leaving an empty stool at the head*

MACBETH Ourself will mingle with society,
         And play the humble host:

[*Lady Macbeth ascends to her throne*

         Our hostess keeps her state, but in best time
         We will require her welcome.
LADY M. Pronounce it for me, sir, to all our friends,
         For my heart speaks they are welcome.

*As Macbeth passes by the door on the left 1 Murderer appears
there. The Lords rise and bow to Lady Macbeth*

MACBETH See, they encounter thee with their hearts' thanks.

	Both sides are even: here I'll sit i'th' midst.	10
	[point to the empty stool	
	Be large in mirth, anon we'll drink a measure	
	The table round.	
	[turns to the door] There's blood upon thy face.	
MURD'R	'Tis Banquo's then.	
MACBETH	'Tis better thee without than he within.	
	Is he dispatched?	
MURD'R	My lord, his throat is cut, that I did for him.	
MACBETH	Thou art the best o'th' cut-throats! Yet he's good	
	That did the like for Fleance: if thou didst it,	
	Thou art the nonpareil.	
MURD'R	Most royal sir,	
	Fleance is 'scaped.	20
MACBETH	Then comes my fit again: I had else been perfect;	
	Whole as the marble, founded as the rock,	
	As broad and general as the casing air:	
	But now I am cabined, cribbed, confined, bound in	
	To saucy doubts and fears. But Banquo's safe?	
MURD'R	Ay, my good lord: safe in a ditch he bides,	
	With twenty trenchéd gashes on his head;	
	The least a death to nature.	
MACBETH	Thanks for that:	
	There the grown serpent lies; the worm that's fled	
	Hath nature that in time will venom breed,	30
	No teeth for th' present. Get thee gone; tomorrow	
	We'll hear ourselves again. *[Murderer goes*	
LADY M.	My royal lord,	
	You do not give the cheer. The feast is sold	
	That is not often vouched, while 'tis a-making,	
	'Tis given with welcome: to feed were best at home;	
	From thence the sauce to meat is ceremony;	
	Meeting were bare without it.	

['The Ghost of Banquo' appears, 'and sits in Macbeth's place'

MACBETH	Sweet remembrancer!	
	Now good digestion wait on appetite,	
	And health on both!	
LENNOX	May't please your highness sit?	

MACBETH	Here had we now our country's honour roofed, 40
	Were the graced person of our Banquo present;
	Who may I rather challenge for unkindness
	Than pity for mischance!
ROSS	His absence, sir,
	Lays blame upon his promise. Please't your highness
	To grace us with your royal company?
MACBETH	The table's full.
LENNOX	Here is a place reserved, sir.
MACBETH	Where?
LENNOX	Here, my good lord. What is't that moves your highness?
MACBETH	Which of you have done this?
LORDS	What, my good lord?
MACBETH	Thou canst not say I did it: never shake 50
	Thy gory locks at me. [*Lady Macbeth rises*
ROSS	Gentlemen, rise, his highness is not well.
LADY M.	[*coming down*] Sit, worthy friends: my lord is often thus,
	And hath been from his youth: pray you, keep seat,
	The fit is momentary, upon a thought
	He will again be well: if much you note him,
	You shall offend him and extend his passion:
	Feed, and regard him not. [*aside*] Are you a man?
MACBETH	Ay, and a bold one, that dare look on that
	Which might appal the devil.
LADY M.	O proper stuff! 60
	This is the very painting of your fear:
	This is the air-drawn dagger which, you said,
	Led you to Duncan. O, these flaws and starts
	(Impostors to true fear) would well become
	A woman's story at a winter's fire,
	Authorized by her grandam. Shame itself!
	Why do you make such faces? When all's done,
	You look but on a stool.
MACBETH	Prithee, see there! Behold! Look! Lo! How say you?
	Why what care I? If thou canst nod, speak too. 70
	If charnel-houses and our graves must send
	Those that we bury back, our monuments
	Shall be the maws of kites. [*the Ghost vanishes*
LADY M.	What! Quite unmanned in folly?

MACBETH If I stand here, I saw him.

LADY M.   Fie, for shame!

MACBETH [*paces to and fro*]
    Blood hath been shed ere now, i'th'olden time,
    Ere humane statute purged the gentle weal;
    Ay, and since too, murders have been performed
    Too terrible for the ear: the time has been,
    That, when the brains were out, the man would die,
    And there an end: but now they rise again,   80
    With twenty mortal murders on their crowns,
    And push us from our stools. This is more strange
    Than such a murder is.

LADY M. [*touches his arm*]   My worthy lord,
    Your noble friends do lack you.

MACBETH   I do forget.
    Do not muse at me, my most worthy friends;
    I have a strange infirmity, which is nothing
    To those that know me. Come, love and health to all;
    Then I'll sit down. Give me some wine, fill full.
                [*as he raises his cup, the Ghost
                reappears in the seat behind him*
    I drink to th' general joy o'th' whole table,
    And to our dear friend Banquo, whom we miss;   90
    Would he were here! To all, and him we thirst,
    And all to all!

LORDS [*drinking*].   Our duties, and the pledge.

MACBETH [*turns to his seat*] Avaunt, and quit my sight! Let the
                         earth hide thee!

                  [*drops the cup*]

    Thy bones are marrowless, thy blood is cold;
    Thou hast no speculation in those eyes
    Which thou dost glare with!

LADY M.   Think of this, good peers,
    But as a thing of custom: 'tis no other;
    Only it spoils the pleasure of the time.

MACBETH What man dare, I dare:
    Approach thou like the ruggéd Russian bear,   100
    The armed rhinoceros, or th'Hyrcan tiger,

Take any shape but that, and my firm nerves
Shall never tremble: or be alive again,
And dare me to the desert with thy sword;
If trembling I inhabit then, protest me
The baby of a girl. Hence, horrible shadow!
Unreal mock'ry, hence!   [*the Ghost vanishes*
              Why, so; being gone,
I am a man again. Pray you, sit still.

LADY M.   You have displaced the mirth, broke the good meeting,
With most admired disorder.

MACBETH   Can such things be,   110
And overcome us like a summer's cloud,
Without our special wonder? You make me strange
Even to the disposition that I owe,
When now I think you can behold such sights,
And keep the natural ruby of your cheeks,
When mine is blanched with fear.

ROSS   What sights, my lord?

LADY M.   I pray you, speak not; he grows worse and worse;
Question enrages him: at once, good night.
Stand not upon the order of your going,   [*they rise*
But go at once.

LENNOX   Good night, and better health   120
Attend his majesty!

LADY M.   A kind good night to all! [*they leave*

MACBETH   It will have blood; they say, blood will have blood:
Stones have been known to move and trees to speak;
Augures and understood relations have
By maggot-pies and choughs and rooks brought forth
The secret'st man of blood. What is the night?

LADY M.   Almost at odds with morning, which is which.

MACBETH   How say'st thou, that Macduff denies his person
At our great bidding?

LADY M.   Did you send to him, sir?

MACBETH   I hear it by the way; but I will send: 130
There's not a one of them but in his house
I keep a servant fee'd. I will tomorrow
(And betimes I will) to the Weird Sisters:
More shall they speak; for now I am bent to know,

By the worst means, the worst. For mine own good
All causes shall give way: I am in blood
Stepped in so far that, should I wade no more,
Returning were as tedious as go o'er:
Strange things I have in head that will to hand,
Which must be acted ere they may be scanned.   140

LADY M.   You lack the season of all natures, sleep.

MACBETH   Come, we'll to sleep. My strange and self-abuse
Is the initiate fear that wants hard use:
We are yet but young in deed.   [they go

SCENE 5

A heath

'*Thunder. Enter the three Witches*', *meeting* HECATE

1 WITCH   Why, how now, Hecat, you look angerly.

HECATE   Have I not reason, beldams as you are,
Saucy and overbold? How did you dare
To trade and traffic with Macbeth
In riddles and affairs of death;
And I, the mistress of your charms,
The close contriver of all harms,
Was never called to bear my part,
Or show the glory of our art?
And, which is worse, all you have done   10
Hath been but for a wayward son,
Spiteful and wrathful, who (as others do)
Loves for his own ends, not for you.
But make amends now: get you gone,
And at the pit of Acheron
Meet me i'th' morning: thither he
Will come to know his destiny.
Your vessels and your spells provide,
Your charms and everything beside.
I am for th'air; this night I'll spend   20
Unto a dismal and a fatal end.
Great business must be wrought ere noon:
Upon the corner of the moon

There hangs a vap'rous drop profound;
I'll catch it ere it come to ground:
And that distilled by magic sleights
Shall raise such artificial sprites
As by the strength of their illusion
Shall draw him on to his confusion.
He shall spurn fate, scorn death, and bear   30
His hopes 'bove wisdom, grace, and fear:
And you all know security
Is mortals' chiefest enemy.

'Music and a song': 'Come away, come away', etc.
A cloud descends

Hark, I am called: my little spirit, see,
Sits in a foggy cloud, and stays for me.
                              [*she flies away on the cloud*
1 WITCH   Come, let's make haste; she'll soon be back again.
                                        [*they vanish*

SCENE 6

A castle in Scotland

'Enter LENNOX *and another Lord'*

LENNOX   My former speeches have but hit your thoughts,
Which can interpret farther: only I say
Things have been strangely borne. The gracious Duncan
Was pitied of Macbeth: marry, he was dead:
And the right valiant Banquo walked too late –
Whom you may say (if't please you) Fleance killed,
For Fleance fled: men must not walk too late.
Who cannot want the thought, how monstrous
It was for Malcolm and for Donalbain
To kill their gracious father? Damnéd fact!   10
How it did grieve Macbeth! Did he not straight,
In pious rage, the two delinquents tear,
That were the slaves of drink and thralls of sleep?
Was not that nobly done? Ay, and wisely too;
For 'twould have angered any heart alive

To hear the men deny't. So that, I say,
He has borne all things well: and I do think
That, had he Duncan's sons under his key
(As, an't please heaven, he shall not) they should find
What 'twere to kill a father; so should Fleance.   20
But, peace! For from broad words, and 'cause he failed
His presence at the tyrant's feast, I hear,
Macduff lives in disgrace. Sir, can you tell
Where he bestows himself?

LORD   The son of Duncan
(From whom this tyrant holds the due of birth)
Lives in the English court, and is received
Of the most pious Edward with such grace
That the malevolence of fortune nothing
Takes from his high respect. Thither Macduff
Is gone to pray the holy king, upon his aid   30
To wake Northumberland and warlike Siward,
That by the help of these (with Him above
To ratify the work) we may again
Give to our tables meat, sleep to our nights;
Free from our feasts and banquets bloody knives;
Do faithful homage and receive free honours:
All which we pine for now. And this report
Hath so exasperate the king that he
Prepares for some attempt of war.

LENNOX   Sent he to Macduff?

LORD   He did: and with an absolute 'Sir, not I',   40
The cloudy messenger turns me his back,
And hums, as who should say, 'You'll rue the time
That clogs me with this answer.'

LENNOX   And that well might
Advise him to a caution, t'hold what distance
His wisdom can provide. Some holy angel
Fly to the court of England and unfold
His message ere he come, that a swift blessing
May soon return to this our suffering country
Under a hand accursed!

LORD   I'll send my prayers with him.
                                                    [they go

ACT 4 SCENE I

A cavern and in the midst a fiery pit with a boiling cauldron above it.
'Thunder', as the Weird Sisters rise, one after the other, from the flames

1 WITCH   Thrice the brinded cat hath mewed.

2 WITCH   Thrice and once the hedge-pig whined.

3 WITCH   Harpier cries: 'Tis time, 'tis time.

1 WITCH   Round about the cauldron go:
          In the poisoned entrails throw. [*they move leftwards about it*
          Toad, that under cold stone
          Days and nights has thirty-one
          Sweltered venom sleeping got,
          Boil thou first i'th' charmèd pot!

ALL   Double, double toil and trouble;   10
          Fire burn and cauldron bubble.   [*they stir the cauldron*

2 WITCH   Fillet of a fenny snake,
          In the cauldron boil and bake:
          Eye of newt and toe of frog,
          Wool of bat and tongue of dog,
          Adder's fork and blind-worm's sting,
          Lizard's leg and howlet's wing,
          For a charm of powerful trouble,
          Like a hell-broth boil and bubble.

ALL   Double, double toil and trouble;   20
          Fire burn and cauldron bubble.   [*they stir*

3 WITCH   Scale of dragon, tooth of wolf,
          Witch's mummy, maw and gulf
          Of the ravined salt-sea shark,
          Root of hemlock digged i'th' dark,
          Liver of blaspheming Jew,
          Gall of goat and slips of yew
          Slivered in the moon's eclipse,
          Nose of Turk and Tartar's lips,
          Finger of birth-strangled babe   30
          Ditch-delivered by a drab,
          Make the gruel thick and slab:
          Add thereto a tiger's chaudron,

For th'ingredience of our cauldron.

ALL   Double, double toil and trouble;
Fire burn and cauldron bubble.   [*they stir*

2 WITCH   Cool it with a baboon's blood,
Then the charm is firm and good.

     '*Enter* HECATE *and the other three Witches*'

HECATE   O, well done! I commend your pains,
And everyone shall share i'th' gains: 40
And now about the cauldron sing,
Like elves and fairies in a ring,
Enchanting all that you put in.

    '*Music and song: Black spirits, etc.*' *Hecate goes*

2 WITCH   By the pricking of my thumbs,
Something wicked this way comes;
Open, locks,
Whoever knocks!

    A door flies open, showing MACBETH *without*

MACBETH   [*enters*] How now, you secret, black, and midnight hags!
What is't you do?

ALL   A deed without a name.

MACBETH   I conjure you, by that which you profess   50
(Howe'er you come to know it), answer me:
Though you untie the winds and let them fight
Against the churches; though the yesty waves
Confound and swallow navigation up;
Though bladed corn be lodged and trees blown down;
Though castles topple on their warders' heads;
Though palaces and pyramids do slope
Their heads to their foundations; though the treasure
Of Nature's germens tumble all together,
Even till destruction sicken; answer me   60
To what I ask you.

1 WITCH   Speak.

2 WITCH   Demand.

3 WITCH   We'll answer.

1 WITCH   Say if th'hadst rather hear it from our mouths,
Or from our masters.

MACBETH   Call 'em, let me see 'em!

I WITCH   Pour in sow's blood, that hath eaten
                 Her nine farrow; grease that's sweaten
                 From the murderer's gibbet throw
                 Into the flame.

ALL   Come, high or low;
                 Thyself and office deftly show.

'Thunder. First Apparition, an armed head' like Macbeth's,
rises from the cauldron

MACBETH   Tell me, thou unknown power –
I WITCH   He knows thy thought:
                 Hear his speech, but say thou nought.   70
I APPAR'N   Macbeth! Macbeth! Macbeth! beware Macduff,
                 Beware the thane of Fife. Dismiss me. Enough.
                              [*'descends'*

MACBETH   Whate'er thou art, for thy good caution thanks;
                 Thou hast harped my fear aright. But one word more –
I WITCH   He will not be commanded: here's another,
                 More potent than the first.

'Thunder. Second Apparition, a bloody child'

2 APPAR'N   Macbeth! Macbeth! Macbeth!
MACBETH   Had I three ears, I'd hear thee.
2 APPAR'N   Be bloody, bold, and resolute: laugh to scorn
                 The power of man; for none of woman born   80
                 Shall harm Macbeth.   [*'descends'*
MACBETH   Then live, Macduff: what need I fear of thee?
                 But yet I'll make assurance double sure,
                 And take a bond of fate: thou shalt not live,
                 That I may tell pale-hearted fear it lies,
                 And sleep in spite of thunder.

'Thunder. Third Apparition, a child crowned, with a tree in his hand'

                             What is this,
                 That rises like the issue of a king,
                 And wears upon his baby-brow the round
                 And top of sovereignty?
ALL   Listen, but speak not to't.
3 APPAR'N   Be lion-mettled, proud, and take no care   90
                 Who chafes, who frets, or where conspirers are:
                 Macbeth shall never vanquished be until

Great Birnam wood to high Dunsinane hill
Shall come against him.   ['*descends*'

MACBETH   That will never be;
Who can impress the forest, bid the tree
Unfix his earth-bound root? Sweet bodements! Good.
Rebellious dead, rise never, till the wood
Of Birnam rise, and our high-placed Macbeth
Shall live the lease of nature, pay his breath
To time and mortal custom. Yet my heart   100
Throbs to know one thing; tell me, if your art
Can tell so much: shall Banquo's issue ever
Reign in this kingdom?

ALL   Seek to know no more.

MACBETH I will be satisfied: deny me this,
And an eternal curse fall on you! Let me know.

       'Hautboys' play as the cauldron descends

Why sinks that cauldron? And what noise is this?

1 WITCH Show!

2 WITCH Show!

3 WITCH Show!

ALL Show his eyes, and grieve his heart;   110
Come like shadows, so depart.

    'A show of eight kings', who pass one by one across the
    back of the cavern as Macbeth speaks, the 'last with a
      glass in his hand'; Banquo's Ghost following

MACBETH Thou art too like the spirit of Banquo: down!
Thy crown does sear mine eyeballs. And thy hair,
Thou other gold-bound brow, is like the first.
A third is like the former. Filthy hags!
Why do you show me this? – A fourth? Start, eyes!
What, will the line stretch out to th' crack of doom,
Another yet? A seventh? I'll see no more:
And yet the eighth appears, who bears a glass
Which shows me many more; and some I see   120
That two-fold balls and treble sceptres carry.
Horrible sight. Now I see 'tis true,
For the blood-boltered Banquo smiles upon me,
And points at them for his. What, is this so?

I WITCH   Ay, sir, all this is so. But why
Stands Macbeth thus amazedly?
Come, sisters, cheer we up his sprites,
And show the best of our delights.
I'll charm the air to give a sound,
While you perform your antic round: 130
That this great king may kindly say
Our duties did his welcome pay.

     'Music. The Witches dance, and vanish'

MACBETH Where are they? Gone? Let this pernicious hour
Stand aye accursèd in the calendar
Come in, without there!

          'Enter LENNOX*'*

LENNOX   What's your grace's will?
MACBETH Saw you the Weird Sisters?
LENNOX   No, my lord.
MACBETH Came they not by you?
LENNOX   No indeed, my lord.
MACBETH Infected be the air whereon they ride,
And damned all those that trust them! I did hear
The galloping of horse. Who was't came by?   140
LENNOX 'Tis two or three, my lord, that bring you word
Macduff is fled to England.
MACBETH   Fled to England!
LENNOX Ay, my good lord.
MACBETH Time, thou anticipat'st my dread exploits:
The flighty purpose never is o'ertook
Unless the deed go with it. From this moment
The very firstlings of my heart shall be
The firstlings of my hand. And even now
To crown my thoughts with acts, be it thought and done:
The castle of Macduff I will surprise,   150
Seize upon Fife, give to th'edge o'th' sword
His wife, his babes, and all unfortunate souls
That trace him in his line. No boasting like a fool;
This deed I'll do before this purpose cool.
But no more sights! [*aloud*] Where are these gentlemen?
Come, bring me where they are.   [*they go*

SCENE 2

Fife. Macduff's castle

'Enter MACDUFF's *Wife, her Son, and* ROSS*'*

L. M'DUFF What had he done, to make him fly the land?
ROSS You must have patience, madam.
L. M'DUFF   He had none:
His flight was madness: when our actions do not,
Our fears do make us traitors.
ROSS   You know not
Whether it was his wisdom or his fear.
L. M'DUFF Wisdom! To leave his wife, to leave his babes,
His mansion and his titles, in a place
From whence himself does fly? He loves us not;
He wants the natural touch: for the poor wren,
The most diminutive of birds, will fight,   10
Her young ones in her nest, against the owl.
All is the fear and nothing is the love;
As little is the wisdom, where the flight
So runs against all reason.
ROSS   My dearest coz,
I pray you, school yourself. But, for your husband,
He is noble, wise, judicious, and best knows
The fits o'th' season. I dare not speak much further,
But cruel are the times, when we are traitors
And do not know ourselves; when we hold rumour
From what we fear, yet know not what we fear,   20
But float upon a wild and violent sea,
Each way and none. I take my leave of you:
Shall not be long but I'll be here again:
Things at the worst will cease, or else climb upward
To what they were before. My pretty cousin,
Blessing upon you!
L. M'DUFF Fathered he is, and yet he's fatherless.
ROSS I am so much a fool, should I stay longer
It would be my disgrace and your discomfort.
I take my leave at once.   [*he hurries forth*

L. M'DUFF	Sirrah, your father's dead, 30
	And what will you do now? How will you live?
SON	As birds do, mother.
L. M'DUFF	What, with worms and flies?
SON	With what I get, I mean, and so do they.
L. M'DUFF	Poor bird! Thou'ldst never fear the net nor lime,
	The pitfall nor the gin.
SON	Why should I, mother? Poor birds they are not set for.
	My father is not dead, for all your saying.
L. M'DUFF	Yes, he is dead: how wilt thou do for a father?
SON	Nay, how will you do for a husband?
L. M'DUFF	Why, I can buy me twenty at any market. 40
SON	Then you'll buy 'em to sell again.
L. M'DUFF	Thou speak'st with all thy wit, and yet i faith
	With wit enough for thee.
SON	Was my father a traitor, mother?
L. M'DUFF	Ay, that he was.
SON	What is a traitor?
L. M'DUFF	Why, one that swears and lies.
SON	And be all traitors that do so?
L. M'DUFF	Every one that does so is a traitor, and must be hanged.
SON	And must they all be hanged that swear and lie? 50
L. M'DUFF	Every one.
SON	Who must hang them?
L. M'DUFF	Why, the honest men.
SON	Then the liars and swearers are fools; for there are liars and swearers enow to beat the honest men and hang up them.
L. M'DUFF	Now God help thee, poor monkey! But how wilt thou do for a father?
SON	If he were dead, you'ld weep for him: if you would not, it were a good sign that I should quickly have a 60 new father.
L. M'DUFF	Poor prattler, how thou talk'st!

'Enter a MESSENGER*'*

MESSENGER	Bless you, fair dame! I am not to you known,
	Though in your state of honour I am perfect
	I doubt some danger does approach you nearly.
	If you will take a homely man's advice,

Be not found here; hence, with your little ones.
To fright you thus, methinks I am too savage;
To do worse to you were fell cruelty,
Which is too nigh your person. Heaven preserve you!   70
I dare abide no longer.   [*he goes*

L. M'DUFF   Whither should I fly?
I have done no harm. But I remember now
I am in this earthly world; where to do harm
Is often laudable, to do good sometime
Accounted dangerous folly: why then, alas,
Do I put up that womanly defence,
To say I have done no harm?

                    '*Enter* MURDERERS'

                              What are these faces?

I MURD'R   Where is your husband?
L. M'DUFF   I hope in no place so unsanctified
Where such as thou mayst find him.
I MURD'R   He's a traitor.   80
SON   Thou liest, thou shag-haired villain.
I MURD'R   What, you egg! [*stabs him*
Young fry of treachery!
SON   He has killed me, mother:
Run away, I pray you.   [*dies*
                    [*Lady Macduff hurries forth 'crying murder',*
                              pursued by the Murderers

                              SCENE 3

England. Before the palace of King Edward the Confessor.
            MALCOLM *and* MACDUFF *come forth*

MALCOLM   Let us seek out some desolate shade, and there
Weep our sad bosoms empty.
MACDUFF   Let us rather
Hold fast the mortal sword, and like good men
Bestride our down-fall'n birthdom: each new morn
New widows howl, new orphans cry, new sorrows
Strike heaven on the face, that it resounds
As if it felt with Scotland and yelled out

Like syllable of dolour.

MALCOLM   What I believe, I'll wail;
What know, believe; and what I can redress,
As I shall find the time to friend, I will.   10
What you have spoke, it may be so perchance.
This tyrant, whose sole name blisters our tongues,
Was once thought honest: you have loved him well;
He hath not touched you yet. I am young, but something
You may deserve of him through me; and wisdom
To offer up a weak, poor, innocent lamb,
T'appease an angry god.

MACDUFF   I am not treacherous.

MALCOLM   But Macbeth is.
A good and virtuous nature may recoil
In an imperial charge. But I shall crave your pardon;   20
That which you are, my thoughts cannot transpose:
Angels are bright still, though the brightest fell:
Though all things foul would wear the brows of grace,
Yet grace must still look so.

MACDUFF   I have lost my hopes.

MALCOLM   Perchance even there where I did find my doubts.
Why in that rawness left you wife and child,
Those precious motives, those strong knots of love,
Without leave-taking? I pray you,
Let not my jealousies be your dishonours,
But mine own safeties: you may be rightly just,   30
Whatever I shall think.

MACDUFF   Bleed, bleed, poor country!
Great tyranny, lay thou thy basis sure,
For goodness dares not check thee: wear thou
                                        thy wrongs,
The title is affeered! Fare thee well, lord:
I would not be the villain that thou think'st
For the whole space that's in the tyrant's grasp,
And the rich East to boot.

MALCOLM   Be not offended:
I speak not as in absolute fear of you:
I think our country sinks beneath the yoke,
It weeps, it bleeds, and each new day a gash   40

Is added to her wounds. I think withal
There would be hands uplifted in my right;
And here from gracious England have I offer
Of goodly thousands. But for all this,
When I shall tread upon the tyrant's head,
Or wear it on my sword, yet my poor country
Shall have more vices that it had before,
More suffer and more sundry ways than ever,
By him that shall succeed.

MACDUFF   What should he be?

MALCOLM It is myself I mean: in whom I know   50
All the particulars of vice so grafted
That, when they shall be opened, black Macbeth
Will seem as pure as snow, and the poor state
Esteem him as a lamb, being compared
With my confineless harms.

MACDUFF   Not in the legions
Of horrid hell can come a devil more damned
In evils to top Macbeth.

MALCOLM   I grant him bloody,
Luxurious, avaricious, false, deceitful,
Sudden, malicious, smacking of every sin
That has a name: but there's no bottom, none,   60
In my voluptuousness: your wives, your daughters,
Your matrons and your maids, could not fill up
The cistern of my lust, and my desire
All continent impediments would o'erbear
That did oppose my will. Better Macbeth,
Than such an one to reign.

MACDUFF   Boundless intemperance
In nature is a tyranny; it hath been
Th'untimely emptying of the happy throne,
And fall of many kings. But fear not yet
To take upon you what is yours: you may   70
Convey your pleasures in a spacious plenty,
And yet seem cold, the time you may so hoodwink:
We have willing dames enough; there cannot be
That vulture in you, to devour so many
As will to greatness dedicate themselves,

Finding it so inclined.

MALCOLM   With this there grows
In my most ill-composed affection such
A stanchless avarice that, were I king,
I should cut off the nobles for their lands,
Desire his jewels and this other's house,   80
And my more-having would be as a sauce
To make me hunger more, that I should forge
Quarrels unjust against the good and loyal,
Destroying them for wealth.

MACDUFF   This avarice
Sticks deeper; grows with more pernicious root
Than summer-seeming lust: and it hath been
The sword of our slain kings: yet do not fear;
Scotland hath foisons to fill up your will
Of your mere own. All these are portable,
With other graces weighed.   90

MALCOLM But I have none. The king-becoming graces,
As justice, verity, temp'rance, stableness,
Bounty, perseverance, mercy, lowliness,
Devotion, patience, courage, fortitude,
I have no relish of them, but abound
In the division of each several crime,
Acting it many ways. Nay, had I power, I should
Pour the sweet milk of concord into hell,
Uproot the universal peace, confound
All unity on earth.

MACDUFF   O Scotland! Scotland!   100

MALCOLM If such a one be fit to govern, speak:
I am as I have spoken.

MACDUFF   Fit to govern!
No, not to live. O nation miserable!
With an untitled tyrant bloody-sceptred,
When shalt thou see thy wholesome days again,
Since that the truest issue of thy throne
By his own interdiction stands accurst,
And does blaspheme his breed? Thy royal father
Was a most sainted king; the queen that bore thee
Oft'ner upon her knees than on her feet,   110

Died every day she lived. Fare thee well!
These evils thou repeat'st upon thyself
Hath banished me from Scotland. O my breast,
Thy hope ends here!

MALCOLM   Macduff, this noble passion,
Child of integrity, hath from my soul
Wiped the black scruples, reconciled my thoughts
To thy good truth and honour. Devilish Macbeth
By many of these trains hath sought to win me
Into his power: and modest wisdom plucks me
From over-credulous haste: but God above   120
Deal between thee and me! for even now
I put myself to thy direction, and
Unspeak mine own detraction; here abjure
The taints and blames I laid upon myself,
For strangers to my nature. I am yet
Unknown to woman, never was forsworn,
Scarcely have coveted what was mine own,
At no time broke my faith, would not betray
The devil to his fellow, and delight
No less in truth than life: my first false speaking   13
Was this upon myself: what I am truly
Is thine and my poor country's to command:
Whither indeed, before thy here-approach,
Old Siward, with ten thousand warlike men,
Already at a point, was setting forth:
Now we'll together, and the chance of goodness
Be like our warranted quarrel! Why are you silent?

MACDUFF Such welcome and unwelcome things at once
'Tis hard to reconcile.

                    'A Doctor' comes from the palace

MALCOLM Well, more anon. Comes the king forth, I pray you?   14
DOCTOR   Ay, sir: there are a crew of wretched souls
That stay his cure: their malady convinces
The great assay of art; but at his touch,
Such sanctity hath heaven given his hand,
They presently amend.

MALCOLM   I thank you, doctor. [*the Doctor goes*
MACDUFF What's the disease he means?

MALCOLM   'Tis called the evil:
A most miraculous work in this good king,
Which often, since my here-remain in England,
I have seen him do. How he solicits heaven,
Himself best knows: but strangely-visited people,   150
All swoln and ulcerous, pitiful to the eye,
The mere despair of surgery, he cures,
Hanging a golden stamp about their necks,
Put on with holy prayers: and 'tis spoken,
To the succeeding royalty he leaves
The healing benediction. With this strange virtue
He hath a heavenly gift of prophecy,
And sundry blessings hang about his throne
That speak him full of grace.

                         ROSS *approaches*

MACDUFF   See who comes here.
MALCOLM My countryman; but yet I know him not.   160
MACDUFF My ever gentle cousin, welcome hither.
MALCOLM I know him now: good God, betimes remove
The means that makes us strangers!
ROSS   Sir, amen.
MACDUFF Stands Scotland where it did?
ROSS   Alas, poor country,
Almost afraid to know itself! It cannot
Be called our mother, but our grave; where nothing,
But who knows nothing, is once seen to smile;
Where sighs and groans and shrieks that rend the air,
Are made, not marked; where violent sorrow seems
A modern ecstasy: the dead man's knell   170
Is there scarce asked for who, and good men's lives
Expire before the flowers in their caps,
Dying or ere they sicken.
MACDUFF   O, relation
Too nice, and yet too true!
MALCOLM   What's the newest grief?
ROSS That of an hour's age doth hiss the speaker;
Each minute teems a new one.
MACDUFF   How does my wife?
ROSS Why, well.

MACDUFF   And all my children?
ROSS   Well too.
MACDUFF   The tyrant has not battered at their peace?
ROSS   No, they were well at peace, when I did leave 'em.
MACDUFF   Be not a niggard of your speech: how goes't?   180
ROSS   When I came hither to transport the tidings
          Which I have heavily borne, there ran a rumour
          Of many worthy fellows that were out;
          Which was to my belief witnessed the rather,
          For that I saw the tyrant's power a-foot.
          Now is the time of help: your eye in Scotland
          Would create soldiers, make our women fight,
          To doff their dire distresses.
MALCOLM   Be't their comfort
          We are coming thither: gracious England hath
          Lent us good Siward and ten thousand men;   190
          An older and a better soldier none
          That Christendom gives out.
ROSS   Would I could answer
          This comfort with the like! But I have words,
          That would be howled out in the desert air,
          Where hearing should not latch them.
MACDUFF   What concern they?
          The general cause? Or is it a fee-grief
          Due to some single breast?
ROSS   No mind that's honest
          But in it shares some woe, though the main part
          Pertains to you alone.
MACDUFF   If it be mine,
          Keep it not from me, quickly let me have it.   200
ROSS   Let not your ears despise my tongue for ever,
          Which shall possess them with the heaviest sound
          That ever yet they heard.
MACDUFF   Humh! I guess at it.
ROSS   Your castle is surprised; your wife and babes
          Savagely slaughtered: to relate the manner,
          Were, on the quarry of these murdered deer,
          To add the death of you.
MALCOLM   Merciful heaven!

What, man! Ne'er pull your hat upon your brows;
Give sorrow words: the grief that does not speak
Whispers the o'er-fraught heart and bids it break.   210

MACDUFF My children too?
ROSS   Wife, children, servants, all
That could be found.

MACDUFF   And I must be from thence!
My wife killed too?

ROSS   I have said.

MALCOLM   Be comforted:
Let's make us med'cines of our great revenge,
To cure this deadly grief.

MACDUFF He has no children. All my pretty ones?
Did you say all? O, hell-kite! All?
What, all my pretty chickens and their dam
At one fell swoop?

MALCOLM Dispute it like a man.

MACDUFF   I shall do so;   220
But I must also feel it as a man:
I cannot but remember such things were,
That were most precious to me. Did heaven look on,
And would not take their part? Sinful Macduff,
They were all struck for thee! Naught that I am,
Not for their own demerits, but for mine,
Fell slaughter on their souls: heaven rest them now!

MALCOLM Be this the whetstone of your sword: let grief
Convert to anger; blunt not the heart, enrage it.

MACDUFF O, I could play the woman with mine eyes,   230
And braggart with my tongue! But, gentle heavens,
Cut short all intermission; front to front
Bring thou this fiend of Scotland and myself;
Within my sword's length set him; if he 'scape,
Heaven forgive him too!

MALCOLM   This tune goes manly.
Come, go we to the king, our power is ready,
Our lack is nothing but our leave. Macbeth
Is ripe for shaking, and the powers above
Put on their instruments. Receive what cheer you may;
The night is long that never finds the day.   [they go 240

ACT 5 SCENE 1

Dunsinane. A room in the castle. 'Enter a Doctor of Physic,
and a Waiting Gentlewoman'

DOCTOR   I have two nights watched with you, but can perceive
         no truth in your report. When was it she last walked?

G'WOMAN Since his majesty went into the field, I have seen her
         rise from her bed, throw her night-gown upon her,
         unlock her closet, take forth paper, fold it, write
         upon't, read it, afterwards seal it, and again return to
         bed; yet all this while in a most fast sleep.

DOCTOR   A great perturbation in nature, to receive at once the
         benefit of sleep and do the effects of watching! In this
         slumbry agitation, besides her walking and other actual   10
         performances, what, at any time, have you heard her say?

G'WOMAN That, sir, which I will not report after her.

DOCTOR   You may to me, and 'tis most meet you should.

G'WOMAN Neither to you nor anyone, having no witness to
         confirm my speech.

                'Enter LADY' MACBETH, *'with a taper'*

         Lo you, here she comes! This is her very guise, and
         upon my life fast asleep. Observe her, stand close.

DOCTOR   How came she by that light?

G'WOMAN Why, it stood by her: she has light by her continually,
         'tis her command.   20

DOCTOR   You see, her eyes are open.

G'WOMAN Ay, but their sense are shut.

DOCTOR   What is it she does now? Look, how she rubs her hands.

G'WOMAN It is an accustomed action with her, to seem thus
         washing her hands: I have known her continue in this
         a quarter of an hour.

LADY M. Yet here's a spot.

DOCTOR   Hark, she speaks! I will set down what comes from
         her, to satisfy my remembrance the more strongly.

LADY M. Out, damnéd spot! Out, I say! One: two: why, then 'tis   30
         time to do't. Hell is murky! Fie, my lord, fie! A soldier,
         and afeard? What need we fear who knows it, when none

can call our power to accompt? Yet who would have
thought the old man to have had so much blood in him?

DOCTOR   Do you mark that?

LADY M.   The thane of Fife had a wife; where is she now? What,
will these hands ne'er be clean? No more o'that, my
lord, no more o'that: you mar all with this starting.

DOCTOR   Go to, go to; you have known what you should not.

G'WOMAN   She has spoke what she should not, I am sure of that: 40
heaven knows what she has known.

LADY M.   Here's the smell of the blood still: all the perfumes of
Arabia will not sweeten this little hand. Oh! oh! oh!

DOCTOR   What a sigh is there! The heart is sorely charged.

G'WOMAN   I would not have such a heart in my bosom, for the
dignity of the whole body.

DOCTOR   Well, well, well, –

G'WOMAN   Pray God it be, sir.

DOCTOR   This disease is beyond my practice: yet I have known
those which have walked in their sleep who have died   50
holily in their beds.

LADY M.   Wash your hands, put on your night-gown, look not
so pale: I tell you yet again, Banquo's buried; he cannot come out on's grave.

DOCTOR   Even so?

LADY M.   To bed, to bed: there's knocking at the gate: come,
come, come, come, give me your hand: what's done,
cannot be undone: to bed, to bed, to bed. [*she goes out*

DOCTOR   Will she go now to bed?

G'WOMAN   Directly.   60

DOCTOR   Foul whisp'rings are abroad: unnatural deeds
Do breed unnatural troubles: infected minds
To their deaf pillows will discharge their secrets:
More needs she the divine than the physician:
God, God forgive us all! Look after her,
Remove from her the means of all annoyance,
And still keep eyes upon her. So, good night:
My mind she has mated and amazed my sight:
I think, but dare not speak.

G'WOMAN   Good night, good doctor.
[*they go*

SCENE 2

The country near Dunsinane. 'Drum and Colours.
Enter MENTEITH, CAITHNESS, ANGUS, LENNOX, *Soldiers'*

MENTEITH   The English power is near, led on by Malcolm,
His uncle Siward and the good Macduff.
Revenges burn in them: for their dear causes
Would to the bleeding and the grim alarm
Excite the mortified man.

ANGUS   Near Birnam wood
Shall we well meet them, that way are they coming.

CAITHNESS   Who knows if Donalbain be with his brother?

LENNOX   For certain, sir, he is not: I have a file
Of all the gentry: there is Siward's son,
And many unrough youths, that even now   10
Protest their first of manhood.

MENTEITH   What does the tyrant?

CAITHNESS   Great Dunsinane he strongly fortifies:
Some say he's mad; others, that lesser hate him,
Do call it valiant fury: but, for certain,
He cannot buckle his distempered cause
Within the belt of rule.

ANGUS   Now does he feel
His secret murders sticking on his hands;
Now minutely revolts upbraid his faith-breach;
Those he commands move only in command,
Nothing in love: now does he feel his title   20
Hang loose about him, like a giant's robe
Upon a dwarfish thief.

MENTEITH   Who then shall blame
His pestered senses to recoil and start,
When all that is within him does condemn
Itself for being there?

CAITHNESS   Well, march we on,
To give obedience where 'tis truly owed:
Meet we the med'cine of the sickly weal,
And with him pour we, in our country's purge,

Each drop of us.

LENNOX   Or so much as it needs
To dew the sovereign flower and drown the weeds.   30
Make we our march towards Birnam.

> ['*exeunt, marching*'

SCENE 3

Dunsinane. A court in the castle. 'Enter MACBETH,
Doctor, and Attendants'

MACBETH Bring me no more reports, let them fly all:
Till Birnam wood remove to Dunsinane
I cannot taint with fear. What's the boy Malcolm?
Was he not born of woman? The spirits that know
All mortal consequence have pronounced me thus:
'Fear not, Macbeth, no man that's born of woman
Shall e'er have power upon thee'. Then fly, false thanes,
And mingle with the English epicures:
The mind I sway by and the heart I bear
Shall never sag with doubt nor shake with fear.   10

A 'servant' enters

The devil damn thee black, thou cream-faced loon!
Where got'st thou that goose look?
SERVANT There is ten thousand –
MACBETH   Geese, villain?
SERVANT   Soldiers, sir.
MACBETH Go prick thy face and over-red thy fear,
Thou lily-livered boy. What soldiers, patch?
Death of thy soul! Those linen cheeks of thine
Are counsellors to fear. What soldiers, whey-face?
SERVANT The English force, so please you.
MACBETH Take thy face hence.   [*servant goes*
                          Seton! [*brooding*] I am sick at heart,
When I behold – Seton, I say! – This push   20
Will cheer me ever, or disseat me now.
I have lived long enough: my way of life
Is fall'n into the sere, the yellow leaf,

And that which should accompany old age,
As honour, love, obedience, troops of friends,
I must not look to have; but, in their stead,
Curses, not loud but deep, mouth-honour, breath
Which the poor heart would fain deny and dare not.
Seton!

SETON enters

SETON   What's your gracious pleasure?
MACBETH   What news more?   30
SETON   All is confirmed, my lord, which was reported.
MACBETH I'll fight, till from my bones my flesh be hacked.
Give me my armour.
SETON   'Tis not needed yet.
MACBETH I'll put it on.
Send out moe horses, skirr the country round,
Hang those that talk of fear. Give me mine armour.
                                    [*Seton goes to fetch it*
How does your patient, doctor?
DOCTOR   Not so sick, my lord,
As she is troubled with thick-coming fancies,
That keep her from her rest.
MACBETH   Cure her of that:
Canst thou not minister to a mind diseased,   40
Pluck from the memory a rooted sorrow,
Raze out the written troubles of the brain,
And with some sweet oblivious antidote
Cleanse the stuffed bosom of that perilous stuff
Which weighs upon the heart?
DOCTOR   Therein the patient
Must minister to himself.

*Seton returns with armour and an armourer, who
presently begins to equip Macbeth*

MACBETH Throw physic to the dogs, I'll none of it.
Come, put mine armour on; give me my staff;
Seton, send out; doctor, the thanes fly from me;
Come, sir, dispatch. – If thou couldst, doctor, cast   50
The water of my land, find her disease,
And purge it to a sound and pristine health,

I would applaud thee to the very echo,
That should applaud again. – Pull't off, I say. –
What rhubarb, senna, or what purgative drug,
Would scour these English hence? Hear'st thou of them?

DOCTOR   Ay, my good lord; your royal preparation
Makes us hear something.

MACBETH   Bring it after me.
I will not be afraid of death and bane
Till Birnam forest come to Dunsinane.   60

                          [*he goes; Seton follows with armourer*

DOCTOR   Were I from Dunsinane away and clear,
Profit again should hardly draw me here.   [*he goes*

SCENE 4

Country near Birnam. 'Drum and Colours. Enter MALCOLM,
SIWARD, MACDUFF, SIWARD'S *Son,* MENTEITH, CAITHNESS,
ANGUS', LENNOX, ROSS, *'and Soldiers, marching'*

MALCOLM   Cousins, I hope, the days are near at hand
That chambers will be safe.

MENTEITH   We doubt it nothing.

SIWARD   What wood is this before us?

MENTEITH   The wood of Birnam.

MALCOLM   Let every soldier hew him down a bough,
And bear't before him: thereby shall we shadow
The numbers of our host, and make discovery
Err in report of us.

SOLDIER   It shall be done.

SIWARD   We learn no other but the confident tyrant
Keeps still in Dunsinane, and will endure
Our setting down before't.

MALCOLM   'Tis his main hope: 10
For where there is advantage to be gone,
Both more and less have given him the revolt,
And none serve with him but constrainèd things
Whose hearts are absent too.

MACDUFF   Let our just censures ·
Attend the true event, and put we on

Industrious soldiership.
SIWARD   The time approaches,
That will with due decision make us know
What we shall say we have and what we owe.
Thoughts speculative their unsure hopes relate,
But certain issue strokes must arbitrate: 20
Towards which advance the war.   ['*exeunt marching*'

SCENE 5

Dunsinane. The court of the castle as before. 'Enter MACBETH,
SETON, *and Soldiers with Drum and Colours*'

MACBETH   Hang out our banners on the outward walls;
The cry is still 'They come': our castle's strength
Will laugh a siege to scorn: here let them lie
Till famine and the ague eat them up:
Were they not forced with those that should be ours,
We might have met them dareful, beard to beard,
And beat them backward home. ['*a cry within of women*'
                             What is that noise?
SETON   It is the cry of women, my good lord.   [*goes*
MACBETH   I have almost forgot the taste of fears:
The time has been, my senses would have cooled   10
To hear a night-shriek, and my fell of hair
Would at a dismal treatise rouse and stir
As life were in't: I have supped full with horrors;
Direness, familiar to my slaughterous thoughts,
Cannot once start me.

SETON *returns*

                 Wherefore was that cry?
SETON   The queen, my lord, is dead.
MACBETH   She should have died hereafter;
There would have been a time for such a word.
Tomorrow, and tomorrow, and tomorrow,
Creeps in this petty pace from day to day,   20
To the last syllable of recorded time;
And all our yesterdays have lighted fools
The way to dusty death. Out, out, brief candle!

Life's but a walking shadow, a poor player
That struts and frets his hour upon the stage,
 And then is heard no more: it is a tale
Told by an idiot, full of sound and fury,
Signifying nothing.

                    'Enter a messenger'

Thou com'st to use thy tongue; thy story quickly.

MESSENGER Gracious my lord,   30
I should report that which I say I saw,
But know not how to do't.

MACBETH   Well, say, sir.

MESSENGER As I did stand my watch upon the hill,
I looked toward Birnam, and anon methought
The wood began to move.

MACBETH   Liar and slave!

MESSENGER Let me endure your wrath, if't be not so:
Within this three mile may you see it coming.
I say, a moving grove.

MACBETH   If thou speak'st false,
Upon the next tree shalt thou hang alive,
Till famine cling thee: if thy speech be sooth,   40
I care not if thou dost for me as much.
I pall in resolution, and begin
To doubt th'equivocation of the fiend
That lies like truth: 'Fear not, till Birnam wood
Do come to Dunsinane'; and now a wood
Comes toward Dunsinane. Arm, arm, and out!
If this which he avouches does appear,
There is nor flying hence nor tarrying here.
I 'gin to be aweary of the sun,
And wish th'estate o'th' world were now undone.   50
Ring the alarum bell! Blow, wind! Come, wrack!
At least we'll die with harness on our back.

                                        [*they hurry forth*

SCENE 6

Dunsinane. Before the castle gate. 'Drum and Colours. Enter
MALCOLM, SIWARD, MACDUFF, *and their army, with boughs'*

MALCOLM Now near enough: your leavy screens throw down,
And show like those you are. You, worthy uncle,
Shall with my cousin your right noble son
Lead our first battle: worthy Macduff and we
Shall take upon's what else remains to do,
According to our order.
SIWARD   Fare you well.
Do we but find the tyrant's power tonight,
Let us be beaten, if we cannot fight.
MACDUFF Make all our trumpets speak; give them all breath,
Those clamorous harbingers of blood and death.   10

They go forward, their trumpets sounding.

SCENE 7

MACBETH *comes from the castle*

MACBETH They have tied me to a stake; I cannot fly,
But bear-like I must fight the course. What's he
That was not born of woman? Such a one
Am I to fear, or none.

Young SIWARD *comes up*

YOUNG S. What is thy name?
MACBETH   Thou'lt be afraid to hear it.
YOUNG S. No; though thou call'st thyself a hotter name
Than any is in hell.
MACBETH   My name's Macbeth.
YOUNG S. The devil himself could not pronounce a title
More hateful to mine ear.
MACBETH   No, nor more fearful.
YOUNG S. Thou liest, abhorréd tyrant, with my sword   10

I'll prove the lie thou speak'st.

               [*they 'fight, and young Siward' is 'slain'*

MACBETH   Thou wast born of woman.
But swords I smile at, weapons laugh to scorn,
Brandished by man that's of a woman born.

He passes on and presently a sound of more
fighting is heard. MACDUFF *comes up*

MACDUFF That way the noise is. Tyrant, show thy face!
If thou beest slain and with no stroke of mine,
My wife and children's ghosts will haunt me still.
I cannot strike at wretched kerns, whose arms
Are hired to bear their staves; either thou, Macbeth,
Or else my sword with an unbattered edge
I sheathe again undeeded. There thou shouldst be;   20
By this great clatter, one of greatest note
Seems bruited. Let me find him, fortune!
And more I beg not.   [*he follows Macbeth. 'Alarums'*

MALCOLM *and* SIWARD *come up*

SIWARD This way, my lord; the castle's gently rendered:
The tyrant's people on both sides do fight,
The noble thanes do bravely in the war,
The day almost itself professes yours,
And little is to do.

MALCOLM   We have met with foes
That strike beside us.

SIWARD   Enter, sir, the castle.

               [*they pass in at the gate.*
                     'Alarum'

SCENE 8

MACBETH *returns*

MACBETH Why should I play the Roman fool, and die
On mine own sword? Whiles I see lives, the gashes
Do better upon them.

MACDUFF *returns, following him*

MACDUFF   Turn, hell-hound, turn.
MACBETH   Of all men else I have avoided thee:
           But get thee back, my soul is too much charged
           With blood of thine already.
MACDUFF   I have no words:
           My voice is in my sword, thou bloodier villain
           Than terms can give thee out!   [*they 'fight'. 'Alarum'*
MACBETH   Thou losest labour.
           As easy mayst thou the intrenchant air
           With thy keen sword impress as make me bleed: 10
           Let fall thy blade on vulnerable crests,
           I bear a charmèd life, which must not yield
           To one of woman born.
MACDUFF   Despair thy charm,
           And let the angel whom thou still hast served
           Tell thee, Macduff was from his mother's womb
           Untimely ripped.
MACBETH   Accursèd be that tongue that tells me so,
           For it hath cowed my better part of man!
           And be these juggling fiends no more believed,
           That palter with us in a double sense,   20
           That keep the word of promise to our ear,
           And break it to our hope. I'll not fight with thee.
MACDUFF   Then yield thee, coward,
           And live to be the show and gaze o'th' time.
           We'll have thee, as our rarer monsters are,
           Painted upon a pole, and underwrit,
           'Here may you see the tyrant'.
MACBETH   I will not yield,
           To kiss the ground before young Malcolm's feet,
           And to be baited with the rabble's curse.
           Though Birnam wood be come to Dunsinane,   30
           And thou opposed, being of no woman born,
           Yet I will try the last. Before my body
           I throw my warlike shield: lay on, Macduff,
           And damned be him that first cries 'Hold, enough'.
                        [*they fight to and fro beneath the castle wall,
                              until at length 'Macbeth' is 'slain'*

SCENE 9

Within the castle

'Retreat and flourish. Enter, with Drum and Colours, MALCOLM, SIWARD, ROSS, *Thanes and Soldiers'*

MALCOLM   I would the friends we miss were safe arrived.

SIWARD   Some must go off: and yet, by these I see,
So great a day as this is cheaply bought.

MALCOLM   Macduff is missing, and your noble son.

ROSS   Your son, my lord, has paid a soldier's debt:
He only lived but till he was a man,   40
The which no sooner had his prowess confirmed
In the unshrinking station where he fought,
But like a man he died.

SIWARD   Then he is dead?

ROSS   Ay, and brought off the field: your cause of sorrow
Must not be measured by his worth, for then
It hath no end.

SIWARD   Had he his hurts before?

ROSS   Ay, on the front.

SIWARD   Why then, God's soldier be he!
Had I as many sons as I have hairs,
I would not wish them to a fairer death:
And so his knell is knolled.

MALCOLM   He's worth more sorrow,   50
And that I'll spend for him.

SIWARD   He's worth no more.
They say he parted well and paid his score:
And so God be with him! Here comes newer comfort.

'Enter MACDUFF, *with Macbeth's head' on a pole*

MACDUFF   Hail, king! For so thou art. Behold, where stands
Th'usurper's curséd head: the time is free:
I see thee compassed with thy kingdom's pearl,
That speak my salutation in their minds;
Whose voices I desire aloud with mine:

        Hail, king of Scotland!

ALL   Hail, king of Scotland! ['*flourish*'

MALCOLM We shall not spend a large expense of time   60
        Before we reckon with your several loves,
        And make us even with you. My thanes and kinsmen,
        Henceforth be earls, the first that ever Scotland
        In such an honour named. What's more to do,
        Which would be planted newly with the time,
        As calling home our exiled friends abroad
        That fled the snares of watchful tyranny,
        Producing forth the cruel ministers
        Of this dead butcher and his fiend-like queen,
        Who, as 'tis thought, by self and violent hands   70
        Took off her life; this, and what needful else
        That calls upon us, by the grace of Grace
        We will perform in measure, time, and place:
        So thanks to all at once, and to each one,
        Whom we invite to see us crowned at Scone.
                         ['*flourish*'. *They march away*